The Legality and Legitimacy of the Use of Force in Northeast Asia

Studies in East Asian Security and International Relations

Edited by

Rüdiger Frank
University of Vienna

VOLUME 2

The titles published in this series are listed at brill.com/seas

The Legality and Legitimacy of the Use of Force in Northeast Asia

Edited by

Brendan Howe
Boris Kondoch

BRILL

LEIDEN · BOSTON
2013

This publication has been typeset in the multilingual "Brill" typeface. With over 5,100 characters covering Latin, IPA, Greek, and Cyrillic, this typeface is especially suitable for use in the humanities. For more information, please see http://www.brill.com/brill-typeface.

ISSN 2213-1051
ISBN 978-90-04-24904-2 (hardback)
ISBN 978-90-04-24905-9 (e-book)

This book is printed on acid-free paper.

CONTENTS

Acknowledgements....vii
List of Contributors....ix

1. Introduction....1
Brendan Howe and Boris Kondoch

2. Aggression, the Prohibition of the Use of Force and Northeast Asia....5
Boris Kondoch

3. East Asian Values and Humanitarian Intervention....43
Brendan Howe

4. Between Harmonious World and "War of Order": Chinese Meanings of Just War and Their Reemergence....75
Nadine Godehardt

5. From Ideology to Pragmatism: China's Position on Humanitarian Intervention in the Post-Cold War Era....117
Jonathan E. Davis

6. The Paradox of Non-use of "Use of Force" Option in Japan's Foreign and Security Policy Consensus....191
Toshiya Hoshino

7. "The Crime of Aggression" and Japan....213
Madoka Futamura

8. Questioning the Legality and Legitimacy of a Preventive Strike by the U.S. to Disarm North Korea of Nuclear Weapons....233
Dan Ernst

Bibliography....265

Index....285

ACKNOWLEDGEMENTS

Brendan Howe and Boris Kondoch

This book resulted from the workshop panel on "Northeast Asian Perspectives on the Legality and the Legitimacy of the Use of Force" held as part of the Korean International Studies Association (KISA) Congress at EwhaWomans University, South Korea. The workshop addressed ethical and legal issues arising from intervention and the use of force in regard to Northeast Asian states. The workshop was hosted and supported by the Korean International Studies Association (KISA) and the Asian Centre for Peace and Security Studies.

The editors would like to recognize the Institute for Development and Human Security, EwhaWomans University, for supporting the foundational conference from which this volume is drawn through the WCU (World Class University) program of the National Research Foundation of Korea funded by the Ministry of Education, Science and Technology (Grant Number: R32-20077). Further support for the international panel and the subsequent book project was supplied by the Asian Political and International Studies Association (APISA); and by an NRF grant on Human Security funded by the Korean Government (MEST) (No. B00017).

LIST OF CONTRIBUTORS

Jonathan Davis received his Juris Doctor from NYU School of Law and his Master in Public Affairs from the Woodrow Wilson School of Public and International Affairs at Princeton University. He currently serves as an Attorney-Adviser in the Office of the Legal Adviser at the U.S. Department of State. Prior to joining the State Department, Mr. Davis practiced international arbitration and litigation as an associate in the New York office of an international law firm.

Dr. Ernst received his Ph.D. from Yale University's Philosophy Department, writing his dissertation under Professor Seyla Benhabib. He has published in various journals including *Israel Law Review; Biomedical Law & Ethics; Trans Humanities;* and *Korean Political Science Association Journal.* He currently lives in New York and is pursuing a Juris Doctorate from NYU.

Madoka Futamura, Academic Programme Officer, Institute of Sustainability, United Nations University (UNU-ISP), Madoka Futamura is an Academic Programme Officer at the Institute of Sustainability, United Nations University (UNU-ISP). She holds a Ph.D. in War Studies from King's College London. She is currently a Global Ethics Fellow of Carnegie Council for Ethics in International Affairs. Her research interests are transitional justice, peacebuilding, international peace and security. Her works include: *War Crimes Tribunals and Transitional Justice: The Tokyo Trial and the Nuremberg Legacy* (London: Routledge, 2008); "The Development of International Criminal Justice and the Role of the UN Security Council: The Case of the Special Tribunal for Lebanon," *The Journal of International Security*, Vol. 37, No. 3, 2009; *Towards a Human Security Approach to Peacebuilding* (UNU Research Brief No. 2, 2010).

Nadine Godehardt, Associate at German Institute for International and Security Affairs in Berlin. She has recently finished her dissertation (*Regions and Intertwined Actors: The Chinese Constitution of Central Asia*) at the University of Hamburg. Her research interests are IR theory, post-regionalism, China's foreign policy in Asia and, particularly, China-Central Asia relations.

Brendan M. Howe, Ph.D. (2004), Trinitiy College, Dublin, is Professor and Department Chair at GSIS, Ewha Womans University. He has been a visiting research fellow at the Centre for International Security Studies, Sydney University; the Research Institute for Strategic Studies, Korea National Defense University; the East-West Centre in Hawaii; and Georgetown University. He previously held posts at Beijing Foreign Studies University and Universiti Malaysia Sarawak. He has published extensively on security decision-making, human security, and the East Asian operating environment including multiple SSCI-ranked articles and books including: "Governance in the Interests of the Most Vulnerable" *Public Administration and Development* Vol. 32, No. 4/5, 2012; "Human Security in North Korea" (with Kahul Kim), *Korea Observer*, Vol. 42, No. 2, 2011; and "Human Security and Human Development in the Lao PDR (with Kearrin Sims)," *Asian Survey*, Vol. 51, No. 2, 2011.

Toshiya Hoshino, Professor and Dean of the Osaka School of International Public Policy, Osaka University. Previously he served as a Minister-Counselor at the Permanent Mission of Japan to the United Nations in charge of political affairs and Senior Research Fellow at the Japan Institute of International Affairs. His recent publications include "Through the Looking Glass? – China's Rise as Seen from Japan," *Journal of Asian Public Policy*, Vol. 5, No. 2, 2012.

Boris Kondoch is Professor at Far East University and Editor of the Journal of International Peacekeeping published by Brill/Martinus Niijhoff. He has an extensive publication experience on international law and international peace-keeping related subjects. He previously edited eight books. Major publications include *inter alia*, "The Responsibility to Protect and Northeast Asia: The Case of North Korea," *The Korean Journal of Defense Analysis*, Vol. 24, No. 4, 2012; "The Applicability of Human Rights Standards to International Policing," *Journal of International Peacekeeping*, Vol. 15, 2011; "The Responsibility of Peacekeepers, Their Sending States, and International Organizations" in D. Fleck, T. Gill (Eds.), *The Handbook of International Law of Military Operations* (Oxford University Press, 2010); *International Peacekeeping, The Library of Essays in International Law* (Ashgate, Aldershot, 2007); and "The United Nations Administration of East Timor," *Journal of Conflict and Security Law* (Oxford University Press), Vol. 6, No. 2, 2001.

CHAPTER ONE

INTRODUCTION

Brendan Howe and Boris Kondoch

The use of force in international relations has been severely curtailed by pragmatic considerations of international order, and further constrained by positive international law. Essentially the international operating environment post-1945 has reinforced the norms of political sovereignty, territorial integrity, and non-intervention. These principles of international governance in the contemporary operating environment have, however, come under attack from two contrasting directions: (1) that they are too restrictive, and that there are in fact other circumstances under which it may be legitimate to use force even if currently it would be illegal to do so; and (2) that governing norms are overly reflective of Western values and perspectives.

Given the rise to prominence of humanitarian intervention and the Responsibility to Protect (R2P) doctrine since the Cold War, combined with the rise of Asia, and particularly Northeast Asia, a region sometimes perceived as the most conflict-prone in the world, this volume offers timely insight into the legality and legitimacy of the use of force from divergent Northeast Asian perspectives. The authors, all of whom are either from the region, or who have many years of experience living and working in the region, offer a diverse and comprehensive evaluation of legal, normative, cultural, and historical insights.

The first part of the book provides an overview on the principle of non-intervention and the prohibition of the use of force within the context of Northeast Asia. In Chapter 2, Boris Kondoch reveals the legal concept of the prohibition of the threat and use of force in international relations to have been one of the key creations of the last century. The chapter begins, however, by tracing the historical foundations of the concepts back to early legal, political or philosophical attempts to regulate war. It identifies the watershed moment of legal distillation as coming with the League of Nations; the first attempt at developing a feasible system of collective security Furthermore the chapter examines the principle of non-intervention as one of the fundamental rules of public international law; although the exact meaning of the principle is unclear, and it remains something of an essentially contested concept. As one of the most conflict-affected regions of the world, Chapter 2 highlights the importance of the discussion for practical international relations in Northeast Asia.

Perhaps not surprisingly, as contemporary discourse has addressed expanding the permissible parameters of just war, particularly in the field of humanitarian intervention, Chapter 2 reveals that in Northeast Asia, the prohibition of aggression and the core concept of internationally illegal use of force have remained uncontested. No government in the region has argued that the rules regulating the use of force have fallen into desuetude and do not apply. Northeast Asian policy stances on non-intervention have been backed by claims of an alternative communal heritage, and both memories of past and fears of future imperialism. Indeed the resistance of Asian countries and commentators to the normative shift in principles of international governance can be seen as part of a wider "Asian values" debate.

Yet in Chapter 3, Brendan Howe addresses the extent to which the strict adherence to the principles of non-intervention in East Asia in general, including both Northeast Asia and Southeast Asia, have increasingly come under attack from internal and external normative communities. The chapter examines the emergence of a global overlapping consensus regarding the need simultaneously to support the concepts of individual human rights, global consensus or shared norms, and a lingering respect for the legal persons of international society, states. This is reflected in the near universal endorsement of related UN legislation, including by regional states. The author notes that this situation has come to pass, not because we are all western liberal individualists now, but rather because all normative traditions, including those in Asia, accept that there are certain practices or operational circumstances which "shock the conscience of humankind" and should be stopped, regardless of whether the national authorities give their consent.

Thus these two foundational chapters introduce the following framing questions from the perspective of Northeast Asia: What are the Asian philosophical concepts regulating the waging of wars? How can they be distinguished from Western concepts of Just War? How have states justified the use of force in international relations? How can Asian values supporting the principle of non-intervention be reconciled with the need to prevent or end genocide or gross violations of human rights? Answers to these questions are greatly elaborated upon by the more case specific chapters encountered in the rest of the book.

In Chapter 4 Nadine Godehardt addresses the meaning of Just War in China and its relevance in Chinese foreign policy. China is a vitally important case study, first, because of its extensive history of and philosophical principles concerning the use of force in international relations. Second, due to its unparalleled recent rise, or more accurately from the perspective of Northeast Asia, its resurgence. And third because of its status as a Permanent Member of the United Nations Security Council and veto holder. Furthermore, although Art. 2(4) of the UN Charter clearly prohibits the threat or use of force in international relations, several instances of the use of force remain controversial including the right to humanitarian intervention. Thus in Chapter 5 Jonathan Davis provides a unique and comprehensive examination of China's position on humanitarian intervention after 1989.

Many international lawyers consider aggression as the crime of crimes. The exact content of the crime or crimes remains, however, unclear. After years of negotiations, states agreed in Kampala in 2010 that aggression under the statute of the International Criminal Court would mean "the planning, preparation, initiation or execution, by a person in a position effectively to exercise control over or to direct the political or military action of a State, of an act of aggression which, by its character, gravity and scale, constitutes a manifest violation of the Charter of the United Nations." Japan has been closely connected with consideration of the nature of aggression, first, and historically, as a paradigmatic example of an aggressor state, more recently as a pacifist state and promoter of human security. In her chapter, the sixth of this volume, Madoka Futamura examines Japan's attitude towards the international efforts towards the criminalization of aggression. In Chapter 6, Toshiya Hoshino further explores the paradox of the non-use of "Use of Force" option in Japan's foreign and security policy consensus. He incorporates analysis of the realization in Tokyo that a comprehensive response is needed to address complicated contemporary security challenges. He claims that the Japanese are seeking to harmonize the pro-active but non-aggressive use of military tools on one side, and the innovative non-military tools on the other side, to pursue a nested peace reflecting the diverse interests of stake-holders.

The volume concludes with a very controversial chapter by Dan Ernst, addressing perhaps the most pressing contemporary strategic hot potato in Northeast Asia – the legality and legitimacy of the use of force against North Korea. Despite many years of negotiations concerning the North Korean nuclear program, the situation on the Korean Peninsula has remained tense. The Democratic People's Republic of Korea (DPRK) is widely viewed as a threat to its neighbors, to regional security, and to its own people. Pyongyang stands accused of actual use of force in launching attacks on a South Korean controlled island and a South Korean naval vessel. In addition its inflammatory rhetoric, sabre rattling, and brinksmanship frequently violates the prohibition on the threat of use of force. Internal governance failures would also seem to be of such magnitude as to violate the responsibility to protect. This chapter considers whether the end of the line has been reached with regard to the DPRK, and that under such conditions, certain military actions may in fact be justified, with specific reference to North Korea's nuclear weapon program and intervention by the United States.

This book does not aim to produce definitive answers to such hotly contested questions, but does seek to raise important issues in a stimulating if controversial way. The debates are ongoing among policy practitioners and legal scholars on many of these keenly or even essentially contested concepts. What the editors and contributors to this volume have attempted to provide is a collection of perspectives from and on Northeast Asia, related to the legality and legitimacy of the use of force in the region.

CHAPTER TWO

AGGRESSION, THE PROHIBITION OF THE USE OF FORCE, AND NORTHEAST ASIA

Boris Kondoch

Introduction

The principle of the non-use of force and the prohibition of aggression in international relations may be considered the most important legal developments of the 20th century. The following chapter will analyse these key rules of international law in the context of Northeast Asia. The first sections examine the historical development of the concept of aggression, from antiquity to the League of Nations, and from the creation of the Military Tribunals at Nuremberg and Tokyo to the establishment of the International Criminal Court. The chapter then focuses on the prohibition of the use of force under the UN Charter and interstate conflicts in Northeast Asia.

Historical Development of the Prohibition of Aggression

Aggression has been regulated by international law since the last century. Most international lawyers agree that aggression refers to the use of force in violation of the UN Charter by a state against another state. The consequences of the use of force have to be serious and large scale in nature. Aggression does not only involve state responsibility[1] but also individual criminal liability.[2] Aggression plays a major role in the context of collective security.

---

[1] S. Kadelbach, "Staatenverantwortlichkeit für Angriffskriege und Verbrechen gegen die Menschlichkeit" in Berichte der Deutschen Gesellschaft für Völkerrecht, *Entschädigung nach bewaffneten Konflikte. Die Konstitutionalisierung der Welthandelsordnung* (C.F. Müller, Heidelberg, 2001), pp. 63–105.

[2] See in detail, for example O. Solera, *Defining the Crime of Aggression* (Cameron May, London, 2007) and M. Hummrich, *Der völkerrechtliche Straftatbestand der Aggression* (Nomos, Baden-Baden, 2001).

From Antiquity to the Theories of Just War

Although the legal concept of prohibition of aggression is a creation of the last century, its origin can be traced back to early legal, political, religious, pacifistic or philosophical attempts[3] to regulate war. The concept of aggression has a firm place in the *just war* tradition.[4] The just war theory may be seen as a theory in "the very loosest sense" with many different sub-traditions and sub-sub-traditions found in Greek custom, *ius gentium*, scholasticism, the doctrine of the holy war[5] and many other schools of thought.[6] The Chinese conception of the just war theory, which has remained an understudied area of research, may be found in Confucianism (a philosophical tradition based on the teachings of Confucius), Mohism (a Chinese philosophy developed by the followers of Mo Ti), Legalism (one of the main Chinese philosophic traditions during the Warring States Period) and Taoism (a Chinese philosophical tradition which emphasizes living in harmony with the Tao). Philosophers like Lao Tzu and Mo Ti (c. 470–390 BCE.) opposed wars.[7] The latter wanted them be prohibited.[8] Wars of conquest and wars for profit were condemned.

Many centuries later, Chairman Mao argued that "[h]istory shows that wars are divided into two kinds, just and unjust. All wars that are progressive are just, and all wars that impede progress are unjust. We Communists oppose all unjust wars that impede progress, but we do not oppose progressive, just wars. Not only do we Communists not oppose just wars; we

---

[3] For an excellent summary of philosophical thoughts on war, see F. Przetacznik, *The Philosophical and Legal Concept of War* (The Edwin Mellen Press, Lewiston, 1994).

[4] See A. Bellamy, *Just Wars: From Cicero to Iraq* (Polity Press, Cambridge, 2006), pp. 3–4, 8.

[5] On the holy war concept according to the old testament of the bible, see Przetacznik, *supra* note 3, pp. 55–58.

[6] See for example, V. Popovski, G.M. Reichberg, N. Turner (eds.), *World Religions and Norms of War* (UNU Press, Tokyo, 2009) and H.M. Hensel (ed.), *The Prism of Just War. Asian and Western Perspectives on the Legitimate Use of Military Force* (Ashgate, Surrey, 2010). On the just causes for Muslims to wage a war of jihad, see M. Rifaat, *International Aggression* (Almqvist & Wiksell International, Stockholm, 1979), pp. 7–11; on the just war theory in Hindu tradition, see S.P. Subedi, "The Concept in Hinduism of 'Just War'," *Journal of Conflict and Security Law*, vol. 8, no. 2, 2003, pp. 339–361.

[7] On the Chinese tradition of Just War in regard to contemporary Chinese foreign policy, see the chapter by Nadine Godehardt and E. MacDonald, "The Same, Only Different: Just War Theory, International Law, and Traditional Chinese Thought," 2004-09-02, paper presented at the annual meeting of the American Political Science Association, accessible at http://www.allacademic.com/meta/p61063_index.html. On the Korean conception of the just war theory, see E.A. Olsen, "Korean Perceptions of Just War" in H.M. Hensel (ed.), ibid., pp. 245–270.

[8] See B. Ferencz, "Aggression" in *EPIL I* (North-Holland, Amsterdam, 1992), pp. 58.

actively participate in them. As for unjust wars, World War I is an instance in which both sides fought for imperialist interests; therefore, the Communists of the whole world firmly opposed that war. The way to oppose a war of this kind is to do everything possible to prevent it before it breaks out and, once it breaks out, to oppose war with war, to oppose unjust war with just war, whenever possible."[9]

However, as pointed out by David A. Graff, "several prominent elements of the Western discourse on just war remained underdeveloped, ambiguous, or the subject of disagreement in the Chinese world. These included competent authority (that is, the identification of precisely which governing authority could legitimately wage a righteous war), proportionality (the expectation that the means adopted should not be disproportionate to the goals being pursued in the conflict), and the entire area of *jus in bello* … ."[10]

The modern concept of just war theory was developed by Christian theologians and philosophers during the Middle Ages. Within the just war tradition, different theorists developed diverging concepts, but they held in common that war was a judicial and procedural redress to a wrong suffered. In the opinion of St. Thomas Aquinas (1225–1274), a "just war" had to satisfy three conditions: a) the authority of a prince (*autoritas principis*); b) a just cause (*causa justa*); and c) righteous intention (*intentio recta*). Like in contemporary international law, only very few types of war were justified.

An important change occurred with the Treaty of Westphalia of 1648, which ended thirty years of fighting between Catholic and Protestant states in their quest for power in Europe and marked the beginning of the modern state system. The concept of equal sovereignty was introduced and the guiding principle was no longer the *recta causa* but the *raison d'état* (the reason of the state). During this period the just war theory based on natural law gradually disappeared, which meant a change from the *bellum iustum* to the *ius ad bellum*. No state could presume to judge whether another's cause was just or not. Every state had the right to wage war because it was considered an essential aspect of state sovereignty. It has to be stressed that the just war doctrine was never part of positive public international law and even during the heyday of the

9 Quoted at http://www.marxists.org/reference/archive/mao/works/red-book/ch05.htm.

10 D.A. Graff, "The Chinese Concept of Righteous War" in H.M. Hensel (ed.), *supra* note 6, pp. 195–216, 196.

just war tradition the concept was not the only view on the thinking of war.[11]

However, the just war-theory never completely disappeared. After the end of the Cold War, there was a revival of the doctrine, when the international community debated the legality and legitimacy of armed interventions after the genocide in Rwanda, NATO's intervention in Kosovo, the terrorist attacks of September 11 and the invasion of Iraq in 2003.[12] The Canadian Commission on Intervention and State Sovereignty, which coined the "Responsibility to Protect" draws heavily on just war thinking, when proposing clearer rules, procedures, and criteria for determining whether, when and how to intervene in case of gross violations of human rights.[13]

From the 19th Century to World War I

The 19th century was a turbulent period in the history of Northeast Asia. It witnessed the rise of Japan and the fall of China. Imperial China declined because foreign powers intervened in its internal affairs and it was defeated in a series of wars (Opium Wars 1839–42, Tonkin War 1893–95, Sino-Japanese War, 1894–95 and the Boxer Rebellion, 1899–1900). While China, Japan and Korea remained among the only few non-colonized states in Asia, they were forced to open doors to trade under foreign threats of military and naval action. At the same time, Russia, China and Japan struggled over control of Korea. China's interference in Korea ended when it lost

---

[11] Early realists like Niccolo Machiavelli (1469–1527) did not impose any legal or moral constrains on the ruler's decision to go to war. Macchiavelli considered which actions were most advantageous to be an effective ruler. War was just which was necessary. For Thomas Hobbes (1588–1679), it made no sense to restrain war in any way, because there was no authority which could have enforced legal or moral rules. The great strategist Carl von Clausewitz (1780–1831) was also not concerned with the ethics or legality of war, see C. von Clausewitz, *On War* (1832), translated and edited by M. Howard and P. Paret (Princeton University Press, Princeton, 1984). For Clausewitz, "war is an act of force, and there is no logical limit to the application of that force. Each side, therefore, compels its opponent to follow suit, a reciprocal action is started which must lead, in theory, to extremes." Ibid., p. 77.

[12] See for example, R.A. Falk, *The Costs of War. International Law, the UN, and the World Order after Iraq* (Routledge, New York, 2008), pp. 27–34, 131–150 and M. Walzer, *Arguing about War* (Yale University Press, New Haven & London, 2004). For important books on the just war theory published before 1989, see for example, P. Ramsey, *The Just War: Force and Political Responsibility* (Scribner's, New York, 1968) and M. Walzer, *Just and Unjust War* (Basic Books, New York, 1977).

[13] Canadian Commission on Intervention and State Sovereignty, *The Responsibility to Protect* (2001), available at http://www.iciss.ca/report-en.asp.

against Japan in the Sino-Japanese War of 1894–5. Japan defeated Russia in the Russo-Japanese War (1904–1905) which was the first victory of a non-Western state over a European one. In the aftermath of the Russo-Japanese War Japan, which had already invaded Korea in the 16th century, finally gained control over the Korean peninsula. In 1906, Korea became a protectorate of Japan and was deprived of the right to pursue its own national foreign policy. Japan officially annexed Korea in 1910. Korea remained part of the Japanese Empire until its liberation in the aftermath of WW II in 1945.

International law at that time did not provide any protection against the threat of, or recourse to, force because aggression and the use of force in international relations were not prohibited. The international system was not based on collective security but on the balance of power, which meant that the only real constraint on states was the opposing power of other states. In addition, diplomacy was another important tool to keep the peace among states.[14]

Until the beginning of the 20th century the recourse to force was considered a matter of sovereign prerogative and the waging of war was recognised as lawful (*ius ad bellum*). International law during this period even recognised the forcible acquisition of territory by conquest under certain conditions.[15] Natural law theories which only permitted a just war under certain conditions (*bellum iustum*)[16] had virtually disappeared. During this period[17] war was considered as a "continuation of politics by

---

[14] Balance of power and collective security are traditional concepts of how to control military power and to deter aggression. Within a system of collective security, states agree that all states would defend the victim of aggression and the aggression would be viewed as an attack against all members within that system. Collective security differs from a system of collective self-defense, which is mainly directed against external threats. Balance of power can be based on the idea that peace and stability are best maintained when military power is equally distributed. One fundamental difference between the two systems is that "the balance principle says that a state should join in resistance to an aggressor only if its own security is affected; the collective security principle says that a state should always because its interests are affected by any aggression." I. Claude, *Power and International Relations* (Random House, New York, 1962), p. 147.

[15] See in detail, S. Korman, *The Right of Conquest. The Acquisition of Territory by Force in International Law and Practice* (Clarendon Press, Oxford, 2003).

[16] See E. de Vattel, *Le Droit des Gens* (Lodres, 1758); H. Grotius, *De Jure Belli ac Pacis* (1625) or the more recent work by the sociologist, M. Walzer, *Just and Unjust Wars* (Second Edition, Basic Books, 1992).

[17] See in detail on the period from 1815 to 1919, S.C. Neff, *War and the Law of Nations. A General History* (Cambridge University Press, Cambridge, 2005), pp. 159–275.

other means."[18] International law had "no alternative but to accept war, independently of the justice of its origin, as a relation which the parties to it may set up if they choose, and to busy itself only in regulating the effects of the relation."[19]

Although the right to wage war was considered an unlimited aspect of state sovereignty during the 19th century, States would still justify their actions, when attacking each other, for example by the right to self-defense, the right to self-preservation, or the right to protect vital interests. Other justifications included the maintenance of the balance of power, an alleged injury to rights or national honour, or dignity. One must also mention the various attempts by States to restrict war and maintain peace during this era. The so-called Concert of Europe was established as an informal organization after the Napoleonic wars. Its objective was to prevent disputes in Europe from escalating into war by containing France, by achieving a balance of power between the great powers of Europe, and by upholding the territorial arrangements decided at the Congress of Vienna in 1814–15. For almost a century, the equilibrium was maintained and no war broke out between the Great Powers in Europe.

In practice, States distinguished between a state of war in a legal sense and other means of compulsion, including retorsion and reprisals. A state of war[20] existed if one of the following conditions had been fulfilled:

(i) if one state expressly declared war against another;
(ii) if one state used force against another state and required third states to comply with the rules of neutrality;
(iii) if one state responded by using force against the resort to force by another state and considered its response as establishing a state of war.[21]

---

[18] C. von Clausewitz, *On War* (1832), Anatol Rapoport (ed.) (Penguin, Baltimore, 1968), p. 402.

[19] W.E. Hall, *A Treatise on International Law* (1924), p. 82 (A.P. Higgins, ed., 8th ed. 1924), quoted in Dinstein, *Aggression and Self-Defense* (Cambridge University Press, Cambridge, Third edition, 2001), p. 69. The view expressed here is very similar to Cicero's famous adage "in war law is silent" made many centuries earlier.

[20] One has to note that there was never a binding definition on war under international law. For a discussion of different definitions, see Prezetacznik, *supra* note 3, pp. 8–28. One of the leading experts on the subject, Yoram Dinstein suggests: "War is a hostile interaction between two or more States, either in a technical or in a material sense. War in the technical sense is a formal status produced by a declaration of war. War in the material sense is generated by actual use of armed force, which must be comprehensive on the part of at least one party to the conflict." See Y. Dinstein, *supra* note 19, p. 15.

[21] See Rifaat, *supra* note 3, pp. 19–25.

Further important developments were the trend towards arbitration[22] and the occurrence of certain restrictions on the waging of war by the end of the 19th century and beginning of the 20th century.[23]

From World War I to World War II

The Versailles Peace Treaty

The major turning point was World War I.[24] This first calamity of the 20th century resulted in the deaths of more than 10 million people. The Versailles Peace Treaty and the subsequent peace treaties with Germany's allies introduced the concept of responsibility for wars of aggression. Unlike other historical peace settlements of previous centuries such as the Treaty of Westphalia (1648), Utrecht (1713), or Vienna (1815), the Versailles Treaty did not include amnesty clauses.

Art. 227 of the Versailles Peace Treaty proposed an international tribunal to hold the German emperor,[25] who was seen as one of the main authors of the war, accountable "for a supreme offence against international morality and the sanctity of treaties,"[26] but not for crimes against

---

22 Ibid., pp. 27–29.

23 The Bryan-Treaties concluded by the United States in 1913 and 1914, prohibited declarations of war or the opening of hostilities until a commission had investigated the merits of the dispute. Art. 2 of the Convention I of the Hague Peace Conferences of 1899 and 1907 required that in case of serious dispute the parties to the convention would resort to good offices and mediation before making "an appeal to arms." Art. 1 of the 1907 Convention obligated not to use force for the recovery of contract debts unless the debt or State refused the offer of arbitration or, after accepting the offer, prevented any compromise from being agreed on, or, after the arbitration, failed to submit the award. Few years earlier, the Foreign Minister of Argentina, Drago had claimed that the Great Powers must not resort to force to seek payments of debts from other countries.

24 World War I was a European Conflict. Japan was one of the major Entente powers. During the course of the war Japan expanded its influence in China and seized German holdings in Shandong and the German held islands: the Carolines, Marianas, Marshalls, Palau and Yap.

25 One century earlier, holding the leadership legally responsible for waging war was almost unthinkable for the statesmen of this period. Napoleon, who turned almost whole Europe against him because of his conquests, was not put on trial but sent to exile. As the German Chancellor, Otto von Bismarck explained "people insist that in conflicts between states, the conqueror should sit in judgement upon the conquered, moral code in hand, and inflict punishment for what he had done ... This is an altogether unreasonable demand. Punishment and revenge have nothing to do with policy. Policy must not meddle with the calling of the nemesis, or aspire to judge's office." quoted in M. Bush, *Our Chancellor* (New York, Scribner and Sons, Vol. 1, 1884), p. 99.

26 The wording of Art. 227 of the Treaty of Versailles has been correctly viewed as a violation of the principle of legality. William Shabas explains, "it is hard to find a better example of a legal norm that deserves the ephitet 'void for vagueness'," W.A. Shabas, "Origins of the Criminalization of Aggression: How Crimes against Peace Became the

international law.[27] The inclusion of Art. 227 was controversial. However, the Allied Commission on the Responsibility of the Authors of the War concluded, before the adoption of the Versailles Treaties, that "(t)he premeditation of a war of aggression ... is conduct which the public conscience reproves and which history will condemn, but ... a war of aggression may not be considered an act directly contrary to positive law ..."[28]

Legal Regulations on the Recourse to War under the Covenant of the League of Nations

The tragic outcome of World War I also led to the creation of the League of Nations and legal restrictions on the recourse to war. The organisation was the first attempt at developing a feasible system of collective security.[29] The preamble of the Covenant of the League of Nations established the obligation for member states "not to resort to war," in order to ensure international peace and security. The members of the League pledged in Art. 10 to uphold the collective security system of the League and to "respect and preserve, as against any external aggression; the territorial integrity and existing political independence" of other states. Art. 10 is the only article in the Covenant, mentioning aggression but without defining the term. Pursuant to Art. 12 of the League Covenant, "the members of the League agree that if there should arise between them any dispute likely to lead to a rupture they will submit the matter either to arbitration or judicial settlement or to inquiry by the Council, and they agree in no case to resort to war until three months after the award by the arbitrators or the judicial decisions or the report by the Council."[30] A principal weakness of the Covenant was that the Council of the League—unlike the Security Council of the United Nations—could not take binding decisions on member states in regard to aggression.

"Supreme International Crime"" in M. Politi, G. Nesta (eds.), *The International Criminal Court and the Crime of Aggression* (Ashgate, Aldershot, 2004), p. 21.

[27] At the end, Kaiser Wilhelm II was never brought to trial and spent the last years of his life in exile in the Netherlands.

[28] Report, Chapter IV, p. 118.

[29] Different mechanisms for the maintenance of international peace and security had been proposed by statesmen, scholars and philosophers, including Pierre Dubois (1250–1322), Émeric Crucé (1590–1648), Abbé de Saint-Pierre and Immanuel Kant (1724–1804). In his famous work *Perpetual Peace* (1795), Kant recommended *inter alia*, a federation open to voluntary membership of any state, a congress to settle disputes and no territorial changes by conquest.

[30] See also Arts. 12, 13, 15 and 16 of the League of Nations.

Art. 15(6) of the Covenant provided that: "Should any Member of the League resort to war in disregard of its covenants under Arts. 12, 13, or 15, it shall *ipso facto* be deemed to have committed an act of war against all other members of the League, which hereby undertake immediately to subject it to severance of all trade or financial relations, the prohibition of all intercourse between their nationals of the covenant-breaking state, and the prevention of all financial, commercial, or personal intercourse between the nationals of the covenant-breaking State and the nationals of any other State, whether a Member of the League or not."

Although under the wording of Art. 15(6) it is crystal clear that sanctions would be automatically applied against the state which resorted to war in violation of the Covenant, practice showed that the article was interpreted differently by the members of the League. It was left to the discretion of each individual state to decide whether another state went to war in violation of the Covenant. This interpretation was also confirmed by Resolution 4 of September 1921.[31] The Council could only advise or recommend on measures against potential or actual aggression.

Even though war was not outlawed altogether, the Covenant created a system which delayed the recourse to violence and introduced the notion of *bellum legale*. Thereby, the Covenant became "the source of and inspiration for developments which in sum destroyed the presumption in favour of the lawfulness of war."[32]

Major Legal Developments during the Period from 1920 to 1945

During the 1920s, further attempts had been made to restrict the right to war. The Draft Treaty on Mutual Assistance of 1923[33] and the Protocol for the Pacific Settlement of International Disputes of 1924, which did not enter into force, declared that aggressive war was an international crime.[34]

---

[31] See League Assembly Resolution 4 of 27 September 1921: League of Nations document A. 1921. P, 453.

[32] I. Brownlie, *International Law and the Use for Force by States* (Oxford University Press, Oxford, 1963), pp. 66.

[33] Art. 1 of the draft treaty states: "The High Contracting Parties declare that aggressive war is an international crime and severally undertake that no one of them will be guilty of its commission. A war shall not be considered as a war of aggression if waged by a State which is party to a dispute and has accepted the unanimous recommendation of the Council, the verdict of the Permanent Court of Justice or an arbitral award against a High Contracting Party, which has not accepted it, provided, however, that the first State does not violate the political independence or the territorial integrity of the High Contracting Party."

[34] It is commonly understood that the Draft Treaty refers to states" responsibility and not to individual criminal responsibility, Brownlie, *supra* note 32, p. 8.

Resolutions of the League Assembly in 1925 and 1927 and the Resolution of the Sixth International Conference in 1928 condemned wars of aggression and declared them prohibited. Several States concluded non-aggression pacts.[35] A famous example was the Locarno Pact of 1925[36] between Germany and Belgium as well as Germany and France. Great Britain and Italy guaranteed the pact.[37] Another example is the Non-Aggression Treaty of 1937 signed by the USSR and China. In 1928, the Pact of Paris, also known as the Briand-Kellogg Pact was signed.[38] The States declared in Art. 1 to "condemn recourse to war for the solution of international controversies" and to "renounce it as an instrument of national policy in their relations with one another."[39] The Pact was a major landmark in the prohibition of war and the use of force, changing international law from *jus ad bellum* to *jus contra bellum*. The Briand-Kellogg Pact, which entered into force in 1929, outlawed war except in self-defense or as a sanction for the violation of the Pact. It rendered aggression an illegal act of States. Prior to the outbreak of World War II, almost all existing States with the exception of Argentina, Bolivia, El Salvador, and Uruguay were bound by the Pact. However, the treaty had major deficiencies which are summarised by Yoram Dinstein:

(i) the issue of self-defense was not clearly addressed in the text;
(ii) no agreed upon limits were set on the legality of war as an instrument of international policy;
(iii) the prohibition of war did not embrace the entire international community; and
(iv) forcible measures short of war were eliminated from consideration.[40]

Despite its weaknesses, the Pact had an important impact on State practice. Many inter-war treaties, in particular those concluded between Latin

[35] Brownlie, ibid., pp. 101–5.

[36] Reprinted in F.L. Israel, *Major Peace Treaties of Modern History, 1648–1967* (Vol. VI, Chelsea House Publishers, 1967), pp. 2385.

[37] Art. 2 of the Locarno Pact provided: "Germany and Belgium, and also Germany and France, mutually undertake that they will in no case attack or invade each other or resort to war against each other."

[38] The pact can be found at http://www.yale.edu/lawweb/avalon/imt/kbpact.htm. For a detailed analysis of the Briand-Kellog Pact, see B. Roscher, "The 'Renunciation of War as an Instrument of National Policy'," *Journal of the History of International Law*, vol. 4, no. 2, 2002, pp. 293–309.

[39] Japan was one of the original signatories of the 1928 Briand-Kellogg Pact.

[40] Dinstein, *supra* note 20, pp. 80.

America States, reaffirmed the legal obligations of the Briand-Kellogg Pact.[41] In the inter-war period, Governments and Statesmen referred to the legal obligations under the treaty, for example in the crises of 1929 between China and the USSR or in the conflict of 1931 between China and Japan. It is widely accepted that by 1939, the provisions of the Briand-Kellogg Pact reflected and recorded a fundamental change in customary international law in respect to the legality of war.[42]

Northeast Asia and the League of Nations

In the context of Northeast Asian, the Manchurian Crisis[43] was of greatest significance.[44] In 1931, Japan invaded parts of Manchuria and occupied the cities of Mukhden and Antung, among others. Japan attempted to justify the invasion by claiming that it had to protect Japanese citizens and property because China had attacked the Southern Manchurian Railway zone. However, as Stephen C. Neff explains, "it justified its actions in various ways, for example as a punitive or hot-pursuit expedition against brigands ("undesirable elements"), or as a police-style measure to impose order in an otherwise anarchic situation – but not as a war against the state of China itself. Its chief contention, though, was that it acted for the purpose of "defending rights and interests on which her (Japan's) very existence depends."[45]

In response, China invoked Art. 11 of the Covenant which declares that "[a]ny war or threat of war, whether immediately affecting any of the Members of the League or not, is hereby declared a matter of concern to the whole League, and the League shall take any action that may be deemed wise and effectual to safeguard the peace of nations. In case any such emergency should arise the Secretary General shall on the request of

---

41 The Treaty to Avoid or Prevent Conflicts between the American States of 1929, the Treaty of Non-Aggression and Conciliation of 1933 and the Savreda-Lamas Pact of 1933. For bilateral treaties during this period, renouncing war, see I. Brownlie, *supra* note 32, pp. 101–105. See also the resolutions adopted within the Inter-American System at the conferences in Havana (1928), Montevideo (1933) and Lima (1938).

42 Brownlie, ibid., pp. 71–74, 107–111; and D. Schindler, "Der Kriegszustand im Völkerrecht der Gegenwart" in *Festschrift v. Heydte* (Duncker & Humblot, Berlin, 1977), pp. 555–576.

43 See in detail, J.T. Sherwood, "An Examination of the Legal Justifications Presented by Japan before the League of Nations in Defense of Her Actions Concerning the Mukden Incident, the Occupation of Manchuria and the Creation of Manchukuo," *Military Law & Law of War Review*, vol. 16, 1977, pp. 204–243.

44 Another issue concerned the annexation of Korea. The Korean provisional government unsuccessfully asked the League to investigate the situation, and raised the issue of Korean liberation, but the League was unwilling to address the Korean question.

45 S.C. Neff, *supra* note 17, p. 305.

any Member of the League forthwith summon a meeting of the Council. It is also declared to be the friendly right of each Member of the League to bring to the attention of the Assembly or of the Council any circumstance whatever affecting international relations which threatens to disturb international peace or the good understanding between nations upon which peace depends."

By the end of 1931, the Council established the Lytton Commission to investigate the Manchurian crisis. In 1932, the Japanese created the puppet state Manchukuo. In January 1932, the U.S. Secretary of State Stimson dispatched notes to the governments of the Republic of China and the Japanese Empire: "… the American Government deems it to be its duty to notify both the Imperial Japanese Government and the Government of the Chinese Republic that it cannot admit the legality of any situation de facto nor does it intend to recognize any treaty or agreement entered into between those Governments, or agents thereof, which may impair the treaty rights of the United States or its citizens in China, including those that relate to the sovereignty, the independence, or the territorial and administrative integrity of the Republic of China, or to the international policy relative to China, commonly known as the open door policy… ."[46]

The so-called Stimson doctrine[47] became a manifestation of American foreign policy so that the United States would not recognize any territorial changes executed by military force. Since the situation in China deteriorated and the great powers lacked the will to further deal with the situation, the dispute was referred to the Assembly. On 11 March 1932, the Assembly declared in a resolution that it was "incumbent upon the Members of the League not to recognize any situation, treaty or agreement, which may be brought by means contrary to the Covenant of the League of Nations or the Pact of Paris."[48] By the same resolution, the Assembly established the "Committee of Nineteen", which had the task of making recommendations upon the receipt of the Lytton report. In October 1932, the Lytton committee issued its report. As one of its key conclusions, the report concluded that Manchuria was an integral part of the Republic of China and that "the military operations of the Japanese troops

---

46 Quoted in Q. Wright, "The Stimson Note of January 7, 1932," *AJIL*, vol. 26, 1932, pp. 342–348, 342.

47 See in detail, D. Turns, "The Stimson Doctrine of Non-Recognition: Its Historical Genesis and Influence on Contemporary International Law," *Chinese Journal of International Law*, vol. 2, no. 1, 2003, pp. 105–143.

48 See League of Nations Official Journal, Special Supplement, no. 101, 1932, pp. 87–88.

during this night ... cannot be regarded as measures of legitimate self-defense. In saying this, does not exclude the hypothesis that the officers on the spot may have thought they were acting in self-defense."[49]

Japan withdrew from the League in 1933 but a truce between China and Japan was signed in the same year. However, Manchukuo remained under Japanese control. When Japan started a full scale war in 1937, the League Sub-Committee of its Far Eastern Advisory Committee investigated the situation and came to the conclusion that Japans recourse to force could not be based on self-defense. The finding was endorsed by the League Assembly.

General Assessment of the League of Nations

The Charter of the League of Nations and the Briand-Kellogg Pact provided "two of the missing components of an effective international system for resolving armed conflict – namely, a requirement that states resolve their differences only by peaceful means and the creation of international machinery to prevent or terminate conflict."[50] The League of Nations introduced an unprecedented framework to distinguish between legal and illegal war based on compliance or non-compliance by member states with procedures under the Covenant. However, neither the system of the League of Nations nor the Briand-Kellogg Pact could prevent Germany's and Japan's wars of aggression, which led to the outbreak of World War II. Even before the outbreak of WWII, the League had failed to stop the Chaco War (1932–35), the intervention by Germany, Italy, and the Soviet Union in the Spanish Civil War (1936–1939), the invasions of Manchuria by Japan in 1931, the invasion of Ethiopia by Italy in 1935, and the invasion of Finland by the Soviet Union in 1939.

The League of Nations failed for a number of reasons: Major powers such as the United States, Germany, the Soviet Union and Japan were not members of the League. Around half of the countries in the world were colonies. At the same time, there was also a lack of commitment to the collective security system of the League. States like France and Britain were more concerned with the balance of power in Europe than with distant conflicts in other parts of the world. Another reason may be seen in

---

49 Quoted in H. Saito, "A Japanese View of the Manchurian Situation," *Annals of the American Academy of Political and Social Science*, vol. 165, 1933, pp. 159–166, 164.

50 M. Matheson, *Council Unbound: The Growth of UN Decision Making on Conflict and Postconflict Issues after the Cold War* (United States Institute for Peace, Washington, 2006), p. 15.

the deficiencies of the Covenant. An obvious flaw in the structure of the Covenant was Art. 5, requiring unanimity in case of major decisions by the Council and the Assembly. It imposed inadequate restrictions on the aggressor state and lacked "teeth" to enforce obligations upon member states. Art. 10 of the Covenant provided that in case of aggression, or in case of any threat or danger of aggression, the Council should advise upon the means how to stop aggression.

According to Hans Kelsen, a fatal error of design was that the Council was at the heart of the organization rather than a Court of Justice which could have peacefully settled disputes by objectively applying international law.[51] Nowadays, the Security Council has the primary but not exclusive responsibility for the maintenance of international peace and security (see Art. 24 of the UN Charter) and the International Court of Justice (ICJ) is one of the six principal organs of the United Nations (see Art. 92 of the UN Charter). The Statute of the ICJ is an integral part of the UN Charter. Although all members states of the United Nations are *ipso facto* parties to the Statute of the ICJ, the Court does only have jurisdiction if that has been conferred by the parties to a dispute.

Developments after World War II

WWII was the most devastating armed conflict in the history of mankind. Even before the outbreak of WWII, Japan had expanded its empire beginning with the occupation in Manchuria. In 1937, the Sino-Japanese War broke out. Four years later, Japan attacked Pearl Harbor after U.S. President Roosevelt imposed an oil embargo on Japan. During the War in the Pacific, Japan succeeded in conquering all of East Asia, including the Philippines, Hong-Kong, Singapore, and Burma. It also attacked Australia. On 15 August 1945, the Japanese emperor, Hirohito, announced Japan's unconditional surrender after the U.S. had dropped atomic bombs on the cities of Hiroshima and Nagasaki.

With the end of World War II in 1945, the issue of ensuring lasting peace and preventing future aggression was revived. One major step was the establishment of the United Nations; the other one was the decision to try the major German war criminals by the International Military Tribunal (IMT) at Nuremberg and the major Japanese war

[51] H. Kelsen, *Law and Peace in International Relations* (Harvard University Press, Cambridge, 1948), pp. 145–168.

criminals by the International Military Tribunal for the Far East (IMTFE) in Tokyo.

The Nuremberg and Tokyo Trials

In the words of the American Chief Prosecutor, Robert M. Jackson, the purpose of the trials was "to make war less attractive to those who held the destiny of peoples in their power"[52] and to deter future aggressions. Individuals were for the first time held individually responsible for the crime of aggression by the International Military Tribunal (IMT) in Nuremberg. The Tokyo Tribunal was established by a Special Proclamation of the Supreme Commander for the Allied Power, General Douglas MacArthur.[53]

The idea of punishing the authors of the Second World War developed during the 1940s. In the Moscow Declaration of 1943, the Allied Powers declared that all Germans who had been responsible for the war would be punished.[54] The Cairo Declaration contained similar statements by the Allied Powers in regard to Japan. As the Potsdam Declaration of 26 July 1945 stressed "(t)here must be eliminated for all time the authority and influence of those who have deceived and misled the people of Japan into embarking on world conquest, for we insist that a new order of peace, security and justice will be impossible until irresponsible militarism is driven from the world" and "stern justice shall be meted out to all war criminals."[55]

Based on a proposal of the United States, aggression was included as an international crime in the London Agreement of 8 August 1945. It appeared as a subcategory of crime against peace in Art. 6(a) of the Nuremberg Charter, which was annexed to the London Agreement:

> The following acts, or any of them, were crimes coming within the jurisdiction of the Tribunal for which there shall be individual responsibility: (a) Crimes against Peace: namely planning, preparation, initiation or waging

---

52 *Report to the President from Justice Robert H. Jackson, Chief of Counsel for the United States in the Prosecution of Axis War Criminals*, *AJIL* (Supplement: Official Documents (July 1945)), vol. 39, 1945, pp. 178–90.

53 Special Proclamation: Establishment of an International Military Tribunal for the Far East annexed to the *Judgement of the International Military Tribunal for the Far East*, Annex No. A-4, Art. 1.

54 The declaration is reprinted in *AJIL* (Supplement: Official Documents, Jan. 1944), vol. 38, 1944, pp. 3–8.

55 The Potsdam Declaration of 26 July 1945 can be accessed at http://www.ndl.go.jp/constitution/e/etc/c06.html.

> of a war of aggression, or war in a violation of international treaties, agreements or assurances, or participation in a Common Plan or Conspiracy for the accomplishment of any of the foregoing.

The Tokyo Charter defined crimes against peace in an almost identical way but made reference to "a declared or undeclared war of aggression." Art. 5(a) of the Tokyo Charter provided as follows:

> Crimes against Peace: namely planning, preparation, initiation or waging of a declared or undeclared war of aggression, or war in a violation of international treaties, agreements or assurances, or participation in a Common Plan or Conspiracy for the accomplishment of any of the foregoing.

Note that the concept of crimes against peace is broader than that of a war of aggression which is only one element of crimes against peace.

Although the prosecution at Nuremberg charged all 22 defendants with crimes against peace, only twelve were convicted. In Tokyo, 28 defendants were charged with crimes against peace and the tribunal found 25 guilty of this crime.[56] The inclusion of aggression remains controversial today. Critics regarded it as a violation of the principle *nullum crimen sine lege, nulla poena sine lege* (no crime without law, without law no punishment) because neither the Briand-Kellogg Pact nor any other international treaty explicitly provided that individuals could incur liability for aggression. The Defense before the Nuremberg Tribunal argued that "ex post punishment is abhorrent to the law of all civilised nations, that no sovereign power had made aggressive war a crime at the time that the alleged criminal acts were committed, that no statute had defined aggressive war, that no penalty had been fixed for its commission, and no court had been created to try offenders."[57] However, the Nuremberg Military tribunal affirmed that Art. 6(a) was declaratory of international law at 1939. It further argued that it was even unnecessary to consider whether it was a crime, because the Nuremberg Charter made the planning and waging of aggressive war in violation of international treaties a crime.[58]

---

[56] In general on the Tokyo trial, see A. Cassese, B.V.A. Röling, *The Tokyo Trial and Beyond* (Polity Press, Cambridge, 1993); N. Boister, R. Cryer, *Documents on the Tokyo International Military Tribunal* (Oxford University Press, Oxford, 2008) and R.H. Minear, *Victor's Justice. The Tokyo War Crimes Trial* (University of Michigan, Ann Arbour, 2001). For the most recent legal study, see N. Boister, R. Cryer, *The Tokyo International Military Tribunal: A Reappraisal* (Oxford University Press, Oxford, 2008). On the controversial role of the Japanese emperor, see H.P. Blix, *Hirohito and the Making of Modern Japan* (Perennial, New York, 2001).

[57] Quoted in M.C. Bassiouni, *Crimes against Humanity* (Kluwer Law International, The Hague, 1999), p. 152.

[58] *Judgment, Nuremberg Trial Proceedings*, available at http://avalon.law.yale.edu/imt/judlawch.asp.

The IMTFE followed the arguments of the Nuremberg Tribunal and dismissed the defense's argument by referring to the Nuremberg judgement. The majority of the judges at the Tokyo Tribunal found that Japan had committed a war of aggression against the Netherlands, the Soviet Union, France, the British Commonwealth and the United States.[59] The strongest critique of the majority's judgement came from the Indian Judge Pal who would have acquitted all the defendants. He rejected the contention in the Tokyo War Crimes trial that wars of aggression were illegal: "In my opinion, no category of crime became illegal or criminal either by the Pact of Paris or as a result of the same. Nor did any customary law develop making any war criminal. Indeed: When the conduct of the nations is taken into account the law will perhaps be found to be that only a lost war is a crime."[60]

The Legacy of the Nuremberg and Tokyo Trials

The trials of the major war criminals at Nuremberg and Tokyo are milestones in the history of civilization and mark an important chapter in international criminal law by setting a precedent for the future.

However, the trials had major defects. Arguably, there was no legal basis for the crime of aggression at that time. One criticism concerned the selection process. Some of the Japanese leaders could not be indicted, because they were either dead (Prince Konoe had committed suicide) or they were considered unfit for trial (General Terauchi and Field Marshall Hisaichi). Leading figures of the financial and industrials conglomerates, the so-called zaibatsu were not indicted because of the lack of clear evidence in regard to their involvement in crimes against peace. Most striking was the omission of the emperor, Hirohito, although attempts had been made to indict him, and he had also offered to take sole responsibility for the war. Finally, Emperor Hirohito was not indicted after the veto of the United States. Although the state of Japan accepted the judgments of the IMTFE in the 1951 San Francisco Peace Treaty,[61] the trial of Japanese war criminals has remained controversial in Japanese society.[62]

---

59 *Judgement*, 49582 a-4.

60 See Pal, *Judgement*, pp. 59. See also the dissenting opinion of Justice Röling, reprinted in N. Boister, R. Cryer, *Documents on the Tokyo International Military Tribunal* (Oxford University Press, Oxford, 2008), pp. 679–807, 684–704.

61 The text of the peace treaty can be found at http://www.taiwandocuments.org/sanfrancisco01.htm.

62 See I. Buruma, *The Wages of Guilt. Memories of War in Germany and Japan* (Phoenix, London, 2002) and M. Futamura, "Memory of War Crimes and War: Japanese Historical

Besides the trials of the major war criminals at Nuremberg and Tokyo, only a few individuals have been indicted for the crime of aggression by U.S. and French military tribunals,[63] as well as by national courts.[64] All trials arose out of the Second World War.

Aggression and the International Criminal Court

In 1998, 120 states adopted the so-called Rome statute creating an International Criminal Court. The court has jurisdiction over genocide, crimes against humanity, war crimes and the crime of aggression. In 2002, the statute entered into force after sixty ratifications. As of August 2012, 121 states including Japan and South Korea have ratified or acceded to the Rome Statute.[65] Russia, the United States, North Korea, and the People's Republic of China are not a party to the Rome Statute. The PRC did not become a member of the International Criminal Court for a number of reasons. The PRC objects, among other reasons, to the fact that the Rome Statute imposes obligations on non-State parties and that war crimes committed in internal conflict fall under the jurisdiction of the court.[66] In regard to the crime of aggression, the PRC argues that the inclusion of the crime of aggression would weaken the role of the Security

---

Consciousness and the Tokyo Trial" in J. Macleod, *Defeat and Memory. Cultural Histories of Military Defeat in the Modern Era* (Palgrave, Hampshire, 2008), pp. 137–153. For an analysis how Japanese legal scholars view the Tokyo Trial, see P. Osten, *Der Tokioter Kriegsverbrecherprozess und die japanische Rechtswissenschaft* (BWV, Berlin, 2003).

63 For a comprehensive analysis of the jurisprudence of the trials, see Part I, II and III of *The Historical Review of Developments Relating to Aggression* (United Nations Publication, New York, 2003).

64 See Brownlie, *supra* note 30, pp. 179. In China, the Japanese military commander Takashi Sakai was indicted by a Chinese military tribunal for conducting military operations in China which were part of Japan's war of aggression. The tribunal applied "Chinese rules governing the trial of War Criminals", see *Re Takashi Sakai, Nanking, Chinese War Crimes Tribunal of the Ministry of National Defense*, 1946, 13 Ann. Dig. 222. According to the Law of October 24, 1946, crimes against peace was defined as "the planning, conspiring or preparing" of an aggressive and therefore unlawful war or doing the same in an aggression against the Republic of China. On the Chinese war trials, see P.R. Picigallo, *The Japanese on Trial. Allied War Crimes Operations in the East 1945–1951* (University of Texas Press, Austin and London, 1979), pp. 158–173.

65 For further reading, see Y.S. Kim, "The Korean Implementing Legislation on the ICC Statute," *Chinese Journal of International Law*, 2011, pp. 161–170 and Kyo Arai, Akira Mayama and Osamu Yoshida, "Japan's Accession to the ICC Statute and the ICC Cooperation Law," *The Japanese Yearbook of International Law*, vol. 51, 2008, pp. 359–383. On Japan and the crime of aggression, see in detail the chapter by Madoka Futamura.

66 See, in detail, Lu Jianping and Wang Zhixiang, "China's Attitude towards the ICC," *Journal of International Criminal Justice*, vol. 3, no. 3, 2005, pp. 608–620.

Council.[67] However, according to Art. 24 of the UN Charter, the Security Council only has primary but not exclusive responsibility for the maintenance of international peace and security.[68]

After years of discussions,[69] the state parties agreed on a definition of aggression at Kampala in 2010 (see Art. 8 *bis* of the ICC statute).[70] The crime of aggression is defined as "the planning, preparation, initiation or execution, by a person in a position effectively to control over to direct the political or military action of a State, of an act of aggression which by its character, gravity and scale, constitutes a manifest violation of the Charter of the United Nations."[71] Any of the acts set forth in the United Nations General Assembly resolution 3314 (XXXIX) of 14 December 1974 qualify as aggression:[72]

---

67 Ibid., p. 617.

68 For further discussion on the role of the Security Council and the ICC in regard to the crime of aggression, instead of many others, see C. McDougall, "When Law and Reality Clash - The Imperative of Compromise in the Context of the Accumulated Evil of the Whole: Conditions for the Excercise of the International Criminal Court's Jurisdiction over the Crime of Aggression," *International Criminal Law Review*, vol. 7, no. 2–3, 2007, pp. 277–333.

69 All relevant documents including the ones related to the Review Conference in Kampala and the Special Working Group on Aggression can be found at http://www.icc-cpi.int/Menus/ASP/Crime+of+Aggression/.

70 The amendment on the crime of aggression can be found at http://iccreviewconference.blogspot.com/2010/06/official-version-of-aggression.html. For a summary of the Kampala conference, see D. Scheffer, "State Parties Approve New Crimes for International Criminal Court," *ASIL Insight*, vol. 14, issue 16, 2010, accessible at http://www.asil.org/files/insight100622pdf.pdf and S. Barriga, L. Grover, "A Historic Breakthrough on the Crime of Aggression," *AJIL*, vol. 105, 2011, pp. 517–533. For critical comments on the definition of the crime of aggression, M.J. Glennon, "The Blank-Prose Crime of Aggression," *The Yale Journal of International Law*, vol. 35, 2010, pp. 71–114. See also the critique of the proposal for the codification of the crime of aggression by Andreas Paulus and the response by Claus Kress in the European Journal of International Law, A. Paulus, "Second Thoughts on the Crime of Aggression," *EJIL*, vol. 20, no. 4, 2010, pp. 1117–1128 and C. Kress, "Time for Decision: Some Thoughts on the Immediate Future of the Crime of Aggression: A Reply to Andreas Paulus," *EJIL*, vol. 20, no. 4, 2010, pp. 1129–1146.

71 Available at http://www.icc-cpi.int/iccdocs/asp_docs/RC2010/RC-WGCA-1-ENG.pdf.

72 However, the U.S. has criticised the definition and rejected the view, that the resolution states customary norms of international criminal law, see *U.S. Policy Toward the Upcoming International Criminal Court Review Conference*, accessible at http://www.asil.org/files/Transcript_ICC_Koh_Rapp_Brooks.pdf; S. Miley, *ICC Nations Lacks Consensus on Aggression*, http://jurist.org/paperchase/2010/06/icc-nations-lack-consensus-on-crime-of-aggression.php and T. Meron, U.S. State Department, *Crime of Aggression: Statement by the United States before the ICC Prepartory Committee*, 6 December 2000, available at http://www.state.gov/s/l/6151.htm.

(a) The invasion or attack by the armed forces of a State of the territory of another State, or any military occupation, however temporary, resulting from such invasion or attack, or any annexation by the use of force of the territory of another State or part thereof;
(b) Bombardment by the armed forces of a State against the territory of another State or the use of any weapons by a State against the territory of another State;
(c) The blockade of the ports or coasts of a State by the armed forces of another State;
(d) An attack by the armed forces of a State on the land, sea or air forces, or marine and air fleets of another State;
(e) The use of armed forces of one State which are within the territory of another State with the agreement of the receiving State, in contravention of the conditions provided for in the agreement or any extension of their presence in such territory beyond the termination of the agreement;
(f) The action of a State in allowing its territory, which it has placed at the disposal of another State, to be used by that other State for perpetrating an act of aggression against a third State;
(g) The sending by or on behalf of a State of armed bands, groups, irregulars or mercenaries, which carry out acts of armed force against another State of such gravity as to amount to the acts listed above, or its substantial involvement therein.

However, it remains unclear which violations of Art. 2(4) of the UN Charter are so manifest that they would fall under the jurisdiction of the International Criminal Court. Many states including the PRC and most international lawyers would agree that humanitarian interventions without Security Council authorizations lack a legal basis in customary international law. However, since humanitarian interventions are sometimes considered to be morally justified this raises the question of whether they could be also considered as examples of aggression.[73]

Another controversial issue concerned the mechanisms that trigger cases concerning the crime of aggression. The aggression amendments

[73] For further discussion, see E. Leclerc-Gagné & M. Byers, "A Question of Intent: The Crime of Aggression and Unilateral Humanitarian Intervention," *Case Western Reserve Journal of International Law*, vol. 41, nos. 2–3, 2009, pp. 379–390 and S.D. Murphy, "Criminalizing Humanitarian Intervention," *Case Western Reserve Journal of International Law*, vol. 41, nos. 2–3, 2009, pp. 341–377.

include three trigger mechanisms: (1) when the Security Council refers a situation to the court, irrespectively whether a State is a party to the Rome Statute; (2) when a State party refers a situation to the ICC; or (3) when the Prosecutor initiates an investigation. The court does have jurisdiction over a crime of aggression, "arising from an act of aggression committed by a State Party, unless that State Party has previously declared that it does not accept such jurisdiction by lodging a declaration with the Registrar."[74] The court cannot exercise jurisdiction over the crime of aggression when committed by a non-party state's national citizen or on a non-party state's territory.

The implementation of jurisdiction over the crime of aggression is delayed until 1 January 2017. After that date the Assembly of State Parties have to agree by two-thirds majority to activate the crime of aggression. One year earlier at least 30 state parties must already have accepted the amendments on aggression.

The United Nations and the Regulation of the Use of Force

In order to prevent aggression, breaches of or threats to peace, the United Nations[75] established a new system of collective security[76] which refers to a sophisticated system of economic, political and military enforcement measures by the Security Council in Chapter VII. The collective security system of the UN Charter rests on four main pillars: (1) the prohibition against the threat or use force between states (see Art. 2(4)); (2) the legal obligation of member states to settle their disputes by peaceful means (see Art. 2(3)); (3) the concept that the Security Council has the primary responsibility for the maintenance of international peace and security (see Art. 24 of the UN Charter); and (4) the legal obligation that member states have the legal obligation to carry out the Security Council's decision

74 See Art. 15 *bis*.

75 The Republic of China was among the founding members of the United Nations. When the Communist Party of China declared the People's Republic of China, it argued that the PRC replaced the Republic of China. However, the PRC was only admitted in 1971. As one of the former enemy states during WW II, Japan could only join the United Nations in 1956. After several failed attempts, North and South Korea joined the UN in 1991.

76 The UN Charter does not contain any express reference to collective security. However, Art. 1(1) of the UN Charter mentions as one of the core aims "collective measures" to suppress acts of aggression and to prevent breaches of the peace. Art. 1(1) includes also adjustments or peaceful settlements of disputes as other paths to maintain peace and security.

(see Art. 25 of the UN Charter). As in any other system of collective security, the United Nations is based on the promise that aggression would be met with opposing force and that members would take collective measures against the aggressor. In addition the United Nations undertakes to prevent aggression by eliminating the causes of conflict, by facilitating the peaceful settlement of disputes, and by promoting disarmament measures.

As pointed out by Philip Bobbitt, "the coming of peace to the society has brought changes to international law."[77] As a consequence, Art. 2(4) was included as the central norm of the UN Charter, which states that "all Members shall refrain in their international relations from the threat or use of force against the territorial integrity or political independence of any state, or in any manner inconsistent with the purposes of the United Nations."[78] The vast majority of international lawyers consider Art. 2(4) of the UN Charter to be a principle of customary international law and agree that this provision constitutes a preemptory norm of international law (*jus cogens*).

The prohibition of the use of force in Art. 2(4) also includes the narrower concept of the prohibition of aggression. The use of force covers wars, forcible measures short of war and even illegal threats of force. The wording of Art. 2(4) stands in contrast to the Kellogg-Briand Pact, which renounced war but not the threat or use of force between States. The difference is explained by Elihu Lauterpacht: "The developments from the words of the Kellogg-Briand Pact to the wording of the Charter were deliberate. It had soon been realised after the adoption of the Kellogg-Briand Pact that the association of the word "war" with a technical condition of states might contend that their use of force, since it fell short of "war" did not violate the prohibition of the Pact. The text words of Art. 2(4) of the Charter was tailored to fill this gap. What was now prohibited was the deliberate initiation of a situation of force. Henceforth, there was to be no room for the argument about whether or not the hostilities amounted to war."[79]

---

[77] P. Bobbitt, *The Shield of Achilles. War, Peace and the Course of History* (Allan Lane, The Penguin Press, London, 2002), p. 355.

[78] The prohibition was reiterated in the Rio Pact of 1947.

[79] E. Lauterpacht, "The Legal Irrelevance of the State of War," *ASIL Proc.*, vol. 62, 1968, pp. 62. On the relevance or irrelevance of war as a legal concept under current international law, see also C. Greenwood, "The Concept of War in Modern International Law," *ICLQ*, vol. 36, 1987, pp. 283–306 and *Im Interview: Rechtswissenschaftler Michael Bothe*

As stated in Art. 2(4) of the UN Charter, only the threat or the use of force, which is inconsistent with the UN Charter is prohibited.[80] The Charter allows the use of force in case of enforcement measures under Chapter VII and reserves the right of individual or collective self-defense under Art. 51 "if an armed attack occurs against a Member of the United Nations."[81]

Despite this narrow framework, several categories of force and their legal justifications remain controversial. Among those are: the right to humanitarian intervention; the right of forcible intervention to protect nationals; the right of military intervention by States, military coalitions or regional organizations in the absence of explicit Security Council authorisation; the right of pre-emptive self-defense; the use of force against non-state actors and in regard to computer network attacks, failed states and *de-facto* regimes.[82]

The Use of Force and Northeast Asia

All states in Northeast Asia with the exception of Japan have used force after 1945. The most tragic event was the Korean War. The following sections discuss the major legal issues arising from the Korean War[83] and

"Als Rechtsbegriff hat der "Krieg" ausgedient," http://www.sueddeutsche.de/kultur/artikel/992/81911/print.html.

[80] See also *Legality of the Threat or Use of Nuclear Weapons*, Advisory Opinion, ICJ Reports 1996, p. 246. In detail, see M. Roscini, "Threats of Armed Force and Contemporary International Law," *NILR*, vol. 54, 2007, pp. 229–277 and N. Stürchler, *The Threat of Force in International Law* (Cambridge University Press, Cambridge, 2007).

[81] The third exception laid down in Arts. 53(1) and 107 of the UN Charter provides for measures against former enemy states. The so-called enemy clause became obsolete; when Italy in 1955, Japan in 1956 and Germany in 1973 were admitted as peace loving nations to the UN, see Art. 4 of the UN Charter.

[82] On the use of force in international relations, see for example, Y. Dinstein, *War, Aggression and Self-Defense* (Cambridge University Press, Cambridge, 4th edition, 2005); T. Franck, *Recourse to Force. State Action against Threats and Armed Attacks* (Cambridge University Press, Cambridge, 2003); C. Gray, *International Law and the Use of Force* (Oxford University Press, Oxford, 3rd edition, 2008); and M.E. O'Connell, *International Law and the Use of Force* (Foundation Press, New York, 2005). See also the commentaries by A. Randelzhofer on Art. 2(4) and 51 of the UN Charter in the B. Simma, *The Charter of the United Nations. A Commentary* (Oxford University Press, Oxford, Second Edition, 2002) and the chapters on the use of force by T. Gill in T. Gill and D. Fleck (eds.), *The Handbook of the International Law of Military Operations* (Oxford University Press, Oxford, 2010). For an excellent article on the methodological debate, see O. Corten, "The Controversies over the Customary Prohibition on the Use of Force: A Methodological Debate", *EJIL*, vol. 16, no. 5, 2006, pp. 803–822.

[83] On the Korean War, see for example B. Cumings, *The Korean War. A History* (Modern Library, 2010); L.M. Goodrich, *Korea: A Study of U.S. Policy in the United Nations* (Council on

then address other instances when states took recourse to force in Northeast Asia.

The Korean War

The DPRK launched the invasion of South Korea on 25 June 1950. The DPRK attempted to justify the invasion by claiming that it had been attacked first by South Korea. However, UN observers rejected the claim and stated that North Korea initiated the conflict.[84] According to SG Trygve Lie, "(t)he reports received from the Commission, as well as reports from sources in Korea, make it plain that military actions have been undertaken by North Korean forces. These actions are a direct violation of ... the principles of the Charter. The present situation is a serious one and is a threat to international peace. The Security Council is in my opinion, the competent organ to deal with it. I consider it the clear duty of the Security Council to take steps necessary to re-establish peace in that area."[85]

The U.S. administration immediately turned to the Security Council. On 25 June 1950, the Security Council adopted SC Resolution 82 determining that North Korea's attack constituted a breach of the peace and calling for the immediate cessation of the hostilities. Furthermore the Council called upon "all members to render every assistance to the United Nations ... and to refrain from giving assistance to the North Korean authorities." On 27 June 1950, the Council adopted SC Resolution 83 and recommended "that the members furnish such assistance to the Republic of Korea as may be necessary to repel the armed attack and to restore international peace and

Foreign Relations, New York, 1956); J. Friedrich, *Yalu. An den Ufern des dritten Weltkriegs* (*Propyläen*, Berlin, 2007); E. Luard, *A History of the United Nations, Vol. 1: The Years of Western Domination 1945–1955* (St. Martin's Press, New York, 1982), pp. 228–274; and W. Stueck, "The United Nations, the Security Council, and the Korean War" in V. Lowe ... [et al.] (eds.), *The United Nations Security Council and War: The Evolution of Thought and Practice since 1945* (Oxford University Press, 2008), pp. 265–279.

84 Nikita Khrushchev who was the First Secretary of the Communist Party of the Soviet Union from 1953–64 ultimately admitted in his memoirs that North Korea started the Korean War: "For many years we insisted that the initiative for starting the Korean War came from South Korea. Some say there is no need to correct this version of events, because it would be of advantage to our enemies. I'm telling the truth now for the sake of history: it was the initiative of Comrade Kim Il Sung, and it was supported by Stalin and many others – in fact by everybody." See N. Krushchev, *The Glasnost Tapes* (Strobe Talbot (ed.), Little Brown, 1990), p. 144.

85 SCOR, 473rd meeting, June 1950.

security in that area." The third and last resolution, SC Resolution 84, recommended that all members should provide military force; requested the U.S. to designate the commander in force: and authorized the Unified Command, at its discretion, to use the United Nations flag in the course of operations. The Security Council could only pass the three resolutions because the Soviet delegate, Jakob Malik, was deliberately absent from the voting. The Soviet Union had boycotted the Security Council in protest against the exclusion of the PRC (at that time China was represented in the Security Council by the Kuomintang group).

China heavily criticised the U.S. involvement in the Korean War. In the words of Mao, "(Truman) shredded all agreements related to the American commitment not to intervene in China's internal affairs ... The United States is unable to justify in any ways its intervention in the internal affairs of Korea, the Philippines, and Vietnam."[86] The PRC considered the UN intervention as a cover up for "United States armed aggression ... and armed intervention in the internal affairs of Korea in violation of world peace."[87] After the return of the Soviet Union delegate Malik to the Security Council on 1 August 1950, he blocked any further action by the Council. In July 1950, the UN forces were able to halt the advance of the North Korean forces. In September 1950, they launched a successful amphibious operation at Incheon and the North Korean defense line collapsed. On 7 October 1950, the General Assembly recommended the pursuit of the North Korean forces into its own territory by approving "all appropriate steps ... to ensure stability throughout Korea ... including the holding of elections, under the auspices of the United Nations, for the establishment of a unified, independent and democratic government in the sovereign State of Korea. When the UN forces advanced to the Yalu River, the PRC intervened by launching a massive attack that forced the UN forces to retreat to the 38th parallel. The PRC justified the intervention as necessary help to North Korea against the 'United States aggression'."[88] The General Assembly found that the PRC had "by engaging in hostilities against United Nations forces there, ... itself engaged in aggression in Korea" and called upon the PRC "to cease hostilities against the United Nations forces and to withdraw

---

86 R. Withnana, *Power, Politics, Law: International Law and State Behaviour during International Crisis* (Martinus Nijhoff Publishers, Leiden, Boston, 2008), p. 90, quoting C.-J. Lee, *China and Korea: Dynamic Relations* (Hoover Press, California, Stanford, 1996), p. 12.

87 S/1583 of 6 July 1950 from PRC Minister of Foreign Affairs, Zhou Enlai to Security Council President. See also S/1703 of 20 August 1950.

88 S/1902 of 11 November 1950.

from Korea."[89] After the retreat to 38th parallel, peace talks begun and the DPRK finally agreed to an armistice at Pamunjon on 27 July 1953.

There is no agreement among legal scholars regarding the legal basis of the UN action in the Korean War.[90] One may either consider Art. 39 in conjunction with Art. 42 of the UN Charter or else view Art. 51 of the UN Charter (collective self-defense) as the legal basis. The Soviet Union and China argued that the Security Council lacked the legal competence to take measures under Chapter VII. The Soviet Union stressed that the SC resolutions "had no legal force since it had been adopted only by six votes, the seventh being that of the "Kuomintang representative."[91] The PRC pointed out that the "... so called United Nations Command ... was endangered illegally in the Security Council under manipulation of the United States during the absence of the permanent members, the Soviet Union and the People's Republic of China ..."[92] The wording of Art. 27(3) of the UN Charter clearly indicates that all decisions of the Council would require the concurring vote of the permanent members. According to Art. 27(3) of the UN Charter, "Decisions of the Security Council on all other matters shall be made by an affirmative vote of nine members including the concurring votes of the permanent members; ... ." However, there had already been a practise developed by 1950, whereby the abstention of a permanent member from voting was deemed still to be a "concurring vote" within the meaning of Art. 27(3). The absence of the Soviet Union could be seen as a violation of Art. 28 of the UN Charter. According to Art. 28(1) of the UN Charter: "The Security Council shall be so organized as to be able to function continuously. Each member of the Security Council shall for this purpose be represented at all times at the seat of the Organization."

---

89 GA Resolution 498(V) of 1 February 1951. See also GA Resolution 500 (V) of 18 May 1951. Both documents are reprinted in I.S. Chung, *Korean Questions in the United Nations* (Seoul National University Press, Seoul, 2002), pp. 58–62.

90 For authors considering the UN action as illegal, see L. Fisher, "The Korean War: On What Legal Basis Did Truman Act?", *AJIL*, vol. 89, 1995, pp. 21–39 and L. Gross, "Voting in the Security Council: Abstention from Voting in the Security Council: Abstention from Voting and Absence from Meeting," *Yale Law Journal*, vol. 60, 1951, pp. 209–257. For authors arguing that the UN action was legal, see M.S. Mc Dougal and R. Gardner, "The Veto and the Charter: An Interpretation for Survival," *Yale Law Journal*, vol. 60, 1951, pp. 285–292 and J.W. Halderman, "Legal Basis for United Nations Armed Forces," *AJIL*, vol. 56, 1962, pp. 971–996. For a short summary on the legal issues, see Y. Pak, *Korea and the United Nations* (Kluwer Law International, The Hague, 2000), pp. 75–91 and for an excellent study on the relationship between state behaviour and international law in the context of the Korean War, see Withana, *supra* note 86, pp. 90–135.

91 *Yearbook of the United Nations*, 1950, p. 225.

92 S/1898 of 6 September 1950.

Northeast Asia and the Use of Force after 1945

The People's Republic of China has traditionally taken a stance of strict non-interference in the affairs of other states and its foreign policy is based on the five principles of peaceful coexistence (i.e., mutual respect for each other's territorial integrity and sovereignty; mutual non-aggression against anyone; mutual non-interference in each other's internal affairs; equality; mutual benefit and peaceful co-existence).[93] During the last decade the PRC has become the major troop contributor among the permanent members of the Security Council to UN peace operations but has remained reluctant to participate in robust operations.[94] The PRC has strongly opposed Western interventions in recent years[95] including the Iraq War in 2003, NATO's intervention in Kosovo in 1998,[96] and the establishment of no-fly zones in Iraq during the 1990s.[97] In regard to the reform of the United Nations, the PRC has argued among others that Art. 51 of the UN Charter should neither be amended nor reinterpreted. In case of urgent threats, the Security Council should address these situations.[98] In practice, the PRC has been reluctant to authorize the use of force through the Security Council. For example, in 2011, the PRC abstained from voting to enforce a no-fly zone over Libya and China's permanent representative, Li Baodong argued that "military action only complicates the situation

---

93 See *Backgrounder: Five Principles of Peaceful Coexistence*, http://news.xinhuanet.com/english/2005-04/08/content_2803638.htm.

94 As of January 2013, the PRC is ranking 15 among the contributors to UN peace operations and providing 1868 peacekeepers, http://www.un.org/en/peacekeeping/contributors/2013/jan13_2.pdf. In general on the PRC's participation in peace operations, see B. Gill and C.-H. Huang, "China's Expanding Role in Peacekeeping, Prospects and Policy Implications," *SIPRI Policy Paper*, 25 November 2009, http://books.sipri.org/files/PP/SIPRIPP25.pdf; Sarah Teitt, "The Responsibility to Protect and China's Peacekeeping Policy," *International Peacekeeping*, vol. 18, no. 3, pp. 298–312 and L. Tiewa, "Marching for a More Open, Confident and Responsible Great Power: Explaining China's Involvement in UN Peacekeeping Operations," *Journal of International Peacekeeping*, vol. 13, nos. 1–2, 2009, pp. 101–130.

95 See Chapter 5 by Jonathan Davis in this volume.

96 The PRC stated in the Security Council that "months ago, without authorization by the Security Council, the United States-led NATO had blatantly launched military strikes against the sovereign States of the Federal Republic of Yugoslavia. In taking that action, NATO had seriously violated the Charter of the United Nations and norms of international law, had undermined the authority of the Security Council, and had, hence, set an extremely dangerous precedent in the history of international relations." SC 4011 meeting, 10 June 1999.

97 SC, 4008th meeting, 21 meeting 1999.

98 See Position Paper of the People's Republic of China on the United Nations Reform, 2005/06/07, accessible at http://www.china-un.org/eng/zghlhg/zzhgg/t199101.htm.

rather than resolves it."[99] In 2012, China vetoed twice SC resolutions calling for tougher sanctions against the Syrian regime. Like Russia China had already vetoed a draft resolution in October 2011 despite the ongoing violence in Syria.[100]

Even when Iraq invaded Kuwait which was one of the clearest cases of aggression after 1945, the PRC opted to abstain from voting when the Security Council adopted Resolution 678 which authorised the use of force to liberate Kuwait.

The PRC has also been involved in military operations on a number of occasions. It was a major party in the Korean War and conducted off-shore island operation against Taiwan in 1954–55 and 1958. Limited uses of force included the invasion of contested territory along the Sino-Indian border in 1962; border clashes between the Soviet Union and the PRC because of a dispute about sovereignty over an island in the Ussuri river in 1969; a military confrontation with the Republic of Vietnam because of a dispute about sovereignty over the Spratly and Paracel islands in 1974;[101] and the armed conflict with Vietnam in 1979.[102] Regarding future scenarios involving the use of force, the PRC has not ruled out the possibility to use force in support of its territorial claim towards Taiwan. Art. 8 of the Anti-Secession Law adopted in 2005 states that "in the event that the 'Taiwan independence' secessionist forces should act under any name or by any means to cause the fact of Taiwan's secession from China, or that major incidents entailing Taiwan's secession from China should occur, or that possibilities for a peaceful reunification should be completely exhausted, the state shall employ non-peaceful means and other necessary measures to protect China's sovereignty and territorial integrity."[103] The PRC has

---

[99] "China 'Stands against Use of Force to Solve Int'l Disputes'," *China Daily*, 7 April, 2011. For further discussion, see Andrew Garwood-Gowers, "China and the 'the Responsibility to Protect': The Implications of the Lybian Intervention," *Asian Journal of International Law*, vol. 2, issue 2, 2012, pp. 375–393.

[100] See UN docs. S/PV.6627 of 4 October 2011; S/2012/77 of 4 February 2012 and SC 10714 of 9 July 2012.

[101] See for a general overview on the military clashes in the South China Sea, EIA, *South China Sea*, http://www.eia.doe.gov/emeu/cabs/South_China_Sea/pdf.pdf, pp. 5–6.

[102] For a short summary of the cases, see A.M. Weisburd, *Use of Force. The Practice of States since World War II* (Penn State Press, 1997), pp. 261–264, 268–269, 272–273 and 281–284. See also S.P. Sharma, "The India-China Border Dispute: An Indian Perspective," *AJIL*, vol. 59, no. 1, 1965, pp. 16–47; T. Robinson, "The Sino-Soviet Border Dispute: Background, Development, and the March 1969 Clashes," *The American Political Science Review*, vol. 66, no. 4, 1972, pp. 1175–1202.

[103] The full text of the Anti-Secession Law can be found at http://english.peopledaily.com.cn/200503/14/eng20050314_176746.html.

consistently argued that the Taiwan question is a purely internal matter of China[104] and therefore Art. 2(4) of the UN Charter did not apply.[105] However, the counter argument would be to regard Taiwan as a stabilized *de facto* regime,[106] which is also protected by Art. 2(4) of the UN Charter.[107]

North Korea has remained the primary threat to peace and security in Northeast Asia. Since the Korean War there have been a number of military crises concerning North Korea including the capture of the U.S. intelligence gathering ship Pueblo in 1968 and military operations along the DMZ, in the Sea of Japan, and in the Yellow Sea. Growing concerns about the human rights situation inside North Korea may lead to humanitarian intervention by foreign powers.[108] However, it is controversial whether a unilateral right to humanitarian intervention which may be understood as "the threat or use of force across state borders by a state (or group of states) aimed at preventing or ending widespread and grave violations of the fundamental human rights of individuals other than its own citizens within whose territory is applied"[109] exists under customary international law.[110] Many scholars agree that allowing individual states to intervene on humanitarian grounds is open to abuse and could lead to the erosion of the existing legal system on the use of force.[111] States have in general

104 See UN doc A/55/420; A/59/879; A/60/255 and A/60/390.

105 See P.C.W. Chan, "The Legal Status of Taiwan and the Legality of the Use of Force in a Cross Taiwan Strait Conflict," *Chinese Journal of International Law*, vol. 8, 2009, pp. 455–492, 484–485.

106 S. Tumarnidze, *Status of the De Facto State in Public International Law. A Legal Appraisal of the Principle of Effectiveness* (2010), pp. 109–131 accessible at http://www.sub.uni-hamburg.de/opus/volltexte/2010/4686/pdf/Doktorarbeit.pdf.

107 Ibid, pp. 317–319.

108 See, for example, D.-J. Jang, Y.-H. Byun, and K.-H. Song, "Human Rights Problems in North Korea: Humanitarian Intervention or Humanitarian Assistance?", paper presented at the annual meeting of the American Political Science Association, 30. August 2007, available at http://www.allacademic.com/meta/p210862_index.html.

109 J.L. Holzgrefe, "The Humanitarian Intervention Debate" in J.L. Holzgrefe, R.O. Keohane, *Humanitarian Intervention. Ethical, Legal, and Political Dilemmas* (Cambridge University Press, Cambridge, 2003), pp. 15–52, 18.

110 Generally on humanitarian intervention, see P. Alston, E. MacDonald, *Human Rights, Intervention, and the Use of Force* (Oxford University Press, Oxford, 2008); S. Chesterman, *Just War or Just Peace? Humanitarian Intervention and International Law* (Oxford University Press, Oxford, 2001); P. Hilpold, "Humanitarian Intervention: Is There a Need for a Legal Reappraisal," *EJIL*, vol. 12, 2001, pp. 437–467 and N.J. Wheeler, *Saving Strangers: Humanitarian Intervention in International Society* (Oxford University Press, Oxford, 2000).

111 For the opposite view, see for example, C. Greenwood, "Humanitarian Intervention: the Case of Kosovo," *Finnish Yearbook of International Law*, vol. 10, 2002, pp. 145–175; R. Lillich, "Forcible Self-help by States to Protect Human Rights," *Iowa Journal of International Law Review*, vol. 53, 1967/1968, pp. 325–251; M. Reisman, "Sovereignty and Human Rights in Contemporary International Law," *AJIL*, vol. 84, 1990, pp. 866–876 and F. Tesón,

not called for humanitarian intervention in regard to North Korea, but the issue has been discussed by academics and could be part of a joint contingency plan between the U.S. and South Korea[112] as a potential scenario after the death of Kim Jong Il and in case of collapse of the North Korean state.[113]

Another future scenario concerning the use of force is that the United States or South Korea could attack in anticipatory self-defense because of North Korea's attempts to build weapons of mass destruction. Any such strike in absence of an armed attack by North Korea would be controversial and most likely condemned by the PRC. It should also be noted that North Korea asserted a right to pre-emptive attacks when in 2002, President Bush had labelled North Korea as a member of the "Axis of Evil"[114] and had considered to launch pre-emptive attacks against North Korea.[115] The right to self-defense is one of the most contentious institutions in contemporary international law. According to Art. 51 of the UN Charter, self-defense requires the existence of an armed attack. However, many scholars agree that an armed attack has to be only imminent and make reference to the *Caroline* formula of 1837, according to which there must be a "necessity of self-defense, instant, overwhelming, leaving no choice, of means, and no moment for deliberation."[116] North Korea itself feels

---

Humanitarian Intervention. An Inquiry into Law and Morality (New York: Transnational Publishers, 1996).

112 The contingency plan is classified and details are not known. According to a South Korean newspaper, the Chosun Ilbo, the plan consists of six scenarios of sudden change in the North including a coup, civil war, a mass exodus of North Koreans, a massive natural disaster, and kidnapping of South Korean citizens by the North. The South Korean Unification Ministry has denied the existence of such a plan. See "Seoul Overhauls N. Korea Contingency Plan," *Chosun Ilbo*, 14 January 2010, http://english.chosun.com/site/data/html_dir/2010/01/14/2010011400307.html and "S. Korea, U.S. Practice Stabilizing N. Korea in Civil War," *Chosun Ilbo*, 6 April 2012. See also S.H. Sheen, "U.S. Contingency Plan for North Korea's Regime Collapse," *IIRI Working Paper Series* 10, October 2011.

113 See B.W. Benett and J. Lind, "The Collapse of North Korea: Military Missions and Requirements," *International Security*, vol. 36, vol. 2, 2011, pp. 84–119; Center for U.S.-Korea Policy (report written by S.-W. Byun), "North Korea Contingency Planning and U.S.-ROK Cooperation," September 2009, available at http://asiafoundation.org/resources/pdfs/DPRKContingencyCUSKP0908.pdf and S. van der Meer, "North Korea after Kim Jong Il: Four Scenarios," *Strategic Insights*, vol. 8, issue 5, 2009, available at http://www.clingendael.nl/publications/2009/20091200_cscp_article_vandermeer_northkorea.pdf.

114 Accessible at http://georgewbush-whitehouse.archives.gov/news/releases/2002/01/20020129-11.html.

115 "N Korea Threatens US with First Strike," *The Guardian*, 6 February 2003.

116 However, it needs to be noted that at the time of the *Caroline* incident international law did not prohibit the use of force among states. Generally on the discussion of pre-emptive and preventive self-defense in the last decade, see M. Bothe, "Terrorism and the Legality of Pre-emptive Force," *EJIL*, vol. 12, 2003, pp. 227–240; R. Falk, "What Future for

constantly threatened by the United States which it labels as the worst peace breaker in the world[117] and has condemned Western interventions including the invasion of Iraq in 2003 and the so-called war on terror.[118]

The Republic of Korea has taken part in a number of military operations. South Korea supported South Vietnam during the Vietnam War by sending the second largest contingent of foreign troops after the United States. It dispatched personnel to the United Nations Operations in Somalia II (UNOSOM II); to the United Nations Mission for the Referendum in Western Sahara (MINURSO); to the United Nations Angola Verification Mission III (UNAVEM III); to the United Nations Military Observer Group in India and Pakistan (UNMOGIP); to the United Nations Observer Mission (UNOMIG); to the United Nations Mission in Liberia (UNMIL); to the United Nations Assistance Mission in Afghanistan (UNAMA); to United Nations Integrated Mission in Timor-Leste (UNMIT); to the United Nations Mission in Nepal (UNMIN); and to the United Nations Interim Force in Lebanon (UNIFIL).[119] As of January 2013 South Korea is providing 431 peacekeepers to the UN and ranking 37 among troop contributing countries.[120]

Japan is prohibited from using military force by its constitution. According to Art. 9 of the National Constitution of Japan, "the Japanese people forever renounce war as a sovereign right of the nation and the threat or

---

the UN Charter System of War Prevention?", *AJIL*, vol. 97, 2003, pp. 590–598; C. Greenwood, "International Law and the Pre-emptive Use of Force: Afghanistan, Al-Quaida, and Iraq," *San Diego Journal of International Law*, vol. 4, 2003, pp. 7–37; and M.E. O'Connell, "The Myth of Pre-emptive Self-Defense," Papers of the *ASIL* Task Force on Terrorism, August 2002 available at http:// www.asil.org. and in the North Korean context, see K.J. Malone, "Preemptive Strikes and the Nuclear Crisis: Legal and Political Limitations on the Use of Force", *Pacific Rim Law & Policy Journal*, vol. 12, no. 3, 2003, pp. 807–834, J.S. Kim, B. Howe, "Pre-emption against Pyongyang: Is a Military First Strike on the Korean Peninsula Legal?", *Journal of Korean Law*, vol. 4, no. 1, 2004, pp. 123–154.

117 See for example, the Statement of the North Korean Vice-Minister of Foreign Affairs, Pak Kil Yon at the GA debate, Sixty-third session of UNGA, 27 September 2008.

118 See for example, the statement of the Democratic People's Republic of Korea in regard to the Report of the International Atomic Energy Agency, General Assembly, 48 meeting, 1 November 2004, A/59/PV.48.

119 See the information provided at the homepage of the Permanent Mission of South Korea to the United Nations, http://un.mofat.go.kr/eng/am/un/bilateral/policy/index.jsp#policy02.

120 See UNDPKO, Ranking of Military and Police Contributions to UN Operations, http://www.un.org/en/peacekeeping/contributors/2013/jan13_2.pdf. For critical remarks on South Korea's role in UN peace operations, see K-Y. Son, "From a Garrison State to a Humanitarian Power?: Security Identities, Constitutive Norms and South Korea's Overseas Troop Dispatches," *The Korean Journal of Defense Analysis*, vol. 23, no. 4, 2011, pp. 557–573 and J.-H. Nam, "Korea's Duty in Peacekeeping. Participation in International Peacekeeping Activities Can Be a Precious Experience for a Divided Nation like Korea," *JoongAng Daily*, 24th April 2008, http://joongangdaily.joins.com/article/view.asp?aid=2888998.

use of force as means of settling international disputes."[121] Therefore any debate concerning the use of force is a difficult topic to address. In practice, Japan supported the liberation of Kuwait from Iraq in 1990 because the military operation had been authorized by SC resolution 678. However, NATO's air campaign over Kosovo in 1999 and the invasion of Iraq in 2003 were controversially debated in Japan.[122]

Since 1992 Japan has also participated in fifteen peace operations. Japanese Self-Defense Force (JSDF) and police officers participated among others in the missions in Cambodia, Mozambique, the Golan Heights, Timor-Leste, and Nepal.[123] As of January 2013, Japan is providing 271 peacekeepers to the UN and ranking 46 among troop contributing countries.[124] Like the PRC and South Korea, Japan has dispatched navy ships to combat piracy off the coast of Somalia.[125] In addition, there is an ongoing debate to review the constitutional barriers because of new security threats.[126] Ever since the North Korean missile tests and the nuclear tests in 2006, Japanese politicians, policy makers, academics and the general public have debated the options how to prevent an attack from North Korea including the development of missile defenses and the possibility of acquiring nuclear weapons as well as the possibility of pre-emptive strikes. When high ranking Japanese policymakers such as the Foreign Minister Taro Aso and the Chief Cabinet Secretary Shinzo Abe argued the need to discuss

---

[121] For further discussion, see J.O. Haley, "Waging War: Japan's Constitutional Constraints," *Constitutional Forum*, vol. 14, issue 2, 2005, pp. 18–34; M.A. Chinen, "Article 9 of the Constitution of Japan and the Use of Procedural and Substantive Heuristics for Consensus," *Michigan Journal of International Law*, vol. 27, no. 1, 2006, pp. 56–114 and C. Martin, "Binding the Dogs of War: Japan and the Constitutionalizing of *Jus ad Bellum*," *U. Pa. J. Int'L.*, vol. 30, 2008, pp. 267–357.

[122] For a detailed discussion, see M. Koji, "Japan" in W. Koji, *Humanitarian Intervention: The Evolving Asian Debate* (Japan Center for International Exchange, Tokyo, 2003), pp. 11–18, accessible at http://www.jcie.org/researchpdfs/HumInterv/human_murata.pdf. See also "FOCUS: Unsteady Koizumi faces Coalition Opposition on Iraq War," accessible at http://www.thefreelibrary.com/FOCUS%3A+Unsteady+Koizumi+faces+coalition+opposition+on+Iraq+war.-a098545590.

[123] Permanent Mission of Japan to the United Nations, *Peace and Security*, accessible at http://www.un.emb-japan.go.jp/topics.en/peace_and_security.html.

[124] Source: http://www.un.org/en/peacekeeping/contributors/2013/jan13_2.pdf.

[125] For further discussion, see L. Black, "Debating Japan's Intervention to Tackle Piracy in the Gulf of Aden: beyond Mainstream Paradigms," *International Relations of the Asia-Pacific*, volume 12, 2012, pp. 259–285.

[126] See in detail, C. Aoi, "Beyond 'Activism-Lite'?: Issues in Japanese Participation in Peace Operations," *Journal of International Peacekeeping*, vol. 13, nos. 1–2, 2009, pp. 72–100 and F.A. Stengel, "The Reluctant Peacekeeper: Japan's Ambivalent Stance on UN Peace Operations," Japan aktuell 2008, accessible at http://www.giga-hamburg.de/dl/download.php?d=/content/publikationen/archiv/ja_aktuell/jaa_0801_fokus_stengel.pdf.

whether pre-emptive strikes would be within the constitutional right of self-defense, the proposal received harsh criticism from Seoul and Beijing.[127] The Chinese spokesperson Jiang Yu considered it as "extremely irresponsible that some high-level politicians of Japan keep on speaking of a pre-emptive strike on another country."[128]

East Asian Peace since 1979

However, starting in 1979, the states in East Asia have experienced a long period of prosperity and peace and have even moved towards greater co-operation. There are manifold reasons why states have not been involved in any major armed conflict. Using force may simply have become too risky; the long absence of war could be premised on economic integration; or the origin might be found in the ideology of "Asian Values" or the ASEAN Way.[129] International lawyers may point out that states in Northeast Asia refrained from using force because of the legal constraint and normative compulsion of Art. 2(4) of the UN Charter. Historians like Stein Tønnesson have argued that peace came in stages and the main explanation for the "East Asia Peace" is that a growing number of international leaders have come to priotize economic growth and economic relations with the USA.[130]

Although no international armed conflict has broken out in Northeast Asia for more than fifty years, the region contains some significant hotspots including the Korean peninsula and the Taiwan Strait. In addition, there are a number of territorial disputes including controversies over the Spratly Islands, Diaoyutai Islands and Dokdo/Takeshima.[131]

---

127 See in detail, D.A. Pinkston, K. Sakurai, "Japan Debates Preparing for Future Preemptive Strikes against North Korea," *The Korean Journal of Defense Analysis*, vol. 18, no. 4, 2006, pp. 95–121. See also "North Korea Rocket Revives Japan Pre-emptive Strike Talk," Reuters, 6 April 2009 and S. Snyder, "Which Country Will Be Israel of East Asia," accessible at http://blogs.cfr.org/asia/2012/04/11/north-koreas-missile-threat-which-country-will-be-the-israel-of-east-asia/.

128 "China Criticizes Japan over Talk of Preemptive Strike on N. Korea," Yonhap News Agency, 13 July 2006.

129 See the chapter by Brendan Howe in this volume.

130 S. Tønnesson, "What Is It that Explains the East Asian Peace since 1979? A Call for a Research Agenda?", *Asian Perspective*, vol. 33, no. 1, 2009, pp. 111–136, T. Kivimäki, "The Long Peace of ASEAN," *Journal of Peace Research*, vol. 38, no. 1, 2001, pp. 5–25.

131 For further reading, see the contributions on maritime security in East Asia in *Global Asia*, vol. 5, no. 4, 2010 and C. Bae, "Island Sovereignties of East Asia: A Comparative Colonial Legacy" in Northeast Asian History Foundation, *Territorial Issues in Europe and in East Asia: Colonialism, War Occupation, and Conflict Resolution* (2009, Seoul). In general, see S. Kim (ed.), *The International Relations of Northeast Asia* (Roman Littlefield Publishers, Lanham, 2004).

Other contentious issues among states in Northeast Asia include the controversial visits to the Yasekuni shrine by Japanese politicians, the debate over Japanese history books, Japan's treatment of comfort women, the naming of the East Sea, the controversial North East project by China and the controversy concerning Baekdu Montain.[132]

Even after the armistice bringing an end to open hostilities North and South Korea were often at the brink of war.[133] Despite the so-called Sunshine Policy developed by the late President Kim Dae Jung and numerous efforts of reconciliation,[134] there are currently no prospects for a stable peace on the peninsula. North Korea conducted missile tests in 1993, 1998, 2006, 2009 and 2012. In 2006[135], 2009,[136] and 2013, North Korea conducted nuclear tests which made it more isolated than before. The test was widely condemned by the international community including the People's Republic of China. On 14 October 2006, the Security Council acting under Chapter VII condemned the test as a threat to the peace and imposed economic and military sanctions by Resolution 1718. After the second nuclear test on 25 May 2009, the sanctions regime on North Korea was further tightened by Security Council Resolution 1874.[137] In response, North Korea claimed that it would no longer be bound by the armistice agreement of 1953.[138] In March 2010, the South Korean navy ship Cheonan had been

---

[132] For further discussion on the conflicting memories and politics of history in Northeast Asia, see the contributions in East Asia Foundation and the Jeju Peace Institute (eds.), *The 5th Jeju Peace Forum: Shaping New Regional Governance in East Asia. A Common Vision for Mutual Benefit and Common Prosperity*, vol. I (ORUEM Publishing House, 2010), pp. 271–335.

[133] N. Michishita, *North Korea's Military-Diplomatic Campaigns, 1966–2008* (Routledge, London, New York, 2010).

[134] In detail on the inter-Korean relations since 1945, see D. Oberdorfer, *The Two Koreas: A Contemporary History* (Basic Books, 2001). On the North-South relations since 1989, see H.G. Lynn, *Bipolar Orders. The Two Koreas since 1989* (Zed Books, London, New York, 2007), pp. 154–171.

[135] On the legality of the 2006 nuclear test, see C.J. Le Mon, "International Law and North Korean Nuclear Testing", *ASIL Insight*, 19 October 2006, http://www.asil.org/insights061020.cfm.

[136] For further discussion of the 2009 Nuclear Tests, see the contributions in *Global Asia*, vol. 4, no. 2, 2009, http://www.globalasia.org/ and the contributions in East Asia Foundation and the Jeju Peace Institute (eds.), *The 5th Jeju Peace Forum: Shaping New Regional Governance in East Asia. A Common Vision for Mutual Benefit and Common Vision for Mutual Benefit and Common Prosperity*, volume III, 2010, pp. 125–142.

[137] See in detail, D.J. Kim, "The North Korean Nuclear Issue and the United Nations," *The Korean Journal of Defense Analysis*, vol. 23, no. 2, 2011, pp. 289–302.

[138] For a legal discussion, see D. Akande, "The Korean War Has Resumed!! (Or So We Are Told)," Blog of the European Journal of International Law, http://www.ejiltalk.org/the-korean-war-has-resumed-or-so-we-are-told/.

sunk by a torpedo. While South Korea claimed that North Korea was behind the incident,[139] North Korea denied any responsibility for the sinking of the Cheonan. In a Presidential statement of July 2010, the Security Council condemned the attack but did not identify the attacker.[140] In November 2010, North and South Korea were at the brink of war when the DPRK fired shells and rockets at the South Korean island, Yeonpyeong. A spokesman of the DPRK Foreign Ministry justified the attack "as a self-defensive measure to cope with the enemy's reckless military provocation of firing shells inside the territorial waters of the DPRK side around Yeonpyeong Islet in the West Sea of Korea."[141] The North Korean claim appeared unsubstantiated and lacked any justification under Art. 51 of the UN Charter. The conflict raised the difficult question how South Korea and the international community could adequately respond to North Korea's violation of the prohibition of the use of force without risking escalation.[142]

On 13 April 2012, North Korea launched a satellite. Three days later the Security Council responded by adopting a presidential statement condemning the launch and announcing to tighten the existing sanctions regime.[143] In March 2013, the Security Council imposed additional sanctions after the third North Korean nuclear test by passing Security Council Resolution 2094. However, it remains the question whether an expanded sanctions regime would be effective and not even counterproductive.[144]

---

139 In his letter to the Security Council, the Permanent Representative of the Republic of Korea to the United Nations, In-kook Park stated that "the armed attack by North Korea against the ROK Navy ship is a flagrant violation of the Charter of the United Nations, the 1953 Korean Armistice Agreement and the 1992 Agreement on Reconciliation, Non-aggression and Exchanges and Cooperation between the South and the North. As such, the armed attack by North Korea constitutes a threat to the peace and security on the Korean Peninsula and beyond." Accessible at http://www.alertnet.org/thenews/newsdesk/N04130942.htm.

140 See S/PRST/2010/13, accessible at http://www.un.org/News/Press/docs/2010/sc9975.doc.htm.

141 Statement Released by Spokesman of DPRK Foreign Ministry, available at http://www.kcna.co.jp/item/2010/201011/news24/20101124-17ee.html.

142 On the strategic implications of the Cheonan and Yeonpyeong incident, see B.E. Bechtol Jr., "The Implications of the Cheonan Sinking," *International Journal of Korean Unification Studies*, vol. 19, no. 2, 2010, pp. 1–40; S. Snyder, S.-W. Byun, "Cheonan and Yeonpyeong. The Northeast Asian Response to North Korea's Provocations", *RUSI Journal*, vol. 156, no. 2, 2011, pp. 74–81.

143 See Presidential Statement of 16 April 2012, SC 10610, accessible at http://www.un.org/News/Press/docs/2012/sc10610.doc.htm.

144 For a critical analysis of the sanctions regime, see M. Noland, "The (Non) Impact of UN Sanctions on North Korea," Working Paper 10, December 2008, Peterson Institute

Conclusions

After almost every significant military operation since the adoption of the UN Charter but also because of the development of new weapon technology,[145] the rise of human rights and new threats to the peace,[146] international lawyers and the United Nations[147] have raised the question whether the rules regulating the use of force have changed or whether they should be modified.[148] Because Art. 2(4) of the UN Charter has been violated so many times, various writers at different times have even developed theories which proclaimed the demise of the UN Charter.[149]

---

for International Economics, accessible at http://www.iie.com/publications/wp/wp08-12.pdf and K.A. Elliott, "Responding to North Korean Provications: Limitations Sanctions," *International Journal of Korean Unification Studies*, vol. 19, no. 2, 2010, pp. 41–60.

145 See for example, T. Marauhn, "The Debate about a Revolution in Military Affairs - A Comment in the Light of Public International Law," Die Friedens-Warte, vol. 77, 2002, pp. 411–435; M.N. Schmitt, "Computer Network Attack and the Use of Force in International Law: Thoughts on a Normative Framework," *Columbia Journal of Transnational Law*, vol. 37, 1999, pp. 885–937; M.E. O'Conell, "Unlawful Killings with Combat Drones: A Case Study of Pakistan (2004–2009)," Notre Dame Law School, Legal Studies Research Paper 09-43, accessible at https://webspace.utexas.edu/rmc2289/LT/Mary%20Ellen%20OConnell%20on%20Drones.pdf; J.J. Paust, "Self-Defense Targeting of Non-State Actors and Permissibility of U.S. Drones in Pakistan," *Journal of Transnational Law and Policy*, vol. 19, 2010, pp. 237–280.

146 K. Wellens, "The UN Security Council and the New Threats to the Peace. Back to the Future," *JCSL*, vol. 8, 2003, pp. 15–70.

147 Two UN reports, the report of the High-Level Panel on Threats, Challenges and Change and the subsequent report by SG Kofi Annan confirmed the legal framework on the use force and advocated no reform of the UN Charter in this respect, accessible at http://www.un.org/secureworld/ and http://www.un.org/largerfreedom/contents.htm.

148 For example, Sean D. Murphy has called for a protean *jus ad bellum* as a normative regime that is less oriented towards a textual codification of the norm and more toward its practical and nuanced application in a complex and global changing environment, S.D. Murphy, "Protean Jus ad Bellum," *Berkeley Journal of International Law*, vol. 27, 2009, pp. 22–52. Anne-Marie Slaughter and Lee Feinstein have suggested that states have a duty to prevent rogue states from acquiring or using WMD. They argue that states may use force under certain circumstances even in absence of SC authorisation, see A.-M. Slaughter, Lee Feinstein, "A Duty to Prevent," *Foreign Affairs*, vol. 83, 2004, pp. 136. See also J. Delbrück, "Effektivität des Gewaltverbots. Bedarf es einer Modifikation der Reichweite des Art. 2(4) UN Charta," *Die Friedens-Warte*, vol. 74, 1999, pp. 139–185; R.N. Gardner, "Neither Bush Nor the 'Jurisprudes'," *AJIL*, vol. 97, 2003, pp. 585–590; W.M. Reisman, "Assesing Claims to Revise the Laws of War", *AJIL*, vol. 97, 2003, pp. 82–90; and J.E. Stromseth, "Law and Force after Iraq: A Transitional Moment," *AJIL*, vol. 97, 2003, pp. 628–642.

149 See for example, the famous article by Thomas Franck, T. Franck, "Who Killed Art. 2(4)? Or: Changing Norms Governing the Use of Force by States," *AJIL*, vol. 64, 1970, pp. 809–837, or M.J. Glennon, *Limits of Law, Prerogatives of Power. Interventionism after Kosovo* (Palgrave, New York, 2001). See also the well-known reply by Louis Henkin to Professor Franck's article, L. Henkin, "The Reports of the Death of Art. 2(4) Are Greatly Exaggerated," *AJIL*, vol. 65, 1971, pp. 544–545.

In Northeast Asia, the prohibition of aggression and the core concept of internationally illegal use of force have remained uncontested. No government in the region has argued that the rules regulating the use of force have fallen into desuetude and do not apply. There are also no novel claims concerning the use of force. States in Northeast Asia have legally justified military action or the threat of force either by reference to Chapter VII of the UN Charter or to Art. 51 of the UN Charter and thereby implicitly confirmed the validity of the prohibition of the use of force. As the International Court of Justice in the *Nicaragua* case explained:

> If a State acts in a way *prima facie* incompatible with a recognized rule, but defends its conduct by appealing to exceptions or justifications contained within the rule itself, then whether or not the state's conduct is in fact justifiable on that basis, the significance of that attitude is to confirm rather than to weaken the rule.[150]

Arguably, the most relevant contentious issues from the perspective of the use of force within the context of Northeast Asia are the right to humanitarian intervention and the right to pre-emptive self-defense. Although all states in Northeast Asia with the exception of North Korea support the so-called Responsibility to Protect,[151] they have not asserted a right to humanitarian intervention. Despite the existing threat from North Korea, there is no consensus between China, Japan and South Korea that the right to pre-emptive self-defense would be permissible under contemporary international law.

---

[150] *Nicaragua* case, para 186.

[151] The full text of the world summit outcome is available at http://daccess-dds-ny.un.org/doc/UNDOC/GEN/N05/487/60/PDF/N0548760.pdf?OpenElement

CHAPTER THREE

EAST ASIAN VALUES AND HUMANITARIAN INTERVENTION

Brendan M. Howe

Introduction

In 2008, controversies over national and international responses to May's devastating cyclone in Burma/Myanmar and Chinese rule in Tibet (with violent demonstrations in Tibet itself, in the surrounding region and, as a result of the Olympic torch relay, across the globe), as well as severe civil unrest in Thailand, the Philippines, and Malaysia, gave an immediacy and urgency to the debate on the clash between state prerogatives, human rights, and the duties of the international community in particular with reference to the East Asian region.

2009 saw an ongoing focus on transnational human security issues in the region, with criticism of the Chinese repatriation of North Korean refugees and the Thai repatriation of ethnic Hmong from Laos. Many victims of the cyclone in Myanmar and also the earthquake which devastated parts of China's Sichuan province in the same month, found themselves victimized a second time by the insufficient responses of regimes that seemed unable or unwilling to provide them with support.[1] Meanwhile, members of the international community are increasingly asserting a right to intervene to protect the human security of individuals against the prerogatives of states.[2] This chapter addresses the philosophical underpinnings for, and future of, non-intervention in East Asia in the face of solidarist claims and pressures from internal and external constituencies.

Traditionally, East Asia has been viewed as a zone of non-intervention where state prerogatives, as the definitive embodiment of political community and shared values, are seen to trump individual human rights. For example Henry Nau notes that the lack of full protection for civil liberties in Asia "reflects the significantly different traditions regarding the relationship of the individual to society. Nowhere in Asia is there a celebration

---

[1] *BBC News*, "Fresh Burma aid appeal two years on from Cyclone Nargis," 3 May 2009, available at: http://news.bbc.co.uk/2/hi/asia-pacific/8657624.stm.

[2] See discussion of international organisations and regimes below.

of political individualism as we know it in the West, either in political thought or in historical events such as the Reformation or Enlightenment."[3] Furthermore, Nau claims that authority patterns "infuse all social relationships – in the family (Confucianism), in religion (Buddhism and Islam), and in the state (Shintoism)."[4] Although perhaps no other region on earth is as culturally and socio-economically diverse, opposition to Western liberal or universal cosmopolitan values emanating from East Asia has been identified collectively as the challenge of "Asian values."[5] A broad resistance to encroachment upon state prerogatives does seem to be reflected in the day-to-day diplomacy of the East Asian region.

In December 1990, when the UN decided to convene a World Conference on Human Rights, several Asian states questioned the applicability of universal human rights in different cultural, economic and social settings. The Asian regional preparatory meeting which took place in Bangkok between 29 March and 2 April 1993 provided an opportunity for Asian governments to put forward their definition of human rights on the global agenda. The Bangkok Declaration, signed by over forty Asian governments, did not reject universal human rights, but the declaration suggested that universality should be considered "in the context of a dynamic and evolving process of international norm-setting, bearing in mind the significance of national and regional particularities and various historical, cultural and religious backgrounds."[6] The Asian states also sought to link development issues with human rights questions and emphasize the importance of non-interference.[7] Indeed, for Kenneth Christie and Denny Roy "development has assumed cult-like status" in East Asia,[8] while for Chu Shulong, "East Asia is one of few areas in the world where most countries strongly defend traditional concepts of national sovereignty and firmly resist foreign intervention in the internal affairs of independent states."[9]

---

[3] Henry R. Nau, *At Home Abroad: Identity and Power in American Foreign Policy* (Ithaca: Cornell University Press, 2002), p. 163.

[4] Ibid., p. 164.

[5] See for instance C.O. Khong, "Asian Values: The Debate Revisited" in *'Asian Values' and Democracy in Asia* (Shizuoka: Proceedings, 1997), available at http://www.unu.edu/unupress/asian-values.html#DEBATE.

[6] *Final Declaration of the Regional Meeting for Asia for the World Conference on Human Rights* (1993), Article 8, available at: http://law.hku.hk/lawgovtsociety/Bangkok%20Declaration.htm.

[7] *The Bangkok Declaration* (1967), Preamble, Articles 4–6, and 17–19, available at: http://www.asean.org/1212.htm.

[8] Kenneth Christie and Denny Roy, *The Politics of Human Rights in East Asia* (London: Pluto Press, 2001), p. 5.

[9] Shulong Chu, "China, Asia and Issues of Sovereignty and Intervention," *Pugwash Occasional Papers*, vol. 2, no. 1, January 2001, p. 1.

The constitutive documents of regional organisations also appear to reflect this non-interventionary approach to human security. The non-interventionary credentials of the Association of Southeast Asian Nations are so firmly entrenched that the approach to regional security taken by the organisation and its member states has become known as the "ASEAN Way" by which is meant, according to the first formal treaty between them (the 1976 Bali Treaty of Amity and Cooperation in Southeast Asia) "a. Mutual respect for the independence, sovereignty, equality, territorial integrity and national identity of all nations; b. The right of every State to lead its national existence free from external interference, subversion or coercion; c. Non-interference in the internal affairs of one another."[10] Likewise, the only formal security treaty organisation among states in Northeast Asia, the Shanghai Cooperation Organisation (SCO) has promoted the "Shanghai Spirit" based on "mutual trust, mutual benefit, equality, consultation, respect for multicivilisations, striving for common development,"[11] and, according to the 2001 Declaration on Establishment of Shanghai Cooperation Organisation, the Members will "mutually respect independence, sovereignty and territorial integrity, not interfere in each other's internal affairs."[12]

States in Asia have frequently acted in accordance with these guidelines. Hence, despite the gross violations of human security perpetrated under Pol Pot's Khmer Rouge, ASEAN member states were unanimous and vociferous in their condemnation of the Vietnamese intervention that put an end to these practices. Likewise, Chinese officials at the United Nations have consistently used the threat of their veto in the Security Council to prevent interventionary initiatives by Western liberal democracies. The Director-General of UNESCO has even given particular credit to Asia as the birthplace of peaceful coexistence, marked by a culture of peace whereby tension is solved not by the use of force but through harmony.[13]

Although, as noted above, there are significant variations in the philosophical traditions of states in the region, there are a number of underlying unifying factors. Broadly speaking, the Asian challenge to solidarism can be seen in cultural, economic and political terms. Culturally, the Asian challenge asserts that the Western liberal or universalist approach ignores

---

[10] *Treaty of Amity and Cooperation in Southeast Asia* (1976), available at: http://www.aseansec.org/TAC-KnowledgeKit.pdf.

[11] *Shanghai Cooperation Organization*, available at: http://www.sectsco.org/EN/.

[12] *Declaration on the Establishment of Shanghai Cooperation Organization* (2001), available at http://www.sectsco.org/.

[13] Sheldon Shaeffer, "Foreword" in Zhou Nan-Zhao and Bob Teasdale (eds.), *Teaching Asia-Pacific Core Values of Peace and Harmony* (Bangkok: UNESCO, 2004), p. v.

the specific cultural traditions and historical circumstances of Asian societies, whose interpretations of human rights are different from those in the West. Economically, the Asian challenge maintains that the priority of developing Asian societies has to be the eradication of poverty. Politically it calls into question the motives of the West accusing them of using human rights merely as an instrument for advancing Western economic or security interests – "power politics in disguise" and a shallow pretence for the use of force against regimes which stand up to Western neo-imperialism.

Essentially, the Asian values debate poses a communitarian epistemological challenge to liberal individualism and solidarism. Communitarians (those who place the community at the centre of human rights discourse either because they view the community of the source of shared conceptions of the good, or because they feel that community is itself a collective good which needs to be protected and promoted) address the necessity of attending to the demands of community alongside of, or prior to, liberty and equality. In other words, we must pay attention to the shared practices and values within each society which constitute a distinct understanding of the common good, its generation, and its distribution, but also, and this particularly resonates with Asian values proponents, society or community is itself a collective good which must at the very least be weighed against other rights. There are human rights, but due to the problem of the particularism of history, culture, and membership, the political community to which individuals belong, rather than uninformed external interference, is the best agency for their defense.[14] For Michael Walzer, the political community (*qua* state) is the closest we can come to a world of common meanings as it is where language, history, and culture come most closely together to produce a collective consciousness.[15]

Thus the implications for any form of intervention let alone the use of force are:

1. Human beings are social beings, and their values are socially generated by the political communities to which they belong.
2. Due to the particularism of history and culture it is not possible for an external agency to reach a just evaluation of the social rules of any political community of which they are not a member.

---

[14] Michael Walzer, *Spheres of Justice: A Defence of Pluralism & Equality* (New York: Basic Books, 1983), p. 5.

[15] Michael Walzer, "The Moral Standing of States: A Response to Four Critics" in Charles Beitz et al. (eds.), *International Ethics* (Princeton: Princeton University Press, 1985), p. 218.

3. The state is the primary and most complete manifestation of political community, as it is where shared meanings come most closely together.
4. We must therefore treat all states as if they are legitimate representatives and manifestations of the will and interests of their citizens.
5. Sometimes an individual, or individual freedoms, may be sacrificed for the good of the community as a whole.
6. No external body has any right therefore to intervene in the affairs of an Asian state on the contested premise of protecting individual human rights as universally imagined.

There are, however, a number of pressures within and upon the region for this state-centric view of security to be modified or even replaced. First, from a liberal/solidarist/normative perspective, calls to respect Asian values in the region can be seen a mere cover to allow despots to violate the human security of their citizens. Second, rationalist interpretations emphasise the increasingly non-state centric nature of threats to security, and this has been borne out by recent regional events such as the Asian financial crisis, "haze" in Southeast Asia, "yellow dust" in Northeast Asia, natural disasters in South Asia, rising sea levels in the Pacific and Indian oceans and of course the 2004 Asian tsunami; as well as global threats such as the current financial crisis, global warming, piracy, crime, and terrorism. Third, from a neoliberal perspective, as Asian countries become increasingly enmeshed in the global financial system, their relative autonomy of action is undermined.[16] Finally, from a constructivist perspective, regional diplomacy in Asia is subject to the influence of a normative shift at the global level that concerns the relationship between the principle of non-interference and the norms of human rights and democracy – a move towards the use of force for humanitarian intervention or normative war-fighting.

The four biggest challenges to regional governments seen to be violating the rights of their citizens come from [1] the evolution of international law; [2] the wider international community as represented by international organizations and regimes and their spokespersons; [3] in the form of some sort of coalition of "liberal" powers willing to engage in economic leverage, normative war fighting or militarized humanitarian intervention; and [4] from the internal constituencies of Asian states themselves.

---

16 Chu, "China, Asia and Issues of Sovereignty and Intervention," p. 1.

International Law

Positive (codified) international law is generally not supportive of the use of force in international affairs. The 1928 Kellogg-Briand Pact essentially outlawed war as an instrument of national policy except (implicitly) when fought in self-defense or when recommended by the Council of the League of Nations. To a considerable extent, this legal position has been inherited by the current United Nations system.[17] Article 2(4) of the UN Charter requires states to refrain from the threat or use of force against the territorial integrity or political independence of a state, or in any other manner inconsistent with the purposes of the United Nations. Pursuant to Article 51, states may only resort to force in the exercise of individual or collective self-defense.[18] Under Articles 53 and 64 of the 1969 Vienna Convention on the Law of Treaties, the prohibition in Article 2(4) of the Charter is part of *jus cogens* – a principle from which no derogation is permitted, and which is often reflected in the drafting of international treaties.[19] For Lyal Sunga:

> a plain reading of Article 2(4) does not support the notion of the legality of unilateral military intervention for humanitarian considerations. In case Article 2(4) is not sufficiently clear in itself, General Assembly resolutions 2625, 3314 and 44/22 reflect the international community's view that Article 2(4)'s prohibition of the use of force in international relations must be interpreted broadly and exceptions to this prohibition have to be read very narrowly.[20]

Essentially, under the UN legal system, the only military intervention that can be justified is one to resist or reverse an act of aggression. Under Chapter VII Article 39, the UN Security Council is responsible for determining threats to international peace, breaches of the peace or acts of

---

[17] Hans Köchler has noted that the Covenant of the League of Nations represented a move from *bellum justum* towards *bellum legale* and was therefore only a partial success towards the goal of abolishing the *jus ad bellum* altogether with the major and decisive step only taken with UN Charter itself eventually implementing the basic provisions of the Briand-Kellogg Pact by integrating the ban of the use of force into a system of collective security. Hans Köchler (ed.), *The Use of Force in International Relations International: Challenges to Collective Security* (Vienna: International Progress Organization, 2006), pp. 13–14.

[18] *Charter of the United Nations* (1945), available at: http://www.un.org/en/documents/charter/.

[19] *Vienna Convention on the Law of Treaties* (1969), available at: http://untreaty.un.org/ilc/texts/instruments/english/conventions/1_1_1969.pdf.

[20] Lyal S. Sunga, "The Role of Humanitarian Intervention in International Peace and Security: Guarantee or Threat?" in Köchler, *The Use of Force in International Relations International*, p. 58.

aggression, and under Article 42 the Security Council – not individual Member States – is empowered to authorize a response.[21] According to codified or "positive" international law therefore, each state has a duty of non-intervention into the affairs of other states. The prohibition against intervention was embodied in General Assembly Resolution 2625, as one of the "Principles of International Law Concerning Friendly Relations Among States."[22] In the Corfu Channel Case, the International Court of Justice (ICJ) denounced any pretend right to intervention in international law; whereas in Nicaragua v. U.S., the judges stated that a linchpin of the Court's argument was that "the principle of non-intervention is an integral part of customary international law."[23]

In order to move beyond the positivist position, we must accept alternative sources of legal justification. This is possible through an examination of customary international law and generally established international norms and rules of behavior that may be considered enabling or binding even if not enshrined in a particular written document. The Paquete Habana Case established that "where there is no treaty and no controlling executive or legislative act or judicial decision [i.e., codified or positive law], resort must be had to the customs and usages of civilized nations, and, as evidence of these, to the works of jurists and commentators."[24] This ruling is reiterated in Article 38 of the Statute of the International Court of Justice, which refers to "international custom, as evidence of a general practice accepted as law," "the general principles of law recognized by civilized nations," and "the teachings of the most highly qualified publicists of the various nations as subsidiary means for the determination of rules of law," alongside the more positive or codified "international conventions, whether general or particular, establishing rules expressly recognized by the contesting states."[25]

---

21 See Köchler, *The Use of Force in International Relations International*, pp. 14–15.

22 General Assembly Resolution 2625 (XXV), *Declaration on Principles of International Law Concerning Friendly Relations among States in accordance with the Charter of the United Nations* (1970), available at: http://www.unrol.org/doc.aspx?n=3dda1f104.pdf.

23 International Court of Justice [ICJ], *The Corfu Channel Case (United Kingdom of Great Britain and Northern Ireland v. Albania (Merits)), Judgement of April 9th 1949*, available at: http://www.icj-cij.org/docket/files/1/1645.pdf; ICJ, *Case Concerning Military and Paramilitary Activities in and against Nicaragua (Nicaragua. v. United States of America (Merits)), Judgement of 27 June 1986*, available at: http://www.icj-cij.org/docket/files/70/6503.pdf.

24 *The Paquete Habana – 175 U.S. 677 (1900)*, available at: http://supreme.justia.com/cases/federal/us/175/677/.

25 ICJ (entered into force on 26 June 1945), *Statute of the International Court of Justice*, available at: http://www.icj-cij.org/documents/index.php?p1=4&p2=2&p3=0.

This means that at least two additional sources of international law must be considered with regard to the use of force: international custom, as evidence of a general practice accepted as law by states, and the works of commentators. If states generally act as if, and leading publicists recognize, that sovereignty is not inviolate, then indeed, an international legal justification of military action in violation of sovereignty is available. If sovereignty can be challenged, and there are certain things that states may not do, then the normative value attached to non-intervention must be weighed against that attached to other commonly held values that are being violated in order to judge the legitimacy of intervention. This implies a crucial theoretical shift from an interpretation of justification which is based purely upon codified international law (legality) towards one embracing wider principles of just war (legitimacy).

League of Nations mandates and UN Trusteeships established an international principle that states could be held accountable for the human rights of those governed. The Nuremberg trials further established a limit to state sovereignty – states could no longer do as they wished with their citizens, and the UN Charter Preamble reaffirms faith in fundamental human rights without discrimination.[26] This is also reflected in the wording of Articles 1(3), 55 and 56. 1948 saw the landmark Universal Declaration of Human Rights passed by the General Assembly, and this was followed in 1966 by the Covenants on Civil and Political Rights and Economic, Social and Cultural Rights.[27] Finally, the Convention on the Prevention and Punishment of the Crime of Genocide has been ratified by the majority of states.[28]

Nick Wheeler has made an attempt to bring together the questions of legality and legitimacy in the context of international law. Concerning the dilemma of what to do about strangers who are subjected to appalling cruelty by their governments, he identifies a marked shift in the normative context of international relations. "As a result of the international legal obligations written into the United Nations system, clear limits were set on how governments could treat their citizens ... [yet due to the weakness

[26] *Charter of the United Nations.*

[27] *Universal Declaration of Human Rights* (1948), available at: http://www.un.org/en/documents/udhr/; *International Covenant on Civil and Political Rights* (1966, entered into force on 23 March 1976), available at: http://www.hrcr.org/docs/Civil&Political/intlcivpol.html; *International Covenant on Economic, Social and Cultural Rights* (1966, entered into force on 3 January 1976), available at: http://www2.ohchr.org/english/law/cescr.htm.

[28] UN General Assembly Resolution 260, *Convention on the Prevention and Punishment of the Crime of Genocide* (1948), available at: http://www.un.org/millennium/law/iv-1.htm.

of legitimate enforcement mechanisms] Intervention by force might be the *only* means of enforcing the global humanitarian norms that have evolved in the wake of the Holocaust."[29]

For Jack Donnelly there is a "remarkable international normative consensus on the list of rights" found in the Universal Declaration of Human Rights, and, according to Dunne and Wheeler, "[w]hat further strengthens Donnelly's claim that there is a normative consensus underlying the human rights regime is the fact that in the daily round of diplomacy, state leaders justify their human rights policies in terms of these standards."[30] For example, the central mission of UNESCO might be "Peace" but this is to be founded on the "intellectual and moral solidarity of mankind" based on "shared values" rather than regional particularism or exceptionalism.[31] One hundred and ninety four have now accepted limits imposed by the 1949 Geneva Conventions upon the waging of war, making them universally applicable.[32] Thus the Conventions themselves, and the fundamental proposition they affirm (that even wars have limits), have become the starting point for global efforts to enforce international humanitarian law. Furthermore, according to the International Court of Justice, the Convention on the Prevention and Punishment of the Crime of Genocide holds to generally accepted values which oblige all states, even those which have few links with the international community, to "punish and prevent genocide."[33]

The Nuremberg trials of Nazi war criminals, despite the dubious backdating of legal principles, helped undermine the principle of sovereignty with regard to a government's treatment of its own people, held individual officials accountable to a wider international court of public opinion, and reinforced the notion of an internationally accepted code of behavior. As put by U.S. Supreme Court Justice Robert Jackson when trying to justify why the criminal statutes relating to wars of aggression and crimes against humanity that he proposed drafting would not be *ex post facto* laws: "What we propose is to punish acts which have been

29 Nicholas Wheeler, *Saving Strangers* (Oxford: Oxford University Press, 2000), p. 1.

30 Tim Dunne and Nick Wheeler (eds.), *Human Rights in Global Politics* (Cambridge: Cambridge University Press, 1999), p. 77.

31 United Nations Educational, Scientific and Cultural Organisation [UNESCO], *Introducing UNESCO: what we are*, available at: http://www.unesco.org/new/en/unesco/about-us/who-we-are/introducing-unesco/.

32 Four Geneva Conventions and Three Additional Protocols are available at: http://www.icrc.org/web/eng/siteengo.nsf/html/genevaconventions.

33 UN General Assembly Resolution 260, *Genocide Convention.*

regarded as criminal since the time of Cain and have been so written in every civilized code."[34]

In 1946 East Asia also experienced a similar exercise in international "justice" in the form of the International Military Tribunal for the Far East (IMTFE), otherwise known as the Tokyo War Crimes Tribunal. Given that the Tribunal was set up by order of General Douglas MacArthur, the Supreme Commander of Allied Forces in the South Pacific, this could still be viewed in the tradition of Western imperialism in Asia. Individuals representing numerous Asian countries (including China, India and the Philippines) did, however, participate as judges and prosecutors. The defendants were accused of crimes against peace, crimes against humanity, and conventional war crimes.[35] In addition, Asian countries (in particular China) held their own trials of Japanese war criminals, convicting and executing far more.

Essentially then, while the constitutive documents of Asian international organizations and codified positive international law continue to reflect a non-interventionary position which accords well with what is often described as "Asian values" this position has come under increasing pressure from the customary elements of international law embodied in the customs and usages of civilized nations, and the works of jurists and commentators. To a certain extent some aspects of international law would appear to place a limit on state sovereignty, impose duties on states regarding how they treat their citizens, and allow or at least decriminalize intervention by external entities whether other states or representatives of the "international community." The latter concept is explored further in the following section on the role of international organizations and regimes in imposing responsibilities upon all governments, including those in East Asia, and duties upon others when these responsibilities are not carried out.

International Organizations and Regimes

The Responsibility to Protect

In the aftermath of the 1990 Gulf War, UN Secretary-General Boutros Boutros-Ghali noted that the time of absolute and exclusive sovereignty

---

[34] Doug Linder, *The Nuremberg Trials,* available at: http://www.law.umkc.edu/faculty/projects/ftrials/nuremberg/nurembergACCOUNT.html.

[35] *Tokyo Trial – Further Readings*, available at: http://law.jrank.org/pages/10812/Tokyo-Trial.html#ixzz0mvHTzFTI.

has passed and that it is "the task of leaders of States today to understand this and to find a balance between the needs of good internal governance and the requirements of an ever more interdependent world."[36] That is to say, no state is immune to the demands and rights of its internal and external constituencies, and the UN, as the embodiment of the international community will not tolerate the hindrance of its "great objectives" of peace and security, justice and human rights and "social progress and better standards of life in larger freedom."[37] Similar sentiments can be found in the Millennium report submitted by the successor to Dr. Boutros-Ghali, Kofi Annan. He also adds that the central task faced by states is to "ensure that globalization becomes a positive force for all the world's people."[38] This Report formed the basis of the Millennium Declaration adopted by Heads of State and Government at the Millennium Summit, held at UN Headquarters in September 2000.[39]

In December 2001, the International Commission on Intervention and State Sovereignty (ICISS) released a report entitled *The Responsibility to Protect*. This declaration included a specific endorsement of humanitarian intervention and the use of force by expressing willingness "to take timely and decisive collective action for this purpose, through the Security Council, when peaceful means prove inadequate and national authorities are manifestly failing to do it."[40] *The Responsibility to Protect* even included a section (6.28–6.40) on what can be done "When the Security Council Fails to Act." According to Sunga, the Commission Report then gave the impression it had accorded scant regard for the basic principles of state sovereignty and non-intervention as it "proceeded to classify and characterize various sorts of deployment of armed force, and then, rather surprisingly, dwelt on a range of operational considerations, logistical questions and issues of military tactics."[41] Thus this initial formulation of the declaration of a Responsibility to Protect (R2P) can be interpreted as a duty to use force to intervene for humanitarian goals.

---

36 Boutros Boutros-Ghali, *An Agenda for Peace: Preventive Diplomacy, Peacekeeping and Peacemaking* (New York: United Nations, 1992), p. 44.

37 Kofi Annan, *In Larger Freedom* (New York: United Nations, 2005), available at: http://www.un.org/largerfreedom.

38 Kofi Annan, *We the Peoples: The Role of the United Nations in the 21st Century* (2000), available at: http://www.un.org/millennium/sg/report/state.htm.

39 UN General Assembly Resolution 55/2, *United Nations Millennium Declaration* (entered into force September 2005), available at http://www.un.org/millennium/.

40 International Commission on Intervention and State Sovereignty, *The Responsibility to Protect* (2001), available at: http://responsibilitytoprotect.org/ICISS%20Report.pdf.

41 Sunga, "The Role of Humanitarian Intervention in International Peace and Security," p. 77.

In the following years this new paradigm has gained momentum and garnered international recognition. In response to this international normative shift, at the High-Level Plenary Meeting for the 2005 World Summit (14–16 September) the world's leaders at the General Assembly agreed on a "responsibility to protect" which included a "clear and unambiguous acceptance by all governments of the collective international responsibility to protect populations from genocide, war crimes, ethnic cleansing and crimes against humanity."[42] Furthermore, the international community promised to take collective action in a timely and decisive manner, "should peaceful means be inadequate and national authorities manifestly fail to protect their populations from genocide, war crimes, ethnic cleansing and crimes against humanity."[43] The World Summit document also noted, however, that such action should be sanctioned through the Security Council, in accordance with the Charter, including Chapter VII. Thus it may be seen as something of a retreat from the original bold formulation proposed by the ICISS. Indeed, Article 139 appears to reaffirm the traditional pre-eminence of the Security Council and the restrictions imposed on UN and other international actions by international law.

Resolution 1674, adopted by the United Nations Security Council on April 28, 2006, "Reaffirm[ed] the provisions of paragraphs 138 and 139 of the 2005 World Summit Outcome Document regarding the responsibility to protect populations from genocide, war crimes, ethnic cleansing and crimes against humanity" and commits the Security Council to action to protect civilians in armed conflict. This resolution was adopted unanimously including by the Asian members. It therefore takes a similarly restrictive line to the World Summit Outcome Document. In diluting the initial R2P proposals, however, it may be that the UN has not only managed to make the whole paradigm fit more comfortably with the existing body of international law, but also that it has made it more palatable to Asian states. This might serve to explain Vietnam's dramatic shift "from a position close to opposition to R2P in 2004–05 to one of relatively positive R2P engagement" at the World Summit and for Resolution 1674.[44]

In fact the majority of states in East Asia have at least engaged with the idea of a responsibility to protect, having shifted from previously hard-line non-interventionary positions. In a recent study Alex Bellamy and Sarah

---

42 General Assembly Resolution 60/1, *World Summit Outcome Document* (2005), available at: http://unpan1.un.org/intradoc/groups/public/documents/un/unpan021752.pdf.

43 Ibid.

44 Alex J. Bellamy and Sarah E. Davies, "The Responsibility to Protect in the Asia-Pacific Region," *Security Dialogue*, vol. 40, no. 6, 2009, p. 561.

Davies have examined the current degree of receptivity to the concept among regional states, identifying Australia, Japan, New Zealand, the Philippines (2004–05) and the Republic of Korea as advocates, Singapore, Indonesia, the Philippines (2006–08) China and Vietnam (2008) as R2P-Engaged, Vietnam (2005–07), Brunei, Cambodia, Laos, Malaysia, and Thailand as Fence Sitters, and only the Democratic People's Republic of Korea and Myanmar as being opposed.[45] Even in these two cases the countries concerned have not explicitly rejected the idea that states have a responsibility to protect their own population.

It must be acknowledged that although Asian states have signed up to international normative documentation this does not necessarily mean that they understand such international principles to imply the same degree of obligation as might be understood among Western advocates. For instance, the Permanent Representative of South Korea to the UN, one of the most ardent supporters of the Responsibility to Protect among Asian states, stressed that "the primary responsibility lies in the individual Government while the international community bears the secondary responsibility," that R2P "distinctly different from humanitarian intervention since it is based on collective actions, in accordance with UN Charter," and that "not all humanitarian tragedies or human rights violations can or should activate R2P."[46] Japan has been instrumental in pushing forward the next step in the evolution of security conceptualization, the human security discourse, and is the largest contributor to the human security related practices and intuitions of the UN. But in Japanese thinking, there is a significant difference between the two perspectives: "while R2P recognizes the necessity for enforcement in certain circumstances, human security rules it out in every occasion," therefore the Japanese focus is one of prevention thereby reducing the need for intervention.[47]

Yet just because these states would prefer to avoid actual military intervention, this does not rule out a shift from a non-interventionary view of international relations as an increased willingness to resort to non-violent intervention whether it be through aid (or its denial), criticism, or behind the scenes diplomacy is nevertheless a significant departure from traditional views of Asian values in international relations. The evolution of

45 Ibid., p. 551.

46 Statement by H.E. Mr. Park In-kook, Permanent Representative of the Republic of Korea to the United Nations, Plenary Meeting of the General Assembly on Responsibility to Protect, 23 July 2009, available at http://www.responsibilitytoprotect.org/Korea_ENG.pdf.

47 Bellamy and Davies, "The Responsibility to Protect in the Asia-Pacific Region" p. 552.

the R2P doctrine itself is reflective of increased engagement between Asian states and the wider international community. As has been mentioned above, the initial ICISS report was very permissive of humanitarian intervention whether or not authorised by the UN Security Council. Not only, however, was this report drafted by an independent body of experts serving in an advisory capacity to the UN, and as such their proposals are not legally binding, it might also be argued that East Asia was under-represented on the panel given that the only member from the region was former President Fidel Ramos of the Philippines. The World Summit document, being a General Assembly resolution was more binding in terms of both legality and, given the near universal representation at the General Assembly, in terms of legitimacy, but was more restrictive in terms of the use of force.

The R2P doctrine or model represents a recognition of a shift in international norms away from state rights, sovereignty and non-interference, towards obligations placed on the governments of all states, including those in East Asia, concerning the wellbeing of their subjects, and upon the elements of global governance, when national governments fail in their duties. Interestingly, this new interventionary perspective also sees a linkage between human rights and development; however, in this case the link may be seen as favouring international intervention if a government is seen as not performing its governance roles adequately in terms of reconciling conflicting interests or generating collective good for its citizens.

Human Security and Development

The United Nations Development Programme (UNDP) has noted that in some cases, protection of national identity has come at the expense of ignoring the concerns of citizens who seek security in their daily lives. For these common citizens, security means "protection from the threat of disease, hunger, unemployment, crime, social conflict, political repression and environmental hazards," the very things that would grant their daily survival.[48] The international community has begun to see security threats not only *between*, but also *within* states, and focus on people in addition to states.[49] The concept of human security and the linkage with economic

[48] United Nations Development Programme [UNDP], *Human Development Report 1994* (New York: Oxford University Press, 1994), p. 22.

[49] According to *World Report on Violence and Health*, only 7 out of 110 conflicts recorded from 1989–2000 were between states, and the rest were civil wars (Geneva: WHO, 2002), p. 218.

wellbeing is in fact rooted in the ideals of the UN, which was founded on the principle that it would always give equal weight to all territories and people. In 1945, the U.S. Secretary of State, Edward Stettinius Jr., reported to his government the conclusions from the San Francisco meeting that led to the establishment of the UN:

> The battle of peace has to be fought on two fronts. The first is the security front where victory spells freedom from fear. The second is the economic and social front where victory means freedom from want. Only victory on both fronts can assure the world of an enduring peace ... No provisions that can be written into the Charter will enable the Security Council to make the world secure from war if men and women have no security in their homes and their job.[50]

The first explicit reference to human security was by the former United Nations Secretary-General Boutros Boutros-Ghali in his 1992 *Agenda for Peace*, in which he called for "an integrated approach to human security" to address root causes of conflict, spanning economic, social and political issues. In this report, the concept was used in relation to preventative diplomacy, peacemaking, peacekeeping and post-conflict recovery. The report drew attention to the broad scope of challenges in post-conflict settings and highlighted the need to address root causes of conflict through a common international moral perception. The report may have considered the importance of a wide network of actors assuming this integrated perspective, but it essentially took a narrow approach to the definition, focusing on physical threats to lives and wellbeing. A decade later, this was followed by the final report of The Commission on Human Security (CHS) established under the chairmanship of Sadako Ogata, former UN High Commissioner for Refugees, and Amartya Sen, Nobel Economics Prize Laureate, entitled *Human Security Now,* which defined human security as follows:

> Human security means protecting fundamental freedoms – freedoms that are the essence of life. It means protecting people from critical (severe) and pervasive (widespread) threats and situations. It means using processes that build on people's strengths and aspirations. It means creating political, social, environmental, economic, military and cultural systems that together give people the building blocks of survival, livelihood and dignity.[51]

---

[50] UNDP, *Human Development Report 1994*.

[51] Commission on Human Security [CHS], *Human Security Now* (New York: CHS, 2003), p. 4.

The UNDP *1994 Human Development Report,* now considered the seminal text on the subject, stressed the need for a broad interpretation of human security, defining it as "freedom from fear" *and* "freedom from want." Here, human security means "safety from such chronic threats as hunger, disease and repression," as well as "protection from sudden and hurtful disruptions in the patterns of daily life – whether in homes, in jobs or in communities."[52] According to this report, human security includes seven components,[53] is preventive, and is people-centred.[54] More recently, in his Millennium Address, Kofi Annan stated that the concept of human security was much broader than just "the absence of violent conflict." In addition he took up the call of freedom from fear, and freedom from want, and placed these concepts centre stage for the global governance mission.[55] Continuing the tradition of recent Secretaries General, Ban Ki-moon, the former Korean Foreign Minister and current Secretary General of the UN made humanitarian considerations like the Responsibility to Protect a key part of his platform during his candidature.[56]

In both policy debate and the academic literature, freedom from want is becoming more important in both absolute and relative terms than freedom from fear. The rationale for focusing on freedom from need as central to human security is that hunger, disease and natural disasters between them kill far more people than war, genocide and terrorism combined. Furthermore, war-related deaths have been declining, and the international community is both more likely to be informed of internal acts of aggression, and more likely to act against them than in previous decades. It is for this reason that the most assertive champions of human security are beginning to provoke controversy by calling for "aid invasions" when states contribute massively negative impacts to the human security of their citizens through deliberate action, incompetence, obstruction, or neglect. If the goal of humanitarian intervention is to minimize human suffering, then "aid invasions" may be more justifiable than those merely enforcing a responsibility to protect.

---

52 UNDP, *Human Development Report 1994,* p. 23.

53 Seven components of human security are: (1) economic security which requires an assured basic income; (2) food security which means all people have both physical and economic access to basic food; (3) health security which means freedom from diseases and infection; (4) environmental security such as freedom from dangers of environmental pollution; (5) personal security which is physical safety; (6) community security which ensures survival of traditional cultures and ethnic groups; and (7) political security which means protection of basic human rights and freedoms, ibid., pp. 24–33.

54 Ibid., pp. 22–23.

55 Annan, *We the Peoples.*

56 Bellamy and Davies, "The Responsibility to Protect in the Asia-Pacific Region," p. 553.

Pressure from Liberal States

In September 1997, Robin Cook, the then British Foreign Secretary, was lambasted by Malaysia's prime minister Dr. Mahathir Mohamad for his so-called ethical foreign policy crusade when he singled out Myanmar's military junta for criticism. According to the Telegraph's Matt Frei, Dr. Mahathir spoke for the region at that time when he told Asia Week: "The West thinks it is so very right and correct that it can sit in judgment of others and even prosecute people ... but the West has got many sins."[57] Mahathir also criticized the major article of faith of those who champion universal values, the Universal Declaration of Human Rights, pointing out that many Asian states were not able to participate in its drafting as they were under the boot of colonial oppression at the time. The buzzwords then were "Asian values" and *sekampung*, the Malay word for togetherness, which together supposedly reflected an alternative heritage emphasizing collective rights and duties to society rather than "Western" individual rights. Dr. Mahathir was, however, forced to back down from his position on the Universal Declaration of Human Rights as a result of internal and external pressures.

There are signs that the actions of Asian governments towards their own citizens that previously were considered internal matters for sovereign states are no longer immune from external scrutiny and criticism. In July 1998, then-Thai Foreign Minister Surin Pitsuwan proposed that ASEAN adopt a policy of flexible engagement, which involved discussions of fellow members' domestic policies. As noted by Dr. Pitsuwan himself, although flexible engagement was rejected to become enhanced interaction, ultimately the new ASEAN political and security community came to the fore, "which is much more intrusive, much more aggressive, much more alien to the ASEAN mental perception than my initial idea in 1998 about flexible engagement."[58] In addition to Thailand, Malaysia and even China have become critical of aspects of Myanmar's governance,[59] Asian states have supported, or at least acquiesced to humanitarian intervention in East Timor, and states in the South Pacific have examined the prospect

---

[57] Matt Frei, "Robin Cook's Moral Crusade Enrages Asia's Fiercest Tiger," *The Daily Telegraph*, 7 September 1997.

[58] *Keynote Address by ASEAN Secretary-General Dr. Surin Pitsuwan*, available at: http://www.rsis.edu.sg/nts/Events/Launch/keynote%20address%20by%20Surin%20Pitsuwan%20-transcript.pdf.

[59] *The New York Times*, "Chinese diplomats criticize Myanmar's new capital," 23 May 2007.

of pooling sovereignty or ceding it to a regional multilateral entity in response to human security crises in Nauru, the Solomon Islands, Fiji, and Papua New Guinea's island province of Bougainville.[60]

Five of the world's leading international jurists commissioned a report from the International Human Rights Clinic at Harvard Law School, calling for the UN Security Council to act on more than fifteen years of condemnation from other UN bodies on human rights abuses in Burma.[61] Meanwhile, Madeleine Albright, the former U.S. Secretary of State, called the response of the Burmese Government to the devastation wrought by Cyclone Nargis, whereby much needed emergency assistance was not distributed to where it was most needed, criminally neglectful, and she raised once again the complex question of when it is right to violate state sovereignty in the interests of the protection of the citizens of the state.[62] U.S. Defense Secretary, Robert Gates used very similar wording, and Gareth Evans, president of the International Crisis Group 2000–09 and a former foreign minister of Australia reflected on whether it was "time for an aid invasion."[63] Finally, French Foreign Minister, Bernard Kouchner, proposed that the Responsibility to Protect be invoked to legitimize the forcible delivery of humanitarian assistance without the consent of the Government of Myanmar.[64]

The May 2009 Europe-ASEAN Meeting (ASEM) in Hanoi, Vietnam was dominated by questions regarding an international response to the continued persecution of Burmese democracy leader, Aung San Suu Kyi by the military junta. Interestingly, criticism of the regime came not only from the Western liberal individualistic states of Europe, but also from Myanmar's fellow ASEAN members. In the week leading up to the meeting, ASEAN released a statement expressing "grave concern" over her treatment, which attracted an old-school Asian values response from the military regime that Thailand (the current chair of ASEAN) was interfering in Myanmar's internal affairs by releasing the organization's critical message.[65] East Timor President Jose Ramos-Horta and the Burma

60 See *The Pacific Plan* endorsed by Leaders at the Pacific Islands Forum meeting in October 2005. Available at: http://www.forumsec.org.fj/resources/uploads/attachments/documents/Pacific_Plan_Nov_2007_version.pdf.

61 International Human Rights Clinic, *Crimes in Burma* (2009), available at: http://www.law.harvard.edu/programs/hrp/documents/Crimes-in-Burma.pdf.

62 Madeleine K. Albright, "The End of Intervention," *The New York Times*, 11 June 2008.

63 Gareth Evans, "Time for an Aid Invasion?" *The Age*, 19 May 2008.

64 Bellamy and Davies, "The Responsibility to Protect in the Asia-Pacific Region," p. 548.

65 *BBC News*, "Burma rejects EU, Asian pressure," 25 May 2009, available at: http://news.bbc.co.uk/2/hi/asia-pacific/8066513.stm.

Lawyers" Council have announced they are ready to go to the International Criminal Court (ICC) to charge Senior General Than Shwe with human rights abuses and violations of international law in Burma.

Meanwhile the liberal Europeans were increasing pressure not only on the target state, Myanmar, but also on other Asian states and organizations to which the regime traditionally turns to support in their resistance against outside interference. The EU's External Relations Commissioner, Benita Ferrero-Waldner, called on Asian countries to "commit themselves to engage with this government in such a way that there be changes" pointing out that China, India and ASEAN were "the real neighbours here. They work with the country, and therefore they have the best influence."[66] ASEAN's ongoing defense of Myanmar has proven a major obstacle to the establishment of a free trade agreement between the two regional blocs, and it may be that under the current economic conditions member countries will see their interests to lie more closely with economic recovery through the reinvigoration of international trade than with the preservation of non-interference.

China is perhaps seen as the last champion of Asian values and bulwark against solidarist interventionary policies. Not only does China have its own human rights and governance issues, but alone among Asian states it potentially has the resources to stand up to Western or universalist critique without the fear of intervention. Even the People's Republic of China is, however, showing signs of normative shift. The opening and growth of China's economy has led to a greater enmeshing of the PRC in multilateral economic and political institutions with subsequent complex interdependence increasing the propensity of China to play the role of responsible regional power. Increasing confidence within China has led to a less defensive posture.[67] China already contributes to regional conflict resolution and mediation initiatives through both formal and informal channels.

In the wake of North Korea's second nuclear test in May 2009 the PRC showed a willingness to get tough with friends and neighbors by siding with Russia and the Western permanent members of the UN Security Council in condemning North Korea's actions. There are grounds for believing that China may change its resistance to foreign interference in

---

[66] *BBC News*, "Burma rejects EU, Asian pressure."

[67] Elizabeth C. Economy, "Leadership Gap in China," *Washington Post*, 1 December 2008, available at: http://www.washingtonpost.com/wp-dyn/content/article/2008/11/30/AR2008113001690.html.

Myanmar either due to a belief that the Junta, like North Korea's regime, has overstepped even the minimal standards of acceptable behavior expected of Beijing's allies, or because Beijing would prefer to focus the expenditure of political capital defending those regimes of more obvious and immediate material benefit such as Sudan. Although certainly not an ardent supporter of potential intervention, China is not the steadfast opponent of principles like the Responsibility to Protect that it is often portrayed. In fact, in its role as a permanent member of the UN Security Council, China has twice endorsed the principle specifically – at the 2005 World Summit and in the reaffirming Security Council Resolution 1674, although with regard to the former they also supported the important qualifications to R2P which were also adopted.[68] Even with regard to Darfur, China supported the deployment of African Union peacekeepers, and its diplomacy was seen as key to getting Sudanese consent for their deployment. Likewise, with regard to Myanmar, China has provided diplomatic support for the use of the Secretary-General's good offices, securing a visa for the Special representative, Ibrahim Gambari; and China remains open to the idea of ASEAN playing a leading role in addressing Myanmar.[69] Furthermore, as discussed in the final section of this chapter, not even China is immune to the penetration and diffusion of universal/solidarist interpretations of human rights among its own population.

Liberal states are able to exert pressure on authoritarian regimes both directly by forcing policy concessions from them in return for trade deals or membership of international organizations and indirectly through appeals to the citizens of target countries. For Whitehead, "in almost all the democratizations that have occurred between the Second World War and the dismantling of the Warsaw Pact, the strategies of regulation and control adopted by the dominant states in the system were of critical importance."[70] Even if the West chooses the path of not intervening in a target country, it remains in a position to impose its wishes through influence over the same multinational organizations Asian governments feel obliged to join. Membership of such exclusive clubs can be conditional upon candidates adopting regimes with which the West feels comfortable – i.e., liberal democracies. Hence former United States President Bill Clinton noted that "multilateral action holds promise as never before"

---

68 Bellamy and Davies, "The Responsibility to Protect in the Asia-Pacific Region," p. 556.

69 Ibid., p. 557.

70 Laurence Whitehead (ed.), *The International Dimensions of Democratization: Europe and the Americas* (New York: Oxford University Press, 1996), p. 15.

and that there now exists an opportunity to "reinvent the institutions of collective security."[71]

For some commentators, even the Gorbachev "revolution" was imposed by the West and that the human rights norms established in 1975 when thirty-five states participating in the Conference on Security and Cooperation in Europe (CSCE) contributed directly to the demise of communism in the former Easter bloc.[72] The 1975 Helsinki Final Act, which set up the CSCE regime, was initially seen as something of a triumph for the Soviet Union (from whence had come much of the initiative for the process) as it guaranteed respect for the national borders and territorial integrity of European states subject only to peaceful change, thereby potentially consolidating Soviet territorial gains in eastern Europe during and in the immediate aftermath of the Second World War. At the insistence of Western powers, however, the Act also set up an international human rights framework that worked to systematically undermine the Soviet totalitarian vision. Whether the Soviet negotiators miscalculated the impact that signing this document would have upon the subject peoples of East Europe, felt it was a price worth paying to potentially divide Western Europe from the United States, or simply felt they had no choice given the stronger position of the Western bloc at this time, ultimately the transformative consequences for Eastern Europe went far beyond what could have been anticipated.

Thus it was not just the general "vitality and attractiveness" of the Western polity, but rather a specific coherent and disputed set of Western requirements, incentives, and reassurances embodied in an international treaty that shaped Moscow's foreign policy options in response to the Soviet Union's systemic crisis.[73] Richard Davy contests that the actions and strength of the West at this time served to stimulate the re-emergence and evolution of civil society in the countries of East-Central Europe.[74] In other words, pressures from international constituencies forced authoritarian regimes to sign up to a human rights declaration, which in turn stimulated the people to hold their governments to account – in line with the human rights guaranteed within the international documentation.

---

[71] Quoted in Charles W. Kegley Jr., "International Peacemaking and Peacekeeping: The Morality of Multilateral Measures," *Ethics & International Affairs*, vol. 10, issue 1, pp. 25–45.

[72] Daniel C. Thomas, *The Helsinki Effect* (Princeton: Princeton University Press, 2001), p. 3.

[73] Whitehead, *International Dimensions of Democratization*, pp. 377–8.

[74] Richard Davy quoted in Whitehead, *International Dimensions of Democratization*, p. 379.

Proponents of both the Six Party Talks and the North Korean Human Rights Act have hoped for something of a Helsinki effect. For instance Roberta Cohen of the Brookings-SAIS Project on Internal Displacement and other policy hawks are keen advocates of a human rights-security linkage when dealing with authoritarian Asian regimes. She cites U.S. President Ronald Reagan's 1982 statement that the "persecution of people must be on the negotiating table or the United States does not belong at that table" as a line that should be taken with the North Korean Government, and claims that the Six-Way Talks could and perhaps should evolve to create a multilateral forum for the Korean Peninsula along the lines of the Helsinki process.[75] The reasoning is that a repressive regime such as that found in the DPRK may agree to be bound by such human rights legislation in the mistaken belief that they can thereby gain international legitimacy without substantial compliance, and yet this "empty" commitment will nonetheless promote "local, transnational, and interstate processes that undermine continued repression."[76]

It is unlikely that any authoritarian regime will repeat the Helsinki Process either because conditions are significantly different and Asian states are therefore less "vulnerable," or because the leaders of such states are well aware of the dangers posed to their regime and are therefore highly unlikely to sign up to a single human rights document of this sort. Nevertheless it is interesting to note that most Asian states are in fact signatories to many of the humanitarian documents listed above. At the very least, as Dr. Mahathir discovered, once a state has signed up to such a treaty, it is difficult later to repudiate its objectives and the implications of interpretation on the international stage.

Furthermore, the existence of these documents, and the fact that many Asian states have signed up to them, may serve to stimulate the final challenge to authoritarian regimes in Asia and the principle of non-intervention: the internal constituencies of these very states; whether individuals, the media, human rights groups, religious groups, and/or non-governmental organizations. U.S. Ambassador Leonard Garment noted in 1976 that "the existence of a formal, written document, to which the Eastern regimes gave their public consent and their formal stamp of legitimacy, has made a difference. The words matter and are beginning to move human minds."[77] In East Asia there is no formal, written document to

[75] Roberta Cohen, "Talking Human Rights With North Korea," *The Washington Post*, 29 August 2004.
[76] Thomas, *The Helsinki Effect*, p. 3.
[77] Ibid., p. 257.

which target regimes may given public consent, but nevertheless internal constituencies may be heartened by the normative turn international affairs have taken in the post-Cold War operating environment. The next section examines in more detail challenges to so-called "Asian values" emanating from within East Asian countries.

Internal Constituencies

The great liberal hope for the region is that as China continues its phenomenal economic progress, a natural and inevitable bi-product will be the emergence of a true Chinese civil society that in turn will press for political liberalization. Lowell Dittmer predicts "under such circumstances, previous experience suggests that a full-blown civil society – albeit still with distinctive Chinese cultural characteristics – is apt to emerge as quickly as bamboo shoots after a spring rain," while Zbigniew Brzezinski agrees: "It is impossible to envision a long-term process of increasing economic pluralism without the appearance of civil society in China that eventually begins to assert its political aspiration."[78] China already faces more than 90,000 protests annually as a result of endemic corruption and ongoing crises in public health and the environment.[79]

Indeed, political pressures for increased public services are so strong and the current provision of education, health care, and pensions so inequitable and dysfunctional that the Chinese government will be compelled to continue to increase the share of output spent on these government services and transfers in the coming decades. China has to perform a delicate balancing act between expanding its economy to avoid domestic unrest and responding to calls, mainly from the West, for the country to act as a "responsible stakeholder."[80] These competing demands on their resources are one reason why the Chinese leadership may wish to pick its battles carefully rather than fight humanitarian intervention whenever and wherever it is proposed.

Authoritarian Asian states face a number of internal normative challenges when attempting to justify policies and actions that may negatively impact upon the human rights of their citizens. First, while it may be possible to talk of pluralistic principles of justice and distribution based

---

[78] Cited in Nau, *At Home Abroad*, p. 165.

[79] Economy, "Leadership Gap in China."

[80] *China Mainland*, available at: http://www.carnegieendowment.org/regions/?fa=viewRegions&region=1000185.

on historically and culturally generated divergent understandings of social goods, these understandings of social goods may historically and culturally have been generated in the interests of only a small and distinct section of the community. Civil society groups in many Asian countries are increasingly vociferous in condemning such unjust privilege and prioritization, whether with regard to caste (India and other South Asian societies), ethnicity (Malaysia), religion (Philippines), age/generation (South Korea), or gender (Japan).

Second, with democratization of the media, it has become harder for governments to perpetrate, cover up, or turn a blind eye to inhumane practices within their jurisdictions or within those of fellow Asian states. Reports and pictures of slavery, human trafficking, or bloated corpses beamed into living rooms may prove too insistent for statesmen to resist, and on a normative level, in the most extreme examples, it is hard to make a case for them to do so. Even communitarians such as Michael Walzer concede something along these lines, stating that "sovereignty also has its limits, which are fixed most clearly by the legal doctrine of humanitarian intervention. Acts or practices that 'shock the conscience of humankind' are, in principle, not tolerated."[81] This process has already taken place in Western liberal democracies as outlined below, and there are signs that a similar normative shift driven by internal constituencies such as the media, NGOs and public opinion is taking place in Asia.

According to Martha Finnemore, in "surveying the global pattern of military intervention since the end of the Cold War, two features stand out. First, most of it is multilateral ... Second, in many cases the geostrategic or economic interests of the intervening states in the target state are negligible."[82] In particular, Finnemore notes the extraordinary costs of the missions to Cambodia (UNTAC) and Somalia (UNOSOM II) as mitigating against material interests of intervening states presenting the determining factor whether or not to intervene.[83] These interventions are, however, also notable for the ultimate failure of collective intervention due to a lack of collective will on the part of the international community. The same can be said of Bosnia in the early 1990s. Lepgold and Weiss catalogue a series of failures on the part of the international

[81] Michael Walzer, *On Toleration* (New Haven: Yale University Press, 1997), p. 21.

[82] See Martha Finnemore, "Military Intervention" in Joseph Lepgold and Thomas Weiss, *Collective Conflict Management and Changing World Politics* (Albany: SUNY Press, 1998), p. 181.

[83] Finnemore, "Military Intervention," p. 181.

community, concluding that "[e]ach of these episodes marked a failure to define and implement an internationalised response to the breakdown of peace."[84]

By contrast, intervention in the Gulf in response to a threat to the material interests of the Atlantic states and the security of the international system they represent was, apparently, successfully concluded. One response to this apparent dissonance is that there was not sufficient correlation of identity between the intervening force and the threatened interests. Not only were Cambodia and Somalia of little concern in economic and security terms, they also proved to be too far removed geopolitically and culturally to maintain a sufficient constituency in favour of intervention. As pointed out by Lepgold and Weiss, collective conflict management must satisfy a critical mass of key states in three ways:

> First, political leaders must believe that they can protect some of their foreign policy stakes multilaterally. Second, it must satisfy the political needs of critical domestic policy factions in the states that are most likely to contribute significantly to the system; without such domestic support, leaders cannot pursue stable and coherent policies. Third, the system also must be compatible enough with societal norms and the manifest wishes of ordinary citizens so that leaders can be confident that they will enjoy necessary popular support.[85]

National interest remained to the fore when the international community decided not to intervene during the 1994 Rwandan genocide. Boutros Boutros-Ghali (UN Secretary-General) identified general "peace-keeping fatigue" as causing unwillingness to contribute troops and fund UN operations.[86] As the world's leader, America faced greater calls upon its resources from the international community and was therefore particularly susceptible. Moreover, the U.S. was experiencing "Somalia Syndrome." American troops had been killed and then had their bodies dragged through the streets of Mogadishu. Somalia drew comparisons with Vietnam, and created a similar anti-interventionist mind-set among American decision-makers, and the wider public. In response the Joint Chiefs of Staff had pushed for a limit on U.S. involvement in any UN mission. The result was Presidential Decision Directive (PDD) 25, which was made public at the beginning of May. This stated that the U.S. would contribute to operations "only where its nation's interests were engaged

---

84 Lepgold and Weiss, *Collective Conflict Management and Changing World Politics*, p. 7.

85 Ibid., p. 6.

86 Boutros-Ghali, *The United Nations and Rwanda*, p. 50.

and that its soldiers would always remain under national command and control."[87]

The UN and Member States were ultimately, however, compelled to take some form of action as a result of pressure from international and domestic public opinion fuelled by information from NGOs and the media. In addition, what prevented other Members of the Security Council from admitting that genocide was taking place was awareness that if such charges were proven, then international law would compel them to intervene, regardless of costs and the dictates of individual national interest. Finally, guilt at the failure to act in this instance increased international normative pressure for action in the next case of "practices that shock the conscience of humankind:" Kosovo.

Madeleine Albright, the U.S. Ambassador to the UN during the Rwandan crisis and Secretary of State during the Kosovo campaign, is perhaps the best example of the transformation wrought upon the rational calculations of key decision-makers as a result of inaction guilt. Through Albright, not only did the U.S. fail to intervene, it also took the lead in restraining the international community as a whole from taking action. Albright informed the Security Council that Washington was opposed to the reinforcement of UNAMIR (the UN mission in Rwanda) under any circumstances, and that the U.S. position was that all UN peacekeepers should be withdrawn.[88] Yet, post-Rwanda Albright became such a fierce advocate of the humanitarian use of military interventionary force, that Kosovo has been termed by many "Madeleine's War." In an interview at Ewha Graduate School of International Studies, Seoul, Korea, on 12 November 2002, Albright confirmed that the previous cases where the United States and the international community had "waited too long to go in" had "played a huge role" in determining policy over Kosovo.[89]

Likewise President Clinton expressed this guilt during a visit to Rwanda in March, 1998 and acknowledged the impact it would have upon future decision-making.[90] Guilt over inaction in Rwanda and similar inaction in Bosnia, combined with pressure from internal and external constituencies meant that the Clinton administration was not going to sit idly by when a

---

[87] Quoted in Wheeler, *Saving Strangers*, p. 224.

[88] Elizabeth Neuffer, *The Key to My Neighbor's House: Seeking Justice in Bosnia and Rwanda* (London: Bloomsbury, 2002), p. 119.

[89] Madeleine K. Albright, interviewed by Brendan Howe (Graduate School of International Studies, Ewha Womans University, Seoul, Korea), 12 November 2002.

[90] *The Associated Press*, "Text of President Clinton's address to genocide survivors at the airport in Kigali, Rwanda," 25 March 1998.

case that seemed to contain elements of both those tragedies next appeared. The intervention in Yugoslavia on behalf of the people of Kosovo demonstrates the impact of historical considerations and the role of internal and external constituencies in pressuring for intervention. Kosovo was to be the first explicitly humanitarian intervention in the post-Cold War world. The eagerness to get involved in Kosovo contrasts most vividly with reluctance over Rwanda and Bosnia, as does the relative absence of considerations of material national interest compared with the Gulf.

Although naturally rich in resources, including large deposits of lead, zinc, nickel and magnesium, the province of Kosovo is one of the poorest regions in the Balkans. It is the most heavily populated region in the Federal Republic of Yugoslavia and suffers from high unemployment.[91] On the other hand, the cost of the war and the damage it caused could, according to third party estimates, be as high as $100 billion. This is equal to over $50,000 for every man, woman and child in Kosovo.[92] Thus by the end of the action, the prize was certainly not going to be worth having in cost-benefit terms, especially when, according to IISS estimates, the utilisation and replacement cost of NATO's campaign amounted to $11 billion with the peace-keeping and support for Kosovo estimated (by the UN) at a further $7.7 billion per annum.[93] Not surprisingly therefore, realists such as Henry Kissinger and Colin Gray repeatedly and convincingly argued against the intervention saying that no vital U.S. military or political interests were at stake, and that "moral outrage is not a sound base for policy" but they nevertheless conceded that "periodically it is so insistent that prudent policy-makers must bow to its demands."[94] Increasingly the democratization of the media and pressures from internal and external civil societies mean that this is true even for authoritarian Asian states.

Despite the humanitarian collateral benefit of Vietnam's intervention in Cambodia in 1978 and India's intervention in East Pakistan (now Bangladesh) in 1971, these actions were initially justified by the actors from a state security perspective, and, as a result, criticised internationally. Likewise, even the Kosovo intervention was opposed by both China and

---

91 Amnesty International, *Kosovo: the Evidence* (London: Amnesty International, 1998), p. 29.

92 Mark Littman, *Kosovo: Law and Diplomacy* (London: Centre for Policy Studies, 1999), p. vii.

93 Littman, *Kosovo: Law and Diplomacy*, pp. 25–26.

94 Patricia Owens, "IR Theory in Practice Case Study: The 1999 Kosovo Crisis" in *Oxford web support material*, Section 1, p. 4 (Oxford: Oxford University Press, 2005).

Russia – hence the necessity of NATO pursuing an essentially illegal if legitimate war in the face of inevitable UNSC vetoes. In an overwhelmingly interconnected region, however, with heavy penetration of states by new media, and with high levels of personal contact between the peoples of different states, ideas and norms are now able to diffuse much more rapidly, and state monopoly control of knowledge and opinion-forming is increasingly undermined.

David Shambaugh has identified international relations in Asia as increasingly a two-level game, whereby societies of the region are interconnected to an unprecedented degree.[95] What Nyan Chanda refers to as the "New Preachers" – NGOs and civil society community activists – have sprouted in many countries in the region to uphold humanitarian causes and issues, and to pressure governments and corporations.[96] These activists have also linked with international bodies and fellow activists in other countries for coordination and support.[97] Thus the authoritarian state's efforts to maintain its power are challenged by the mutually reinforcing trends of the constant diffusion of information and the rise of civil society activism.[98]

The third internal challenge to authoritarian government in Asia is that, even if the majority of an Asian population supports the prioritization of collective good over individual rights within the epistemological framework of their community-generated normative understanding, in all such societies responsibility is a two-way street. While individuals are perceived as having duties towards the community rather than rights against it, nevertheless the collective state, or its representatives, likewise has a duty towards the citizens to look after (rather than prey upon) their collective goods. Predatory democracies, kleptocracies, and totalitarian dictatorships are as much an abomination to Eastern communitarian "contracts" or understandings as they are to Western social contracts.

For example, South Korea is often held up as the purest example of a Confucian society. In fact according to Sung Chul Yang, such traditional authoritarianism, "characterized by a centralized bureaucratic monarchy, may indeed be one of the most enduring political traditions in Korea."[99]

[95] David Shambaugh, "International Relations in Asia: The Two-Level Game" in Shambaugh and Yahuda, *International Relations of Asia*, p. 3.

[96] Nyan Chanda, "Globalization and International Politics in Asia" in Shambaugh and Yahuda, *International Relations of Asia*, p. 307.

[97] Ibid., p. 308.

[98] Ibid., p. 309.

[99] Sung Chul Yang, *The North and South Korean Political Systems – A Comparative Analysis* (Seoul: Hollym International Corp., 1999), p. 14.

Yet we are faced with an interesting conundrum that for a people so wedded to Confucian conservatism and respect for authority it seems strange that they should so readily take to the streets in defiance of their social superiors. One possible answer to this conundrum is that Confucian values are supposed to be reciprocal. While respect is owed to social superiors this also imposes a corresponding degree of duty and responsibility towards the wellbeing of social inferiors. The anger felt in Korean protests is generated by a heightened degree of disappointment and frustration with those who have been placed in an elevated position and yet have broken the Confucian obligations to the rest of society.

This is not to suggest, however, that as a result of Rwanda and Kosovo, political leaders will authorise any and all humanitarian missions put before them, or that state-centric considerations would cease to play a role in structuring the decision-making of even democratic states let alone those under more authoritarian systems of government or those, like East Asian countries, with stronger non-interventionary traditions. Rwanda demonstrated the ongoing relevance of material considerations while revealing an awareness of how normative considerations could form part of the operating environment within which rational decisions were made. Yet the above analysis does reveal a shift in the weight given to normative considerations when addressing the formation of foreign policy, evident first within liberal regimes, but also, increasingly apparent among other states, including those in Asia.

Conclusion

Asian values survive in the constitutive documents of regional international organizations, and in many of the foreign policy priorities of Asian states. They are also to be found forming the epistemological foundations of communitarian societies. They do not, however, permit Asian governments to violate the rights of their citizens with impunity. Indeed those authorities which hide behind claims of Asian Values to justify such abuses are facing an increasing challenge from internal and external communities as well as from the changing nature of international law which may even lead to militarized humanitarian intervention. Just as European values which used to justify the disenfranchisement of women, racism, serfdom, and slavery, became anachronistic, so too may practices of states which undermine rather than protect the human security of their citizens, whether in Asia or elsewhere. There is an overlapping value consensus in

Asia reflecting concepts of harmony as expressed in Japanese "*wa*," Chinese "*he*" and Korean "*sang-saeng*," but harmony can be challenged by internal factors as much as external ones.[100] Severe violations of the internal harmony of an Asian society may require external intervention, even to the extent of the use of force, in order to restore the natural balance.

A global overlapping consensus is emerging regarding the need simultaneously to support the concepts of individual human rights, global consensus or shared norms, and a lingering respect for the legal persons of international society, states.[101] This is reflected in the near universal endorsement of related UN legislation. On 6 May 2008, in a speech supportive of the concepts and critical of attachments to state sovereignty in the region ASEAN Secretary-General Dr. Surin Pitsuwan explicitly links human security, the responsibility to protect and humanitarian intervention, emphasising how the world has changed and that ASEAN and indeed the Asia-Pacific can do no less.[102] On 14 September 2009, in the course of the closing plenary of its 63rd session, the UN General Assembly adopted resolution A/63/L80 Rev.1 entitled "The Responsibility to Protect" which had been co-sponsored by 67 member states from every region in the world, including a number of states from the Asia-Pacific region. Only seven states sought to play down the importance of the document, stressing that in their opinion the resolution was strictly procedural, and none of these came from the Asia-Pacific region.[103]

What is needed is a way to reflect these competing demands upon our evaluation of justice. Perhaps we can accept the claims of communitarians and relativists that we are historically and culturally situated, and that indeed in Asia these forces are particularly strong, yet nevertheless identify there being certain universal human wrongs which require a forceful response from the international community. This is not because we are all western liberal individualists now, but rather because all normative traditions, including those in Asia, accept that there are certain practices or operational circumstances which "shock the conscience of humankind" and should be stopped, regardless of whether the national authorities give

100 UNESCO Director-General, Mr. Koichi Matsuura cited in "Preface" in Nan-Zhao and Teasdale, *Teaching Asia-Pacific Core Values of Peace and Harmony*, p. vii.

101 See John Rawls, "The Idea of an Overlapping Consensus," *Oxford Journal of Legal Studies*, vol. VII, no. 1, spring 1987, pp. 1–27.

102 *Keynote Address by ASEAN Secretary-General Dr. Surin Pitsuwan.*

103 Global Centre for the Responsibility to Protect, *GCR2P Summary on Statements on Adoption of Resolution RES A/63/L80 Rev.1* (2009), available at: http://globalr2p.org/media/pdf/GCR2P_Summary_of_Statements_on_Adoption_of_Resolution_on_R2P.pdf.

their consent. If the national authorities resist the restoration of harmony, then the use of force may be considered justifiable by some if not all of the states in the region.

Nevertheless Asian perspectives on the focus and emphasis of intervention do appear to differ from the agenda being pushed from the West in that prevention is emphasised over the use of force, development over security, a broad interpretation rather than a narrow interpretation with regard to human security and a slow evolution and codification of international law. Asian states have demonstrated a capacity and willingness to change their positions on these issues, but any attempt to rush this transformation as for instance some of the more zealous advocates did with regard to the aftermath of Cyclone Nargis in Myanmar is likely to strengthen conservative reaction and scepticism in the region against opinions championed by more "progressive" voices.[104]

104 Bellamy and Davies, "The Responsibility to Protect in the Asia-Pacific Region," p. 567.

CHAPTER FOUR

BETWEEN HARMONIOUS WORLD AND "WAR OF ORDER": CHINESE MEANINGS OF JUST WAR AND THEIR REEMERGENCE

Nadine Godehardt

Introduction

The determining principles of Chinese foreign policy are, amongst others, peace, development, and cooperation (*heping, fazhan, hezuo*).[1] Although promoting peace is a universal goal, hardly any state emphasizes its peaceful and defensive orientation as consistently as does the People's Republic of China (PRC).[2]

The concept of a harmonious society (*hexie shehui*) further highlights the constant significance of economic success and the general political direction of China. A harmonious Chinese society, however, can only be accomplished in agreement with a peaceful and stable international environment—a harmonious world (*hexie shijie*).[3] The new security concept (*xin anquan guan*) further underscores this goal. It emphasizes the need for more cooperation, particularly through a stronger Chinese engagement in regional or international economic and security institutions.[4]

---

[1] See as one example the official statement of the Ministry of Foreign Affairs of the People's Republic of China: Peace, Development and Cooperation. In Commemoration of the 35th Anniversary of Restoration of Lawful Seat of the People's Republic of China in the United Nations, 2006, available at http://www.fmprc.gov.cn/ng/wjb/zzjg/gjs/gjsxw/t278484.htm, last accessed on 4 December 2007. Zhaoxing Li, Peace, Development and Cooperation. Banner for China's Diplomacy in the New Era, 08/2005, available at http://www.fmprc.gov.cn/eng/zxxx/t208032.htm, last accessed on 4 June 2008.

[2] See official statements about the Chinese policy of peace and development and harmonious society 中国的和平发展道路 (China's Way of Peace and Development), available at http://www.gov.cn/zwgk/2005-12/22/content_134060.htm, last accessed on 6 June 2008 and for more detailed information about harmonious society and government innovations see, for example, http://www.china.com.cn/aboutchina/zhuanti/hxsh/node_7043253.htm, last accessed on 6 June 2008.

[3] Willy Lam, "Socialism with a Harmonious Face: Hu Jintao's Plan for Reform," *China Brief*, vol. 4, no. 20, 2004, pp. 5–7., *Harmonious Society*, China Daily, 29 September 2007, available at http://english.peopledaily.com.cn/90002/92169/92211/6274603.html, last accessed 3 August 2012.

[4] Ministry of Foreign Affairs of the People Republic of China: China's Position Paper on the New Security Concept, available at http://www.mfa.gov.cn/eng/wjb/zzjg/gjs/gjzzyhy/2612/2614/t15319.htm, last accessed 3 August 2012.

However, China's plea for harmony very much relies on the country's domestic stability. It still describes the foundation of China's increasing "going out" mentality, which "marks a shift in the leadership's understanding of China's position in the world."[5] China is no longer a detached outsider of world politics but is increasingly becoming an engaged insider. China's voice matters and her new role is widely discussed in the academic debate.[6]

The image of China's peaceful rise, which the Chinese government is keen to advance in the world, stands in contrast to the Western view of China's ascent as a threat. China's economic and military growth is often regarded as a potential threat to the (East) Asian security structure and as a challenge to the U.S. American, European or Western understanding of the world.[7] The uncertainty about China's true military capabilities and political intentions further supports the image of a "dangerous" China. Hence China's ascent (and yet to a lesser extent India's ascent) challenges the traditional Eurocentric worldview. Analysts speak of a power shift from the West to the East.[8] Bestsellers have been written entitled *The Post-American World* by Fareed Zakaria or *The New Asian Hemisphere. The Irresistible Shift of Global Power to the East* by Singaporean Diplomat Kishore Mahbubani. Zakaria focuses on the "rise of the rest" which he underscores is not only an economic phenomenon but also one that "has political, military, and cultural consequences"[9] and is going to condition a post-American world order in the future. Meantime, Mahbubani focuses on the interdependence between Asia's rise and Western modernization.[10]

---

[5] Yongniang Zheng & Keat Tok Sow, "Harmonious Society and Harmonious World: China's Policy Discourse under Hu Jintao," *Briefing Series* (University of Nottingham), 1–9.

[6] Thomas J. Christensen, "Posing Problems without Catching Up. China's Rise and Challenges for U.S. Security Policy," *International Security*, vol. 25, no. 4, 2001, pp. 5–40; Bates Gill & Yanzhong Huang: "Sources and Limits of Chinese 'Soft Power'," *Survival*, vol. 48, no. 2, 2006, pp. 17–36; Evan Medeiros & Taylor Fravel, China's New Diplomacy, *Foreign Affairs*, vol. 82, no. 6, 2003, pp. 22–35.

[7] For a critical discussion of the China threat theory see Khalid R. Al-Rhodan, "A Critique of the China Threat Theory: A Systematic Analysis," *Asian Perspective*, vol. 31, no. 2, 2007, pp. 41–66.

[8] Martin Jacques, *When China Rules the World. The Rise of the Middle Kingdom and the End of the Western World* (London et al., Penguin, 2009); Robert Ross & Feng Zhu, *China's Ascent. Power, Security, and the Future of International Politics* (Ithaca: Cornell University Press, 2008).

[9] Fareed Zakaria, *The Post-American World* (London et al., Penguin, 2009)., p. xxiii.

[10] Kishore Mahbubani, *The New Asian Hemisphere: The Irresistible Shift of Global Power to the East.* (New York: Public Affairs, 2008), p. xiii.

Even though the PRC is more active in international and regional organizations—and better integrated in the international community—than ever before, China's struggle for power, recognition and status constantly raises questions about the narrative behind Beijing's peaceful rise rhetoric.[11] Domestically, the drastic measures taken against the so-called three evils, fundamentalism, separatism, and terrorism, have further stoked distrust of China's plea for harmony.[12] Furthermore, the political practices and rhetoric in Xinjiang, Tibet, or Taiwan often differ clearly from the proclaimed principles of gaining mutual trust, peaceful development and harmonious society/world.

In the field of International Relations (IR), offensive realists have decisively influenced the discussion and have emphasized the possibility of a coming conflict between China and the United States.[13] From their perspective, China is a revisionist state like all great powers and seeks hegemony in the system.[14] By contrast, Alastair Iain Johnston states that China is increasingly conforming to international and regional norms, and for that reason China is not a revisionist power.[15] Whether China's foreign policy is benign or malignant remains "profoundly uncertain."[16] This leads to the question of when, exactly, the use of violence or even wars is justified in Chinese thinking. Although the Chinese understanding of Just War has rarely been studied,[17] the investigation of the idea of Just War in

11 See also Susan L. Shirk, *China: Fragile Superpower* (Oxford et al: Oxford University Press, 2008).

12 See Chien-peng Chung: "Confronting Terrorism and Other Evils in China: All Quiet on the Western Front?", *The China and Eurasia Forum Quarterly*, vol. 4, no. 2, 2006, pp. 75–87.

13 Richard Bernstein & Ross H. Munro, "China 1: The Coming Conflict with America," *Foreign Affairs*, vol. 76, no. 2, 1997, pp. 18–32.

14 John Mearsheimer, *The Tragedy of Great Power Politics* (New York, 2001), p. 21.

15 Alastair I. Johnston, "China as a Status Quo Power?", *International Security*, vol. 27, no. 4, 2003, pp. 5–56.

16 Aaron L. Friedberg, "The Future of U.S.-China Relations. Is Conflict Inevitable?", *International Security*, vol. 30, no. 2, 2005, pp. 7–45.

17 Most of the examinations deal with Chinese warfare and the meaning of war in general. Some examples of a specific analysis of the Just War problematic are Daniel A. Bell, "Just War and Confucianism. Implications for the Contemporary World" in Bell, Daniel A. (ed.), *Confucian political ethics* (Princeton 2007), pp. 226–257; Mark E. Lewis, "The Just War in Early China" in B. Torkel (ed.), *The Ethics of War in Asian Civilizations* (London/New York, 2006), pp. 185–200.; Mark E. Lewis, *Sanctioned Violence in Early China* (Albany, New York, 1990); Karen Turner, "War, Punishment and The Law of Nature in Early Chinese Concepts of the State," *Harvard Journal of Asiatic Studies*, vol. 53, no. 2, 1993, pp. 285–324; 吴征宇 (Wu Zengyu): 正义战争理论的当代意义论析 ("Contemporary Meaning of the Just War Theory"), 现代国际关系 (*Contemporary International Relations*), no. 8, 2004, pp. 12–17.; 张露 (Zhang Lu): 中西正义战争思想比较分析 ("A Comparison of Chinese and Western Just War Thought"), 现代国际关系 (*Contemporary International Relations*), no. 4, 2005, pp. 15–20.

Chinese traditional thinking can, nevertheless, contribute to the analysis of China's current foreign policy. In this context, the Chinese concept of Just War must be analyzed with respect to the understanding of political order in traditional China, which mainly centered on an ideal emperor who held the Mandate of Heaven and whose power knew no boundaries. The examination of the Chinese understanding of Just War imparts knowledge about a notion that is often naturally used from a European or Western perspective. In addition, this analysis highlights how the Chinese understanding of *Tianxia*, particularly with regard to the Chinese meanings of Just War, which displays just one aspect of the *Tianxia* system, reemerge in the politics of the modern Chinese territorial state. It points to the PRC's particular political interconnectedness as domestic problems in Tibet or Xinjiang are difficult to separate from other issues: regional problems in Central or South Asia as well as regional crises on the North Korean Peninsula or in the South China Sea; or international discussions about, for instance, humanitarian interventions, the Responsibility to Protect or terrorism that also have an impact on China's political practices and rhetoric.

The focus of this analysis is the Chinese tradition of Just War and its benefits for an enhanced understanding of contemporary Chinese political practices. Thus, this paper aims to derive deeper insight into current patterns of Chinese political practices from the Chinese understanding of Just War. Although my perspective is limited to only one aspect of the tremendously vast Chinese culture, the underlying questions are also essential for political theorists.[18] Consequently, an empirical examination of China's actual participation in warfare is not of interest; rather, the chapter analyzes the classical writings of Chinese philosophy in order to understand the general characteristics of Just War in the Chinese tradition. The Chinese meaning of Just War is examined by means of philosophical texts from the Spring and Autumn Period as well as the Warring States Period (722 B.C.–221 B.C.). The writings of interest are the Confucian classics, Confucius, Mencius, and Xunzi, as well as the seven military classics.[19]

---

[18] For instance, Kenneth N. Waltz tries to answer the question regarding the causes of war and peace. See Kenneth N. Waltz, *Man, The State and War. A Theoretical Analysis* (New York, 2001 [1959]). With a broader focus on security, see also Barry Buzan, *People, States and Fear: An Agenda for International Security in the Post-Cold War Era*, 2nd edition (New York, 1991).

[19] Ralph D. Sawyer, *The Seven Military Classics of Ancient China* (transl. by Ralph D. Sawyer with Mei-chün Sawyer, Boulder/San Francisco/Oxford, 1993); Pin Sun, *Military Methods* (transl. by Ralp D. Sawyer with Mei-chün Sawyer, Boulder/San Francisco/Oxford, 1995); Confucius, *Analects of Confucius* (Beijing, 1994); *Hsün-tzu* (transl. by Hermann

The current policy of a harmonious society/world (*hexie shehui/hexie shijie*) also refers to these writings. Although traditional ideas constitute only one aspect of the official discourse in China (alongside, for instance, Maoist thinking), these concept have recently reemerged in Chinese academic and political discourse.[20] Hence, it is still necessary to take these ideas seriously.

The Concept of War in China: The Debate on China's Strategic Culture

The debate on strategic culture addresses the relationship between a certain national culture and the strategic thinking of a respective country. This primarily started with Jack Snyder's famous analysis of Russian strategic culture.[21] Snyder's idea of different unique strategic cultures stems from the view that people are socialized differently and, thus, develop a distinct mode of strategic thinking. Regarding China, analysts focus on the possibility that China's foreign policy orientation is based on the idea that China's civilization is *per se* peaceful. Thus, the underlying and crucial question is how (and if!) war or conflict is then justified. Moreover, the growing interest in this debate is also based on the somewhat persistent, particularly Western, distrust towards the narrative behind Beijing's continuous "peace rhetoric".

Chinese Strategic Culture: "Cultural Moralists"[22]

The Western and Chinese secondary literature generally emphasizes the unimportant role of military force in Chinese tradition.[23] John K. Fairbank,

---

Köster, Kaldenkirchen, 1967); 孟子 (Mengzi), 陈成国 (Chen Chengguo): 四书五经 (*Four Books and Five Classics*), (Hunan Changshao, 2002), pp. 61–139.

20 For instance 赵汀阳 (Zhao Tingyang): 怀世界研究. 作为第一哲学的政治哲学 (*Investigations of the Bad World: Political Philosophy as First Philosophy*), (Beijing: Zhongguo Renmindaxue Chubanshe, 2009).

21 Jack Snyder, *The Soviet Strategic Culture: Implications for Limited Nuclear Operations, Rand Cooperation 1977*, available at http://www.rand.org/pubs/reports/R2154.html, last accessed on 5 August, 2012.

22 This phrase has been introduced by Tiejun Zhang. His concept of "cultural moralism" refers to Confucian ideas and stands in contrast to Alastair I. Johnston's "cultural realism." See Tiejun Zhang, *Reconstruction the Great Wall. Chinese Security Strategy in the Early 21st Century* (Goteborg, 2003), p. 32.

23 For an overview of the central literature see Alastair I .Johnston, *Cultural Realism. Strategic Culture and Grand Strategy in Chinese History* (Princeton, 1995) and also Michael D Swaine & Ashley J. Tellis, *Interpreting China's Grand Strategy. Past, Present, and Future* (Project Air Force RAND, Santa Monica, 2000), p. 45.

for instance, states that in China war was and is to be considered as a last resort.[24] Thus, the use of force shall only be justified if neither the classical Confucian teachings nor the practice of rewards and punishment[25] are successful. Otherwise, in the past, the use of force simply displayed the moral weakness of the emperor, and he would lose the Mandate of Heaven. The Mandate of Heaven was *the* symbol of the emperor's authority in traditional China. It constituted the core of the Chinese traditional understanding of the state. As Herlee G. Creel emphasizes:

> The doctrine of the Mandate of Heaven became the cornerstone of the Chinese Empire. Henceforward China was a state—and, since it ideally embraced "all under heaven", the only state—created by, and maintained under the direct supervision of, the highest deity, Heaven. Its ruler was the Son of Heaven. His office bestowed the highest lorry [sic] possible to man.[26]

The emperor represented the highest level of morality, and because of his virtuousness he held the Mandate of Heaven. The emperor further symbolized the unity of harmony and stability within the political order. His own moral behavior coincided with his own personality, and, as a result, the emperor's virtue was recognized beyond the country's boundaries. The acceptance of his authority by others was the essential reason why war was no longer necessary. If the emperor, therefore, held the Mandate of Heaven, his virtuousness was a reason for the insignificance of military force and war, but if the emperor was forced to wage a war, it then proved that he could not preserve the harmony of his nation and between nations. Fairbank concludes, "Herein lies the pacifist bias of the Chinese tradition. War is not easy to glorify because ideally it should never have occurred."[27] This also shows the difficulty of identifying *the* Chinese concept of war. According to most authors war is condemned in Chinese tradition. For instance, Adelmann and Shih mention that "war was seen as an aberration."[28] They emphasize the pacifist focus of the Chinese war concept.

---

24 John K. Fairbank, "Introduction: Varieties of the Chinese Military Experience," in Frank A. Kiermann & John K. Fairbank (eds.), *Chinese Ways in Warfare* (Cambridge Mass., 1974), pp. 1–26.

25 "Rewards and Punishment" was introduced by the Legalists (*fajia*), who represent the realist strand of Chinese philosophy. The concept implies that the emperor should use rewards or punishments towards his people according to the circumstances. In a broader sense, "Rewards and Punishments" underlines the flexibility of Chinese criminal law.

26 Herlee G. Creel, *The Origins of Statecraft in China* (*vol. 1*) *The Western Chou Empire* (Taipei, 1970), p. 93.

27 Fairbank, "Introduction," p. 7.

28 Jonathan R. Adelmann & Chih-yu: *Symbolic War: The Chinese Use of Force. 1840–1980* (Taipei, 1993), p. 31.

They stress two aspects in particular that are in contrast to the West.[29] The first is that non-violent solutions are preferred to direct confrontations. The second is that there exists a general preference for defensive warfare, and that wars of aggression are morally condemned.

Due to these two aspects, psychological warfare has a higher significance than physical warfare or bloodshed. The authors furthermore compare Chinese warfare with an art and confront the "war as art" with the Western understanding of "war as tactics." According to this idea, victory is not gained through violence but through stratagem.[30]

Adelmann and Shih focus primarily on the question of *how* war is waged, and they conclude that the means of war are intended to avoid the use of military force. This justifies their argument that from a Chinese perspective violence and war are condemned and outlawed ("war was seen as an aberration"). From the question of how war is waged, Adelmann and Shih draw their conclusion about the general meaning of war. But this argumentation raises the following criticism.

Adelmann and Shih's analysis responds to the question of *whether* war (or violence) is part of the Chinese military tradition. They identify the idea of psychological warfare—which basically means war is war without fighting ("victory by stratagem, not force")—as the greatest difference from the West. Like that of Fairbank, Adelmann and Shih's argumentation attempts to develop a pacifist idea of war, but this pacifist doctrine cannot explain the fact that even in China war is possible. However, the question remains under which circumstances the use of force is justified. The authors further do not sufficiently explain what defensive warfare actually means which is one of the shortcomings of the cultural moralists.

Chinese Strategic Culture: The Realists

Since the mid-1990s the pacifist view of China's military tradition, as argued by Fairbank and others, has frequently been challenged. Because *if* this pacifist and defensive orientation describes the guidelines and characteristics of Chinese security policy up to the present day, and *if further*, as according to Andrew Scobell, this characteristic means that only the Chinese civilization is peaceful,[31] *then* the question of how the Chinese

29 See here and in the following Adelmann & Shih, *Symbolic War*, p. 32.

30 Adelmann & Shih, *Symbolic War*, p. 33.

31 Andrew Scobell refers to the Chinese Defense White Paper in 1998, but in the 2004 version there are similiar statements. See Andrew Scobell, "The Chinese Cult of Defense," *Issues & Studies*, vol. 37, no. 5, 2001, pp. 100–127. In the Chinese scientific debate the

government explains an anti-secession law that implies the possibility of war against Taiwan is a legitimate one.[32] China's self-image as a peace-loving nation, in contrast to foreign representations of the country, has not changed much. Various factors, such as the ongoing economic boom, increasing political engagement, and military armament, have fuelled the U.S.-led discussion of China as a "strategic threat."[33] Alastair I. Johnston and Andrew Scobell use this distrust as the starting point for their analysis.

In his book *Cultural Realism* Alastair I. Johnston explores the actual use of force in Chinese military thought. His central question is, "How does one explain the frequency of violence in Chinese historical strategic behaviour while at the same time maintaining that traditional Chinese strategic thought is uniquely antimilitaristic?"[34] As a result, Johnston mentions two requirements for the development of strategic thinking in China: on the one hand a Confucian, pacifist orientation and on the other the so-called Parabellum[35] paradigm, which refers to the Western concept of Realpolitik. Johnston chooses a dichotomous approach to study Chinese strategic culture.[36] He focuses on the Song dynasty's collection of military classics, because in his opinion it is important to search for the earliest transcripts in Chinese history where the idea of strategic culture was

---

connection between current policy and traditional thinking describes a basic approach. See 罗建波 (Luo Jianbo): 构建中国崛起的对外文化战略 ("Establishing an external cultural strategy currently rising in China'), 现代国际关系 (*Contemporary International Relations*), no. 3, 2006, p. 36.

[32] See Anti-Secession law Art. 8: "[...] the state shall employ non-peaceful means and other necessary measures to protect China's sovereignty and territorial integrity. The State Council and the Central Military Commission shall decide on and execute the non-peaceful means and other necessary measures as provided for in the preceding paragraph and shall promptly report to the Standing Committee of the National People's Congress."

[33] See Denny Roy, "Hegemon on the Horizon? China's Threat to East Asian Security," *International Security*, vol. 19, no. 1, 1994, pp. 149–168; Thomas J. Christensen, "Chinese Realpolitik," *Foreign Affairs*, vol. 75, no. 5, 1996, pp. 37–52 and more recently Thomas J. Christensen, "Posing Problems without Catching Up. China's Rise and Challenges for U.S. Security Policy," *International Security*, vol. 25, no. 4, 2001, pp. 5–40. As an example of the Chinese discourse see 楼春豪 (Lou Chunhao): 进攻性现实主义 "中国威胁论" 的实质 ("The Essence of the Offensive Realism view on the 'China Threat Debate'"), 国际关系学院研 9i, 生部 (*Journal of University of International Relations*), no. 3, 2006, pp. 14–18.

[34] Alastair I .Johnston, *Cultural Realism. Strategic Culture and Grand Strategy in Chinese History* (Princeton, 1995), p. 27.

[35] Parabellum means "*si pacem, parabellum*"(Engl.: If you seek peace, prepare for war.), see Alastair I. Johnston, "Cultural Realism and Strategy in Maoist China' in Peter J. Katzenstein (ed.), *The Culture of National Security: Norms and Identity in Word Politics* (New York, 1996), p. 217, fn. 2.

[36] Johnston speaks of the "dichotomized nature of Chinese strategic culture." Johnston, *Cultural Realism*, p. 173.

elaborated.[37] Johnston examines these Chinese military classics and questions their pacifist bias, which other authors (Fairbank, Adelmann/Shih) often imply *a priori*.

Based on three general elements of strategic culture,[38] Johnston distinguishes the central paradigm of a Chinese strategic culture as follows: first, the condition of war shall be condemned and avoided; second, the enemy shall be cultivated; and third, force shall only be used as a last resort. If armed force has to be used against external security threats, it should generally be defensive. Johnston draws the conclusion that force is not respected as an effective instrument and is quite contrary to a moral and virtuous basis for the domestic political system, which in turn leads to a peaceful society. But in view of the military strategists, Johnston reconsiders:

> In the military texts the use of the military instrument (*bing* 兵) is considered highly efficacious, indeed necessary, for dealing with security threats. This is not to say that war or violence is the sole basis of the state security, but there is a strong expectation that violence inheres in human social processes, [...]. Thus the status of violence in these texts is higher than implied in the secondary Western and Chinese literature. It is also higher than implied in the Confucian-Mencian notion of internal rectification as the basis for external security that infuses much of this secondary literature."[39]

Johnston opposes the pacifist doctrine with a realist approach which characterizes the use of force as a social phenomenon. Thus, Johnston joins realism with Chinese culture. This forgotten connection is one of his greatest achievements.

As important as the confrontation of the Confucian (moral) approach with the realist ideas of the military strategists is, their relation is not finally resolved. Moreover, the question arises as to what the dichotomy of Chinese strategic culture actually demonstrates, since elements of the

---

[37] Johnston, *Cultural Realism*, p. 40. Johnston states that he only needs to analyze the military classics, because these works already comprehend elements of other traditions (e.g., Confucianism, Legalism or Daoism), see Johnston, *Cultural Realism*, p. 45: "Indeed, there is in some cases very little difference between the content of these military classics and the other texts on statecraft that have been traditionally categorized as philosophical classics." See also Alastair I. Johnston, "Thinking about Strategic Culture', *International Security*, vol. 19, no. 4, 1995, pp. 32–64.

[38] The three general elements are the role of war within human relations, the nature of the enemy, and the effectiveness of military violence. For a comprehensive introduction of "strategic culture" see Johnston, *Cultural Realism*, p. 5–31; 37.

[39] Johnston, *Cultural Realism*, p. 72 f.

moral viewpoint are also recovered in the realist ones.[40] Johnston's dichotomy explains only that from a Confucian perspective the use of force is considered ineffective and from a military strategist perspective seems to be effective. This merely underlines the fact that war in China also describes a social phenomenon, and it is furthermore another response to the question—although from a realist perspective—of whether war or force generally plays a role in Chinese tradition.

The discussion of Just War[41] further demonstrates how difficult it is to identify the meaning of Just War within this dichotomous approach. Consequently, Johnston uses the concept of Just War to highlight Chinese zero-sum politics[42] and misses the opportunity to explain the correlation between these two approaches. Although he discovers that for the military strategist, as for the Confucian writers, war sometimes is necessary, Johnston has difficulties understanding why war as a political instrument is condemned but then, under unavoidable circumstances, also justified.

Most of the contradictions in Johnston's argumentation are related to his insufficient examination of Just War theory. The dimensions of the European concept of Just War can be introduced with the help of the following two questions: first, when or under which circumstances is war acceptable (*jus ad bellum*)? Second, how is the justified war waged (*jus in bello*)?[43] Regarding a deeper understanding of Just War in China it could be useful whether the Chinese argumentation of the use of violence come close to or prefer any of these questions or even develops a different ideal-type of Just War. However, since a war that is fought can only be a Just War, the justification of war – at least with respect to the military strategists – is already resolved, as Johnston himself points out.[44] Thus, the question

[40] See Johnston, *Cultural Realism*, p. 66: "Most of the texts [the military classics, N.G.] repeat in various forms the statement that weapons are inauspicious instruments and are only used under unavoidable circumstances."

[41] Johnston mostly speaks of "righteous war" (Chin. 义战, *yizhan*), but the connection to the Just War theory is obvious. Besides, other scientists translate the Chinese term "*yizhan*" as Just War, and the explicit difference between the two phrases is not explained by Johnston.

[42] See Johnston, *Cultural Realism*, p. 71.

[43] A third perspective is the termination of war (or *jus post bellum*) For a comprehensive overview see Brian Orend, "Jus Post Bellum', *Journal of Social Philosophy*, vol. 31, no. 1, 2000, pp. 117–137; Kellogg E. Davida, "Jus post Bellum: The Importance of War Crime Trials', *Parameters*, vol. 32, no. 3, 2002, pp. 87–99; Brian Orend, *The Morality of War* (Ontario, 2006); Michael Walzer, *Just and Unjust Wars. A Moral Argument with Historical Illustrations*, 3rd edition (New York, 2003).

[44] See Johnston, *Cultural Realism*, p. 68: "Indeed, in the military texts, the *only* conditions under which force can be legitimately employed is to fight a "righteous war' (yi zhan 義戰) [...]."

when a war is acceptable is not much of interest; instead, the classics rather deal with the question of *how* a Just War actually has to be waged (*jus in bello*). It is, therefore, less important that violence plays a more central role for the military strategist than for the Confucians and more important to determine how the use of force or the means of war are judged. This basic distinction of Just War could have shed some light on Johnston's attempt to correlate a Confucian approach with a realist one.

Andrew Scobell clearly opposes Johnston's concept of cultural realism. In his book *China's Use of Military Force. Beyond the Great Wall and the Long March*,[45] he argues that Johnston primarily pursues a unilateral approach because he mainly considers the Chinese military classics; Johnston's realist view of Chinese strategic culture represents his central aspect of analysis. Scobell further argues that Johnston underlines the symbolic character of Confucianism only within Chinese military tradition.[46] In contrast to this unilateral approach, Scobell emphasizes "that both strands of strategic culture are operative, and that the 'Confucian-Mencian' one reflects deeply held beliefs."[47]

Scobell highlights a close link between the Chinese tradition of criminal law and the present defense policy. According to Scobell, Chinese criminal law refers to two different schools of thought, namely Confucianism and legalism.[48] Scobell therefore concludes that a dualistic argumentation is essential for the analysis of Chinese strategic culture. He states, "If China's criminal justice policy has historically been shaped by the interplay between two divergent philosophies, then surely this is also possible in the case of defense policy."[49] Using both philosophical traditions, Scobell adopts his understanding of a Chinese strategic culture, which he describes as "Cult of Defense." His central questions are as follows:

---

45 Andrew Scobell, *China's Use of Military Force. Beyond the Great Wall and the Long March* (Cambridge, 2003).

46 Scobell, *Use of Military Force*, p. 20: "Yet Johnston seeks to explain away the presence of a "Confucian-Mencian' strand in strategic writings."

47 Scobell, *Use of Military Force*, p. 20.

48 Legalism (Chin. 发家 *fajia*) is a Chinese philosophical school which deduces its ideas from the political praxis during the Warring States Period. Hence Legalist ideas stand in direct opposition to Confucian ones. The most important representatives are Shang Yang and Han Feizi. For further information see Yang Shang, *The Book of Lord Shang. A Classic of the Chinese School of Law* (transl. by Duyvendak, London, 1928); Feizi Han, *Die Kunst der Staatsführung. Die Schriften des Meisters Han Fei* (transl. by Wil-mar Mögling, Leipzig, 1994).

49 Scobell, *Use of Military Force*, p. 22.

> Is China a peaceful, defensive-minded power or a bellicose, expansionist state? Has China become more belligerent in recent decades? How can contemporary depictions of a bellicose China be reconciled with earlier descriptions of a dominant pacifist tradition?[50]

In contrast to the "Cult of Offensive" which was pursued by the European elite during the First World War, the "Cult of Defense" is rooted in the cultural—not ideological—tradition of China. Scobell's "Cult of Defense" is paradoxical, because it includes not only defensive measures but also offensive actions. "Moreover, the effect of the present 'Cult of Defense' is, paradoxically, not a preference for what are clearly defensive military policies and actions but rather those that are actually offensive."[51] This understanding of defense policy, which actually implies offensive military strikes, coincides with the ambiguous Chinese political rhetoric. It shows that the concept of defense is used flexibly, and basically points out the pragmatic perception of defense in China.

Scobell's "Cult of Defense" consists of "three core philosophical elements and four guiding strategic principles."[52] The former make up the central elements of Chinese military tradition, which also represent the Confucian tradition: first, the Chinese are peace-loving people; second, they are not aggressive or expansionist; and third, they use force only in the case of self-defense. The latter four guiding principles underline the fact that China (1) fights only Just Wars, (2) values national unity, (3) is surrounded by domestic and foreign enemies, and (4) adheres to the concept of "active defense."[53] In contrast to the three core elements, these four guiding strategic principles justify the use of force. However, Scobell does not give any references to explain the central idea of his "Cult of Defense." Even though he emphasizes the usage of Just War from Confucius to Mao Zedong, he cannot document the specific Confucian aspect in the Chinese concept of Just War. He examines current military confrontations between China and other countries, but his empirical case studies cannot disprove Johnston's hermeneutic cultural realist approach.

In addition, Scobell does not deal with the different dimensions of Just War. First, the (European) idea and origin of Just War is not introduced. Representatives of the European concept of Just War—traditional as well

50 Scobell, *Use of Military Force*, p. 15.

51 Scobell, *Use of Military Force*, p. 26.

52 See here and in the following Andrew Scobell, "The Chinese Cult of Defense," *Issues & Studies*, vol. 37, no. 5, 2001, pp. 100–127.

53 Scobell, "The Chinese Cult of Defense," p. 113.

as modern ones—distinguish between three dimensions of Just War: the justice to war (*jus ad bellum*), laws concerning practices while engaged in a war (*jus in bello*), and justice after war (*jus post bellum*). Each of these dimensions highlights a specific question of Just War, and only if all conditions are fulfilled can a war be called a Just War. Second, the way in which the Chinese understand the different dimensions of Just War remains uncertain. Third, Scobell avoids distinguishing the originally Chinese meaning of Just War from the political rhetoric used in his case studies (such as the Chinese involvement in Vietnam). Scobell's conclusion regarding the common role of Just War within current Chinese politics is questionable. Because *if, as* according to Scobell, "just wars are good wars, and unjust wars are bad ones,"[54] the Chinese understanding of Just War is still not translated.

The Role of Just War in China's Academic Discourse

Generally, there is huge interest in works about military history, military thought, or warfare in China;[55] nevertheless, examinations of the meaning of Just War are uncommon. Why does the question of 义战 (*yi zhan*), "just war or righteous war," not receive much consideration in China? The first answer would be: 春秋无义战 (*chunqiu wu yizhan*).[56] This quote by Mengzi and the many books about the Chinese tradition in warfare show that the examinations of Just War in China seldom investigate the notion of war; rather, they look at the relation between justice and war. Although there are articles which discuss the different perspectives of Chinese philosophers regarding the notion of war or analyze the relationship between morality, virtue, and war,[57] these articles do not help to comprehensively

[54] Scobell, "The Chinese Cult of Defense', p. 121.

[55] For an examination of Sunzi's and Mozi's military thought see 于泽民 (Yu Zemin): 两千年军事思想的沟通. 中国古典战略今用 (*The Understanding of 2000 Years Chinese Military Thought. The Present Usage of Classical Chinese Strategy*), (Beijing, 2006). Further, a collection of historical works and comments 周振甫 (Zhou Zhenfu): 古代战纪选 (*A Selection of Classical War Records*), (Nanjing, 2005).

[56] Chin. 春秋无义战 (*Chunqiu wu yizhan*) means: "During the Spring and Autumn Period there were no just wars". See 孟子 (Mengzi), 陈成国 (Chen Chengguo): 四书五经 (*Four Books and Five Classics*), (Hunan Changshao, 2002), p. 132.

[57] See for instance 时殷弘 (Shi Yinhong): 关于战争与和平的伦理传统: 西方与中国 ("Theoretical Tradition of War and Peace. China and the West'), 世界经济与政治 (*World Economics and Politics*), no. 10, 1999; For a collection of Confucian statements about war, see 倪乐雄 (Ni Lexiong), 孔子与战争 ("Confucius and War'), 军事历史研 9i, (*Military Historical Record*), no. 4, 1999, pp. 93–104. In view of the origin of international law

explain the phenomenon of Just War in China. In particular, the question of the justification of and the rules for the justification of war are not mentioned.[58] After all, from a Confucian perspective, war—if waged by the emperor—is implicitly justified

Therefore, if Chinese academics analyze Just War, they often describe the European understanding of Just War. Wu Zhengyu, for instance, traces the origin and development of the European Just War tradition. He also emphasizes the current significance of the Just War theory, especially with regard to international law. With a view to ethics in warfare, Zuo Gaoshan introduces the meaning of *jus ad bellum* and *jus in bello*. In this context, Zuo Gaoshan also discusses the justification of defensive warfare, particularly the question of whether the Iraq War can be regarded as defensive warfare. Furthermore, he introduces the dimension of *jus post bellum* and considers the different responsibilities which arise after the termination of war.[59]

Contrary to the former authors, Zhang Lu deals with the Chinese understanding of Just War. After a brief overview of the European tradition of

---

and sovereignty during the Spring and Autumn Period as well as the Warring States Period, a discussion regarding Mozi's ideas by 桑东辉 (Sang Donghui): 也谈春秋战国时期的诸侯国是否为主权国家. 以《墨子》为例, 以国际法为视角 ("From the perspective of international law using Mozi as an example: The renewed discussion about whether the Feudal States of the Chunqiu and Warring States Period represent Sovereign States or not"), 国际政治研究 (*Studies of International Politics*), no. 2, 2006, pp. 137–149. For the numerous articles about the meaning of Sunzi for politics in current-day China, see for instance 姚有志 (Yao Youzhi)/马德宝 (Ma Debao), 《孙子兵法》与当代中国主流战争理论 ("Sun Zi's Art of War and Mainstream Contemporary Chinese Theories of War"), 中国军事科学 (*China Military Science*), no. 6, 2004, pp. 9–16.

[58] See 王联斌 (Wang Lianbin), 中华武德文化研 9i, 论纲 ("Theory Outline of the Chinese Military Virtue Culture Research"), 军事历史研 9i, (*Military Historical Record*) no. 4, 2005, pp. 150–159; 宫玉振 (Gong Yuzheng), 文化流变与中国传统兵家的形态更替 ("Cultural Transformation and the Substitution of the Chinese Traditional Military Theory"), 军事历史研究 (*Military Historical Record*), no. 1, 2000, pp. 172–180. Gong presents the different schools of Chinese philosophy. He discusses the concept of Just War, especially in relation to Confucianism, and emphasizes the connection between the military strategist Wuzi and the ideas of Confucianism.

[59] See 左高山 (Zuo Gaoshan): 正义的战争与战争的正义. 关于战争伦理的反思 ("Just War and Justice of War. About the recollection of war morality"), 伦理学研究 (*Studies in Ethics*), no. 6, 2005, pp. 43–48 and 吴征宇 (Wu Zengyu): 正义战争理论的当代意义论析 ("Contemporary Meaning of the Just War Theory"), 现代国际关系 (*Contemporary International Relations*), no. 8, 2004, pp. 12–17. In this context the article of Zhu Zhijiang should be mentioned, because following different perspectives on realism, militarism, pacifism, and the Just War theory he generates a relation between morality and war. See 朱之江 (Zhu Zhijiang), 论道德视角下的战争 ("Discussion about war from a moral viewpoint"), 军事历史研究 (*Military Historical Research*), Nr. 1, 2005, pp. 142–152.

Just War, his analysis aims to introduce the Chinese tradition of Just War. In Zhang Lu's opinion, the different views on war are dependent on the different evaluations of human nature in Chinese philosophy,[60] although he does not sufficiently prove this hypothesis. Zhang summarizes five basic assumptions from the Chinese academic debate about Just War in China: (1) There are just and unjust wars. (2) The people's consent is the most important criteria for the justification of war. (At this point, two aspects of Zhang Lu's standpoint are difficult to understand: the emphasis on the people's *consent* on the one hand and the emphasis that the people's consent is the *most important* criteria for the justification of war on the other hand. He does not clarify the correlation between both aspects.) (3) War that supports justice. (4) The caution of waging war and the condemnation of aggressive warfare. (5) The ultimate goal of war is not only the punishment of war crimes, but also the establishment of universal morality and justice.[61] Zhang Lu further compares the European and the Chinese traditions of Just War. He intends to show that the European criteria for Just War were already famous within the classic Chinese philosophy. The main difference consists of the Chinese opposition to the idea of hegemony and power politics.[62] Finally, Zhang Lu emphasizes the peaceful orientation of the Chinese tradition, but he still does not introduce rules or criteria for a Chinese meaning of Just War.

The Chinese Tradition of Just War: Confucianism and Military Strategists

The Spring and Autumn Period, as well as the Warring States Period, represent the origin of Chinese philosophy since the most important schools of thought were founded during this period. The cruelty and social unrest

---

[60] See 张露 (Zhang Lu), 中西正义战争思想比较分析 ("A Comparison of Chinese and Western Just War Thought'), 现代国际关系 (*Contemporary International Relations*), no. 4, 2005, pp. 15–20. Following Zhang, there are philosophers who characterize human nature as good or bad, others who claim that the origin lies within human nature, and again others who maintain an ambiguous attitude towards human nature. The relation between human nature and the idea of Just War is, however, controversial. Author's interview with Professor Yang Lihua, Beijing University, October 2006.

[61] See 张露 (Zhang Lu), "A Comparison of Chinese and Western Just War Thought," p. 18.

[62] See 张露 (Zhang Lu), "A Comparison of Chinese and Western Just War Thought," p. 20.

in most of the kingdoms at that time resulted in a high level of creativity.[63] The careful examination of these classics is, therefore, the foundation for the discussion of the Chinese concept of Just War.[64]

Confucianism

The different Confucian writings mainly deal with questions regarding the structure of the political order and the establishment of the emperor's authority—in other words, with the question of how the kingdom shall be ruled. When the emperor holds the Mandate of Heaven (*Tianming*),[65] his authority will extend to every man living under heaven (*tianxia*).[66] The notion of *Tianxia* constitutes the core of the Chinese traditional concept of political order. As Edward Wang clearly points out, "*Zhongguo* indicated the center of the world, hence the 'central state' or 'middle kingdom,' while *tianxia* referred to the extended Chinese world, despite its ecumenical claim."[67] *Tianxia*, therefore, comprises the whole known geographic space from a mere Chinese perspective. According to Joseph Chan, "the Confucian conception of *Tianxia* refers to an ideal moral and political order admitting of no territorial boundary – the whole world to be governed by a sage according to principles of rites (*li*) and virtues (*de*)."[68] This 'sage' stands for the Chinese Emperor, who is appointed by heaven (*Tian*). He holds the Mandate of Heaven (*Tianming*), which legitimizes his authority. Thus, the Emperor is the Son of Heaven (*Tianzi*) and he likewise represents the highest level of morality. His authority essentially depends on his virtue and his ability to act in the terms of the Mandate of Heaven. Ideally, the Emperor will rule and attract all under heaven (*Tianxia*), because "If people under your reign are happy, people will be attracted to come from afar."[69] His authority surpasses territorial boundaries.

---

63 Herlee G. Creel, *The Origins of Statecraft in China (vol. 1) The Western Chou Empire* (Taipei, 1970), p. 42: "It would probably be generally agreed that for most practical purposes the Chinese tradition may be said to have begun with the Chou."

64 The Chinese classics are considered to consist of the Confucian writings, the Maoist and Legalist writings, and the military classics written during the Warring States Period. In this article I will focus on the Confucians' and military strategists' perspectives.

65 Chin. 天命 (*tianming*).

66 Chin. 天下 (*tianxia*).

67 Edward Wang, "History, Space, and Ethnicity: The Chinese Worldview," *Journal of World History*, vol. 10, no. 2, 1999, pp. 285–305.

68 Joseph Chan, "Territorial boundaries and Confucianism," in Daniel A. Bell (ed.), *Confucian-Political Ethics* (Princeton, NJ: Princeton University Press, 2008), p. 69.

69 Confucius, *Analects of Confucius* (Beijing, 1994), XIII, 16.

Hence his moral superiority is a prerequisite for his selection, the basis of his authority and further serves as the rule for his actions.

It follows that from a traditional Chinese perspective domestic and foreign political practices cannot be separated. Within the *Tianxia* system foreign relations are rather perceived as a reflection of internal relations. John K. Fairbank points out that, the "[…] Chinese tended to think of their foreign relations as giving expression externally to the same principle of social and political order that were manifested internally within the Chinese state and society."[70] Instead of territorial boundaries, relations between different entities are better expressed by a hierarchical relationship between the center (Emperor) and the periphery (tributary states). Thus, Edward Wang rightly argues that "in the Chinese perception of the world, there was always a center-periphery consideration that helped situate the *zhongguo* in the known world, the *Tianxia*."[71]

Following this narrative, internal (civil) and external wars are also difficult to distinguish from one another. Moreover, internal and external wars coincide with this understanding of authority. The union of internal and external political practices is the central phenomenon within Confucian writings. Nevertheless, this perception of authority, which establishes an empire without boundaries, can be identified in various cultures. It is not a unique phenomenon,[72] although the moral justification of authority indeed is.

For the identification of Just War criteria it must again be emphasized that the emperor's authority within a state and towards other states was not regarded differently. From a Confucian perspective, power and authority are not enforced by violence; rather, Confucian authority is based on a moral acceptance of power. A moral and supreme emperor seizes power without the use of force. So with regard to foreign affairs and the question of war, the Confucian emperor is victorious without fighting. It is, therefore, important to recognize the fundamental correlation between

---

[70] John K. Fairbank, *The Chinese World Order: Traditional China's Foreign Relations* (Cambridge, Mass.: Harvard University Press, 1968), p. 3.

[71] Wang, "History, Space, and Ethnicity: The Chinese Worldview," p. 290.

[72] See for instance the scientific debate about the Imperium Romanum or "*Imperium sine fine*" (Engl. "Empire without boundaries") Andrew Lintott, *Imperium Romanum. Politics and administration* (London/New York, 1993), p. 1: "According to Cicero, […] it was asserted that the land in which Scipio lived was bound to rule the earth." It is important to realize that this phenomenon is not specifically Chinese, but rather universal. Despite Rome it is also found in Traditional Persia. See Pierre Briant, *Histoire de l'empire Perse. De Cyrus à Alexander* (Paris, 1996); Herfried Münkler, *Imperien: die Logik der Weltherrschaft – vom Alten Rom bis zu den Vereinigten Staaten* (Hamburg, 2007).

internal and external affairs while analyzing the Confucian writings about questions of (Just) War.

Although the Confucians, especially Mengzi, emphasize that wars of conquest and wars for profit are condemned, it seems that there is a difference between war and "punishment." For this reason, a "punitive expedition"[73] is valued differently from general warfare and represents the type of war which is morally justified. A punitive war is different because the reason for war lies in the moral decline of the political order. This means that an attack can be justified when the harmony between the emperor and his people is disturbed. Annexation by another kingdom or rebellion against an immoral and unjust emperor is legitimized because it is viewed as the emperor's righteous punishment.

Confucius highlights the moral decline within a political community as a just reason to wage a war. Once Confucius told the emperor of Lu that the emperor of Qi was murdered by a senior official who wanted to gain power in the Kingdom of Qi. Confucius gave the advice that this immoral offence needed to be punished to restore the internal order of Qi. From Confucius' viewpoint, a "punitive expedition"—or in other words, a war—against Qi was justified.[74]

According to Confucius, a crime which potentially affects the political system of another kingdom is a legitimate reason to send a "punitive expedition." This argument alludes to two things: First, there is the tremendous role of domestic politics in connection with the justification of war. This means a moral offence, a violation of Confucian traditions or the overall Tianxia-order could legitimize an attack by another state. Second, war is possible, even likely, without a previous act of aggression. These understandings of "war" or as the Confucians say "punishments" lead to some difficulties. *If* a State X is ruled by Confucian measures and another State Y is not, then the Confucians discuss the possibility of State X sending a punitive expedition to State Y. Although this particular "punishment" is considered to be different from a conventional war, it still implies the use of force. In other words, the Confucians legitimize punitive warfare because of a "potential danger." In this context the idea of punishment extends beyond the understanding of war. Hence, the internal collapse of one state is automatically understood as a threat to another state. When a state tries to diminish this danger, it means sending a "punitive

---

[73] Chin. 诛伐 (*zhufa*).

[74] See Confucius, *Analects of Confucius*, XIV, 21.

expedition." So the case of "punitive expeditions" appears to be similar to the idea of prevention; however, punishment is fundamentally contrary to prevention. Its essence lies in the fact that the implementation of the penalty *follows* the crime. The different interpretations of "punitive expedition" as, for instance, annexation, rebellion, defense, or prevention, disguise the actual understanding of war which is justified by the Confucians. Most reviews and analyses of the Chinese concept of Just War use "punitive expedition" as the common translation of the Confucian term for a justified war. Even though this translation is literally correct, it seems inappropriate in regard to the context. The internal organization of the political order is the main subject in Confucianism, even with regard to the justification of war. Thus, it makes sense to use the expression "war of order" instead of "punitive expedition."

The Confucian idea of political order is based on humanity (*ren*), righteousness (*yi*), and traditional conventions (*li*). The emperor's absolute authority is the reason for the insignificance of war. If the use of force is not necessary, then why are armed forces nevertheless a part of the Confucian political order?[75] This contradiction between the ideal of a Confucian political order and the possibility of war at the same time is somewhat naturally accepted by the Confucians. It clearly underpins the different starting points of Western and Chinese thinking. In conclusion, it is important to recognize that war plays a decisive role in Confucianism. Despite the emphasis on peaceful preferences, Confucius also highlights the military's position:

> Zi-Gong asked what was needed for government. Confucius said, "Sufficient food, sufficient armaments, and common people's trust in government." Zi-Gong asked, "Suppose you were forced to get rid of one of the three, which one would you get rid of first?" Confucius said, "Armaments."[76]

Even though the military is the first need which is dispensable, it is still part of the righteous government. It follows that the use of force is not excluded *a priori*. Although war is not a classic Confucian topic, there still exist criteria which obviously justify a "war of order."

Military Strategists

The most influential writings about Chinese military thought were written during the Warring States Period, in which war and cruelty occurred

[75] *Hsün-tzu* (transl. by Hermann Köster, Kaldenkirchen: Steyler Verlag, 1967).
[76] Confucius, *Analects of Confucius*, XII, 7.

frequently. With some exceptions, the vast majority of the military classics were also created in this period.[77] These military classics deal with the state's organization and administration. Similar to the works of the Confucians, these classics focus on the emperor's position and ideal leadership as their starting point. With the exception of Sunzi, all military strategists first discussed the internal organization of political order and then emphasized the necessity of armed forces to guarantee stability and security in Tianxia. The authors chiefly stressed the analysis of tactics which could be used during a war, for instance, the means of the emperor and the position of his army or his general. A fundamental goal of the military strategists was to limit the use of force. War is still condemned in these writings, but it is argued that Just Wars need to be waged. Military strategies were, therefore, necessary, especially when victory should be realized with a minimum of costs.

When referring to the question of Just War, the military strategists need to be considered for two reasons. Although it seems that the legitimacy of military actions is not a central subject of their writings, the military strategists developed certain conditions which justified the use of their strategies. First, it had to be a Just War. Second, they underlined what means of war should generally be used and how these means should be judged. Thus, the military strategists—in contrast to the European tradition of Just War—also considered the independence of the justification of war (*jus ad bellum*) from the means of war (*jus in bello*) in particular. The proportionality of means was further examined in the context of stratagem and deception.

In contrast to the Confucian writings, the relation between *wen* and *wu*[78]—more precisely, the role of the military within the social order—is the most important topic of the military classics. According to the

[77] The exceptions are 黃石共三略 (Huang Shi Gong San lue), which was written in Han dynasty (206–220 B.C.) and the 唐太 f問對李衛公 (Tang Taisong wen dui Li Weigong), written during the Tang dynasty (618–907 A. D.). Another work *The Secret Teachings of Tai Gong* was created in the eleventh century, though Sawyer's translation is based on a transcript from the Warring States Period. See Ralph D. Sawyer, *The Seven Military Classics of Ancient China* (transl. by Ralph D. Sawyer with Mei-chün Sawyer, Boulder/San Francisco/Oxford, 1993), p. 23. At the beginning of the 1970s the transcript of Sun Bin's *Military Methods* was rediscovered. See Pin Sun, *Military Methods* (transl. by Ralp D. Sawyer with Mei-chün Sawyer, Boulder/San Francisco/Oxford, 1995).

[78] Chin. 文 (*wen*) means civil; Chin. 武 (*wu*) means military. These characters describe the two sides of the dilemma. The role of armed forces within the social (or civil) order was the most important topic for the military strategists. See about *wen* and *wu* Fairbank: Introduction, p. 2 f.

methods of Sima, the basis of authority is not only a harmonious society, but also warfare: "Authority comes from warfare, not from harmony among men."[79] Although the internal order still consists of harmony, the external position of a kingdom can only be secured with the help of warfare. "Within, [the government] gains the love of the people, the means by which it can be preserved. Outside, it acquires awesomeness, the means by which it can wage war." Nevertheless, war may not be waged arbitrarily, because this would cause the decline of authority. "Thus, even though a state may be vast, those who love warfare will inevitably perish. Even though calm may prevail under Heaven, those who forget warfare will certainly be endangered!" Sunzi also mentions that war is a social phenomenon but possesses destructive powers at the same time. "Warfare is the greatest affair of state, the basis of life and death, the Way [Tao] to survival or extinction. It must be thoroughly pondered and analyzed."[80] As a result, the reasons for war are of particular significance.

Wuzi, for instance, specifies five general reasons for war: to protect the emperor's reputation, to gain benefits, hatred, civil unrest, and war as a result of famine. Moreover, Wuzi points out five types of war: Just Wars which save mankind from chaos; aggressions which are exercised with the acceptance of the people; wars which mobilize the army out of rage; wars which are waged only for profit; and "contrary wars" which are fought even when the people are in a state of emergency or weakened because of famine.[81]

The concept of Just War was not only a political instrument for the military strategists but also the foundation for the development of their strategies. The general criteria for Just War mentioned by the different military strategists are as follows: the emperor's authority, which finally decides on the use of force; war as defensive warfare and therefore as a direct reaction to an aggressive attack by another state; and the use of force as a last resort. In addition, war has to be useful for the people, because the people guarantee the emperor's power.[82] Yet another aspect expressed by the military strategists is that war should only be fought when victory is certain. The aim of war is victory or—in a broader sense—peace.

79 See here and in the following Sawyer, *The Seven Military Classics of Ancient China*, Chapter 2, "The Methods of Ssu-ma', p. 126.

80 Sawyer, *The Seven Military Classics of Ancient China*, p. 157.

81 See Sawyer, *The Seven Military Classics of Ancient China*, p. 208 and Johnston: "Cultural Realism', p. 67.

82 The important role of the people is mentioned in various writings. See Sawyer, *Seven Military Classics of Ancient China*, Introduction, p. 32. See also in the Methods of the Sima,

The Ambiguous Meaning of Defensive Warfare

Defense is a legitimate reason to raise a war, but defense is not consistently understood as a reaction to previous aggression. From a Confucian perspective, the meaning of defense allows further interpretations. On the one hand, defense represents a criterion for Just War, but on the other hand, the criteria for defense itself are not examined. The various means of war recognized by the military strategists clearly underline this assumption. It therefore seems that defense is significantly more than just a reaction to previous aggression. Defense according to the military strategists prevents direct confrontations; it makes victory possible before war actually breaks out. At first glance this appears to be a contradiction, but it actually describes the core of Chinese military thought. Winning without fighting requires that defensive measures are undertaken before the enemy's first strike. Following this interpretation, defense also implies direct action.[83]

Thus, the true art of war is to defeat the enemy without fighting. As Sunzi states, "For to win one hundred victories in one hundred battles is not the acme of skill. To subdue the enemy without fighting is the acme of skill."[84] But even Just War still means war, although it should be reduced to a minimum. This is the reason why warfare begins before the first gunshot. Preventive measures are used to avoid actual combat. Referring to the Chinese concept of Just War, this would definitely extend the meaning of defense as a righteous cause of war. Sunzi further mentions, "Thus, what is of supreme importance in war is to attack the enemy's strategy. The next best is to disrupt his alliances. The next best is to attack his army. The worst policy is to attack cities. Attack cities only when there is no alternative."[85]

Sunzi does not clarify what "to attack the enemy's strategy" or "to disrupt its alliances" exactly means. One interpretation could be that Sunzi supports mainly diplomatic solutions, but in the context of other statements from the *Art of War* a more offensive reading is possible.

Sawyer, *Seven Military Classics of Ancient China*, p. 126: "Authority comes from warfare, not from harmony among men. For this reason if one must kill men to give peace to the people, then killing is permissible. If one must attack a state out of love for their people, then attacking is permissible."

[83] According to Andrew Scobell, the "ambiguous understanding of defence" describes the basic perception of strategic culture in China. See Scobell, *China's Use of Military Force*, p. 26.

[84] Tzu Sun, *The Art of War* (transl. by. Samuel B. Griffith, Oxford, 1963), III, 3.

[85] Tzu Sun, *The Art of War*, III, 4–7.

The various Sunzi commentators point out that "to attack the strategy" can also mean to destroy the enemy's material resources.[86] In addition, the enemy should be attacked while he is still planning the aggression; in other words, the potential threat should be nipped in the bud. Consequently, this preventive idea seems necessary to ensure that force is actually used as a last resort. With regard to the matter of defense, the potential threat of an aggressive strategy is reason enough to "actively defend" oneself. Knowledge about the enemy's situation, army, and potential behavior is, therefore, of particular importance in order to gain victory. For this reason, *espionage* constitutes a significant part of warfare, because strategies cannot be attacked without information about the adversary's intentions. Sunzi also mentions the role of "foreknowledge." "What is called 'foreknowledge' cannot be elicited from spirits, nor from gods, nor by analogy with past events, nor from calculations. It must be obtained from men who know the enemy situation."[87] Secret agents or secret services in general are central means of war, especially when the enemy is to be beaten with minimum costs.

Another aspect which is highlighted by the military strategists is the use of stratagems or deception during acts of war. The military strategists stress the role of stratagems as being deceptions which disguise the true strategies of action. In the context of the understanding of espionage, it seems that deception plays a more essential role. Although there are criteria for fighting a Just War, the impression that almost every means seems justified to win a war is evident. Sunzi further identifies deception as the fundamental basis of warfare.[88] The meaning of deception, therefore, includes not only the concealment of information; deception also describes an active measure of war and the starting point for the development of war strategy. Burles and Shulsky also underline that it is more about forcing the enemy to act the way you want him to act, so that the enemy's behavior serves to your own advantage.[89]

---

86 For more on Sunzi's commentators see Tsu Sun, *Wahrhaft siegt, wer nicht kämpft* (transl. by Ingrid Fischer-Schreiber, Freiburg 1990), pp. 50–54; p. 93.

87 Tzu Sun, *The Art of War*, XIII, 3–4.

88 Tzu Sun, *The Art of War*, I, 17 and I; 18–27: "Therefore, when capable, feign incapacity; when active, inactivity. When near, make it appear that you are far away; when far away, that you are near. Offer the enemy a bait to lure him; feign disorder and strike him. [...] Attack where he is unprepared; sally out when he does not expect you. These are the strategist's keys to victory. It is not possible to discuss them beforehand."

89 See Burles, Mark & Abram N. Shulsky: *Patterns in China's Use of Force. Evidence from History and Doctrinal Writings* (Washington 2000), Appendix, pp. 79–95, esp. p. 89.

Orthodox and unorthodox tactics during war are measures to simply control the enemy. For the military strategists Sunzi, Sun Bin, and Tai Gong, unorthodox means of war describe a central measure for gaining victory. As Sunzi says, "Generally, in battle, use the normal [orthodox, N.G.] force to engage; use the extraordinary [unorthodox, N.G.] to win."[90] Sawyer explains that orthodox tactics imply textbook confrontations, for instance, fighting at the front. Unorthodox tactics, on the other hand, illustrate a flexible and surprising use of armed forces. Sawyer concludes,

> Thus, [...], the orthodox may be used in unorthodox ways, and an orthodox attack may be unorthodox when it is unexpected precisely because it is orthodox—whereas a flanking or indirect assault would be thereby be considered normal therefore orthodox.[91]

The surprise effect of flexible warfare is a decisive guarantee of victory. Hence, the pragmatic counterpart of deception as a strategic basis of warfare lies in the use of unorthodox tactics. Neither deception nor unorthodox measures are condemned; these means of war are justified by the military strategists.

General Characteristics of Just War in the Chinese Tradition[92]

After analyzing the different Chinese philosophical perceptions, it becomes clear that even in China's traditional thinking, war and violence can be justified. Confucius actually introduces the possibility of a "punitive expedition," although the criteria for a preventive intervention remain questionable. The classic Confucian writings mainly deal with the maintenance and organization of political order; it is, therefore, necessary to determine the Chinese meaning of Just War from the description of political community in traditional China.

In accordance with an era of relative political stability during the Western Zhou dynasty (1122–771 B.C.),[93] the (ideal) Confucian emperor represents the unity of harmony and stability. He is the core of the

90 Tzu Sun, *The Art of War*, V, 5.

91 Sawyer, *The Seven Military Classics of Ancient China*, Notes to Sun-tzu's *Art of War*, Fn. 33, p. 427. See also Pin Sun, *Military Methods* (transl. by. Ralph D. Sawyer with Mei-chün Sawyer, Boulder/San Francisco/Oxford 1995), p. 233.

92 For his comments and suggestions on the following two sections, I would like to thank Dr. Oliver Lembcke.

93 "Die Zhou Dynastie folgt den beiden vorangegangenen Dynastien der Xia und Shang. Wie vornehm und kultiviert! Ich folge Zhou. "(The Zhou Dynasty succeeds the two

traditional Chinese political order and his virtue serves as an example for the "common man" (*xiao ren*). On the other hand, the people are indebted to the emperor's authority. Consequently, the hierarchical order determines the relationship between the emperor and the people. He surely rules *for* the people, but is not legitimated *by* the people; the hierarchical relations are characterized by mutual responsibilities, not by rights and duties. The emperor holds the Mandate of Heaven (*tianming*) and because of his moral authority gains power without fighting. The domestic harmony which is highlighted in the Confucian understanding of peace also influences the perception of the empire's external stability. "The Chinese world order, therefore, was as much an ethical as a political phenomenon. Harmony internationally as well as domestically was the product of the emperor's virtue."[94]

Recently, Zhao Tingyang's work on rethinking Tianxia further underpins this understanding. Zhao tries to translate the traditional understanding into a modern political theory. Although he does not ground his view of Tianxia in one particular strand of Chinese traditional thinking, Zhao's analysis of Tianxia summarizes many viewpoints mentioned earlier. In his understanding of *Tianxia* the term stands for a wider meaning of "world" and consists of three meanings.[95] First, *Tianxia* refers to the topographic expansion, everything under the sky or simply the geographic world. Second, the social understanding of *Tianxia* points to the necessary support of the "hearts of all people" (*minxin*). *Minxin* secures the political legitimacy of the *Tianxia* and mostly depends on virtuous governance. Therefore, the relationship between the common agreement of the people (*Minxin*) and the rule of virtue (*Dezhi*) is co-constitutive.[96] Third, the most important meaning of *Tianxia* is the establishment of a world institution (*Shijie zhixu*) and only with the final creation of a world institution the *Tianxia* system is fully accomplished.

Beside this relatively broad three meanings, Zhao mentions a set of important principles that further explain the features of the *Tianxia*

---

previous dynasties of the Xia and Shang. How distinguished and civilized! I follow Zhou.) *Konfuzius: Gespräche* (transl. by Ralf Moritz, Leipzig, 1982), III, 14.

94 Suisheng Zhao, *Power Competition in East Asia: from the Old Chinese World Order to Post-cold War Regional Multipolarity* (London, 1997), p. 8.

95 Tingyang Zhao, "A Political World Philosophy in terms of All-under-heaven (Tianxia)," *Diogenes,* vol. 56, no. 5, 2009, pp. 9–10; 赵汀阳 (Zhao Tingyang): 怀世界研究. 作为第一哲学的政治哲学 ("Investigations of the Bad World: Political Philosophy as First Philosophy"), (Beijing: Zhongguo Renmindaxue Chubanshe, 2009), pp. 82–7.

96 Zhao Tingyang, "Investigations of the Bad World," p. 98.

system. The first one is the principle of "all inclusiveness" (*Wuwai*) which states that every person, family or state is part of *Tianxia*. Nothing is considered to be outside. Nobody is excluded. Tianxia becomes the common interest of every person. The common interest goes in line with the many existing personal interests because of the underlying conformance of both.[97] As Zhao emphasizes, "'all-under-heaven' is meant to be of all and for all, and never of and for anybody in particular."[98] The condition of *Wuwai* also secures peace and prosperities among the countries in the *Tianxia*; it refers to the transformation of many states into one world entity by attraction rather than coercion.[99]

In a *Tianxia* system where every place is internal, Zhao characterizes relations between different entities as relations between the far and the distance (*Yuanjin qinshou guanxi*). Zhao refers to what is generally described with the image of core-periphery relations that originally indicates the difference between the core and the periphery in cultural and geographic terms. Later this image often changed into an idea of discrimination of the core towards the periphery or simply a presupposed supremacy of the core towards the periphery.[100] However, it is crucial that the relation between the near and the far is not understood in a purely geographic sense. Closeness and distance can also be perceived in cultural terms; thus, the "core" could also be identified as a mutual understanding of certain values.[101] The development of these relationships is a process of constant change and transformation. Consequently, "all-inclusiveness" does not simply stand for enforced conformity.

The second principle deals with the institutional character of the *Tianxia*, the question of order (*Zhi*) and disorder (*Luan*). *Zhi* represents the Chinese quest for establishing a good social order that is accepted by the people; *Luan* stands either for the absence of any social order or for the unavoidable situation of revolution.[102] In addition, the institutions should facilitate cooperation and keep the possibility of conflict low.

Cooperation in the *Tianxia* order is furthermore based on two political strategies. First, the strategy of virtue (*De Celüe*) that in a long-term perspective seems to be more effective than the use of force since it mainly

97 Zhao Tingyang, "Investigations of the Bad World," p. 90.

98 Zhao Tingyang, "A Political World Philosophy in terms of All-under-heaven," p. 11.

99 William A. Callahan, "Chinese Visions of World Order: Post-hegemonic or a New Hegemony?", *International Studies Review*, vol. 10, 2008, p. 752.

100 Zhao Tingyang, "Investigations of the Bad World," p. 92.

101 I am grateful to Francesco Sisci for this remark.

102 Zhao Tingyang, "Investigations of the Bad World," p. 103.

builds on the common agreement of all people (*Minxin*). Thus, the strategy of virtue very much relies on the confidence and support of the common people.[103] On the other hand, good or virtuous governance also maximizes the benefits of all people and creates an advantageous environment for the people. In short, the strategy of virtue refers to the differentiation between the common people who get more benefits and the sovereign who then obtains the power to rule.[104]

Second, Zhao introduces the strategy of harmony (*He Celüe*) which focuses on the question how to build cooperation out of differing interests. Cooperation is inevitable linked to the implementation of harmony. Harmony (*He*) is seen as the most essential principle in Chinese thinking. In contrast to the idea of sameness (*Tong*), harmony refers to the diversity of things that make cooperation possible. It follows that harmony grows out of the improvement and transformation of differences while "sameness reduced possibilities to only one thing."[105] Hence, harmony (*He*) represents an ontological principle while sameness (*Tong*) stands for a psychological effect (i.e., all simply emerge into one). Both should not be confused. This distinction is crucial because harmony is contrary to sameness not referring to an enforced conformity which would destroy the substance of culture in the first place. Culture develops and is rather shaped by relations within the *Tianxia*.

Thus, ideally, no other political community could or would elude the harmony of the Chinese emperor. Zhao's argumentation again shows that authority in Tianxia is regionally unlimited and that harmony is the key feature of the traditional Chinese political order. Due to boundless claims to authority and the "all-inclusiveness" of the Tianxia, the Chinese tradition lacks a distinction between international and domestic conflicts; both are primarily considered as disturbances of harmony. Peace is, therefore, the absence of disturbance— and regarded as synonymous with harmony, which is represented by the emperor. Peace, however, is not a political concept rather an ontological status; it cannot be actively founded by the emperor.[106] But if the harmony is challenged, the emperor has the

103 Zhao Tingyang, "Investigations of the Bad World," p. 111–115.

104 Zhao Tingyang, "Investigations of the Bad World," p. 114.

105 Zhao Tingyang, "A Political World Philosophy in Terms of All-under-heaven," p. 14.

106 As it was, for instance, developed by Thomas Hobbes, see Thomas Hobbes, *Leviathan: Oder Stoff, Form und Gewalt eines kirchlichen und bürgerlichen Staates* (edited by Irene Fetscher, Frankfurt am Main, 2006 [1651]).

duty to restore political order, an act which can also include the use of violence.

Consequently, the traditional focus on the maintenance of political order is central to the Chinese understanding of Just War, because continuous disorder is considered more dangerous than the use of military violence. "The internal disintegration of a nation is more dangerous than its external aggression […]. Furthermore, internal disintegration is likely to invite aggression from without and in that case the State is defenceless for there is no unity within."[107] It follows that violence and war are justified when the emperor intends to eliminate the disorder. In this context, the justified war is referred to as a "punitive expedition." Furthermore, the aggression of another political community must not precede the actual use of violence, because it is the maintenance of political order which can lead to a military intervention, even when it is the domestic decline of political order in a neighboring state that entails a potential threat. Moreover, a military intervention can be raised with the intention to contain the potential danger of anarchy. In these cases of preventive intervention it makes sense to use the expression "war of order" instead of "punitive expedition"; the rules for such an intervention still remain uncertain.

The means of war also highlight the traditional Chinese attitude towards the use of violence, especially the ambiguous understanding of defense. Defensive warfare not only implies a reaction to previous aggression, but also denotes an active military strike. According to the military strategists and the Confucians, the meaning of war is to achieve victory without fighting; defensive warfare begins even before the first movement of the enemy. This understanding of defense implies that a potential threat can be solved preemptively and highlights the possible use of preventive violence. A central aim is to control the enemy's actions before a potential threat becomes a real one.[108] In this context, defeating the enemy without fighting implies that the use of military violence should be restricted to an absolute minimum. These means do not exclude violence, but they should still avoid bellicose actions: (1) On the one hand, deception describes the withdrawal of information, the concealment of tactics,

---

107 Leonard S. Hsü, *The Political Philosophy of Confucianism. An Interpretation of the Social and Political Ideas of Confucius, His Forerunners, and His Early Disciples* (London/Dublin/New York, 1932), p. 73.

108 On the one hand this aspect is difficult to combine with the Just War theory, but on the other hand it points out a current debate: whether—or when—a preventive or preemptive strike could be justified.

or an ambush. On the other hand, the Chinese understanding of deception extends beyond this general understanding. Deception is further viewed as the basis of warfare. This includes, for instance, the active control of the enemy's resources or influencing the enemy's actions in a way that serves one's own goals. The Chinese idea of deception or stratagems is not kept secret, because deception or stratagems are not interpreted negatively but rather as a sign of intelligence. (2) The orthodox and unorthodox methods are closely linked to the meaning of deception. It is essential that unorthodox tactics such as deploying troops flexibly and surprisingly if it ensures victory and success are justified. Hence, war waged by the emperor seems to be more similar to a police action than a military one. Defense can be understood as preventive and also includes direct action with the help of unorthodox methods. War, justice, and prevention stand closely together in Chinese tradition. Thus, the term "war of order" gets closer to the core of what expresses a Chinese understanding of a Just War since it does not conceal the possibility of preventive intervention.

Just War in a Harmonious World

Uncertainties about China's true foreign policy orientation still dominate the academic debate; even the representatives of different approaches in IR theory cannot find a clear answer. Consequently, the numerous analyses about China's rise range between peaceful or bellicose claims of China's future engagement in Asia and in the world.

Aaron L. Friedberg shows that this uncertainty about China's future path is one of the most controversial issues in IR.[109] "It is possible to identify liberals who expect confrontation and conflict, realists who believe that the relationship will basically be stable and peaceful, and constructivists who think that events could go either way."[110] Friedberg aims to categorize the liberal, realist, as well as constructivist approaches around either an optimistic or pessimistic perception of Chinese foreign policy.[111] For liberal optimists, the growing economic interdependence between China and the United States has strengthened the mutual interest in peace between the two countries and in the Asia-Pacific region. Further, the

109 Aaron L. Friedberg, "The Future of U.S.-China Relations. Is Conflict Inevitable?", *International Security*, vol. 30, no. 2, 2005, pp. 7–45.

110 Friedberg, "The Future of U.S.-China Relations', p. 10.

111 A similar attempt was made by Thomas J. Christensen, but he only distinguishes between a positive-sum perspective "in which the United States, China, and other regional

embeddedness of China in international institutions such as the WTO and regional institutions such as the ARF, ASEAN+3 or the East Asian Summit will promote "contact, communication and, over time, greater mutual understanding and even trust."[112] Both aspects, interdependence and institutions, would also promote the process of democratization in China. On the contrary, realists' attitudes are mostly pessimistic. In this context, Friedberg particularly emphasizes China's incredible economic and military ascent, which is threatening not only because of its speed, but also because of "its growing mass and enormous potential."[113] He subsequently argues that rising powers aim to expand their power and, consequently, challenge the established powers. In the tradition of offensive theorists, a confrontation between rising and established powers is seldom resolved peacefully. From this perspective, China's predominant goal would be to push the United States out of their sphere of influence in East Asia. Realist optimists, however, argue that even though the balance of power between the U.S. and China needs to be monitored, China's power capabilities are weaker in reality than many analysts have claimed. While China's economy and military power is growing, the power of the United States has not stopped growing.[114] According to the realist optimists, a rising power does not necessarily act aggressively. Rising powers can have different political intentions and their aims can be limited.[115] Therefore, realist optimists describe the dominant security dilemma as muted. The liberal pessimists question the structure of the Chinese political system and its potential for democratization. The PRC is still an authoritarian state. Furthermore, the Chinese government supports the growth of a strong nationalist

---

actors have strong incentives to increase mutual trust, transparency, and economic ties, thereby minimizing the likelihood of avoidable military conflicts that serve no nation's long-term interests" and a zero-sum perspective "in which the continued relative increase in Chinese power poses the most formidable long-term danger to the national security and economic interest of the United States and its allies in the region [...]." Thomas J. Christensen, "Fostering Stability or Creating a Monster? The Rise of China and U.S. Policy toward East Asia," *International Security*, vol. 31, no. 1, 2006, p. 81.

112 Friedberg, "The Future of U.S.-China Relations," p. 14.

113 Friedberg, "The Future of U.S.-China Relations," p. 17.

114 See for instance Gerald Segal, "Does China Matter?", *Foreign Affairs*, vol. 78, no. 5, 1999, pp. 24–36; Khalid R. Al-Rhodan, "A Critique of the China Threat Theory: A Systematic Analysis," *Asian Perspective*, vol. 31, no. 2, 2007, pp. 41–66.

115 For the Chinese case, see David Shambaugh, who states that "China's regional power and influence need not result in a reciprocal decrease in U.S. power and influence. Acquiring and wielding power and influence in a non-bipolar system [...] is not a zero-sum game." David Shambaugh, "China Engages Asia. Reshaping the Regional Order," *International Security*, vol. 29, no. 3, May 2004, pp. 64–99.

sentiment towards Taiwan, Japan, and the United States. Even if China's political system were to transform into a more democratic one, the impact on U.S.-China relations would not automatically be a given. And "if China does not change [...] certain persistent features of America's domestic regime appear likely to incline the United States toward conflict with the PRC."[116] This would turn the democratic peace argument around. Liberal pessimists worry that this situation would lead to a "vicious cycle of mutually reinforcing suspicions and fears."[117]

Constructivist optimists argue that people can change the environment by following their beliefs and ideas. Even though China's traditional thinking is determined by the "parabellum paradigm,"[118] the constructivist optimists claim that Chinese politicians can change their attitude via increasing international embeddedness and institutional contact. Constructivist pessimists, however, maintain that concerning China, "positive change is likely to be a long time in coming."[119] Therefore, the interaction with the outside world could also harden relations with the U.S. or China's political intentions because of the experience of shocks and crises.

Friedberg's attempt to categorize the dominant patterns of the theoretical debate still gives a good impression of the difficulty of determining China's future foreign policy intentions. He tries to synthesize the six different positions and further emphasizes that "each of the six positions captures some aspect of reality and that most, and perhaps all, of the causal mechanisms that they describe are at work simultaneously."[120] But the question which Friedberg also cannot answer is whether the PRC itself has an idea of its future foreign policy orientation. The general uncertainty can therefore be united in one question: What is China's concept of (regional and international) order? Friedberg's categorization is one step in the right direction, but his classification of the different perspectives is not always without doubt. On the one hand, it could be questioned whether the representatives of the different IR theories always stand for only one of Friedberg's six positions or whether most of them do not already combine different approaches. On the other hand, the dominant IR approaches all rely on a rather Eurocentric starting point which makes it indeed difficult to simply use these approaches to explain the Chinese

[116] Friedberg, "The Future of U.S.-China Relations," p. 31.
[117] Friedberg, "The Future of U.S.-China Relations," p. 33.
[118] Johnston, *Cultural Realism*.
[119] Friedberg, "The Future of U.S.-China Relations," p. 37.
[120] Friedberg, "The Future of U.S.-China Relations," p. 39.

concept of political order. Hence, the examination of the different IR theories, though important, can only shed limited light on China's future political practices.

In contrast to Friedberg's focus on IR theories, Johnston emphasizes the underlying cultural pattern of Chinese traditional foreign policy, which supports his "parabellum paradigm" hypothesis. He combines cultural aspects with a realist perspective on China's foreign policy practices. This connection between Chinese traditional thinking and contemporary political attitudes is usually a strong argument among Chinese academics like Zhao Tingyang and is also often mentioned in official documents which highlight the peaceful and harmonious orientation of the PRC.[121] Furthermore, authors such as David Kang also try to link China's traditional idea of order with China's contemporary role in the region as well as in the world.[122]

In *China Rising: Peace, Power, and Order in East Asia*, David Kang discusses the question why East Asian states are not balancing against a rising China. He claims, "the balancing hypothesis finds little empirical support in modern East Asia."[123] Contrary to pessimistic approaches, he underlines that China is rising peacefully and that East Asian states view China as a more benign power than is generally expected. With his specific perspective on East Asia, Kang challenges classic approaches of IR theory and in particular neorealist interpretations of East Asian Order. Kang refers to the hierarchical tradition in Asia, and China's central role within this hierarchy. Following John K. Fairbanks classical argument, he argues that, "East Asian regional relations have historically been hierarchic, more peaceful, and more stable than those in the West."[124] Hierarchy, following

---

121 See for example, Ministry of Foreign Affairs of the People Republic of China: Peace, Development and Cooperation. In Commemoration of the 35th Anniversary of Restoration of Lawful Seat of the People's Republic of China in the United Nations, 2006, available at http://www.fmprc.gov.cn/ng/wjb/zzjg/gjs/gjsxw/t278484.htm, last accessed on 4 December 2007; Zhaoxing Li, *Peace, Development and Cooperation. Banner for China's Diplomacy in the New Era*, 08/2005, available at http://www.fmprc.gov.cn/eng/zxxx/t208032.htm, last accessed on 4 June 2008; 中国的和平发展道路 ("China's Way of Peace and Development"), available at http://www.gov.cn/zwgk/2005-12/22/content_134060.htm, last accessed on 6 June 2008; 孙学峰 (Sun Xuefeng): 和谐世界理念与中国国际关系理论研究 ("The Concept of a Harmonious World and the Study of Chinese International Relations Theory'), 教学与研究 (*Education and Research*), vol. 11, 2007.

122 Recently published by David C. Kang, *China Rising. Peace, Power, and Order in East Asia* (New York, 2007), p. 23.

123 Kang, *China Rising*, p. 23.

124 David Kang, "Hierarchy, balancing and empirical puzzles in Asian international relations," *International Security*, vol. 28, 2003, p. 166.

Kang's understanding, describes a specific distribution of power that is accepted by the involved units. As he highlights, "In hierarchy, independent sovereign nations accept the central position of the largest power in the system but are fully functional on their own terms."[125]

Based on Kang's specific perspective on East Asia, hierarchy in good times represents a more stable system. East Asia is, therefore, not following the European experience and, from this perspective, Kang clearly contradicts Friedberg's dictum that "Europe's past is Asia's future."[126] He rather refers to the tradition of East Asian international relations before the intrusion of the Western powers in the nineteenth century. Kang discusses the developments in East Asia between the thirteenth and nineteenth centuries to show how the region became what it is today. Hence, he identifies criteria such as the geographical scope, the major actors and the distribution of powers that characterize the level of interaction within the traditional East Asian international system. Kang uses the historical constellations with China as the preponderant power in East Asia to underscore his hierarchy argument and contradict the balance of power hypothesis. He argues that although East Asia "was a system primed for intense balance of power politics," balancing or alliance formation against China has not occurred. "Conflict tended to occur not to check rising Chinese power but rather as a consequence of decaying Chinese order."[127] It follows that a stable China somewhat stands for a stable Asia. Secondary powers had no need to fight China; rather, they benefited from China's central role. With regard to the tributary system, Kang shares the view that tribute states gained as much as they invested, which further stabilizes China's role. It follows that Asian international relations stress formal hierarchy but at the same time also share informal equality – in contrast to the European tradition, which was dominated by formal equality and informal hierarchy.[128]

Except for the tributary system Kang does not divulge any additional principles that explain hierarchy as a fundamental concept in East Asian international relations.[129] Although he refutes Acharya's claim that he has

---

125 David Kang, "The Theoretical Roots of Hierarchy in International Relations," *Australian Journal of International Affairs*, vol. 58, 2004, p. 348.

126 Aaron L. Friedberg, "Ripe for rivalry? Prospect for peace in a multipolar Asia," *International Security*, vol. 18, 1993, pp. 5–33.

127 Kang, *China Rising*, pp. 30–7.

128 Kang, "The theoretical roots of hierarchy in international relations," pp. 339–40.

129 Furthermore, his perspective on the tributary system is rather static.

not simply inverted Friedberg's argument ("Europe's past is Asia's future" becomes "Asia's past is Asia's future"), he does focus on Asian history, because "there are good reasons to think that Asian states may not function like European states."[130]

However, it is hardly true that balancing never occurred at any point in Chinese history. To the contrary, the overcoming of the balance of power during the Warring States period, through the success of Qin Shihuangdi and the establishment of the first Chinese dynasty (*Qin*), laid the foundation for the course of political developments in East Asia until the intrusion of the Western powers in the nineteenth century. Consequently, Kang's view on East Asian history rather conceals the more important question of *why* China and Europe, despite facing similar problems, experienced different outcomes. It follows that Kang is skilled in highlighting where the East Asian developments differ from Europe but he cannot exactly show why. Kang's view on East Asia conceals that Imperial China regarded herself as the core of the then known world, in other words like a civilization without boundaries. Very much in contrast to Modern China that – at least on paper – displays a sovereign nation-state within the international system.

With regard to Friedberg's discussion, I provide an enhanced matrix where I combine Friedberg's classifications with the different perspective on China's political order as well as meanings of Just War. The matrix particularly highlights the clash of claims between Chinese and Western academics since the former exclusively emphasize China's peaceful orientation and the latter mainly take a more skeptical view of China's contemporary foreign policy practices.

The benign character of Chinese politics is, therefore, found not only in official documents and statements but also in Chinese academic analyses, which are keen to spread the image of a peaceful China into the academic world.[131] For example, a stronger emphasis on the connection between Chinese culture and current Chinese political practices makes it possible to generate ideal-types of "war of order" or "harmony" that are grounded in Chinese culture. After all, ideal-types, following Max Weber, are an abstraction from the world and are culturally grounded. They are not

[130] Amitav Acharya, "Will Asia's Past Be Its Future?", *International Security*, vol. 28, no. 3, 2003, pp. 149–164.

[131] See for an overview Sébastian Billioud, "Confucianism, 'Cultural Tradition', and Official Discourse in China at the start of the New Century," *China Perspectives*, vol. 69, no. 3, 2007, pp. 50–65.

Chart 1. Perspectives of Chinese Foreign Policy Practices in Modern and Traditional China.

Pattern	Modern China		Traditional China	
	China	West	China	West
Peaceful/ Cooperation/ Harmony	Harmonious society/ harmonious world (official documents); cultural moralism (Tiejun Zhang); Tianxia as model of the world (Zhao Tingyang)	Liberal optimists, constructivist optimists	Cultural moralism (Tiejun Zhang)	Interpretations in view of Chinese classical writings (John K. Fairbank, Adel-mann/Shih). "War was seen as aberration." (Adelmann/Shih)
Bellicose/ Conflict/ Revisionist/	X	Realist pessimists, liberal pessimists	X	Interpretations which refer to Confucianism and the military strategists as determining patterns of Chinese traditional foreign policy (Alastair Iain Johnston, Andrew Scobell).
Peaceful and bellicose/ Status quo	X	Realist optimists, constructivist pessimists	X	Interpretations which refer to Confucianism and the military strategists as determining patterns of Chinese traditional foreign policy (Alastair Iain Johnston, Andrew Scobell).

Source: Author's compilation.

referring to something concrete that exists in the world, they are rather a "utopia" (a non-place) that helps to show how far or close reality differentiates from the respective ideal-type.[132] It is crucial that ideal-types never display empirical actuality and that they are even less part of a pattern that simply categorizes actuality. In fact, ideal-types are conceptual, idealized, and perspectivized devices that help us to clarify certain characteristics about actuality such as Chinese contemporary political practices.[133] It follows that ideal-types are never true; instead, they should be useful.

In this context, the examination of Chinese meanings of Just War is in fact a first step into this direction, it, however, can only shed light on a few aspects of contemporary Chinese policy practices. Hence, based on the examination of Just War or "war of order" and the understanding of political order in China's traditional thinking, we can only assume how far or close China's current political practices differentiates from the generated traditional notions.

Today, most Chinese regard the country's continuous rise as the obligatory reestablishment of China's lost status in the world. This patriotic view is based on a strong belief in China's ability to finally overcome the "century of shame and humiliation."[134] The period of European domination – when the imperial government was forced to sign unequal treaties and granted foreigners privileges of extraterritoriality – and later Japanese occupation slowly undermined the empire's self-understanding as hub of their known world. From a Chinese perspective, Imperial China already occupied great power status. Even at the eve of the first Opium War Qing-China made up approximately one third of the world's total GDP which at that time was still six times more than the share of the British Empire.[135] Hence, China's current rise is not regarded as a new historical phenomenon but rather as a way to regain the country's lost international status.

However, the intrusion of foreigners or the "clash of civilization" in the nineteenth century led to the end of the Tianxia-system, to the abolish-

---

[132] Max Weber, *Gesammelte Werke zur Wissenschaftslehre* (Tübingen: J.C.B. Mohr, 1922), p. 191.

[133] Weber, *Gesammelte Werke zur Wissenschaftslehre*, p. 194.

[134] The century of shame and humiliation refers to the time from the nineteenth century until the foundation of the People's Republic of China (PRC) in 1949.

[135] The Qing dynasty was the last ruling dynasty. The last emperor Puyi abdicated on February 12, 1912.

ment of the tribute system, and to the consolidation of a "modern political order." Consequently, the two Opium Wars followed by the signing of the treaties of Nanjing (1842) and Tianjin (1858) forced the imperial government to reconsider their relations to the outside – non-civilized – world. The treaty system enforced the Western domination, dissolved the full sovereignty of the Qing-court and further undermined the emperor's authority. It secured various rights regarding for instance the loosening of tariff regulations or the stationing of foreign legations on Chinese ground. "Since the Treaty of Nanking, the more clear-minded of the generally ignorant and conservative Chinese officials were beginning to realize that a closed door policy towards the foreigners was no longer possible (...)."[136] In 1861, the imperial government finally established the *Zongli Yamen*; an office that particularly managed foreign relations. The *Zongli Yamen* also was the first step for Imperial China to abolish the Sinocentric worldview and instead acknowledge sovereignty and equality as the basis of foreign relations. However, the foundation of the *Zongli Yamen* was not China's free elected entrance into the Family of Nations but rather "the beginning of China's being drawn forcibly, albeit half-willingly, into the expanding European international system."[137] Hence, Imperial China acted on behalf of foreign pressure. After the First World War, Republican China was then elected into the League of Nations and regained at least judicially its international status. Still, as Zhang Yongjing rightly argues, "China entered the international society not by meticulously fulfilling that standard [European standard of civilization, N.G.] but by revolt in a changing international milieu, against the regimes Europe introduced to regulate its relations with the non-European world."[138] Hence, it becomes clear that certain concepts such as nation-states, sovereignty, or equality have been mainly introduced to China by the West. Moreover, the Western intrusion shattered the Sino-centric worldview. Zhang Yongjing rightly claims that "[w]hen *Tianxia* (all-under-heaven) shrank to *guojia* (state), *the* Chinese world became *a* China in *the* world."[139]

---

136 S.M. Meng, *The Tsungli Yamen: Its Organization and Functions.* (Cambridge, Mass.: Harvard University Press, 1970), p. 19.

137 Yongjin Zhang, "China's Entry into International Society: Beyond the Standard of Civilization', *Review of International Studies,* vol. 17, 1991, p. 5.

138 Zhang, "China's Entry into International Society," p. 16.

139 Yongjin Zhang: "System, Empire and State in Chinese International Relations," *Review of International Studies,* vol. 27, 2001, p. 61.

Today, the PRC leadership persistently defends the idea of "sovereignty" which according to Shan Wenhua is marked by three main "Chinese characteristics": First, due to the humiliating and shameful experience during the Qing-Dynasty, the Chinese government nowadays sees the principle of sovereignty at the "very center of international law". Second, they particularly uphold the inviolability of state sovereignty. Third, they further stress the mutual and reciprocal character of sovereignty which is implemented in the principle of "mutual respect of sovereignty and territorial integrity" that refers to one of the Five Principles of Peaceful Co-existence (the other four principles are mutual non-aggression, mutual non-interference in each other's internal affairs, equality and mutual benefit, and peaceful coexistence).[140] Since the establishment of the People's Republic of China by Mao Zedong, national integrity, the maintenance of national sovereignty and domestic stability have been the most important objectives of Chinese political practices.

These objectives are, amongst others, challenged by recurring self-immolations of Tibetan monks or violent protests of the Uyghur minority in Xinjiang as well as by the ongoing discussions of the political status of Taiwan. The situation in Xinjiang is indeed an important example, because it underscores how intertwined China's domestic and regional stability in fact is. After a series of terrorist attacks by Uyghur separatists' movements during the 1990s the situation seemed to be quiet at the beginning of the 2000s. Particularly after the East Turkestan Islamic Movement (ETIM) was recognized as a terrorist organization by the United States and the UN in 2001, and due to the success of China's strike hard campaigns in Xinjiang. However, in July 2009, the heaviest riots since 1949 broke out in Urumqi. They left 200 deaths and over 1700 injuries. This outburst of violence between Uyghurs and Han-Chinese again made it very clear and how delicate the situation in fact is, and how fast the assumed stability can be crumbled.

Furthermore, the 2010 Kyrgyz crises reminded the Chinese officials of the conflict potential in the country's immediate Western neighborhood. In the aftermath of the revolution in April 2010, it came to heavy clashes between Kyrgyz and Uzbek in Southern Kyrgyzstan, especially in the city of Osh in late May/June 2010. During this period it was very difficult for the interim government to actually gain control over the South. The Kyrgyz

---

140 Wenhua Shan, "Redefining the Chinese concept of sovereignty" in Gungwu Wang & Yongnian Zheng (eds.), *China and the New International Order*. (London et al., Routledge, 2008),p. 58.

security forces took drastic measures. Due to these chaotic circumstances, the Kyrgyz interim government asked China and the Shanghai Cooperation Organization (SCO) (next to Russia and the Comprehensive Security Treaty Organization, CSTO) to intervene and help to stabilize the situation. The SCO, however, reacted very slowly and only with an approximately 240 words strong statement emphasizing a peaceful solution to the riots and the prevention of spillover effects. The Chinese government offered help but only in the rather symbolic realm of US$5 million. This clearly shows the limited capabilities of the SCO and the lack of interest of the Chinese government to actively engage or even solve incidents such as the riots in Southern Kyrgyzstan. But the 2010 Kyrgyz riots raised serious doubts among Chinese academics about the country's rigid adherence to the non-intervention principle.[141] Many experts underpinned China's lack of capabilities to react appropriately to the Kyrgyz crisis both alone or in the framework of the SCO. Their main concern was how the Chinese government can and should respond in a case of violent insurgency that takes place in the immediate neighborhood. With regard to the uncertain situation in Afghanistan after 2014 and its potential impact on the regional neighborhood including China, this question is still of great importance. Consequently, the Chinese government aims to avert problems in their immediate regional neighborhood like the North Korean Peninsula, Central/South Asia, or the South China Sea since these problems could have a direct impact on the country's domestic stability.

Hence, the concept of a harmonious world underlies Chinese efforts to actively influence the international as well as regional order. It constitutes a general change of policy in China, because Deng Xiaoping's primary goal was to regain a stable economy. Therefore, his foreign policy followed the motto "hiding one's capacity while biding one's time" (*taoguang yanghui yousuo zuowei*). With the idea of a harmonious world, "Beijing is trying to synchronize its internal and external outlooks, so that its international behaviors are no more than extensions of its self-belief and domestic politics."[142]

Internationally, the Chinese government continues to support the principle of sovereignty. Beijing maintains a strict respect for noninterference in domestic affairs, especially in terms of authorizations within the scope

[141] Interviews conducted by the author with several Chinese experts from August till December 2011 in Beijing, Shanghai and Urumqi.

[142] Zheng & Tok Sow, "Harmonious Society and Harmonious world," p. 6.

of Chapter VII of the UN Charter.[143] China's position in the report of the International Commission on Intervention and State Sovereignty, "Responsibility to Protect" (R2P), leaves no doubt about its primary orientation: stability. China argues, "It is inadvisable to make hasty judgments that the State concerned is unable to protect its own citizen and rush to intervene."[144] The primacy of stability in traditional China converges today with the classical paradigm of sovereignty on the international level. Consequently, the Chinese government avoids violating the national integrity of other states by keeping up the principle of non-intervention. We can also observe this practice in China's reserved reactions towards the Libyan civil war in 2011 or the recent voting in the UN General Assembly against the use of force in Syria.

However, the establishment of a harmonious world depends on the particular political context. Internationally, China presents herself as a status quo power, but with regards to the regional context, the country does not only seek stability but also tries to actively engage with its neighbors through a range of regional institutions. China's regional policy of "cooperative dependencies" seems to have successfully established a harmonious society in a harmonized regional neighborhood. In this respect, China certainly represents a regional power (see Chart 2).

Conclusion

The correlation between harmony and stability is a central aspect of political thinking in traditional China. Peace is synonymous with harmony and describes the absence of disturbances. Consequently, the use of violence can be justified because the political order needs to be restored. Even though violence stands in contrast to the ideal of a virtuous emperor, wars

143 See the overview by Bonny Ling, "China's Peacekeeping Diplomacy," *International Relations and Institutions*, no. 1, 2007, available at http://hrichina.org/public/PDFs/CRF.1.2007/CRF-2007-1_Peacekeeping.pdf., last accessed on 5 December 2007. For a recent analysis of China's attitude towards UN Peacekeeping Operations see Yin He, China's Changing Policy on UN Peacekeeping Operations, *Asia Studies* (Institute for Security and Development Policy, Stockholm, July, 2007), available at http://www.silkroadstudies.org/new/docs/Silkroadpapers/2007/YinHe0409073.pdf., last accessed on 5 December 2007; Bates Gill & James Reilly, "Sovereignty, Intervention and Peacekeeping: The View from Beijing," *Survival*, vol. 42, no. 3, 2000.pp. 41–59.

144 Overview of Member States' position, available at http://www.reformtheun.org/index.php?module=uploads&func=download&fileId=148, last accessed on 10 July 2008. Further information to R2P available at http://www.iciss.ca/report-en.asp and http://www.responsibilitytoprotect.org/, last accessed on 10 July 2008.

Chart 2. Different context = different political practices?

Context	Modern China	Traditional China (no difference between internal and external relations)
Domestic	Harmony, stability, sovereignty, national integrity	Harmony converges with stability, Harmony does not know boundaries, Empire,
Regional	Regional power, harmonized region, economic interdependence	Peace = Harmony, War = disturbance of harmony/stability
International	Status quo power (stability), non-intervention principle	

Source: Author's compilation.

in respect of order are Just Wars. Therefore, political order is the reason that determines whether the use of violence or war is justified.

The power of a Confucian emperor is regionally unlimited. Harmony does not know boundaries. The emphasis on boundaries, territory, and sovereignty distinguishes the modern Chinese state from the traditional Chinese empire. But the significance of a stable political order still determines political thinking in the PRC. Internationally, stability converges with the classic paradigm of sovereignty and China's plea for the non-intervention principle. Regionally, China seeks to harmonize her immediate regional neighborhood and build strategic dependencies by actively engaging in regional cooperation mechanisms. Thus, China's political practices need to be differentiated according to the different political contexts within which the country is situated.

As a result, the analysis of Just War in China could represent one way of shedding light on the ambiguity of Chinese foreign policy. It underlines why notions of China's peaceful development or the idea of a harmonious society/harmonious world are difficult to classify and foster the image of Chinese politics as benign or malignant. However, the examination of the Chinese meaning of Just War only makes sense when it is analyzed in connection with the Chinese concept of political order. The importance of the traditional understanding of "order" in China (the Tianxia system) has merely been introduced in this analysis; further research needs to deal in more detail with the Chinese view of order and its relevance to the contemporary understanding of political practice in China.

CHAPTER FIVE

FROM IDEOLOGY TO PRAGMATISM: CHINA'S POSITION ON HUMANITARIAN INTERVENTION IN THE POST-COLD WAR ERA

Jonathan E. Davis*

Introduction

The rise of the People's Republic of China (PRC) raises many questions about the country's perceptions of international law, as well as how China conceives of its role as a great power in the international system. With its growing economic, political, and military power, as well as its increasing assertiveness in international relations, China is an important actor on a broad range of issues that transcend national borders. Historically, China has expounded an absolutist conception of sovereignty, which stands in contrast to the sovereignty-eroding characteristics of many solutions to today's most pressing transnational problems.[1] Whether and how China adapts its traditional views of sovereignty to meet these challenges will say a lot about China's rise and its future role in the international system.

One particularly instructive lens through which to examine China's changing attitudes toward sovereignty and intervention is its response to humanitarian crises, which have been—and are almost certain to remain—a common feature of international relations in the post-Cold War world. The role China plays in future humanitarian crises will depend in large part on its position on the limits of sovereignty and the international legal constraints on humanitarian intervention.

* J.D., NYU School of Law; M.P.A., Woodrow Wilson School of Public and International Affairs, Princeton University. The author is an Attorney-Adviser in the Office of the Legal Adviser at the U.S. Department of State. The views expressed in this chapter are the author's alone and do not represent the views of the U.S. Department of State or the U.S. Government. An earlier version of this work was published in the *Vanderbilt Journal of Transnational Law*, vol. 44, no. 2, March 2011, pp. 217–283.

[1] *See generally* Jerome Alan Cohen, "China and Intervention: Theory and Practice," *University of Pennsylvania Law Review*, vol. 121, no. 3, January 1973, pp. 471–505; *see also infra* text accompanying notes 19–32.

Surprisingly little has been written about China's position on humanitarian intervention, notwithstanding the country's ability to shape or obstruct the development of international norms in this area. As one commentator put it, "[e]ither China is perceived to be irrelevant to emerging post-Cold War norms in this area or it is viewed as simply an insurmountable obstacle, so far out of step with the rest of the world that it should be ignored."[2] This chapter suggests just the opposite. With its great-power status and privileged position as a permanent member of the United Nations Security Council, China has considerable influence over the development of the international law of humanitarian intervention. Additionally, although China's position often conflicts with the position of those who promote a right of humanitarian intervention, it is hardly "far out of step" with global trends. In fact, China's position on humanitarian intervention corresponds to that of a large number of other states.

This chapter examines China's state practice and official pronouncements in the following post-Cold War cases frequently cited by academics when considering the international legal status of humanitarian intervention: the no-fly zones established in Iraq after the first Gulf War; the conflicts in Somalia, Haiti, Rwanda, Bosnia, Kosovo, and East Timor; the development of the "responsibility to protect"; and the conflicts in Darfur, Libya, and Syria. During these events, China was forced to decide whether to support, acquiesce in, or oppose outside intervention to relieve the suffering. Each of these events led Beijing to define and clarify its attitude toward core international legal principles, including state sovereignty and nonintervention.

This chapter demonstrates that while China continues to champion strong conceptions of state sovereignty and noninterference in interstate relations, its actions since the Cold War evince a willingness to acquiesce in, and even actively support, multilateral humanitarian interventions that obtain both Security Council authorization and target state consent. Furthermore, Beijing has adopted certain tenets of the concept of "the responsibility to protect," suggesting that China is not as inflexible on sovereignty and intervention as some suppose.

---

[2] Michael C. Davis, "The Reluctant Intervenor: The UN Security Council, China's Worldview, and Humanitarian Intervention" in Michael C. Davis, Wolfgang Dietrich, Bettina Scholden, and Dieter Sepp (eds.), *International Intervention in the Post-Cold War World* (Armonk, NY: M.E. Sharpe, 2004), pp. 241–253, at pp. 243–244 ("It is noteworthy that in the plethora of academic articles and books addressing humanitarian intervention the position of China on these issues is hardly mentioned.").

This is not to say that China shows signs of supporting the further development of the international law of humanitarian intervention; rather, China is likely to remain a "persistent objector" to claims of a unilateral right of humanitarian intervention for the foreseeable future. On a more practical level, however, these trends suggest that Beijing may be willing to undertake, support, or acquiesce in military action to prevent or end atrocities, crimes against humanity, genocide, or other humanitarian catastrophes if its two preconditions to intervention—Security Council authorization and target state consent—are met. This concession may be of little comfort to those seeking a robust norm of humanitarian intervention, especially given China's ability to block Security Council authorizations and the high bar of target state consent. Yet signs of greater flexibility in Beijing's position—including its willingness to consider situations of humanitarian need as threats to international peace and security and to use its growing global influence to secure target state consent—indicate that China might not stand in the way of multilateral action in future cases of extreme humanitarian suffering.

Ultimately, China's rising power cuts both ways, placing Beijing in a strong position to shape the future development of international norms on humanitarian intervention as well as to block or oppose future interventions. As a result, Beijing's position on humanitarian intervention cannot be ignored.

Humanitarian Intervention and International Law

The legal status of humanitarian intervention remains unsettled under international law.[3] For the purposes of this chapter, humanitarian intervention is defined as the use of force by a state (or group of states) in another sovereign state's territory to protect the host state's citizens from gross human rights abuses, mass atrocities, crimes against humanity, or genocide. Thus defined, humanitarian intervention is in direct tension

---

[3] *See* Simon Chesterman, *Just War or Just Peace?: Humanitarian Intervention and International Law* (New York: Oxford University Press, 2001); Jennifer M. Welsh, "Introduction" in Jennifer M. Welsh (ed.), *Humanitarian Intervention and International Relations* (New York: Oxford University Press, 2004); *see generally* Ryan Goodman, "Humanitarian Intervention and Pretexts for War," *American Journal of International Law*, vol. 100, no. 1, January 2006, pp. 107–141 (addressing the issue of whether international law should permit states to intervene to stop or ameliorate dire humanitarian crises without UN approval).

with the norms of state sovereignty and nonintervention that arose out of the settlement at Westphalia in 1648.[4]

The origins of modern humanitarian intervention can be traced to British and French interventions in the nineteenth century.[5] However, there is little support for the claim that a customary international legal right of humanitarian intervention arose during the nineteenth or early twentieth century as a result of state practice and *opinio juris*.[6]

Even if a right of humanitarian intervention had developed by the early twentieth century, the enactment of the United Nations Charter cast serious doubt on the continued validity of any such right under international law.[7] Article 2(1) of the Charter implicitly incorporates the customary international law principle of nonintervention by reaffirming the "sovereign equality" of all member states.[8] Additionally, Article 2(4) explicitly prohibits the use of force, with only two exceptions: the use of force in self-defense and the use of force pursuant to a Security Council-authorized enforcement action under Chapter VII of the Charter.[9] Furthermore,

---

4 The principle of nonintervention is recognized as part of customary international law. *See Military and Paramilitary Activities in and Against Nicaragua* (*Nicaragua v. U.S.*), 1986 ICJ 14, ¶ 202 (June 27) ("The principle of non-intervention involves the right of every sovereign State to conduct its affairs without outside interference; though examples of trespass against this principle are not infrequent, the Court considers that it is part and parcel of customary international law.").

5 *See* Gary J. Bass, *Freedom's Battle: The Origins of Humanitarian Intervention* (New York: Alfred A. Knopf, 2008), pp. 5–8; *see also* Martha Finnemore, *The Purpose of Intervention: Changing Beliefs About the Use of Force* (Ithaca, NY: Cornell University Press, 2003), pp. 58–66. For a comprehensive overview of the origins and development of the idea of humanitarian intervention, see Chesterman, *supra* note 3, at pp. 7–44.

6 Chesterman, *supra* note 3, at pp. 43–44 ("More than anything, humanitarian intervention appears to occupy a lacuna in the primitive international legal regime of the time."). It is well established that the formation of a new rule of customary international law requires that a certain behavior must (i) "amount to settled practice" and (ii) be accompanied by *opinio juris sive necessitatis*, or the stated belief that such acts were undertaken because they were believed to be obligatory under international law. *See Nicaragua*, 1986 ICJ ¶ 207 ("Either the States taking such action or other States in a position to react to it, must have behaved so that their conduct is "evidence of a belief that this practice is rendered obligatory by the existence of a rule of law requiring it."").

7 Chesterman, *supra* note 3, at pp. 45–47.

8 U.N. Charter art. 2, para. 1.

9 Id. art. 2, para. 4 ("All Members shall refrain in their international relations from the threat or use of force against the territorial integrity or political independence of any state, or in any other manner inconsistent with the Purposes of the United Nations."). The prohibition on the use of force is a *jus cogens* principle of international law. *Nicaragua*, 1986 ICJ ¶ 190. Article 51 of the Charter provides for an exception to the prohibition on the use of force for the "inherent right of individual or collective self-defense." U.N. Charter art. 51. The other exception—Security Council-authorized enforcement actions—is embodied in Article 39: "The Security Council shall determine the existence of any threat to the peace,

Article 2(7) incorporates a principle of noninterference by prohibiting the United Nations from intervening "in matters which are essentially within the domestic jurisdiction of any state."[10] Chapter VII, the only exception to this noninterference principle, authorizes the Security Council to declare any situation to be "a threat to international peace and security" and thereafter take enforcement measures, including the use of force.[11]

Certain commentators argue, in light of both the Charter's constraints on the use of force and insufficient state practice and *opinio juris* in the post-Charter era to establish a new norm of customary international law, that international law does not recognize a right of humanitarian intervention.[12] In part, opposition to the recognition of a right to humanitarian intervention arises out of a concern that granting such a right will lead to its abuse.[13] Nonetheless, a significant number of scholars argue that a right of humanitarian intervention exists in the post-Charter era. Some proponents argue that Article 2(4) of the Charter left open a loophole for humanitarian intervention,[14] while others argue that a right of humanitarian intervention has emerged as a norm of customary international law through sufficient state practice and *opinio juris* during the 1990s and 2000s.[15] Still others posit a theory of "sovereignty as responsibility," which holds that if a state proves unable or unwilling to prevent mass atrocities

---

breach of the peace, or act of aggression and shall make recommendations, or decide what measures shall be taken in accordance with Articles 41 and 42, to maintain or restore international peace and security." Id. art. 39.

10 Id. art. 2, para. 7:

> Nothing contained in the present Charter shall authorize the United Nations to intervene in matters which are essentially within the domestic jurisdiction of any state or shall require the Members to submit such matters to settlement under the present Charter; but this principle shall not prejudice the application of enforcement measures under Chapter VII.

Id.

11 Id. arts. 39, 41–42.

12 See, e.g., Chesterman, *supra* note 3, at p. 226 ("[T]here is no "right" to humanitarian intervention in either the UN Charter or customary international law."). Professor Chesterman finds that "[t]here is, in short, minimal state practice and virtually no *opinio juris* that supports a general right of humanitarian intervention." Id. at p. 235.

13 Id. at p. 231:

> [I]t is *more* dangerous to hand states a "right"—even of such a limited nature—than simply to assert the cardinal principle of the prohibition of the use of force and let states seek a political justification for a particular action if they find themselves in breach of that norm.

Id.

14 Id. at pp. 47–53.

15 Id. at pp. 57–65.

or genocide from taking place within its territory, certain rights of sovereignty are lost and constraints on the use of force are relaxed, allowing intervention in order to bring an end to humanitarian catastrophes.[16]

This chapter does not seek to resolve the debate on the status of a claimed right of humanitarian intervention—or of the related "responsibility to protect"—under international law. Rather, this chapter accepts such ideas as contested and focuses instead on the evolution of China's position on humanitarian intervention since the end of the Cold War. It thus aims not only to contribute to the general debate on the status of humanitarian intervention under international law but also to contribute to a better understanding of whether and under what conditions China might undertake or support such interventions. In the process, this chapter also examines Chinese attitudes toward state sovereignty. Although some commentators distinguish between a unilateral right of humanitarian intervention and enforcement actions with humanitarian objectives authorized by the Security Council,[17] this chapter adopts the broader view of humanitarian intervention that encompasses both types of interventions.[18]

Part III briefly examines China's historical attitudes toward sovereignty and intervention, from its founding in 1949 until the end of the Cold War. Part IV examines China's state practice and official pronouncements during seven humanitarian crises that are frequently cited by commentators as evidence of a developing customary international law norm of humanitarian intervention. Part V addresses China's more recent responses to the evolution of "the responsibility to protect," the humanitarian crisis in Darfur, and the conflicts in Libya and Syria. Finally, Part VI analyzes the elements of continuity and change in China's post-Cold War attitudes toward humanitarian intervention, as well as the various determinants of its position on humanitarian intervention under international law.

---

16 Id. at pp. 53–57.

17 Id. at p. 5.

18 See, e.g., Fernando Tesón, *Humanitarian Intervention: An Inquiry into Law and Morality* (Ardsley, NY: Transnational Publishers, 1997), p. 234; W. Michael Reisman, "Hollow Victory: Humanitarian Intervention and Protection of Minorities," *Proceedings of the Annual Meeting of the American Society of International Law*, vol. 91, pp. 431–437, April 1997, at p. 431; Jennifer M. Welsh, "The Security Council and Humanitarian Intervention" in Vaughan Lowe, Adam Roberts, Jennifer Welsh, and Dominik Zaum (eds.), *The United Nations Security Council and War: The Evolution of Thought and Practice Since 1945* (New York: Oxford University Press, 2008), pp. 535–562, at p. 535.

Historical Chinese Attitudes Toward Intervention

Since its founding in 1949, the PRC's foreign policy has been characterized largely by adherence to a rigid conception of state sovereignty and steadfast insistence on the principle of noninterference in other states' internal affairs.[19] This stance is unsurprising considering the experience of China during its "century of humiliation," when it was subjected to repeated interventions by foreign powers and significant infringements on its sovereignty.[20] Certain experiences in the PRC's early history—including, in the 1950s, U.S. military intervention in the Taiwan Straits and covert support of the 1959 uprising in Tibet—reinforced Beijing's strict stance on sovereignty and nonintervention.[21]

In the early 1950s, China articulated its anti-interventionist posture in a set of guideposts for interstate relations known as the "Five Principles of Peaceful Coexistence."[22] Now enshrined in China's Constitution, these principles include respect for sovereignty and territorial integrity, nonaggression, and noninterference in other states' internal affairs.[23] These principles continue to play a role, at least rhetorically, in China's foreign policy.

During its first decade, the PRC also began to develop a nascent policy on permissible foreign interventions, including the position that target state consent was a *sine qua non* for the legality of any intervention.[24]

---

[19] *See generally* Cohen, *supra* note 1. Interestingly, Professor Cohen found that while feudal states in pre-imperial China also generally accepted a principle of noninterference, they "frequently invoked [an] exception [that] permitted intervention against a ruler who oppressed his own people." Id. at p. 474 (citing Te-hsu Ch'eng, "International Law in Early China (1122–249 BC)," *Chinese Social and Political Science Review*, vol. 11, 1927, pp. 44–46).

[20] Id. at p. 476.

[21] Id. at p. 477.

[22] Chinese Premier and Foreign Minister Zhou Enlai first proposed these principles during meetings with Indian delegations between December 1953 and June 1954. Simei Qing, *From Allies to Enemies: Visions of Modernity, Identity, and U.S.–China Diplomacy, 1945–1960* (Cambridge, MA: Harvard University Press, 2007), p. 254.

[23] The Preamble to the PRC Constitution states:

> China consistently carries out an independent foreign policy and adheres to the five principles of mutual respect for sovereignty and territorial integrity, mutual non-aggression, non-interference in each other's internal affairs, equality and mutual benefit, and peaceful coexistence in developing diplomatic relations and economic and cultural exchanges with other countries.

Xianfa (Constitution of the People's Republic of China), pmbl. para. 12 (2004).

[24] *Compare* Cohen, *supra* note 1, at p. 482 (citing a Chinese legal scholar's statement that the Soviet Union's military intervention in Hungary in 1956 was lawful because the intervention came at the request of the formal Hungarian government), *with* id. at p. 488

Beijing's support for wars of national liberation and its condemnation of racist regimes stand as limited exceptions to its relatively strict anti-interventionist stance during the Cold War.[25]

In 1971, the PRC replaced the Taiwan-based Kuomintang government in China's seat at the United Nations and on the Security Council.[26] In the following decade, Beijing continued to espouse strict conceptions of sovereignty and noninterference. For example, the PRC opposed UN peacekeeping efforts by refusing to participate in Security Council deliberations or votes on peacekeeping, or to contribute money or resources to UN missions.[27]

In the early 1980s, as Deng Xiaoping launched his "reform and opening" program, hints of an erosion of the PRC's absolutist conception of sovereignty began to appear.[28] For example, in a 1981 international law textbook, Chinese legal scholars Wang Tieya and Wei Min referred to the prevention of genocide as one of the international obligations of states and noted that "necessary measures to suppress these behaviors [including genocide] were consistent with generally recognized principles

(describing China's condemnations of the Soviet invasion of Czechoslovakia in 1968 as an illegal violation of Czechoslovak sovereignty). China's different positions on the legality of the Soviet interventions in Hungary and Czechoslovakia also can be explained as a manifestation of the Sino–Soviet split in the early 1960s, rather than as the development of a principled position on the requirement of target state consent to foreign intervention. *See* Jonathan D. Spence, *The Search for Modern China* (New York: W.W. Norton & Co., 1999), pp. 553–559 (discussing the Sino–Soviet split).

[25] For a discussion of the PRC's support of "liberation struggles" and an attempt to reconcile that posture with Beijing's generally anti-interventionist stance, see Cohen, *supra* note 1, at pp. 489–505.

[26] Spence, *supra* note 24, at p. 596.

[27] M. Taylor Fravel, "China's Attitude Toward U.N. Peacekeeping Operations Since 1989," *Asian Survey*, vol. 36, no. 11, November 1996, pp. 1102–1121, at pp. 1103–1104; *see* Bates Gill and James Reilly, "Sovereignty, Intervention and Peacekeeping: The View from Beijing," *Survival*, vol. 42, no. 3, Autumn 2000, pp. 41–59, at pp. 41, 43–44 (noting that China participated in its first vote on peacekeeping in 1981); Pang Zhongying, "China's Changing Attitude to UN Peacekeeping," *International Peacekeeping*, vol. 12, no. 1, Spring 2005, pp. 87–104, at pp. 87, 89–90. During this period, however, the Security Council authorized no operations that could be considered humanitarian interventions, and the Council was largely quiet on three cases that commentators sometimes characterize as humanitarian interventions: India's 1971 intervention in Bangladesh (East Pakistan), Tanzania's 1978–79 intervention in Uganda, and Vietnam's 1978–79 intervention in Cambodia (Kampuchea). Although commentators often cite these cases as examples of humanitarian intervention due to the substantial humanitarian payoffs that supposedly resulted, none of the intervening states justified their actions on the basis of a unilateral right of humanitarian intervention, and relied instead on a justification of self-defense. Chesterman, *supra* note 3, at p. 84.

[28] Jiangyu Wang, "China and the Universal Human Rights Standards," *Syracuse Journal of International Law and Commerce*, vol. 29, no. 1, Fall 2001, pp. 135–158, at pp. 146–147.

of international law and should not be considered as intervening in the internal affairs of a state."[29] Following the Tiananmen Square events of 1989, however, whatever space may have existed for advancing a more liberal conception of sovereignty narrowed, and the trauma of those events reinforced the Chinese leadership's absolutist conception of sovereignty.[30] Still, it should be noted that China officially maintained a somewhat more liberal stance toward intervention through 1991, when a PRC human rights white paper declared:

> China has always held that to effect international protection of human rights, the international community should interfere with and stop acts that endanger world peace and security, such as gross human rights violations caused by colonialism, racism, foreign aggression and occupation, as well as apartheid, racial discrimination, genocide, slave trade and serious violation of human rights by international terrorist organizations.[31]

However, outside of the circumstances specifically mentioned in the white paper, Beijing made clear that China remained

> [f]irmly opposed to any country making use of the issue of human rights to sell its own values, ideology, political standards and mode of development, and to any country interfering in the internal affairs of other countries on the pretext of human rights, the internal affairs of developing countries in particular, and so hurting the sovereignty and dignity of many developing countries.[32]

Chinese Attitudes Toward Humanitarian Intervention in the 1990s

This Part examines China's acts and official pronouncements during seven humanitarian crises of the 1990s. These cases are typically cited by scholars when considering the international legal status of humanitarian intervention: (A) the northern and southern no-fly zones over Iraq after the first Gulf War; (B) Somalia; (C) Haiti; (D) Rwanda; (E) Bosnia; (F) Kosovo; and (G) East Timor.

---

[29] Id. at p. 146 (quoting Wang Tieya and Wei Min (eds.), *Guoji Fa* (*International Law*) (1981), p. 268).

[30] Id. at p. 147.

[31] Information Office of the State Council of China, "White Paper on Human Rights in China—Part X: Active Participation in International Human Rights Activities," 1991, http://www.china.org.cn/e-white/7/7-L.htm, accessed 28 October 2012.

[32] Id.

Iraq: The Northern and Southern No-Fly Zones

Following the UN-authorized, U.S.-led expulsion of Iraqi forces from Kuwait in 1991, the United States, the United Kingdom, and France established "no-fly zones" (NFZs) over northern and southern Iraq to prohibit Iraqi aircraft from entering those airspaces.[33] Both NFZs were established without explicit UN authorization.[34] The United States, the United Kingdom, and France justified their actions in part by alleging the continued validity of Security Council Resolution 678—authorizing member states, under Chapter VII, "to use all necessary means" to effect the withdrawal of Iraqi troops from Kuwait, as demanded previously in Resolution 660[35]—in combination with Resolution 688—demanding an immediate end to Saddam Hussein's repression of Iraq's civilian population.[36] All three countries stressed the humanitarian objectives of the NFZs: the Northern Zone was designed to protect Iraq's Kurdish population, and the Southern Zone was designed to protect Iraqi Shiites and Marsh Arabs.[37] The United Kingdom even went so far as to claim that an emerging principle of international law permitted military intervention to prevent humanitarian catastrophes.[38]

Due to the parties' reliance on implied authorizations in previous Security Council resolutions, the case of the Iraqi NFZs did not present an unambiguous claim of a unilateral right of humanitarian intervention,[39]

---

[33] Jane E. Stromseth, "Iraq's Repression of Its Civilian Population: Collective Responses and Civilian Challenges" in Lori Fisler Damrosch (ed.), *Enforcing Restraint: Collective Intervention in Internal Conflicts* (New York: Council on Foreign Relations Press, 1993), pp. 77–117, at p. 94.

[34] Jules Lobel and Michael Ratner, "Bypassing the Security Council: Ambiguous Authorizations to Use Force, Cease-Fires and the Iraqi Inspection Regime," *American Journal of International Law*, vol. 93, no. 1, January 1999, pp. 124–154, at pp. 126, 132–133.

[35] S.C. Res. 678, ¶ 2, U.N. Doc. S/RES/678 (29 November 1990); *see also* S.C. Res. 660, ¶ 2, U.N. Doc. S/RES/660 (2 August 1990) (demanding Iraqi withdrawal of troops from Kuwait).

[36] S.C. Res. 688, ¶¶ 1–2, U.N. Doc. S/RES/688 (5 April 1991).

[37] *See* Chesterman, *supra* note 3, at pp. 196–200; Michael Wines, "U.S. and Allies Say Flight Ban in Iraq Will Start Today," *New York Times*, 27 August 1992; John F. Harris and John Mintz, "U.S. Warplanes Patrol Wider "No-Fly" Zone," *Washington Post*, 5 September 1996.

[38] Christine Gray, "The Use of Force and the International Legal Order," in Malcolm D. Evans (ed.), *International Law* (Oxford: Oxford University Press, 2d ed., 2006), pp. 589–620, at p. 595 ("We believe that humanitarian intervention without the invitation of the country concerned can be justified in cases of extreme humanitarian need.").

[39] *See* Christine Gray, "From Unity to Polarization: International Law and the Use of Force Against Iraq," *European Journal of International Law*, vol. 13, no. 1, 2002, pp. 1–19, at pp. 9–11, 16–18 (noting that the American and British governments claimed that the NFZs were established in furtherance of Resolution 688, and that "states did not treat the US, UK and French action with respect to the no-fly zones in Iraq as practice helping to establish a

but it nonetheless represents an important test case for Chinese attitudes in the immediate post-Cold War period. Although China voted in favor of Resolution 660, demanding Iraq's unconditional withdrawal from Kuwait,[40] it abstained from voting on Resolution 678, which authorized military action to enforce Resolution 660's demand.[41] This abstention demonstrated Beijing's distinct reluctance to endorse the Security Council's authorization of the use of force by member states under Chapter VII. Notably, China also abstained from voting on Resolution 688, a non-Chapter VII resolution calling for Saddam to end the repression of Iraq's civilian population.[42] During the Security Council debate on Resolution 688, China expressed concern about the humanitarian situation in Iraq, as well as the flood of refugees into Turkey and Iran.[43] However, China objected that the resolution violated the principle of noninterference enshrined in Article 2(7) of the UN Charter, stating that "the Security Council should not consider or take action on questions concerning the internal affairs of any state."[44] Thus, even though Resolution 688 was not a Chapter VII measure, and despite the affirmation of all member states "to respect the sovereignty, territorial integrity and political independence of Iraq,"[45] China abstained.[46]

Two factors help to explain China's abstention. First, China may have been especially sensitive about any erosion of the noninterference principle in 1991, less than two years after the events of Tiananmen Square. Second, Resolution 688 was unprecedented: it was the first time the Security Council declared a humanitarian crisis to be a threat to international peace and security.[47] Although Resolution 688 did not invoke

right of humanitarian intervention"). *But cf.* Christopher Greenwood, "International Law and the NATO Intervention in Kosovo," *International and Comparative Law Quarterly*, vol. 49, no. 4, October 2000, pp. 926–934, at pp. 929–930 (citing the Iraqi NFZs as precedents for humanitarian intervention).

40 U.N. SCOR, 45th Sess., 2932d mtg. at p. 27, U.N. Doc. S/PV.2932 (2 August 1990).

41 U.N. SCOR, 45th Sess., 2963d mtg. at pp. 64–65, U.N. Doc. S/PV.2963 (29 November 1990).

42 U.N. SCOR, 46th Sess., 2982d mtg. at p. 52, U.N. Doc. S/PV.2982 (5 April 1991).

43 Id. at pp. 55–56.

44 Id.

45 S.C. Res. 688, *supra* note 40, pmbl. para. 7.

46 U.N. SCOR, 46th Sess., 2982d mtg., *supra* note 46, at p. 52. According to one source, Resolution 688 contained no enforcement language "to persuade China to abstain rather than veto." Brian Frederking, *The United States and the Security Council: Collective Security Since the Cold War* (New York: Routledge, 2007), p. 90.

47 Max Hilaire, *United Nations Law and the Security Council* (Burlington, VT: Ashgate, 2005), p. 218.

Chapter VII, it stated that the exodus of refugees from Iraq "threaten[ed] international peace and security" in the region.[48] China's abstention likely reflected concern that the Security Council's willingness to consider even the external effects of internal repression set a dangerous precedent.

Yet, in spite of China's abstention and its opposition to the Security Council's interference in Iraq's internal affairs, Beijing voiced no objections to the NFZs at the time of their establishment.[49] Later China did issue statements indicating its unease with the NFZs. For example, in August 1992, the Chinese Foreign Ministry spokesman noted China's "serious concern" over developments in southern Iraq and stated that no step should be taken that "jeopardize[d] Iraq's unification and territorial integrity."[50] Additionally, China reiterated its concern about Iraqi sovereignty and territorial integrity after a U.S. warplane shot down an Iraqi fighter in the Southern Zone in December 1992.[51] Nonetheless, China did not protest the United States' use of force to enforce the NFZ.[52] According to two commentators, "What [China] would neither authorize nor assist de jure, they would acquiesce in de facto."[53]

Over time, however, Beijing's opposition to the NFZs grew more explicit, as Western justifications for continued enforcement of the NFZs shifted from humanitarianism to the containment of Saddam's regime.[54] Years later, in 2000, China expressed "its condemnation" of the establishment of the Iraqi NFZs, stating that the NFZs "violate[d] the UN Charter and norms of international relations and [were] in defiance of and trampling on Iraq's sovereignty."[55] In that statement, China referred to Western justifications for the NFZs—to prevent Saddam from suppressing domestic minorities in the north and to protect Iraqi Shiites in the south—as an

48 Id.

49 James Cockayne and David M. Malone, "The Security Council and the 1991 and 2003 Wars in Iraq," in *The United Nations Security Council and War*, *supra* note 18, pp. 384–405, at pp. 384, 393.

50 "Iraq 'No-Fly Zone' China 'Concerned'," *Xinhua Gen. Overseas News Service*, 31 August 1992.

51 "Spokesman on U.S. Warplane Shooting Down Iraqi Fighter," *Xinhua General Overseas News Service*, 28 December 1992.

52 James Cockayne and David M. Malone, "Creeping Unilateralism: How Operation Provide Comfort and the No-Fly Zones in 1991 and 1992 Paved the Way for the Iraq Crisis of 2003," *Security Dialogue*, vol. 37, no. 1, March 2006, pp. 123–141, at pp. 133–134.

53 Id. at p. 129.

54 For a discussion of the changing justifications for the NFZs, see Cockayne and Malone, *supra* note 49, at p. 393.

55 Chinese Ministry of Foreign Affairs, "Fact Sheet: The Iraq Issue," 2000, http://www.iraqwatch.org/government/China/china-mfa-iraqfacts.htm, accessed 28 October 2012.

"excuse" and a "pretense," respectively.[56] In contrast to China's strong opposition to the NFZs well after their establishment, Beijing's position on the NFZs at the time of their creation and throughout the 1990s was much more muted.

Somalia

The case of Somalia provides further evidence of China's early post-Cold War views on humanitarian intervention. Significantly, China supported all Security Council resolutions on Somalia between January 1992 and November 1994, despite the fact that those resolutions dealt with the purely internal humanitarian situation in Somalia, in contrast with Resolution 688's focus on the external humanitarian consequences of internal strife in Iraq.[57] One of the Security Council's early actions in Somalia was to establish a Chapter VI peacekeeping mission—the United Nations Operation in Somalia (UNOSOM)—to monitor a ceasefire agreement signed in Mogadishu in March 1992.[58] UNOSOM, however, quickly proved ineffective in ending the violence.[59] In December 1992, facing an increasingly dire humanitarian situation in Somalia, the Security Council adopted Resolution 794, which authorized a U.S.-led humanitarian intervention.[60]

Resolution 794 set a groundbreaking precedent in two ways. First, it marked the Security Council's first Chapter VII authorization of the use of force without host state consent.[61] Second, it was the first time the Security Council authorized the use of force based on purely humanitarian concerns.[62] Although China supported the UN-authorized, U.S.-led humanitarian intervention in Somalia—known as the United Task Force

---

56 Id.

57 The Security Council adopted seventeen resolutions on the situation in Somalia during this period; all but one passed unanimously. Welsh, *supra* note 18, at pp. 538–539.

58 *See* S.C. Res. 751, ¶ 3, U.N. Doc. S/RES/751 (24 April 1992) (requesting the Secretary-General to deploy a group of fifty observers).

59 Chesterman, *supra* note 3, at pp. 141–142.

60 S.C. Res. 794, ¶¶ 6–13, U.N. Doc. S/RES/794 (3 December 1992).

61 Chesterman, *supra* note 3, at p. 142.

62 Welsh, *supra* note 18, at p. 539; S.C. Res. 794, *supra* note 60, ¶ 10 ("Determining that the magnitude of the human tragedy caused by the conflict in Somalia, further exacerbated by the obstacles being created to the distribution of humanitarian assistance, constitute[d] a threat to international peace and security," the Council, acting under Chapter VII, authorized member states "to use all necessary means to establish as soon as possible a secure environment for humanitarian relief operations in Somalia.").

(UNITAF)[63]—it expressed reservations about the Security Council authorizing member states to use force for humanitarian purposes.[64] More importantly, China made clear that its support for the intervention was predicated on the fact that the intervention was "an exceptional action in view of the unique situation in Somalia"—a clear reference to the absence of a functioning Somali government.[65]

In March 1993, the Security Council adopted Resolution 814, which expanded UNOSOM's force size and mandate in order to take over responsibilities from UNITAF.[66] In effect, Resolution 814 established UNOSOM II, the first UN peacekeeping operation authorized to undertake enforcement actions under Chapter VII.[67] Again, in explaining its support for the operation, China cited "the unique situation of the absence of any effective, functioning government in Somalia" as the reason for its vote "in favour of the United Nations taking strong, exceptional measures in Somalia."[68] Additionally, China reiterated its reservations about the Security Council's novel invocation of Chapter VII in a peacekeeping context.[69] As China's positions on Resolutions 794 and 814 make clear, its support for both the UN-authorized, U.S.-led humanitarian intervention in 1992 and the 1993 Chapter VII peacekeeping mission, UNOSOM II, was

---

[63] U.N. SCOR, 47th Sess., 3145th mtg. at pp. 17–18, U.N. Doc. S/PV.3145 (3 December 1992).

> Taking into account the long-term chaotic situation resulting from the present lack of a Government in Somalia, and in view of our deep sympathy with the Somali people in their anguish, we endorse the requests of most African countries and the recommendations of the Secretary-General, that is, that the United Nations should take prompt, strong and exceptional measures for the settlement of the Somali crisis.

Id. at pp. 16–17.

[64] Id. at p. 18.

[65] Id. In fact, in an apparent concession to the views of China and like-minded states, Resolution 794 made explicit reference to the "unique character of the present situation in Somalia," the "complex and extraordinary nature of the situation in Somalia," and the "exceptional response" of the international community. S.C. Res. 794, *supra* note 60, pmbl. China also called for the mission to cease promptly upon the establishment of a secure environment for the delivery of humanitarian relief.

[66] Hilaire, *supra* note 47, at p. 50.

[67] S.C. Res. 814, ¶¶ 5–14, U.N. Doc. S/RES/814 (26 March 1993).

[68] U.N. SCOR, 48th Sess., 3188th mtg. at p. 21, U.N. Doc. S/PV.3188 (26 March 1993).

[69] Id. at p. 22 ("It is our understanding that this authorization is based on the needs of the unique situation in Somalia and should not constitute a precedent for United Nations peace-keeping operations."). China reiterated its resistance to the Council's authorization of the use of force for UNOSOM II's operations during a Council debate on the extension of its mandate. *See* U.N. SCOR, 49th Sess., 3385th mtg. at pp. 5–6, U.N. Doc. S/PV.3385 (31 May 1994) (stating that UNOSOM II's "humanitarian mandate remains unchanged, and the principle of using non-coercive measures should be observed in the performance of that mandate").

dependent on the absence of a legitimate, functioning government in Somalia and, therefore, on the impossibility of obtaining host state consent. As a result, China's support for the interventions in Somalia demonstrated a willingness, at most, to countenance humanitarian intervention where there was no legitimate state authority to approve or reject foreign humanitarian action.

Haiti

Although the 1994 intervention in Haiti by a UN-authorized, U.S.-led multinational force was more than just a humanitarian mission,[70] China's stance on two important Security Council resolutions regarding the Haiti intervention provides insight into its early post-Cold War position on the principle of noninterference. Haiti plunged into chaos following a September 1991 *coup d'état* that drove its democratically elected president, Jean-Bertrand Aristide, into exile.[71] By 1993, humanitarian conditions had deteriorated drastically, leading to an exodus of refugees that put immense pressure on the Security Council to address the ongoing political and humanitarian crisis.[72]

In June 1993, acting under Chapter VII, the Security Council unanimously adopted Resolution 841, imposing a fuel and arms embargo on Haiti and freezing the financial assets of the new Haitian government.[73] During the Security Council's debate on that resolution, Beijing characterized the crisis in Haiti as "essentially a matter which falls within the internal affairs of that country, and therefore [one that] should be dealt with by the Haitian people themselves."[74] Still, China supported the resolution based on "the unique and exceptional situation in Haiti"—an apparent reference to the fact that the sanctions had been requested by the "legitimate" Haitian permanent representative to the United Nations (i.e., the representative of Aristide's exiled government) in a letter to the UN Secretary-General.[75] China also indicated that the Security Council's

70 S.C. Res. 940, ¶¶ 4–10, U.N. Doc. S/RES/940 (31 July 1994).

71 Chesterman, *supra* note 3, at p. 152.

72 Id. at pp. 152–155.

73 S.C. Res. 841, ¶¶ 5–14, U.N. Doc. S/RES/841 (16 June 1993).

74 U.N. SCOR, 48th Sess., 3238th mtg. at p. 20, U.N. Doc. S/PV.3238 (16 June 1993).

75 Id. at p. 21. The Organization of American States originally established these sanctions in 1991. The Haitian permanent representative to the United Nations sought to make them "universal and mandatory" in his request to the Secretary-General. Welsh, *supra* note 18, at p. 542.

consideration of the matter was proper given similar requests by the Organization of American States.[76] As in the case of Somalia, China emphasized that its support did not constitute a change in its position on the principle of noninterference.[77]

On July 31, 1994, the Security Council, acting under Chapter VII, adopted Resolution 940, authorizing a U.S.-led multinational force "to use all necessary means to facilitate the departure from Haiti of the military leadership ... [and] the prompt return of the legitimately elected President and the restoration of the legitimate authorities of the Government of Haiti."[78] The Security Council's language makes clear that Resolution 940 was motivated by more than simply humanitarian aims, citing not only grave concerns about "the significant further deterioration of the humanitarian situation in Haiti," but also objectives that included "the restoration of democracy in Haiti and the prompt return of the legitimately elected President, Jean-Bertrand Aristide."[79] In authorizing this unprecedented mission to reestablish a democracy, the Security Council highlighted "the unique character of the present situation in Haiti and its deteriorating, complex and extraordinary nature, requiring an exceptional response."[80]

China abstained from voting on Resolution 940.[81] Up to that point, China had supported all Security Council resolutions on Haiti, including all sanctions measures.[82] Here, however, China strongly objected to the

---

76 U.N. SCOR, 48th Sess., 3238th mtg., *supra* note 74, at p. 20.

77 Id. at p. 21.

> The Chinese delegation, as its consistent position, does not favour the Security Council's handling [of] matters which are essentially internal affairs of a Member State, nor does it approve of resorting lightly to such mandatory measures as sanctions by the Council. We wish to point out that the favourable vote the Chinese delegation cast just now does not mean any change in that position.

Id.

78 S.C. Res. 940, *supra* note 70, ¶ 4. On September 19, 1994, a U.S.-led multinational force entered Port au Prince in Operation Uphold Democracy per Resolution 940. On March 31, 1995, the UN Mission in Haiti (UNMIH) replaced the U.S.-led force, although U.S. troops remained on the island until March 1996 under the command of UNMIH in Operation New Horizons (in which the U.S. commander was also the commander of the UN forces).

79 Id. pmbl. paras. 4, 8.

80 Id. ¶ 2.

81 U.N. SCOR, 49th Sess., 3413d mtg. at p. 12, U.N. Doc. S/PV.3413 (31 July 1994).

82 Prior to the adoption of Resolution 940, all Security Council resolutions on Haiti were adopted unanimously. *See* S.C. Res. 841, *supra* note 73, ¶¶ 5–8 (establishing a trade embargo on arms and petroleum products); S.C. Res. 861, ¶ 1, U.N. Doc. S/RES/861 (27 August 1993) (suspending Resolution 841's trade embargo); S.C. Res. 862, ¶ 2, U.N. Doc. S/RES/862 (31 August 1993) (authorizing deployment of an "advance team" to Haiti to prepare for a larger mission); S.C. Res. 867, ¶¶ 1–2, U.N. Doc. S/RES/867 (23 September 1993) (establishing UNMIH); S.C. Res. 873, ¶ 1, U.N. Doc. S/RES/873 (13 October 1993)

Security Council's invocation of Chapter VII to authorize member states to use force to resolve the situation in Haiti, and it noted that the resolution was "disconcerting because this would obviously create a dangerous precedent."[83] As with Resolutions 678 and 688 on Iraq, China emphasized its preference for "a peaceful solution" over "the resort to pressure at will or even the use of force."[84]

Yet, while noting that military action in Haiti did not conform to the UN Charter's preference for the peaceful resolution of disputes, China refrained from invoking sovereignty or noninterference principles in the Security Council debate.[85] This is especially puzzling given that Resolution 940 represented the first and only time that the Security Council has authorized the use of force to restore democracy in a member state.[86] One explanation, however, may be that the intervention came at the request of the "legitimate" government of Haiti in exile,[87] thus providing an element of consent.

China sought to clarify its position in November 1994 when it explained its favorable vote on Resolution 964, which authorized the strengthening of an advance team of the UN peacekeeping mission, the UN Mission in Haiti (UNMIH).[88] In a statement before the Security Council, China's representative highlighted the principle of noninterference:

> China has consistently ... opposed interference in the internal affairs of other countries and the use or threat of the use of force in international relations. We expounded this position when the Council adopted [R]esolution 940 (1994), which authorized military action in Haiti. Still less should [R]esolution 964 (1994), which has just been adopted, be understood as an affirmation of this so-called formula.[89]

(terminating the suspension of Resolution 841's trade embargo); S.C. Res. 875, ¶ 1, U.N. Doc. S/RES/875 (16 October 1993) (calling for strict enforcement of Resolution 841's embargo); S.C. Res. 905, ¶ 2, U.N. Doc. S/RES/905 (18 March 1994) (extending UNMIH's mandate); S.C. Res. 917, ¶¶ 2–3, U.N. Doc. S/RES/917 (6 May 1994) (expanding sanctions against Haiti); S.C. Res. 933, ¶ 1, U.N. Doc. S/RES/933 (30 June 1994) (further extending UNMIH's mandate).

83 U.N. SCOR, 49th Sess., 3413d mtg. at p. 10, U.N. Doc. S/PV.3413 (31 July 1994).

84 Id.

85 Id.

86 Sebastian von Einsiedel and David M. Malone, "Haiti," in David M. Malone (ed.), *The UN Security Council: From the Cold War to the 21st Century* (Boulder, CO: Lynne Rienner Publishers, 2004), pp. 467–482, at p. 467.

87 Michael Byers, *War Law: Understanding International Law and Armed Conflict* (London: Atlantic Books, 2005), p. 32.

88 U.N. SCOR, 49th Sess., 3470th mtg. at p. 5, U.N. Doc. S/PV.3470 (29 November 1994).

89 Id. *See also* U.N. SCOR, 49th Sess., 3430th mtg. at p. 6, U.N. Doc. S/PV.3430 (29 September 1994).

In light of this record, China's position on the intervention in Haiti perhaps should be viewed as an exceptional case in which China's muted opposition to, or acquiescence in, the intervention can be attributed to the presence of the consent of Haiti's "legitimate" government in exile. In any case, the example of Haiti demonstrates Beijing's concern that such intervention could set a precedent that would lead to the eventual erosion of the noninterference principle.

Rwanda

Unique among the cases examined in this chapter, Rwanda is, first and foremost, an instance of *non*intervention rather than intervention—shamefully so, considering the international community's inaction in light of its awareness of the unfolding genocide and the scale of human tragedy involved.[90]

In October 1993, China voted with a unanimous Security Council to establish the UN Assistance Mission in Rwanda (UNAMIR), a Chapter VI peacekeeping force with the mandate to monitor a ceasefire agreement between the Rwandan government and the Tutsi-led Rwandan Patriotic Front (RPF); both parties consented.[91] Shortly after genocidal violence erupted in early April 1994, the Security Council unanimously adopted Resolution 912, which infamously reduced UNAMIR forces from 2,500 to 270 troops.[92] Although the Security Council record is silent on China's views here, it is notable that Beijing—like other members of the Security Council—showed no inclination to characterize the unfolding events as a genocide, instead acquiescing in the Security Council's characterization of the crisis as a civil war.[93]

In a subsequent reversal of course, in May 1994, the Security Council unanimously adopted Resolution 918, which authorized UNAMIR's expansion to 5,500 troops and enlarged its mandate to include the protection of refugees and civilians at risk and the establishment of humanitarian "safe

---

[90] For sustained critiques of the international community's failure to respond to the Rwandan genocide, see Phillip Gourevitch, *We Wish to Inform You that Tomorrow We Will Be Killed with Our Families: Stories From Rwanda* (New York: Picador, 1998); Samantha Power, *A Problem From Hell: America and the Age of Genocide* (New York: HarperCollins Publishers, 2003), pp. 329–389; Samantha Power, "Bystanders to Genocide: Why the United States Let the Rwandan Tragedy Happen," *Atlantic Monthly*, September 2001, p. 84.

[91] S.C. Res. 872, ¶¶ 2–3, U.N. Doc. S/RES/872 (5 October 1993).

[92] S.C. Res. 912, ¶ 8, U.N. Doc. S/RES/912 (21 April 1994); U.N. Secretary-General, *Special Report of the Secretary-General on the U.N. Assistance Mission for Rwanda*, ¶ 16, U.N. Doc. S/1994/470 (20 April 1994).

[93] *See* Welsh, *supra* note 18, at p. 545.

areas."[94] Voting in favor of the expanded mandate, China cited the "increasingly grave" humanitarian situation and noted that "the situation in Rwanda has worsened quickly, with civil war engulfing the whole country and its people being plunged into an abyss of misery, creating a huge exodus of refugees into neighboring countries."[95]

However, due in part to the ghosts of the failed peacekeeping mission in Somalia, the expanded UNAMIR force never materialized.[96] Instead, in late June 1994, the Security Council adopted Resolution 929, authorizing the deployment of a multinational French-led force.[97] By that time, the genocide had largely run its course, with estimates of 500,000 to one million Tutsis and moderate Hutus slaughtered.[98] Adopted under Chapter VII, Resolution 929 authorized member states to use "all necessary means to achieve the humanitarian objectives" set out in the resolution, including to secure and protect displaced persons, refugees, and civilians at risk.[99]

China abstained, offering several reasons for its vote.[100] First, China clung to the characterization of the crisis as a civil war and argued that negotiation between the parties was the "only way of solving the crisis," emphasizing that "[r]esort to armed force or mandatory measures would only worsen the situation."[101] Second, clearly demonstrating China's preference for a traditional peacekeeping force over a member state-led force with Chapter VII enforcement powers, Beijing argued for the deployment

---

94 S.C. Res. 918, ¶ 5, U.N. Doc. S/RES/918 (17 May 1994).

95 U.N. SCOR, 49th Sess., 3377th mtg. at p. 9, U.N. Doc. S/PV.3377 (16 May 1994). China reaffirmed its support for UNAMIR's humanitarian mandate by voting in favor of Resolution 925 in early June 1994. *See* S.C. Res. 925, ¶ 10, U.N. Doc. S/RES/925 (8 June 1994) (requesting that UNAMIR continue to work closely with the UN Department of Humanitarian Affairs); U.N. SCOR, 48th Sess., 3388th mtg. at p. 12, U.N. Doc. S/PV.3388 (8 June 1994).

96 *See* "Report of the Independent Inquiry Into the Actions of the United Nations During the 1994 Genocide in Rwanda," in letter dated December 15, 1999 from the U.N. Secretary-General addressed to the President of the Security Council, at p. 25, U.N. Doc. S/1999/1257 (16 December 1999) ("By [July 25], over two months after [R]esolution 918 (1994) was adopted, UNAMIR still had only 550 troops, a tenth of the authorized strength."); Power, "Bystanders to Genocide," *supra* note 90, at p. 90 (discussing how the intervention in Somalia influenced later thinking regarding intervention in Rwanda).

97 S.C. Res. 929, ¶¶ 1–3, U.N. Doc. S/RES/929 (22 June 1994).

98 This figure is an estimate only; the exact number of victims of the Rwandan genocide is unknown. See, e.g., Power, *A Problem From Hell*, *supra* note 90, at p. 334 ("[S]ome 800,000 Tutsi and politically moderate Hutu were murdered.").

99 S.C. Res. 929, *supra* note 97, ¶ 3.

100 U.N. SCOR, 49th Sess., 3392d mtg. at p. 4, U.N. Doc. S/PV.3392 (22 June 1994). Brazil, New Zealand, Nigeria, and Pakistan also abstained from voting on Resolution 929. Id. at p. 5.

101 Id. at p. 4.

of an expanded UNAMIR in lieu of authorizing military intervention by a member state for humanitarian purposes.[102] Third, China noted the lack of consent of the conflicting parties to the deployment of the multinational force.[103] In the end, despite Rwanda's unprecedented humanitarian crisis, Beijing proved unwilling to support the Security Council's authorization of a member state-led humanitarian intervention in the absence of consent of the parties concerned.

Bosnia

The international intervention in Bosnia from 1992 to 1995 was neither initially nor later primarily a humanitarian intervention.[104] Nonetheless, at times UN peacekeeping operations in Bosnia during this period demonstrated characteristics of humanitarian intervention, and an examination of Beijing's position is therefore useful for understanding Chinese attitudes toward sovereignty and intervention in the early to mid-1990s.

In February 1992, the Security Council adopted Resolution 743, establishing the UN Protection Force (UNPROFOR) to oversee ceasefire agreements signed at Geneva in late 1991 and Sarajevo in early 1992.[105] China voted in favor of the initial UNPROFOR resolution.[106] In order to understand China's position on subsequent resolutions enlarging UNPROFOR's mandate, it is important to note that Resolution 743 was not a Chapter VII enforcement measure: the Security Council established UNPROFOR as an ordinary Chapter VI peacekeeping mission, with the consent of the Federal

---

[102] Id.

[103] Id.

[104] As defined earlier in this chapter, "humanitarian intervention" is the use of force by a state (or group of states) in another sovereign state's territory for the purposes of protecting the other state's citizens from gross human rights abuses, mass atrocities, crimes against humanity, or genocide. *See supra* text accompanying notes 6–7. Initially, the UN peacekeeping force in Bosnia was *not* authorized to use force except in self-defense. S.C. Res. 743, U.N. Doc. S/RES/743 (21 February 1992) (neither referring to Chapter VII nor otherwise authorizing the use of force, even in self-defense). Additionally, while the original mandate of the UN force included humanitarian assignments, it was established as "an interim arrangement to create the conditions of peace and security required for the negotiation of an overall settlement of the Yugoslav crisis." Id. ¶ 5; *see also* Nicholas Morris, "Humanitarian Intervention in the Balkans," in *Humanitarian Intervention and International Relations*, *supra* note 3, pp. 98–119, at pp. 98, 103. As described *infra* notes 109–112, the Security Council repeatedly enlarged the force's mandate to encompass the protection of civilians from ethnic cleansing and mass atrocities, including authorizing the UN peacekeeping units to use force in the fulfillment of this expanded mandate.

[105] S.C. Res. 743, *supra* note 104, ¶ 8.

[106] U.N. SCOR, 47th Sess., 3055th mtg. at p. 4, U.N. Doc. S/PV.3055 (21 February 1992).

Republic of Yugoslavia (FRY).[107] UNPROFOR's original mandate included maintaining conditions for successful peace talks and securing three demilitarized "safe havens," known as UN Protected Areas (UNPAs), in the former Yugoslav republic of Croatia.[108]

Faced with mass civilian casualties, ethnic cleansing, and a burgeoning refugee population, the Security Council regularly expanded UNPROFOR's mandate over the next three years to encompass increasingly complex operations.[109] These operations included the protection of aid workers and humanitarian convoys and the establishment and protection of "safe areas" around Sarajevo and five Bosnian towns, including Srebrenica.[110] This "mission creep" blurred the line between traditional peacekeeping and "peace enforcement" operations.[111] Moreover, it interposed

107 Resolution 743 did, however, state "that the situation in Yugoslavia continues to constitute a threat to international peace and security as determined in [R]esolution 713 (1991)." S.C. Res. 743, *supra* note 104, pmbl. para. 5. Resolution 713 called on all UN member states to implement a "general and complete embargo on all deliveries of weapons and military equipment to Yugoslavia." S.C. Res. 713, ¶ 6, U.N. Doc. S/RES/713 (25 September 1991).

108 S.C. Res. 743, *supra* note 104, ¶ 5. The UNPAs were established in Eastern Slavonia, Western Slavonia, and Krajina.

109 Michael W. Doyle and Nicholas Sambanis, *Making War and Building Peace: United Nations Peace Operations* (Princeton, NJ: Princeton University Press, 2006), pp. 165–166.

110 *See* S.C. Res. 758, ¶ 8, U.N. Doc. S/RES/758 (8 June 1992) (enlarging UNPROFOR's mandate and strength, and calling on all parties to create conditions for delivery of humanitarian supplies to Sarajevo and other destinations, including establishment of a security zone around Sarajevo's airport); S.C. Res. 761, ¶¶ 4–5, U.N. Doc. S/RES/761 (29 June 1992) (authorizing the deployment of additional personnel to ensure the "security and functioning" of Sarajevo's airport to facilitate the delivery of humanitarian aid); S.C. Res. 776, ¶ 2, U.N. Doc. S/RES/776 (14 September 1992) (increasing UNPROFOR's strength and enlarging its mandate to include protection of International Committee of the Red Cross convoys); S.C. Res. 819, ¶¶ 1–14, U.N. Doc. S/RES/819 (16 April 1993) (declaring Srebrenica a "safe area"); S.C. Res. 824, ¶¶ 3–6, U.N. Doc. S/RES/824 (6 May 1993) (declaring that Sarajevo and other "threatened areas," including, Tuzla, Žepa, Goražde, Bihać, and Srebrenica, should be treated as "safe areas" by all parties); S.C. Res. 836, ¶¶ 4–11, U.N. Doc. S/RES/836 (4 June 1993) (enlarging UNPROFOR's mandate to include protection of designated "safe areas"). In particular, Resolution 836—a Chapter VII resolution—authorized UNPROFOR,

> acting in self-defense, *to take the necessary measures, including the use of force*, in reply to bombardments against the safe areas by any of the parties or to armed incursion into them or in the event of any deliberate obstruction in or around those areas of the freedom of movement of UNPROFOR or of protected humanitarian convoys.

Id. ¶ 9 (emphasis added). Effectively, this enlargement of UNPROFOR's mandate allowed it to use force to protect the "safe areas." Id.

111 *See generally* Alex J. Bellamy and Paul Williams, *Understanding Peacekeeping* (Malden, MA: Polity Press, 2d ed., 2010), pp. 193–202; Trevor Findlay, "The New Peacekeepers and the New Peacekeeping," in Trevor Findlay (ed.), *Challenges for the New Peacekeepers* (Oxford: Oxford University Press/SIPRI, 1996), pp. 1–31; Nugroho Wisnumurti, "The United

UNPROFOR troops between conflicting parties, as well as between hostile forces and civilians, in situations where the consent of some or all parties had eroded or was nonexistent.[112] In other words, UNPROFOR operations frequently exhibited characteristics of humanitarian intervention, and China's position on the expansion of UNPROFOR's mandate during this period therefore sheds light on the evolution of China's attitudes toward humanitarian intervention in the post-Cold War era.

China voted in favor of a number of resolutions enlarging UNPROFOR's mandate throughout 1992, including those that expanded its mandate to include the protection of Sarajevo's airport to ensure the security of humanitarian airlift operations,[113] the monitoring of "pink zones" controlling access to the UNPAs,[114] the assumption of border control functions,[115] and the demilitarization of Prevlaka Peninsula near Dubrovnik.[116] However, this support for an enlarged mandate to facilitate humanitarian relief clashed with both China's disinclination to support Chapter VII enforcement actions and its insistence on obtaining the conflicting parties' consent to any enlargement of UNPROFOR's mandate. Thus, China abstained from the votes on resolutions authorizing member states to "take … all measures necessary," including the use of force, to support certain humanitarian objectives.[117] China's representative made clear that it was concerned not only that UNPROFOR ran "the risk of plunging into armed conflict," but also that the expansion of UNPROFOR's mandate had "not received the express consent of the parties concerned in Bosnia and Herzegovina."[118]

Nations and Peace Enforcement: Prescription for Disorder or Path Towards a New World Order?", *Brown Journal of World Affairs*, vol. 3, Winter/Spring 1996, pp. 67–76, at pp. 67–69.

112 *See* Bellamy, *supra* note 111, at pp. 193–202, 280–88; Wisnumurti, *supra* note 111, at pp. 71–72.

113 S.C. Res. 761, *supra* note 110, ¶¶ 1–3.

114 S.C. Res. 762, ¶ 3, U.N. Doc. S/RES/762 (30 June 1992).

115 S.C. Res. 769, ¶¶ 1–2, U.N. Doc. S/RES/769 (7 August 1992).

116 S.C. Res. 779, ¶ 2, U.N. Doc. S/RES/779 (6 October 1992). The Prevlaka Peninsula is located in Croatia.

117 S.C. Res. 770, ¶ 2, U.N. Doc. S/RES/770 (13 August 1992) (authorizing the use of force to facilitate delivery of humanitarian assistance to Sarajevo and other parts of Bosnia and Herzegovina) (India and Zimbabwe also abstained from voting); S.C. Res. 776, *supra* note 110, ¶ 2. (referring to Resolution 770, which invoked Chapter VII, and expanding UNPROFOR's mandate to include the protection of International Committee of the Red Cross humanitarian convoys) (India and Zimbabwe also abstained from voting). *See also* U.N. SCOR, 47th Sess., 3106th mtg. at 50, U.N. Doc. S/PV.3106 (13 August 1992); U.N. SCOR, 47th Sess., 3114th mtg. at pp. 10–12, U.N. Doc. S/PV.3114 (14 September 1992).

118 U.N. SCOR, 47th Sess., 3114th mtg. at p. 10, U.N. Doc. S/PV.3114 (14 September 1992).

As fighting intensified in Bosnia in early 1993, the Security Council moved to provide UNPROFOR with greater powers to address increasingly complex conditions on the ground.[119] In the face of reports of "ethnic cleansing" and deteriorating humanitarian conditions, China softened its position on the enlargement of UNPROFOR's mandate and voted in favor of several Chapter VII measures designating "safe areas," as well as resolutions authorizing the expanded use of force by UNPROFOR— including air power—not only for purposes of self-defense, but also to protect the safe areas and ensure the freedom of movement of UN and humanitarian convoys.[120] However, China still expressed unease with the Security Council's reference to Chapter VII, and it noted that the situation in Bosnia was "an exceptional case and therefore does not constitute a precedent for future United Nations peace-keeping operations."[121] In several cases, China, while reiterating its reservations about invoking Chapter VII to authorize the use of force, explicitly noted that its favorable vote was due to the resolutions' humanitarian objectives.[122]

Despite these affirmative votes, China's support for enforcement resolutions with humanitarian objectives remained limited. For example, in

---

119 *See* John F. Burns, "Serbs Intensify Sarajevo Attack; U.N. Fears A Final All-Out Push," *New York Times*, 23 March 1993 (describing UNPROFOR's struggle to contain the escalating violence in Bosnia); John F. Burns, "Vicious 'Ethnic Cleansing' Infects Croat-Muslim Villages in Bosnia," *New York Times*, 21 April 1993 (same); Chuck Sudetic, "Serbian Forces Said to Overrun Muslim Villages," *New York Times*, 3 June 1993 (same).

120 *See* U.N. SCOR, 48th Sess., 3199th mtg. at p. 3, U.N. Doc. S/PV.3199 (16 April 1993); S.C. Res. 819, *supra* note 110 (designating Srebrenica and its surroundings as a "safe area," while also explicitly reaffirming "the sovereignty, territorial integrity and political independence of Bosnia and Herzegovina"); S.C. Res. 824, *supra* note 110 (designating Sarajevo and the towns of Goražde, Tuzla, Žepa, and Bihać as "safe areas"); S.C. Res. 807, U.N. Doc. S/RES/807 (19 February 1993) (authorizing the use of force in self-defense); S.C. Res. 836, *supra* note 110 (authorizing the use of force, including air power, to protect safe areas and facilitate the delivery of humanitarian aid); U.N. SCOR, 48th Sess., 3228th mtg. at p. 48, U.N. Doc. S/PV.3228; S.C. Res. 958, U.N. Doc. S/RES/958 (19 November 1994) (authorizing member states to use "all necessary measures, through the use of air power, in an[d] around the safe areas in the Republic of Bosnia and Herzegovina," to support UNPROFOR in the performance of its mandate).

121 U.N. SCOR, 48th Sess., 3174th mtg. at p. 21, U.N. Doc. S/PV.3174 (19 February 1993). Thereafter, the PRC continued to express reservations about the applicability of Chapter VII to UN peacekeeping operations and to note that the invocation of Chapter VII for UNPROFOR operations did not constitute a precedent for future UN peacekeeping missions. See, e.g., U.N. SCOR, 48th Sess., 3189th mtg. at p. 16, U.N. Doc. S/PV.3189 (30 March 1993) ("It is our view that the application of Chapter VII is due to the special and specific needs of Croatia and should not constitute a precedent for the peace-keeping operations of the United Nations.").

122 U.N. SCOR, 48th Sess., 3228th mtg. at p. 49, U.N. Doc. S/PV.3228 (4 June 1993); U.N. SCOR, 49th Sess., 3461st mtg. at p. 7, U.N. Doc. S/PV.3461 (19 November 1994).

October 1992, China abstained from voting on Resolution 781, which established a no-fly zone (NFZ) over Bosnia to prevent attacks by Serbian warplanes.[123] Significantly, Resolution 781 represented the first time that the Security Council imposed an NFZ over another member state's sovereign territory. In explaining its abstention from voting on Resolution 781, China noted that it did not oppose "in principle" the establishment of an NFZ to facilitate humanitarian relief operations and protect civilians, but it emphasized that "the consent of all relevant parties" was absent.[124] Similarly, in March 1993, China abstained from voting on Resolution 816, which invoked Chapter VII to authorize member states to enforce the NFZ using "all necessary measures."[125] In explaining its abstention, China again emphasized the lack of consent of the "parties concerned" and also noted its "reservations on the invocation of Chapter VII to authorize countries to use force in implementing the no-fly zone."[126]

The requirement of consent also factored into China's votes to extend UNPROFOR's mandate. In one Security Council debate, China stated that a "precondition" for the continued deployment of UN peacekeeping forces was "the prior request or consent from the host countries or the parties concerned."[127] Still, China's favorable votes on a number of enforcement resolutions—especially those with humanitarian objectives—indicated a degree of flexibility in its position on consent, as resolutions adopted under Chapter VII implicitly do not require the consent of the parties concerned.[128]

Nonetheless, when China perceived that proposed actions impinged on sovereignty and territorial integrity, its support for those actions became contingent on the consent of the parties.[129] For example, in December

---

123 S.C. Res. 781, ¶ 1, U.N. Doc. S/RES/781 (Oct. 9, 1992).

124 U.N. SCOR, 47th Sess., 3122d mtg. at p. 7, U.N. Doc. S/PV.3122 (9 October 1992).

125 S.C. Res. 816, ¶ 4, U.N. Doc. S/RES/816 (31 March 1993). On April 12, NATO commenced operations to enforce the Bosnian NFZ. William Drozdiak, "NATO to Patrol Bosnian Skies Starting Monday," *Washington Post*, 9 April 1993.

126 U.N. SCOR, 48th Sess., 3191st mtg. at p. 22, U.N. Doc. S/PV.3191 (31 March 1993).

127 U.N. SCOR, 48th Sess., 3286th mtg. at p. 8, U.N. Doc. S/PV.3286 (4 October 1993).

128 Rosalyn Higgins, "A General Assessment of United Nations Peace-Keeping," in Antonio Cassese (ed.), *United Nations Peace-Keeping* (Alphen aan den Rijn, The Netherlands: Sijthoff & Noordhoff, 1978), pp. 1–14, at p. 5; Marianne von Grünigen, "Neutrality and Peace-Keeping," in *United Nations Peace-Keeping, supra*, pp. 125–153, at p. 136; Yoel Arnon Tsur, "The United Nations Peace-Keeping Operations in the Middle East From 1965 to 1976," in *United Nations Peace-Keeping, supra*, pp. 183–221, at p. 207.

129 China repeatedly demanded deference to sovereignty and territorial integrity during Security Council debates. See, e.g., U.N. SCOR, 50th Sess., 3575th mtg. at p. 8, U.N. Doc. S/PV.3575 (8 September 1995); U.N. SCOR, 49th Sess., 3454th mtg. at p. 13, U.N. Doc.

1995, when China voted in favor of establishing the Implementation Force (IFOR)—the NATO-led multinational force deployed to Bosnia following the 1995 London peace agreement[130]—it attributed its support to "the urgent wishes of the party concerned and the fact that this draft resolution calls for extraordinary action in extraordinary circumstances."[131] As the case of the Bosnian crisis shows, China was grappling with defining the boundaries of its adherence to the principle of noninterference, demonstrating both a greater flexibility on intervention and a lingering reluctance to sanction the use of force for humanitarian purposes in contexts of eroded consent.

Kosovo

NATO's 1999 unilateral military intervention in Kosovo marked the boldest claim to a freestanding right of humanitarian intervention to date. It also marked the high point of China's opposition to the idea of humanitarian intervention. Following the Federal Republic of Yugoslavia's (FRY) rejection of the Rambouillet Accord in early 1999, NATO launched a bombing campaign designed to drive Serbian forces from Kosovo in order to make way for an international peacekeeping force that would protect both Kosovar Albanian and Serbian communities in Kosovo and allow refugees to return home.[132] NATO's bombing campaign ran from March 24 to June 10, 1999, during which time ethnic cleansing in Kosovo escalated and added to the refugee problem.[133] At no point did NATO receive UN authorization for its military intervention.[134] On June 12, FRY President Slobodan

S/PV.3454 (8 November 1994); U.N. SCOR, 49th Sess., 3428th mtg. at p. 24, U.N. Doc. S/PV.3428 (23 September 1994); U.N. SCOR, 49th Sess., 3367th mtg. at pp. 54–55, U.N. Doc. S/PV.3367 (21 April 1994); U.N. SCOR, 49th Sess., 3356th mtg. at p. 10, U.N. Doc. S/PV.3356 (31 March 1994); U.N. SCOR, 49th Sess., 3344th mtg. at p. 11, U.N. Doc. S/PV.3344 (4 March 1994); U.N. SCOR, 48th Sess., 3200th mtg. at pp. 31–32, U.N. Doc. S/PV.3200 (17 April 1993).

130 U.N. SCOR, 50th Sess., 3607th mtg. at pp. 13–14, U.N. Doc. S/PV.3607 (15 December 1995).

131 Id.

132 Javier Solana, "NATO's Success in Kosovo," *Foreign Affairs*, vol. 78, no. 6, November/December 1999, pp. 114–120, at pp. 116–117.

133 See, e.g., William Booth and James Rupert, "Exodus Swells, Straining Capacity of Refugee Camps," *Washington Post*, 18 April 1999; James Rupert, "Refugees Report Roadside Slaughter," *Washington Post*, 29 April 1999; R. Jeffrey Smith and William Booth, "Yugoslavia Steps Up Expulsions," *Washington Post*, 17 April 1999; R. Jeffrey Smith, "New Wave of Kosovo Exiles Tells of Atrocities by Serbs," *Washington Post*, 15 April 1999; Daniel Williams, "Brutal Conditions Enveloping Kosovo," *Washington Post*, 27 March 1999.

134 *See generally* Louis Henkin, "Kosovo and the Law of 'Humanitarian Intervention,'" *American Journal of International Law*, vol. 93, no. 4, October 1999, pp. 824–828, at pp. 825–826.

Milošević finally acceded to conditions that paved the way for a NATO peacekeeping force—the Kosovo Force (KFOR)—to enter the province.[135]

Of all NATO members, the United Kingdom most vocally proclaimed a unilateral right of humanitarian intervention.[136] The U.K. Secretary of Defense at the time stated that "[i]n international law, in exceptional circumstances and to avoid a humanitarian catastrophe, military action can be taken, and it is on that legal basis that military action was taken."[137] Similarly, on the day NATO commenced its bombing campaign, the U.K. permanent representative to the United Nations argued that NATO's intervention was legal and that in situations "of overwhelming humanitarian necessity, military intervention is legally justifiable."[138] The United States provided similar justifications for NATO's intervention, although, unlike the United Kingdom, it did not argue explicitly for a freestanding right of humanitarian intervention.[139] Separately, Germany and France took the position that the NATO campaign did not set a precedent for a right of humanitarian intervention.[140]

---

135 Thomas W. Lippman, "Yugoslavs Begin Kosovo Retreat," *Washington Post*, 11 June 1999 Daniel Williams and William Drozdiak, "NATO Peace Force Hastens Into Kosovo," *Washington Post*, 12 June 1999; Daniel Williams, "Yugoslavs Yield to NATO Terms," *Washington Post*, 4 June 1999.

136 Professor Brownlie, however, notes that Kosovo is not a clear-cut example of humanitarian intervention due to the mixed motives expressed by NATO member states. Ian Brownlie, *Principles of Public International Law* (Oxford: Oxford University Press, 7th ed., 2008), pp. 742–744 (further stating that in 1999 "there was little or no authority and little or no state practice to support the right of individual States to use force on humanitarian grounds in international law"). *See also* Michael J. Matheson, "Justification for the NATO Air Campaign in Kosovo," *Proceedings of the Annual Meeting of the American Society of International Law*, vol. 94, April 2000, p. 301, at p. 301.

137 Malcolm N. Shaw, *International Law* (Cambridge: Cambridge University Press, 6th ed., 2008), p. 1157.

138 Brownlie, *supra* note 136, at p. 743.

139 Id.

140 Gray, *supra* note 38, at pp. 595–596 ("As regards Kosovo, there was little express support from states for an autonomous doctrine of humanitarian intervention, other than from the UK."). Professor Gray also writes,

> Most States arguing in the Security Council and in the ICJ did not rely on humanitarian intervention alone as an autonomous justification for the use of force; they seemed to rely on a combination of humanitarian and implied authorization by the Security Council. The Netherlands and others stressed that the action followed directly from Security Council Resolution 1203; it could not be described as unilateral.

Id. A statement by NATO's Secretary-General in March 1999 provided diverse justifications for the campaign, including the FRY's refusal to accept the terms of the Rambouillet Accord or comply with other demands of the "international community," in addition to

For China, however, the story was not as simple as that of the Serbian state systematically cleansing Kosovo of ethnic Albanians. From China's perspective, Serbia was defending its sovereignty against internal challenges—a position that China almost certainly viewed with sympathy given its own internal challenges to sovereignty, including in Tibet, Xinjiang, and Taiwan. Thus, China was adamant that the situation in Kosovo was an internal affair of the FRY. For example, in a statement before the General Assembly in December 1998, China stated that "Kosovo is a part of the [FRY], and respect for the [FRY's] sovereignty and territorial integrity and noninterference in its internal affairs under any pretext are in conformity with the principles of the United Nations Charter."[141]

China repeated this sentiment regularly at the United Nations, including in defense of its abstention from voting on Resolution 1160, in which the Security Council determined, for the first time, that the conflict in Kosovo constituted a threat to international peace and security and imposed an arms embargo on the FRY under Chapter VII.[142] China's statement evinced sensitivity to the supposed "internationalization" of a domestic secessionist movement under the guise of responding to a humanitarian crisis, and its fear that the resolution might set a precedent for international intervention in its own affairs led Beijing to oppose the Council's designation of the situation in Kosovo as a threat to international peace and security.[143]

---

arguing that the FRY's failure to meet these demands made NATO's intervention "necessary to avert a humanitarian catastrophe." Linda D. Kozaryn, "NATO Orders Air Strikes to End "Humanitarian Catastrophe,"" *American Forces Press Service*, 24 March 1999 (quoting Javier Solana, NATO Security-General, Statement (23 March 1999)).

141 U.N. GAOR, 53d Sess., 85th plen. mtg. at p. 22, U.N. Doc. A/53/PV.85 (9 December 1998).

142 S.C. Res. 1160, ¶ 8, U.N. Doc. S/RES/1160 (23 September 1998). In the Security Council meeting on Resolution 1160, China's representative stated that "Kosovo is an integral part of the territory" of the FRY and that "[t]he question of Kosovo is, in its essence, an internal matter" of the FRY, and he noted that China does "not think that the situation in Kosovo endangers regional and international peace and security." U.N. SCOR, 53d Sess., 3868th mtg. at p. 11, U.N. Doc. S/PV.3868 (31 March 1998). China also abstained from Resolution 1199 for the same reasons. *See* U.N. SCOR, 53d Sess., 3930th mtg. at pp. 1, 3, U.N. Doc. S/PV.3930 (23 September 1998) (explaining that China's abstention was based on concerns about infringing Kosovo's sovereignty and the Council's invocation of Chapter VII). For other PRC statements calling the situation in Kosovo an internal affair of the FRY, see U.N. GAOR, 52d Sess., 70th plen. mtg. at p. 32, U.N. Doc. A/52/PV.70 (12 December 1997); U.N. GAOR, 51st Sess., 82d plen. mtg. at pp. 29–30, U.N. Doc. A/51/PV.82 (12 December 1996).

143 U.N. SCOR, 53d Sess., 3930th mtg., *supra* note 142, at p. 3.

> [M]any countries in the region are multi-ethnic. If the Security Council becomes involved in a dispute without being requested to do so by the countries of the

China objected again when, in fall 1998, NATO threatened military action against the FRY to encourage a ceasefire and speed the deployment of a monitoring and verification mission in Kosovo.[144] In an October 1998 Security Council debate, China stated clearly its position that NATO's threats of military action constituted unlawful interference in the FRY's internal affairs, and it condemned NATO for acting without consulting with or seeking the authorization of the Security Council.[145] NATO's actions, China stated, "violated the purposes, principles and relevant provisions of the United Nations Charter, as well as international law and widely acknowledged norms governing relations between States."[146] In particular, China noted that NATO's challenge to the Security Council's authority "created an extremely dangerous precedent in international relations," and reiterated its position that the question of Kosovo must be settled in a manner that respected the sovereignty and territorial integrity of the FRY.[147]

In the lead-up to NATO's military campaign, China decried the "double standards" of Western claims of a right of humanitarian intervention.[148] In a January 1999 Security Council statement, which reflected China's self-designated role as spokesperson of the developing world, China lambasted the international community for paying "great attention to the humanitarian situation in the former Yugoslavia" while unconscionably forgetting "the hundreds of thousands of our African brothers and sisters who also require the international community's special care."[149] To China, NATO's

---

> region—or goes even further and unfairly applies pressure on or threatens actions against the Government of the country concerned—it would create a bad precedent and have wider negative implications.

Id.

[144] U.N. SCOR, 53d Sess., 3937th mtg. at p. 14, U.N. Doc. S/PV.3937 (24 October 1998). China maintained that it was "not in principle opposed to a technical resolution [on] the Kosovo question, but [was] opposed to [the] exercise of pressure on the FRY that amount[ed] to interference in its domestic affairs." Id. China also noted that the resolution contained no authorization to use or threaten to use force in the FRY. Id.

[145] Id. China abstained from voting on Resolution 1203, which endorsed agreements for a ceasefire as well as for the establishment of the Kosovo Verification Mission (an unarmed contingent of peace monitors from the Organization for Security and Cooperation in Europe), based on its opposition to NATO's threats of military action. S.C. Res. 1203, ¶¶ 1, 7–8, U.N. Doc. S/RES/1203 (24 October 1998).

[146] U.N. SCOR, 53d Sess., 3937th mtg., *supra* note 144, at p. 14.

[147] Id. China also made clear its position that Resolution 1203 did "not entail any authorization to use force or to threaten to use force against the Federal Republic of Yugoslavia" and stated that it should not be interpreted as doing so. Id.

[148] U.N. SCOR, 54th Sess., 3968th mtg. at p. 7, U.N. Doc. S/PV.3968 (21 January 1999).

[149] Id.

claims of a right of humanitarian intervention were merely a pretense, and it warned that "in international relations, there is a tendency to politicize humanitarian questions and to use them as a pretext to interfere in the internal affairs of sovereign countries. This can only arouse great concern."[150]

When NATO launched its bombing campaign in the FRY in March 1999, China's condemnation was immediate. In a March 24 Security Council meeting, China denounced NATO's intervention as "a blatant violation of the United Nations Charter and of the accepted norms of international law."[151] China reiterated that the Kosovo situation was "an internal matter" of the FRY and that its settlement "should be based on respect for the sovereignty and territorial integrity of the Federal Republic of Yugoslavia."[152] Furthermore, China stated that it "oppose[d] interference in the internal affairs of other States, under whatever pretext or in whatever form."[153] China's rhetoric also took an ideological turn in response to these events, as when China objected "to the use or threat of use of force in international affairs and to power politics whereby the strong bully the weak."[154] China further criticized NATO's usurpation of the Security Council's exclusive prerogative to identify threats to international peace and security and to authorize corresponding enforcement actions, including the use of force.[155]

On March 26, China voted in favor of a draft resolution, submitted by Belarus, India, and Russia, condemning NATO's attack as a violation of the UN Charter.[156] The measure failed, with only China, Namibia, and Russia voting in favor.[157] In one sense, the draft resolution's failure lent legitimacy to the principle that intervention without Security Council authorization is permissible in cases of overwhelming humanitarian need. Still, while

150 Id.

151 U.N. SCOR, 53d Sess., 3988th mtg. at p. 12, U.N. Doc. S/PV.3988 (24 March 1999). China reiterated this position before the Security Council two days later. U.N. SCOR, 53d Sess., 3989th mtg. at p. 9, U.N. Doc. S/PV.3989 (26 March 1999) ("The Chinese Government strongly opposes such an act, which constitutes a blatant violation of the principles of the Charter of the United Nations and of international law, as well as a challenge to the authority of the Security Council.").

152 U.N. SCOR, 53d Sess., 3988th mtg., *supra* note 151, at p. 12.

153 Id.

154 Id.

155 Id. ("We are firmly opposed to any act that violates this principle and that challenges the authority of the Security Council.").

156 U.N. SCOR, 53d Sess., 3989th mtg., *supra* note 151, at p. 6. Specifically, the draft resolution stated that NATO's unilateral use of force constituted a "flagrant violation" of Articles 2(4), 24, and 53 of the UN Charter. Id. at p. 3.

157 Id. at p. 6.

the United Nations never condemned NATO's intervention, it is equally important to note that NATO's intervention never received any formal UN endorsement.[158] Condemnation was left to individual states, such as China and Russia, or groups of states, such as the G-77.[159]

In June 1999, China issued its fullest denunciation of NATO's intervention in Kosovo in response to the Security Council's adoption of Resolution 1244, a Chapter VII resolution authorizing member states and relevant international organizations to establish an international security presence in Kosovo under UN auspices.[160] China did not block the resolution but abstained from voting.[161] In its statement before the Council, China repeated its position that, in the absence of UN authorization, NATO's military strikes against the FRY "seriously violated the Charter ... and norms of international law" and thus set "an extremely dangerous precedent in the history of international relations."[162] China's permanent representative declared, "This war, waged in the name of humanitarianism ... in fact produced the greatest humanitarian catastrophe in post-Second-World-War Europe and ... seriously undermined peace and stability in the Balkans."[163] Again, China emphasized that settlement of the Kosovo question should be based on "respect for the sovereignty and territorial integrity" of the FRY.[164]

China's position on the ethnic dimension of NATO's intervention was particularly striking:

---

158 On the status of the doctrine of humanitarian intervention after Kosovo, Professor Shaw writes, "It can be concluded that the doctrine of humanitarian intervention in a crisis situation was invoked and not condemned by the United Nations, but it received meager support. It is not possible to characterize the legal situation as going beyond this." Shaw, *supra* note 137, at p. 1157.

159 A September 1999 G–77 statement reads: "The Ministers [of the G–77] stressed the need to maintain clear distinctions between humanitarian assistance and other activities of the United Nations. They rejected the so-called right of humanitarian intervention, which had no basis in the UN Charter or in international law." "Ministerial Declaration of the Twenty-Third Annual Meeting of the Ministers for Foreign Affairs of the Group of 77," ¶ 69 (24 September 1999). The G–77 statement represented the views of 132 states.

160 S.C. Res. 1244, ¶ 7, U.N. Doc. S/RES/1244 (10 June 1999).

161 China abstained rather than vetoing the resolution because NATO had suspended its bombing campaign, the FRY agreed to a peace plan, and the draft resolution "reaffirmed the purposes and principles of the United Nations Charter, the primary responsibility of the Security Council for the maintenance of international peace and security and the commitment of all Member States to the sovereignty and territorial integrity of the Federal Republic of Yugoslavia." U.N. SCOR, 54th Sess., 4011th mtg. at p. 9, U.N. Doc. S/PV.4011 (10 June 1999).

162 Id. at p. 8.

163 Id.

164 Id.

> We are not in favour of discrimination against or the oppression of any ethnic group. At the same time, we are also opposed to any act that would create division between different ethnic groups and undermine national unity. Fundamentally speaking, ethnic problems within a State should be settled in a proper manner by its own Government and people, through the adoption of sound policies. They must not be used as an excuse for external intervention, much less used by foreign States as an excuse for the use of force.[165]

Additionally, China emphasized that the principles of respect for sovereignty and noninterference in other states' internal affairs had not eroded in the post-Cold War era:

> Since the end of the cold war, the international situation has undergone major changes, but those principles are by no means outdated. On the contrary, they have acquired even greater relevance. At the threshold of the new century, it is even more imperative for us to reaffirm those principles. In essence, the "human rights over sovereignty" theory serves to infringe upon the sovereignty of other States and to promote hegemonism under the pretext of human rights. This totally runs counter to the purposes and principles of the United Nations Charter. The international community should maintain vigilance against it.[166]

Given both the ready analogy of Kosovo to Taiwan and NATO's willingness to circumvent the Security Council and thereby nullify Beijing's ability to veto the use of force, NATO's intervention in the FRY likely cut especially close to Chinese sensitivities about claims of a unilateral right of humanitarian intervention. While Kosovo marked the high point of Chinese opposition to humanitarian intervention in the post-Cold War era, the particular sensitivities it raised remain relevant to China's position today.

East Timor

China's support for the UN-authorized, Australian-led humanitarian intervention in East Timor in 1999, as well as the subsequent UN peacekeeping operation, offers an interesting counterpoint to its opposition to NATO's intervention in Kosovo earlier that year. Following a May 1999 agreement between Indonesia and Portugal on how to settle the status of East Timor, the Security Council, with China's support and Indonesia's consent, established the UN Mission for East Timor (UNAMET) in order to assist with a referendum that would decide whether the East Timorese desired

165 Id. at pp. 8–9.
166 Id. at p. 9.

independence or a relationship of special autonomy with Indonesia.[167] Nearly 80 percent of East Timorese voters endorsed independence in the UN-sponsored plebiscite.[168] Almost immediately, armed militias, backed by the Indonesian military, began a campaign of violence to reverse the decision.[169]

As violence spread and the refugee population grew, it became apparent that the Indonesian government was unwilling or unable to control the situation or protect East Timorese civilians and UNAMET convoys from attack.[170] Initially, Jakarta resisted international pressure either to improve security or to accept an international peacekeeping force.[171] For its part, China took the position that any international intervention would require the consent of the Indonesian government. In a Security Council debate on September 11, 1999, China noted its grave concern "over the continuing violence and resulting humanitarian crisis in East Timor," but stated two preconditions for support of an international intervention: "The deployment of any peacekeeping force should be at the

---

[167] S.C. Res. 1246, ¶ 1, U.N. Doc. S/RES/1246 (11 June 1999) (adopted unanimously). UNAMET consisted of a civilian police contingent to advise the Indonesian police force on security, military liaison officers to advise the Indonesian armed forces, and civilian personnel to monitor the freedom and fairness of the scheduled referendum. The Security Council twice extended UNAMET's mandate. S.C. Res. 1257, ¶ 1, U.N. Doc. S/RES/1257 (3 August 1999) (extending UNAMET's mandate through Sept. 30, 1999); S.C. Res. 1262, ¶ 1, U.N. Doc. S/RES/1262 (27 August 1999) (further extending UNAMET's mandate through Nov. 30, 1999).

[168] Seth Mydans, "In East Timor, Decisive Vote for a Break from Indonesia," *New York Times*, 4 September 1999.

[169] Welsh, *supra* note 18, at p. 551; Seth Mydans, "Timorese Flee as Militias Seem to Gain Upper Hand," *New York Times*, 3 September 1999; Seth Mydans, "Violence as East Timor Awaits Vote Count," *New York Times*, 2 September 1999; Seth Mydans, "Militias Raise Tensions After Timor Votes," *New York Times*, 1 September 1999.

[170] Barbara Crossette, "As Support for Intervention Grows, Indonesia Persuades U.N. to Delay Evacuation of Mission," *New York Times*, 9 September 1999; Seth Mydans, "Jakarta Concedes a Loss of Control Over Timor Forces," *New York Times*, 12 September 1999; Philip Shenon, "President Asserts Jakarta Must Act or Admit Troops," *New York Times*, 10 September 1999.

[171] Barbara Crossette, "U.N. Says Jakarta's Opposition to Peacekeepers Is Weakening," *New York Times*, 12 September 1999; Barbara Crossette, "Annan Warns Indonesians that Inaction May Lead to Criminal Charges," *New York Times*, 11 September 1999; Barbara Crossette, "U.N. Says a Quarter of East Timorese Have Fled," *New York Times*, 8 September 1999; Barbara Crossette, "Security Council Presses Indonesia to Restore Order," *New York Times*, 6 September 1999; Mark Landler, "The Fate of East Timor: The Indonesian View; Jakarta Military Is Taking Central Role in Crisis," *New York Times*, 10 September 1999; Seth Mydans, "Indonesia Says No to Timor Peacekeepers," *New York Times*, 9 September 1999; David E. Sanger, "Indonesia Is Warned It Could Lose Western Aid," *New York Times*, 8 September 1999.

request of the Indonesian Government and endorsed by the Security Council."[172]

On September 12, in a dramatic reversal of its position three days before,[173] the Indonesian government consented to the deployment of international peacekeepers in East Timor.[174] Beijing praised Jakarta's decision as "rational, respectable and responsible,"[175] and on September 15, China voted in favor of Resolution 1264, a Chapter VII measure authorizing the establishment of an Australian-led, multinational peacekeeping force—the International Force in East Timor (INTERFET)—to restore peace and security in East Timor.[176] Two days later, China announced its intention to contribute up to two hundred civilian police to a future UN mission in East Timor, marking China's first participation in a UN peacekeeping operation since 1992, in Cambodia.[177] China deployed the police contingent after the Security Council, in Resolution 1272, authorized the establishment of the UN Transitional Administration in East Timor (UNTAET).[178]

Some commentators suggest that Beijing's support for humanitarian intervention in East Timor demonstrated a relaxation of its position on sovereignty and noninterference in other states' internal affairs.[179] This

---

172 U.N. SCOR, 54th Sess., 4043d mtg. at p. 13, U.N. Doc. S/PV.4043 (11 September 1999); *see also* Chen Yali, "China: No Violence in East Timor," *China Daily*, 10 September 1999 ("The international community may help in stabilizing the situation if the Indonesian Government so demands. But before a request is made, any outside intervention should take caution so the infringement upon national sovereignty that was obvious in the Kosovo case is not repeated.").

173 Mydans, *supra* note 171.

174 Seth Mydans, "Indonesia Invites a U.N. Force to Timor," *New York Times*, 13 September 1999.

175 Xi Mi, "China: Positive Gesture Made," *China Daily*, 15 September 1999.

> The outburst of violence in East Timor after its recent vote has somewhat tarnished Indonesia's image.... If it does not take prompt action, the next victim will not only be the East Timor people, but also Indonesia's own fundamental interests.... [Jakarta] has now decided to honor a pledge by inviting international peacekeepers to East Timor. This decision, painful as it might be, is rational, respectable and responsible.

Id.

176 S.C. Res. 1264, ¶ 3, U.N. Doc. S/RES/1264 (15 September 1999). Resolution 1264 also reaffirmed the sovereignty and territorial integrity of Indonesia. Id.

177 "China: Nation to Send Police to E. Timor," *China Daily*, 17 September 1999.

178 S.C. Res. 1272, ¶ 1, U.N. Doc. S/RES/1272 (25 October 1999).

179 These commentators appear to mistakenly view the UN intervention in East Timor as a violation of Indonesian sovereignty and therefore conclude that China's participation in the UNTAET mission indicates a softening of Beijing's position toward humanitarian intervention. See, e.g., Allen Carlson, *Unifying China, Integrating with the World: Securing*

interpretation, however, ignores the fact that the intervention received both Indonesia's consent and the Security Council's authorization, both of which were prerequisites for China's support.[180] To be sure, Indonesia's dramatic about-face indicates that significant pressure was applied in order to convince Jakarta to accept an international peacekeeping force. Thus, to the extent that China proved willing to accept "induced" consent as legitimate consent to intervention, the case of East Timor reflects a degree of flexibility in China's previously strict insistence on noninterference, although this flexibility is less evident than some commentators have suggested.[181]

Chinese Attitudes Toward Humanitarian Intervention in the 2000s

This Part examines China's acts and official pronouncements with respect to (A) efforts to redefine humanitarian intervention as "the responsibility to protect" following NATO's intervention in Kosovo; (B) the humanitarian crisis in Darfur; and the conflicts in (C) Libya and (D) Syria.

The Responsibility to Protect

NATO's intervention in Kosovo catalyzed a fresh debate about the permissibility of humanitarian intervention under international law. In particular, the stridency of opposition to NATO's actions prompted advocates of humanitarian intervention to rethink their approach. A decade after the

Chinese Sovereignty in the Reform Era (Stanford, CA: Stanford University Press, 2005), p. 176 (citing China's "quiet, supportive role in facilitating humanitarian intervention in East Timor" and its support for Security Council Resolutions 1264 and 1272 only months after its vocal opposition to NATO's action in Kosovo as evidence that "Chinese foreign policy circles at this time basically accepted the legitimacy of human rights and humanitarian intervention"); Evan A. Feigenbaum, "China's Challenge to *Pax Americana*," *Washington Quarterly*, vol. 24, no. 3, Summer 2001, pp. 31–43, at p. 34 ("In mid-1999, the UN experience in East Timor signaled that China's orthodox view of sovereignty might be less intractable than Beijing's rhetoric would otherwise indicate. China sent observers, for example, to participate in a UN peace enforcement operation that violated what was still sovereign Indonesian territory.").

[180] *See* Feigenbaum, *supra* note 179, at p. 34 (recognizing that the intervention accommodated "China's mostly nonnegotiable principles of sovereignty"—consent of the sovereign and UN authorization—thereby preserving China's "orthodoxy intact"); Gill and Reilly, *supra* note 27, at p. 46 (finding China's "two core conditions of host nation acquiescence and Security Council approval met").

[181] The term "induced consent" is borrowed from Welsh, *supra* note 18, at p. 552.

end of the Cold War, they sought to reconceptualize humanitarian intervention and build international consensus around the concept's legitimacy.[182] The result was a concept called "the responsibility to protect" (R2P).[183]

A statement before the UN General Assembly in October 1999 by China's permanent representative, Qin Huasan, most clearly lays out China's position on humanitarian intervention at that time.[184] Qin's speech was in large part a reaction to a September 1999 speech by UN Secretary-General Kofi Annan that implored the international community to reach a consensus on how to approach humanitarian intervention.[185] In his speech, Qin called for "vigilance" against "such arguments as "humanitarian

---

182 See Gareth Evans, "From Humanitarian Intervention to the Responsibility to Protect," *Wisconsin International Law Journal*, vol. 24, no. 3, 2006, pp. 703–722, at p. 708.

> We sought to turn the whole weary debate about the right to intervene on its head and to re-characterize it not as an argument about any right at all but rather about a responsibility—one to protect people at grave risk—with the relevant perspective being not that of the prospective interveners but, more appropriately, of those needing support.

Id. (footnote omitted); *see also* Carsten Stahn, "Responsibility to Protect: Political Rhetoric or Emerging Legal Norm?", *American Journal of International Law*, vol. 101, no. 1, January 2007, pp. 99–120, at pp. 102–103 ("The commission [on state sovereignty] proposed dealing with this problem by recharacterizing sovereignty, that is, by conceiving of sovereignty as responsibility rather than control.").

183 Professor Shaw notes that "the responsibility to protect" "may be seen as an effort to redefine the principles of humanitarian intervention in a way that seeks to minimize the motives of the intervening powers." Shaw, *supra* note 137, at p. 1158. Similarly, Professor Alvarez writes, "The concept sought to deflect attention from the controverted "right" of some states to intervene, to the duties of all states to protect their own citizens from avoidable catastrophes, and for third parties to come to the rescue." José E. Alvarez, "The Schizophrenias of R2P," in Philip Alston and Euan Macdonald (eds.), *Human Rights, Intervention, and the Use of Force* (Oxford: Oxford University Press, 2008), pp. 275–284, at p. 275. For more comprehensive overviews of "the responsibility to protect," see Alex J. Bellamy, *Responsibility to Protect: The Global Effort to End Mass Atrocities* (Malden, MA: Polity Press, 2009), pp. 31–45; Gareth Evans, *The Responsibility to Protect: Ending Mass Atrocity Crimes Once and For All* (Washington, DC: The Brookings Institution, 2008), pp. 38–50.

184 U.N. GAOR, 54th Sess., 27th plen. mtg. at p. 12, U.N. Doc. A/54/PV.27 (6 October 1999).

185 *See* "U.N. Secretary-General, Secretary-General Presents His Annual Report to the General Assembly," U.N. Press Release SG/SM/7136 (20 September 1999).

> To those for whom the greatest threat to the future of the international order is the use of force in the absence of a Security Council mandate, one might ask – not in the context of Kosovo – but in the context of Rwanda: If, in those dark days and hours leading up to the genocide, a coalition of States had been prepared to act in defense of the Tutsi population, but did not receive prompt Council authorization, should such a coalition have stood aside and allowed the horror to unfold?

Id. In a more immediate response to Annan's September 20 speech, Chinese Foreign Minister Tang Jiaxuan took issue with the idea of humanitarian intervention, denouncing

intervention" and "human rights over sovereignty" that [have] cropped up recently [and] set human rights against sovereignty."[186] While acknowledging that the world had changed profoundly since the end of the Cold War, Qin argued that "the principles of respect for State sovereignty and noninterference in internal affairs are far from outdated" and that any willful weakening of these principles "will undoubtedly have dangerous consequences in international relations."[187]

Reflecting on both China's history as a victim of foreign intervention and its status as a voice of the developing world, Qin also warned of the risk of such a doctrine being cynically manipulated by powerful, intervening states:

> In today's world only a very small number of rich, large and strong countries have both the ambition and the power to interfere in other countries' affairs. For small and weak countries, sovereignty is their last defence against foreign bullying. If this defence were to be broken, acts of the rich bullying the poor and the strong bullying the weak would be given the green light, and there would be no peace in the world.[188]

Qin also criticized the application of "different standards in different regions" when it came to the exercise of humanitarian intervention, and he suggested that such double standards betrayed the ulterior motives of Western states in promoting a right of humanitarian intervention.[189]

---

again the illegality of NATO's intervention in Kosovo, calling it an "ominous precedent," and criticizing the increased tendency toward interventionism it represented. U.N. GAOR, 54th Sess., 8th plen. mtg. at p. 16, U.N. Doc. A/54/PV.8 (22 September 1999). Noting that a "cold war mentality still lingers on" and that "[h]egemonism and power politics have manifested themselves in new expressions," Tang warned that "if the notion of "might is right" should prevail, a new gunboat policy would wreak havoc, [and] the sovereignty and independence by virtue of which some small and weak countries protect themselves would be jeopardized." Id. at pp. 15–16. Tang also stated:

> The history of China and other developing countries shows the sovereignty of a country is the prerequisite for and the basis of the human rights that the people of that country can enjoy. When the sovereignty of a country is put in jeopardy, its human rights can hardly be protected effectively. Sovereign equality, mutual respect for State sovereignty and non-interference in the internal affairs of others are the basic principles governing international relations today. In spite of the major changes in the post-Cold-War international situation, these principles are by no means out of date.

Id. at p. 16.

186 U.N. GAOR, 54th Sess., 27th plen. mtg., *supra* note 184, at p. 12.

187 Id.

188 Id.

189 Id. ("Maybe under the fig-leaf of humanitarian intervention some are actually seeking to promote their own strategic, military or economic interests. This, if true, is what the people of the world should watch out for.").

Calling humanitarian intervention a "new concept" (as opposed to a norm or principle of international law), Qin stated China's position that any further development of this concept "should be based on the Charter of the United Nations and basic norms governing international relations"—an implicit reference to respect for sovereignty and noninterference in internal affairs.[190] Similarly, China stated that unilateral interventions and enforcement actions that bypassed the Security Council unequivocally violated the UN Charter and international law.[191]

It was in this post-Kosovo climate that the Canadian-sponsored International Commission on Intervention and State Sovereignty (ICISS) launched a series of roundtables worldwide to build consensus on the contours of a right of humanitarian intervention and make the doctrine less susceptible to abuse by grounding it in a normative legal framework.[192] One such roundtable was held on June 14, 2001, at the China Institute of International Studies in Beijing, and the rapporteur's report from that meeting demonstrates a strong current of Chinese opposition.[193] Chinese interlocutors argued that humanitarian intervention was "a total fallacy" that lacked any legal basis under international law, particularly in light of the UN Charter's restrictions on the use of force.[194] Additionally, Chinese participants rejected the notion of "human rights transcending sovereignty" as a Western philosophy that represented "highly politicized thinking with ulterior political motives" and failed to take into account

---

190 Id.

191 Id. This point was also made by Chinese President Jiang Zemin in a special address to the Security Council in September 2000. *See* U.S. SCOR, 55th Sess., 4194th mtg. at p. 7, U.N. Doc. S/PV.4194 (7 September 2000). *See also* Ministry of Foreign Affairs of China, "Joint Statement Signed by the Chinese and Russian Heads of States," 16 July 2001, http://www.fmprc.gov.cn/eng/wjdt/2649/t15772.htm, accessed 28 October 2012 (declaring that "China and Russia will make joint efforts to strengthen the leading role of the United Nations and its Security Council in international affairs and oppose any attempt to undermine the basic norms of international relations by resorting to such arguments as "humanitarian intervention" and "limited sovereignty" and so on").

192 Evans, *supra* note 182, at pp. 706–712.

193 International Commission on Intervention and State Sovereignty [ICISS], *The Responsibility to Protect: Research, Bibliography, Background* (Ottawa, Canada: International Development Research Centre, 2001), pp. 391–394. For a list of Chinese participants present at the roundtable, see id. at 391. As one participant in the ICISS initiative noted, "The Chinese government had opposed The Responsibility to Protect throughout the ICISS process and insisted that all questions relating to the use of force defer to the Security Council." Alex J. Bellamy, "Whither the Responsibility to Protect? Humanitarian Intervention and the 2005 World Summit," *Ethics and International Affairs*, vol. 20, no. 2, Summer 2006, pp. 143–169, at p. 151.

194 ICISS, *supra* note 193, at p. 392.

non-Western views.[195] Chinese participants further noted that, in practice, Western powers had employed double standards on international human rights issues; to some, it was "clear that certain Western powers [had] played with noble principles to serve their own hegemonic interests."[196] They also objected to humanitarian intervention on a more pragmatic level, arguing that it had proved "counterproductive to halting massive killings in targeted countries, for it can facilitate interventionists exploiting the legality for their own purposes and encourage warring parties inside a country to take an irresponsible stand in mediation processes."[197]

Although Chinese participants rejected humanitarian intervention, they strongly endorsed an alternative concept of "humanitarian assistance," and they argued for a clear distinction between the two in order to keep the latter "free of ulterior political motives."[198] They also suggested that humanitarian assistance be defined by respect for state sovereignty, including the prerequisite of obtaining all parties' consent prior to undertaking humanitarian actions; the requirement of Security Council authorization in all cases involving military personnel; impartiality on the part of any third parties involved; and application of the principle of nonuse of force, except in self-defense in the course of peacekeeping operations.[199]

In December 2001, six months after the Beijing roundtable, the ICISS published *The Responsibility to Protect*, a report promoting the idea of "sovereignty as responsibility" and concluding that when a population is suffering serious harm, and the state in question is unwilling or unable to avert it or is itself the perpetrator, the principle of nonintervention yields to an international "responsibility to protect."[200] The ICISS report divided the R2P into three component responsibilities: the responsibility to prevent, the responsibility to respond, and the responsibility to rebuild.[201] Furthermore, the report laid out six criteria for military intervention for humanitarian purposes: just cause, right intention, last resort, legitimate authority, proportional means, and a reasonable prospect of success.[202]

---

195 Id.

196 Id.

197 Id.

198 Id. at p. 393.

199 Id. at pp. 393–394. The Chinese interlocutors also proposed, *inter alia*, that the international community reaffirm the principles of respect for state sovereignty and noninterference in internal affairs as stated in Article 3(4) of the UN Charter. Id.

200 ICISS, *The Responsibility to Protect: Report* (Ottawa, Canada: International Development Research Centre, 2001), p. 69.

201 Id. at p. xi.

202 Id. at pp. xii–xiii.

Despite the goal of ICISS of achieving consensus on a new normative framework for humanitarian intervention, the report's conclusions still appeared to conflict with China's long-standing commitment to noninterference in other states' internal affairs, and the repackaging of humanitarian intervention as the R2P seemed to do little to address China's core concerns. However, in a nod to China's position, the ICISS report concluded that the Security Council was the most appropriate body to authorize such interventions.[203] Moreover, the report suggested that the international community should focus on making the Security Council work better than it had in the past.[204] Just as importantly, the report did not argue for a unilateral right of humanitarian intervention, but rather discussed the R2P solely within the framework of the United Nations.[205]

Although aspirational at the time of its promulgation in 2001, the R2P gained traction in subsequent years. In December 2004, the UN Secretary-General's sixteen-member High-Level Panel on Threats, Challenges and Change (HLP) endorsed

> the emerging norm that there is a collective international responsibility to protect, exercisable by the Security Council authorizing military intervention as a last resort, in the event of genocide and other large-scale killing, ethnic cleansing or serious violations of international humanitarian law which sovereign Governments have proved powerless or unwilling to prevent.[206]

The HLP's report further stated that "[t]he principle of nonintervention in internal affairs cannot be used to protect genocidal acts or other atrocities, such as large-scale violations of international humanitarian law or large-scale ethnic cleansing, which can properly be considered a threat to international security and as such provoke action by the Security Council."[207] It is important to note that the HLP conceived of the R2P as "exercisable by

203 Id. at p. 49.
204 Id.
205 Id. at pp. xii–xiii.
206 High-Level Panel on Threats, Challenges and Change, "A More Secure World: Our Shared Responsibility," ¶ 203, U.N. Doc. A/59/565 (2 December 2004) (emphasis omitted).

> [The R2P] lies, first and foremost, with each individual State .... [I]f national authorities are unable or unwilling to protect their citizens, then the responsibility shifts to the international community to use diplomatic, humanitarian and other methods to help protect the human rights and well-being of civilian populations.

U.N. Secretary-General, "In Larger Freedom: Towards Development, Security and Human Rights for All," ¶ 135, U.N. Doc. A/59/2005 (21 March 2005).
207 High-Level Panel on Threats, Challenges and Change, *supra* note 206, ¶ 200.

the Security Council," thus envisioning humanitarian intervention as falling within an existing exception to the prohibition on the use of force—actions authorized by the Council—rather than as a new exception.[208] Notably, Qian Qichen, China's former Foreign Minister, was a member of the HLP.[209] Although Qian's support for the HLP's recommendations reportedly was "passive" at the time, it later would prove important in securing Beijing's support for the endorsement of the R2P.[210]

In January 2005, Chinese Ambassador Wang Guangya applauded the HLP's conclusion that "individual sovereign States" continue to be "the front-line actors in dealing with all the threats we face."[211] Most significantly, Wang agreed that "[s]overeign states have the *primary* responsibility of protecting their own citizens," apparently conceding that Beijing accepted that the international community has a residual responsibility to protect civilian populations if a sovereign state fails to fulfill its primary responsibility.[212] Wang also made clear China's position that any residual responsibility, if it existed, lay with the Security Council.[213] While stating that the United Nations must place a "particular emphasis on timely assistance in serious humanitarian crises," Wang cautioned:

---

[208] Kofi Annan approved of this formulation in his 2005 report, "In Larger Freedom." *See* U.N. Secretary-General, *supra* note 206, ¶ 126 ("The task is not to find alternatives to the Security Council as a source of authority but to make it work better."); *see also* id. ¶ 135 (noting that when a national authority fails in its duty to protect its population—and when international "diplomatic, humanitarian and other methods" likewise fail—"the Security Council may out of necessity decide to take action under the Charter of the United Nations, including enforcement action, if so required").

[209] High-Level Panel on Threats, Challenges and Change, *supra* note 206, Annex II.

[210] Evans, *supra* note 183, at p. 45 (stating that "without [Qian Qichen's] immense prestige back in Beijing, it is difficult to believe that, given the traditional strength of its concerns about nonintervention, China would have been quite as relaxed on this issue as it proved to be at the World Summit").

[211] "Statement by Ambassador Wang Guangya on the Report of the High-Level Panel," 27 January 2005, http://www.china-un.org/eng/zghlhg/zzhgg/t181639.htm, accessed 28 October 2012.

[212] Id. (emphasis added). The speeches of China's representative Zhang Yishan during Security Council debates in 2005 on the protection of civilians in armed conflict also reflect China's acceptance of this tenet of the R2P. *See* U.N. SCOR, 60th Sess., 5319th mtg. at p. 29, U.N. Doc. S/PV.5319 (9 December 2005) ("Individual states have the primary responsibility to protect their own citizens."); U.N. SCOR, 60th Sess., 5209th mtg. at p. 16, U.N. Doc. S/PV.5209 (21 June 2005) ("[T]he primary responsibility for protecting civilians lies with the Governments concerned.").

[213] "Statement by Ambassador Wang Guangya," *supra* note 211 ("The purposes and principles of the UN Charter should continue to be safeguarded and the rights and responsibilities of sovereign States continue to be respected. We believe that this is an important guideline.").

> [I]t is inadvisable to make hasty judgment that the State concerned is unable or unwilling to protect its own citizens and rush to intervene. The basic principles of sovereign equality and non-interference in internal affairs of other States as stated in the Charter have to be strictly respected. The matter should be carefully judged and handled by the Security Council in view of the specific circumstances. In deciding on coercive actions, the Security Council should exercise particular caution and deal with situations on a case-by-case basis and not by any hard and fast rules.[214]

Thus, China signaled a growing willingness to accept the broad outlines of the R2P, albeit with strong caveats that any intervention must receive Security Council approval and that the Security Council should respond to humanitarian crises cautiously and on a case-by-case basis. The latter caveat indicated Beijing's preference that the Security Council's approach to humanitarian intervention should remain ad hoc and exceptional rather than become "normalized."

China proved reluctant to accept the further crystallization of the R2P into a formal international legal norm, and it likewise opposed the formulation and adoption of specific criteria for determining when, where, and how humanitarian intervention should take place.[215] In other words, to the extent that China countenanced humanitarian intervention, it sought to regulate humanitarian intervention in the realm of politics, rather than law, and to confine humanitarian intervention to a political forum that it could control through the exercise of its permanent veto power. Still, in perhaps the most significant signal of China's growing acceptance of the R2P, Beijing included a section entitled "The Responsibility to Protect" in its June 2005 position paper on UN reform.[216] In that paper, China stated

---

214 Id.

215 *See* Alex J. Bellamy, "Responsibility to Protect or Trojan Horse? The Crisis in Darfur and Humanitarian Intervention," *Ethics and International Affairs*, vol. 19, no. 2, September 2005, pp. 31–54, at p. 36 (noting that, in addition to China, the United States, the United Kingdom, France, and Russia also were reticent to formalize criteria for intervention under the rubric of the R2P); *see also* Jennifer M. Welsh, "Implementing the Responsibility to Protect: Where Expectations Meet Reality," *Ethics and International Affairs*, vol. 24, no. 4, Winter 2010, pp. 415–430, at p. 425 ("Russia and China, joined by three nonpermanent members (Algeria, the Philippines, and Brazil) reminded the Council [in 2006] that the [World Summit] Outcome Document had given the general assembly the mandate for continuing discussion of RtoP (a sure recipe for ensuring very slow movement on implementation)".); U.N. SCOR, 63d Sess., 5898th mtg. at p. 9, U.N. Doc. S/PV.5898 (27 May 2008) ("Many members are currently deeply concerned about the concept of the responsibility to protect, and the relevant discussions should therefore be pursued in the United Nations. The Security Council is in no position to interpret or expand the concept of the responsibility to protect at will, much less to abuse it.").

216 "Position Paper of the People's Republic of China on the United Nations Reforms," 7 June 2005, http://www.china-un.org/eng/xw/t199101.htm, accessed 28 October 2012; *see*

that "[e]ach state shoulders the primary responsibility to protect its own population," but it also explicitly acknowledged that "[w]hen a massive humanitarian crisis occurs, *it is the legitimate concern of the international community to ease and defuse the crisis*."[217] The position paper also stated that international responses to humanitarian crises "should strictly conform to the UN Charter" and should respect "the opinions of the country and the regional organization concerned."[218] The paper reiterated China's position that decisions to intervene should fall to the Security Council alone,[219] which was consistent with the evolving doctrine of the R2P.[220]

The R2P gained its first official recognition in the landmark 2005 World Summit Outcome document, a consensus document agreed upon by all 191 nations.[221] Significantly, the document stated that "[e]ach individual State has the responsibility to protect its populations from genocide, war crimes, ethnic cleansing and crimes against humanity."[222] However, the Outcome document made clear that the R2P was not a legal exception to the Security Council's primacy in matters of the use of force:

> In this context, we are prepared to take collective action, in a timely and decisive manner, *through the Security Council, in accordance with the Charter, including Chapter VII*, on a case-by-case basis and in cooperation with relevant regional organizations as appropriate, should peaceful means be

also James Traub, "The World According to China," *New York Times Magazine*, 3 September 2006, p. 27 (reporting that China's UN ambassador conceded that the R2P had become a matter of international law but also noted that "you have to decide how to apply this").

217 Position Paper, *supra* note 216 (emphasis added).

218 Id. This language has been echoed in statements by China's UN representatives. *See* U.N. SCOR, 61st Sess., 5577th mtg. at pp. 7–8, U.N. Doc. S/PV.5577 (4 December 2006) ("[I]n accordance with the Charter of the United Nations and international humanitarian law, the responsibility to protect civilians lies primarily with the Governments of the countries concerned."). China's representative also noted that the international community or other external parties "should not infringe upon the sovereignty and territorial integrity of the countries concerned, nor should they enforce intervention by circumventing the Governments of such countries." Id.; *see also* U.N. SCOR, 61st Sess., 5476th mtg. at p. 9, U.N. Doc. S/PV.5476 (28 June 2006) ("The primary responsibility to protect civilians lies, first, with the Governments concerned. The international community and other parties, while providing support and assistance, should not undermine the sovereignty and territorial integrity of the countries concerned."); U.N. SCOR, 60th Sess., 5319th mtg., *supra* note 212, at p. 30 (stating that all efforts to protect civilians in armed conflict "should not violate the principles enshrined in the Charter; nor should they infringe upon the sovereignty and territorial integrity of Member States").

219 Position Paper, *supra* note 216.

220 ICISS, *supra* note 200, at p. 49.

221 2005 World Summit Outcome, G.A. Res. 60/1, ¶ 139, U.N. Doc. A/RES/60/1 (16 September 2005).

222 Id. ¶ 138.

> inadequate and national authorities manifestly fail to protect their populations from genocide, war crimes, ethnic cleansing and crimes against humanity.[223]

Earlier in 2005, there had been indications that China might resist an endorsement of the R2P in the Outcome document.[224] Additionally, Chinese President Hu Jintao's speech at the September 2005 World Summit suggested a hard line on the R2P, when he argued that "we should all oppose acts of encroachment on other countries" sovereignty, forceful interference in a country's internal affairs, and willful use or threat of military force."[225] In the end, however, China acceded to the Outcome document's endorsement of the R2P, but not before Beijing's wariness about the concept influenced the document's drafting.[226] In December 2005, China reaffirmed its acceptance of the broad outlines of the R2P, but it referred to the R2P as a "concept" rather than an emerging norm.[227]

In a significant step, the Security Council, in April 2006, incorporated the R2P into Resolution 1674 by reaffirming paragraphs 138 and 139 of the Outcome document, which recognized the responsibility to protect populations from genocide, war crimes, ethnic cleansing, and crimes against

---

223 Id. ¶ 139 (emphasis added).

224 In response to an Outcome document draft in June 2005, Chinese Ambassador Wang Guangya indicated that "differences of views" continued to exist about the R2P, that "further consultations [were] necessary," and that "prudence [was] required for the statement on this question in the draft." "Statement by Ambassador Wang Guangya at the Informal Meeting of the General Assembly on the Draft Outcome Document of the September Summit," 21 June 2005, http://www.fmprc.gov.cn/eng/wjdt/zyjh/t200845.htm, accessed 28 October 2012.

225 "Written Speech by H.E. Hu Jintao, President of the People's Republic of China, at the High-Level Plenary Meeting of the United Nations" 6oth Session," 14 September 2005, http://www.fmprc.gov.cn/eng/wjdt/zyjh/t213091.htm, accessed 28 October 2012.

226 *See* Bellamy, *supra* note 193, at p. 166 ("[T]he document's drafters separated the sections on the use of force and the responsibility to protect (they were conjoined in "In Larger Freedom") in order to reassure China and India."). Additionally, Bellamy writes,

> Between "In Larger Freedom" and the first drafts of the outcome document, the commitment to criteria was reduced to a commitment to continue discussing criteria. Then, in the final version, even this commitment was removed. To all intents and purposes, this appears to have been a major diplomatic victory for the anti-interventionists (especially China and Russia), who had opposed criteria from the outset, believing that they opened up the possibility for abuse.

Id.

227 U.N. SCOR, 60th Sess., 5319th mtg., *supra* note 212, at p. 30 ("The consensus opinion of the international community, as well as its justifiable demand, is that swift steps must be taken to mitigate and put an end to large-scale humanitarian crises and gross violations of human rights.").

humanity.[228] Resolution 1674 thereby committed the Security Council to protect civilians in armed conflict.[229] Although China supported Resolution 1674, it later asserted that the version of the R2P articulated in the resolution was "not the same as the simple concept of the responsibility to protect, about which many countries continue to have concerns."[230] This is a puzzling statement, although it could be interpreted as China's acceptance of the applicability of the R2P in situations of severe humanitarian need, but not in situations that fail to rise to that level.[231]

China, retreating somewhat from this lukewarm acceptance of the R2P, has since urged the Security Council to approach the concept "with caution" and argued that the Outcome document gave only a "very cautious" endorsement of the R2P.[232] Furthermore, China has stressed that it would be inappropriate "to expand, willfully interpret or even abuse this concept," which Resolution 1674 "only reaffirmed in principle ... without any further elaboration."[233] In this vein, Beijing has indicated a preference that further discussions of the R2P take place in the General Assembly, as provided for in the Outcome document, rather than in the Security Council.[234] However, despite this backpedaling, China's interaction with the developing concept of the R2P demonstrates its embrace of certain elements of the R2P, albeit with a continued reluctance to see the concept

---

228 S.C. Res. 1674, ¶ 4, U.N. Doc S/RES/1674 (28 April 2006).

229 Id. The R2P was also reaffirmed and incorporated into Resolution 1706 in August 2006. *See* S.C. Res. 1706, ¶¶ 1, 8–9, U.N. Doc. S/RES/1706 (31 August 2006) (enlarging the mandate for the UN Mission in Sudan (UNMIS) and urging member states to deploy assistance in order to secure the effective implementation of the Darfur Peace Agreement).

230 U.N. SCOR, 61st Sess., 5476th mtg., *supra* note 218, at p. 10.

231 China stated that the "simple" R2P concept was the one elaborated on in the Outcome document, and noted, "In-depth discussion of the issue should continue in the General Assembly so that differing opinions can be heard and doubts cleared up. In that role, the Security Council cannot and should not replace the General Assembly." Id. Again, China's insistence that any further discussion of the R2P should take place in the General Assembly rather than the Security Council likely reflected its opposition to the formulation and adoption of specific criteria for intervention under the concept's rubric. *See supra* note 236 and accompanying text.

232 U.N. SCOR, 61st Sess., 5577th mtg., *supra* note 218, at p. 8.

233 Id.

234 Id.; *see also* U.N. SCOR, 62d Sess., 5703d mtg. at p. 17, U.N. Doc. S/PV.5703 (22 June 2007).

> At present, there are still differing understandings and interpretations of this concept among Member States. The Security Council should therefore refrain from invoking the concept of the responsibility to protect. Still less should that concept be misused. The Security Council should respect and support the General Assembly in continuing to discuss the concept in order to reach broad consensus.

Id.

crystallize into a rule of international law.[235] As the case of Darfur suggests, this socialization process may have affected China's approach to humanitarian crises in practice.

Darfur

No event has focused as much attention on Chinese attitudes toward humanitarian intervention as the crisis in Darfur, in western Sudan. Darfur presents an interesting case for the analysis of China's evolving position on humanitarian intervention because it demonstrates elements of both flexibility and intransigence in China's position. Although China insisted that any military intervention in Darfur receive Khartoum's consent, it also demonstrated a greater willingness to use its influence over the Sudanese government to secure that consent. In doing so, China showed a softening of its stance on noninterference, while keeping intact its insistence on host state consent. Although it is too soon to determine whether this reluctant activism represents a shift in China's posture on humanitarian intervention, the case nonetheless demonstrates Beijing's willingness to take a less ideological and more pragmatic approach to the resolution of humanitarian crises.

In early 2003, rising tensions in the Darfur region of western Sudan erupted in armed clashes between Sudanese government forces and rebel groups.[236] The conflict spread in the following year, as government-allied Arab Janjaweed militias raided Darfurian villages and refugee camps in a campaign of village burning, rape, and civilian massacres.[237] By December 2003, conditions had deteriorated so drastically that UN Under-Secretary-General for Humanitarian Affairs and Emergency Relief Jan Egeland declared Darfur "one of the worst humanitarian crises in the world."[238]

---

[235] For one of the PRC's more recent statements related to the R2P, see U.N. SCOR, 64th Sess., 6066th mtg. at p. 7, U.N. Doc. S/PV.6066 (14 January 2009).

> Governments bear the primary responsibility for protecting their civilians. While the international community and external forces can provide constructive support, they must follow the provisions of the Charter, fully respecting the wishes and refraining from undermining the sovereignty and territorial integrity of the countries concerned, and even more so from forceful intervention.

Id.

[236] *See generally* Samantha Power, "Dying in Darfur: Can the Ethnic Cleansing in Sudan Be Stopped?", *New Yorker*, 30 August 2004, pp. 56–73 (discussing the violence in Darfur).

[237] Id.

[238] "Humanitarian and Security Situations in Western Sudan Reach New Lows, UN Agency Says," *UN News Service*, 5 December 2003.

In a Security Council briefing in April 2004, Egeland stated that the government-backed Janjaweed militias were engaging in a coordinated, "scorched-earth" campaign of ethnic cleansing against Darfur's black African population.[239]

In July 2004, the Security Council finally took action and adopted Resolution 1556, declaring the situation in Darfur a "threat to international peace and security and to stability in the region."[240] Adopted under the Council's Chapter VII powers, Resolution 1556 endorsed the African Union's (AU) proposed deployment of a protection force to Darfur and demanded that Khartoum disarm the Janjaweed militias and bring to justice those responsible for violations of human rights and international humanitarian law, as well as other atrocities.[241] Resolution 1556 also imposed an arms embargo on the Janjaweed and other militias operating in Darfur.[242] Finally, the Security Council stated its intention to consider further actions, including actions pursuant to Article 41 of the UN Charter, in the event of Khartoum's noncompliance.[243]

China abstained from the vote on Resolution 1556.[244] During the Security Council debate, China's representative, Zhang Yishan, argued that resolving the Darfur crisis required, *inter alia*, "a comprehensive agreement based on respect for the Sudan's sovereignty and territorial integrity."[245] Echoing Resolution 1556's language—as well as that of the R2P[246]—Zhang noted that "China believe[d] that the Government of the Sudan bears primary responsibility for resolving the Darfur situation and that the international community should make every effort to assist the Government of the Sudan."[247] Nonetheless, China abstained because of the resolution's mandatory provisions, citing concern that the measures

---

239 "Sudan: Envoy Warns of Ethnic Cleansing as Security Council Calls for Ceasefire," *UN News Service*, 2 April 2004.

240 S.C. Res. 1556, pmbl. para. 21, U.N. Doc. S/RES/1556 (30 July 2004).

241 Id. ¶ 6.

242 Id. ¶ 7.

243 Id. ¶ 6.

244 U.N. SCOR, 59th Sess., 5015th mtg. at p. 3, U.N. Doc. S/PV.5015 (30 July 2004).

245 Id. at p. 2. Chinese efforts appear to have secured a clause in Resolution 1556 affirming the Council's "commitment to the sovereignty, unity, territorial integrity, and independence of Sudan." S.C. Res. 1556, *supra* note 240, pmbl. para. 4.

246 *See* S.C. Res. 1556, *supra* note 240, pmbl. para. 9 ("*Recalling* in this regard that the Government of Sudan bears the primary responsibility to respect human rights while maintaining law and order ... ."); ICISS, *supra* note 200, at p. xi ("[T]he primary responsibility for the protection of its people lies with the state itself.").

247 U.N. SCOR, 59th Sess., 5015th mtg., *supra* note 244, at p. 2.

would undermine diplomatic efforts and only complicate the situation in Darfur.[248]

China repeated this mantra when it abstained from voting on subsequent Darfur-related resolutions, always objecting that pressure on Khartoum would undermine progress toward a political settlement and make matters worse.[249] Interestingly, however, China did not object that the pressure on Khartoum infringed Sudanese sovereignty, and its rhetoric reflected pragmatic concerns rather than ideological disagreement over the noninterference principle. For example, during one Security Council debate, China's representative argued that the international community "should increase humanitarian assistance to Darfur rather than create a situation that could lead to the closing of the door to relief and assistance."[250]

Still, sovereignty and noninterference norms were important to Beijing's position on Darfur. Although China strongly supported the deployment of the African Union Mission in Sudan (AMIS) as well as the expansion and strengthening of the AU peacekeeping force,[251] the AMIS deployed to Darfur with Khartoum's consent.[252] In a Security Council meeting a day

---

248 Id.

249 *See* U.N. SCOR, 61st Sess., 5423d mtg. at p. 3, U.N. Doc. S/PV.5423 (25 April 2006). In explaining China's abstention on Resolution 1672, which placed travel restrictions and financial sanctions on individuals involved in the Darfur conflict, China's representative said:

> If, as a result of the Security Council's sanctions resolution, any party to the Abuja talks has second thoughts about signing such a peace accord, the conflict in the Darfur region will inevitably be prolonged or even intensify. The Security Council would have to assume responsibility for such an eventuality.

Id. China also abstained on Resolution 1591, which imposed further travel and financial asset sanctions. U.N. SCOR, 60th Sess., 5153d mtg. at p. 5, U.N. Doc. S/PV.5153 (29 March 2005) ("[J]ust maintaining pressure without regard for the complexity of the issue and the specific circumstances of the Darfur crisis could end up further complicating the situation and making it even more difficult to resolve."). Likewise, China abstained on Resolution 1564, which threatened sanctions if Khartoum declined to accept an expanded AU mission in Darfur and failed to end the violence. U.N. SCOR, 59th Sess., 5040th mtg. at pp. 4–5, U.N. Doc. S/PV.5040 (18 September 2004) ("It has been our consistent view that, instead of helping to solve complicated problems, sanctions may make them even more complicated… . [T]he Security Council and the international community should focus on encouraging the Sudanese Government to continue to cooperate, rather than doing the opposite.").

250 U.N. SCOR, 59th Sess., 5040th mtg., *supra* note 249, at p. 4.

251 *See* id. at p. 5 ("We support expanding the African Union's deployment in Darfur … .").

252 Paul D. Williams, "Military Responses to Mass Killing: The African Union Mission in Sudan," *International Peacekeeping*, vol. 13, no. 2, June 2006, pp. 168–183, at p. 176.

after the May 2006 signing of the Darfur Peace Agreement, China's Foreign Minister Li Zhaoxing stated that "the consent and cooperation of the Sudanese Government are prerequisites for the deployment of a United Nations operation."[253] Not once did China countenance the possibility of unilateral humanitarian intervention or even a UN peace enforcement operation.[254] Rather, Beijing sought to limit the mandate of any future UN mission to monitoring the implementation of a peace agreement upon the consent of the parties involved.[255] In explaining its May 2006 vote in favor of Resolution 1679, which endorsed the African Union's decision to transition to a UN peacekeeping force in Darfur as soon as possible,[256] China stated that despite the resolution's invocation of Chapter VII, deployment of a UN force to Darfur would nonetheless require "the agreement and cooperation of the Sudanese Government."[257] In a Security Council meeting in August 2006, China stated again that its support for a UN force in Darfur was contingent on Khartoum's consent.[258]

In August 2006, China's strict insistence on the Sudanese government's consent to any intervention in Darfur led it to abstain from voting on Resolution 1706.[259] Resolution 1706 expanded the size and mandate of the UN Mission in Sudan (UNMIS)—which, with Khartoum's consent, had already deployed in Southern Sudan to monitor a separate peace agreement there[260]—to include a deployment to Darfur to support both the implementation of the Darfur Peace Agreement of May 2006 and the N'djamena Ceasefire Agreement.[261] By threatening its veto, China

253 U.N. SCOR, 61st Sess., 5434th mtg. at p. 7, U.N. Doc. S/PV.5434 (9 May 2006).

254 See, e.g., U.N. SCOR, 61st Sess., 5439th mtg. at p. 3, U.N. Doc. S/PV.5439 (16 May 2006) ("[O]ur country's Minister for Foreign Affairs, Mr. Li Zhaoxing, laid out China's position at last week's Security Council meeting of foreign ministers. We believe that, if the United Nations is to deploy a peacekeeping operation in Darfur, the agreement and cooperation of the Sudanese Government must be obtained.").

255 U.N. SCOR, 60th Sess., 5153d mtg., *supra* note 249, at p. 5.

256 S.C. Res. 1679, ¶ 3, U.N. Doc. S/RES/1679 (16 May 2006).

257 U.N. SCOR, 61st Sess., 5439th mtg., *supra* note 254, at p. 3.

258 U.N. SCOR, 61st Sess., 5519th mtg. at p. 5, U.N. Doc. S/PV.5519 (31 August 2006) ("The transition of AMIS to a United Nations mission is a good and pragmatic approach. Such a transition can be possible and the mission can be deployed only when the consent of the Government of National Unity [of Sudan] is obtained.").

259 Id. at p. 2.

260 Security Council Resolution 1590 established UNMIS to monitor and support the implementation of the 2005 Comprehensive Peace Agreement that ended the civil war between north and south Sudan. S.C. Res. 1590, ¶ 1, U.N. Doc. S/RES/1590 (24 March 2005).

261 S.C. Res. 1706, *supra* note 229, ¶ 8. Additionally, Resolution 1706 authorized the use of "all necessary means" to protect UN personnel, humanitarian workers, and civilians under threat of physical violence. Id. ¶ 12.

reportedly managed to secure a clause in Resolution 1706 stating that the Security Council "*invite*[*d*] the consent of the Government of National Unity [the Sudanese government] for this deployment."[262] Nonetheless, that language proved insufficient to gain China's support, as did the Security Council's reaffirmation of its "strong commitment to the sovereignty, unity, independence, and territorial integrity of Sudan, which would be unaffected by transition to a United Nations operation in Darfur."[263] To China, that language failed to state with sufficient clarity that Khartoum's consent was a *sine qua non* for the deployment of a UN force. In particular, Beijing sought language that "required," rather than "invited," the Sudanese government's consent prior to authorizing a UN deployment.[264] In any case, Khartoum's consent was not forthcoming, rendering 1706 a resolution manqué.[265]

By late fall, the May 2006 Darfur peace deal was unraveling, and violence was escalating and spilling across the border into neighboring Chad.[266] Pressure was mounting on China to play a constructive role in the humanitarian crisis, and there were signs that Beijing was reevaluating its position.[267] First, during an emergency Security Council meeting in

---

[262] Id. ¶ 1 (emphasis added); *see also* Stephen Rademaker, "Unwitting Party to Genocide: The International Criminal Court Is Complicating Efforts to Save Darfur," *Washington Post*, 11 January 2007 (discussing how China's veto threat created the need to provide for the Sudanese government's consent before deploying UN peacekeepers).

[263] S.C. Res. 1706, *supra* note 229, pmbl. para. 3.

[264] U.N. SCOR, 61st Sess., 5519th mtg., *supra* note 258, at p. 5.

> However, we have consistently urged the sponsors to clearly include "with the consent of the Government of National Unity" in the text of the resolution, which is a fixed and standardized phrase utilized by the Council when deploying United Nations missions. We also urged the sponsors to carefully reconsider the timing of the vote. Regrettably, they failed to earnestly heed China's sincere efforts. Due to our principled reservations on the timing of the vote and on the text itself, China could not but abstain from the voting.

Id.

[265] *See* U.N. SCOR, 61st Sess., 5520th mtg. at p. 11, U.N. Doc. S/PV.5520 (11 September 2006) ("[W]e should continue to seek the consent and cooperation of the Sudanese Government regarding the deployment of United Nations peacekeeping troops."); Daniel B. Schneider, "U.N. Council Votes to Send Troops to Darfur; Sudan Objects," *New York Times*, 1 September 2006 (noting that following the adoption of Resolution 1706, China continued to insist that any UN deployment in Darfur be predicated on Sudan's consent and cooperation, and that no UN peacekeeping operation should be imposed).

[266] U.N. SCOR, 61st Sess., 5520th mtg., *supra* note 265, at p. 19 ("Because of those factions, violence has resumed, especially in the north, on the borders with Chad.").

[267] *See* Jim Yardley, "China Defends Sudan Policy and Criticizes Olympics Tie-In," *New York Times*, 8 March 2008 ("Calls for political leaders to boycott the Olympics have mostly gone unheeded, but the criticism has pushed Beijing to take a more active, and public, role in resolving the Darfur conflict."); see also "China Presses Sudan Over Darfur," *New York*

November 2006, China's representative Wang Guangya reportedly played a critical role in gaining Khartoum's acceptance of a plan to deploy a hybrid UN–AU force in Darfur.[268] Then, in February 2007, President Hu Jintao visited Khartoum and reportedly pressured Sudanese President Omar Hassan al-Bashir to cooperate with the United Nations and permit the deployment of a UN peacekeeping force in Darfur.[269] In April, Chinese Assistant Foreign Minister Zhai Jun visited Khartoum for more talks with the Sudanese government, resulting in an agreement for the deployment of three thousand UN peacekeepers to Darfur, including a contingent of Chinese military engineers.[270] Additionally, under pressure from the international community and facing a campaign to designate the 2008 Beijing Olympics the "Genocide Olympics," China appointed a special envoy to Darfur, Liu Guijin, in May 2007.[271] Beijing's newly constructive role also reportedly was a key factor in obtaining President al-Bashir's June 2007 consent to the deployment of a hybrid UN–AU peacekeeping force in Darfur.[272]

On July 31, 2007, China joined a unanimous Security Council in adopting Resolution 1769, which authorized the deployment of that hybrid peacekeeping force, the UN Assistance Mission in Darfur (UNAMID).[273]

Times, 12 June 2008 (stating that China's diplomacy toward Sudan was "unusually strong, given China's close ties to Sudan, where it is a major investor in the oil industry and to whom it sells arms"); Lydia Polgreen, "China, in New Role, Uses Ties to Press Sudan on Troubled Darfur," *New York Times*, 23 February 2008 ("China has begun shifting its position on Darfur, stepping outside its diplomatic comfort zone to quietly push Sudan to accept the world's largest peacekeeping force, diplomats and analysts say.").

[268] Colum Lynch, "China Filling Void Left by West in U.N. Peacekeeping," *Washington Post*, 24 November 2006 (reporting that China's UN ambassador, Wang Guangya, "played a critical role in persuading the Sudanese government to allow an expanded U.N. presence in the Darfur region" and quoting U.S. special envoy to Sudan, Andrew Natsios, praising Wang's efforts to secure Khartoum's cooperation).

[269] Howard W. French, "Chinese Leader to Visit Sudan for Talks on Darfur Conflict," *New York Times*, 25 January 2007.

[270] Stephanie Kleine-Ahlbrandt and Andrew Small, "China's New Dictatorship Diplomacy: Is Beijing Parting with Pariahs?", *Foreign Affairs*, vol. 87, no. 1, January/February 2008, pp. 38–56, at p. 47.

[271] Id.

[272] "A Hopeful Wind of Change," *Economist*, 12 May 2007, p. 50; Helene Cooper, "Darfur Collides with Olympics, and China Yields," *New York Times*, 13 April 2007; Lydia Polgreen and Warren Hoge, "Sudan Relents on Peacekeepers in Darfur," *New York Times*, 13 June 2007; "Too Few, Too Late?", *Economist*, 21 April 2007, p. 52.

[273] U.N. SCOR, 62d Sess., 5727th mtg. at p. 10, U.N. Doc. S/PV.5727 (31 July 2007); *see also* U.N. SCOR, 62d Sess., 5784th mtg. at p. 15, U.N. Doc. S/PV.5784 (27 November 2007) ("It has been China's consistent position that a political settlement of the question of Darfur should be sought through dialogue and consultation on the basis of respect for the sovereignty and territorial integrity of the Sudan.").

In its statement before the Security Council, China made clear that Khartoum's consent was crucial to its vote.[274] Thus, on one level, the case of Darfur demonstrates that consent to intervention remains one of China's baselines, while on another level, it demonstrates a distinct shift in China's role in addressing humanitarian crises. After initially shielding Sudan from international pressure, China later proved willing to use its diplomatic leverage with Khartoum to secure Sudan's consent to the deployment of a UN peacekeeping force, a shift that signaled a moderation of China's position on the principle of noninterference in practice.

Libya

The UN-sanctioned, NATO-led intervention in Libya in 2011 appeared, at least initially, to be the culmination of the decade of effort by advocates of the R2P to coalesce support for the idea that the international community has a duty to intervene and protect civilians whose lives are threatened by the very government charged with the primary responsibility to protect them. In retrospect, it is a cautionary tale that highlights the limits of acceptance of the R2P, including by China. Indeed, in light of subsequent backlash, the intervention in Libya—which led to the ousting of Muammar el-Qaddafi—may come to be seen as the high point of the R2P, with the concept now in at least temporary, if not permanent, disfavor.

The case for intervention in Libya was clear-cut. As anti-government protests spread across Libya in February 2011, they were met with a violent crackdown by Libya's leader, Colonel Qaddafi, who infamously channeled rhetoric from the Rwandan genocide when he labeled anti-government protesters "cockroaches" and vowed to hunt them down and kill them "house by house."[275] In late February, the Security Council acted by unanimously adopting Resolution 1970 under Chapter VII of the Charter, which imposed an arms embargo on Libya and asset freezes and travel bans on Qaddafi and other top Libyan leaders and also referred the situation in Libya to the International Criminal Court (ICC), only the second time the Council had referred a member state to the world court.[276] Notably, it also explicitly invoked Libya's responsibility to protect its population, but

---

274 U.N. SCOR, 62d Sess., 5727th mtg., *supra* note 273, at p. 10 ("The consensus reached by the United Nations–African Union–Sudan tripartite dialogue mechanism on the hybrid operation is the political prerequisite on the basis of which this resolution is adopted.").

275 Kareem Fahim and David D. Kirkpatrick, "Qaddafi Orders Brutal Crackdown as Revolt Grows," *New York Times*, 23 February 2011.

276 S.C. Res. 1970, U.N. Doc. S/RES/1970 (26 February 2011).

omitted any reference to the international community's duty to protect Libyan civilians if Qaddafi's government failed to do so.[277]

China's support for Resolution 1970 was significant not only because of the ICC referral but also because the Security Council acted in response to political violence and violations of human rights in Libya that resembled, at least superficially, the PRC's Tiananmen Square crackdown in 1989.[278] In a terse, post-vote statement, Beijing's representative stated that its favorable vote was predicated on "the special situation in Libya at [the] time and the concerns and views of the Arab and African countries."[279]

In the subsequent weeks, the civil conflict between pro-Qaddafi government forces and anti-government rebels deepened, and the threat to civilians grew. On March 12, following calls by the anti-Qaddafi rebels and the international community, the Arab League asked the UN to impose a no-fly zone (NFZ) over Libya.[280] On March 17, 2011, the Security Council adopted Resolution 1973, a Chapter VII resolution that authorized—without the Qaddafi government's consent—the establishment of an NFZ over Libya and the use of "all necessary measures" to protect civilians from attack and enforce compliance with the NFZ.[281] The resolution expressly "exclud[ed] a foreign occupation force of any form on any part of Libyan territory."[282] It passed with ten countries in favor and five countries abstaining: Brazil, China, Germany, India, and Russia.[283]

Like Resolution 1970, Resolution 1973 expressly invoked Libya's responsibility to protect but was silent regarding the international community's corresponding duty.[284] In explaining its abstention, China said that it "support[ed] the Security Council's adoption of appropriate and necessary action to stabilize the situation in Libya ... and to halt acts of violence against civilians" and noted that it "attache[d] great importance" to the Arab League and African Union's support for the establishment of an NFZ.[285] Despite regional support, however, China stated without

---

[277] Id. pmbl. para. 9 ("[r]ecalling the Libyan authorities" responsibility to protect its populations").

[278] *See* Jason Dean, "China's Vote on Libya Signals Possible Shift," *Wall Street Journal*, 28 February 2011 (describing China's vote as "an unusual endorsement by Beijing of sanctions against another government over the treatment of its people").

[279] U.N. SCOR, 66th Sess., 6491st mtg. at p. 4, U.N. Doc. S/PV.6491 (26 February 2011).

[280] Ethan Bronner and David E. Sanger, "No-Flight Zone in Libya Backed by Arab League," *New York Times*, 13 March 2011.

[281] S.C. Res. 1973, ¶¶ 4, 8, U.N. Doc. S/RES/1973 (17 March 2011).

[282] Id. at pmbl., ¶ 4.

[283] U.N. SCOR, 66th Sess., 6498th mtg. at p. 3, U.N. Doc. S/PV.6498 (17 March 2011).

[284] S.C. Res. 1973, *supra* note 281, pmbl.

[285] U.N. SCOR, 66th Sess., 6498th mtg., *supra* note 283, at p. 10.

clarifying that it "ha[d] serious difficulty with parts of the resolution," noting its opposition to the use of force and its position that any UN action should abide by the Charter and international law and "respect the sovereignty, independence, unity and territorial integrity of Libya."[286]

On March 19, NATO countries began launching airstrikes against Libyan government forces.[287] Although at first largely limited to securing the NFZ and preventing rebel-controlled cities in eastern Libya from being overrun, the airstrikes later expanded to include attacks against pro-Qaddafi forces in close support of rebel offensives toward Tripoli. China quickly expressed unease and "regret" at the growing scope of the airstrikes, arguing that they exceeded the UN mandate and imperiled the lives of civilians.[288] At the same time, Chinese state-run media stridently opposed the intervention and argued that Resolution 1973 was a pretext for the West's "hegemonic intentions."[289] In subsequent Security Council discussions on the protection of civilians in armed conflicts, China repeatedly accused NATO of overstepping its mandate and reaffirmed the importance of observing the principles of "objectivity and neutrality" in protecting civilians, further stating that "[t]here must be no attempt at regime change or involvement in civil war by any party under the guise of protecting civilians."[290]

China's abstention on Resolution 1973—and therefore its acquiescence in a UN-backed military action against another government for humanitarian purposes—appeared to signal a liberalization of its position on

---

286 Id.

287 *See* Elisabeth Bumiller and David D. Kirkpatrick, "Allied Airstrikes Pound Libyan Ground Forces," *New York Times*, 23 March 2011; David D. Kirkpatrick, Steven Erlanger, and Elisabeth Bumiller, "Allies Open Air Assault on Qaddafi's Forces in Libya," *New York Times*, 19 March 2011.

288 Andrew Jacobs, "China Urges Quick End to Airstrikes in Libya," *New York Times*, 22 March 2011. *See also* "Chinese President Meets French Counterpart, Saying Force Is No Solution to Libyan Issue," *Xinhua*, 30 March 2011 (quoting Chinese President Hu Jintao as saying that "[i]f military action brings disaster to civilians and causes a humanitarian crisis, then it runs counter to the purpose of the UN resolution").

289 Jacobs, *supra* note 288 (quoting, *inter alia*, a People's Daily article as stating that "humanitarian intervention is only an excuse for military intervention into other countries" domestic affairs" and that intervening states "claim to be motivated by morality but in fact they are driven by narrow political and economic interests"). *See also* Chris Buckley, "China Seizes on Libya for Propaganda War Against West," *Reuters*, 23 March 2011 (describing criticism of the intervention in China's state-run press as a "propaganda campaign" aimed in part at dissuading copycat pro-democracy or anti-regime protests in China); Andrew Jacobs and Jonathan Ansfield, "In China, Security Muffles Calls for Change," *New York Times*, 28 February 2011.

290 U.N. SCOR, 66th Sess., 6531st mtg. at pp. 20–21, U.N. Doc. S/PV.6531 (10 May 2011); U.N. SCOR, 66th Sess., 6650th mtg. at pp. 24–25, U.N. Doc. S/PV.6650 (9 November 2011).

noninterference and humanitarian intervention.[291] Regional support for the intervention, particularly that of the Arab League and the African Union, was critical to China's favorable vote on Resolution 1970 and its abstention on Resolution 1973. Qaddafi's threat to massacre civilians and high-level defections of Libyan government officials may also have played a large role in China's votes.[292] But this apparent victory for collective action by the UN to prevent atrocities against civilians did not come without a cost, as the perceived incongruity between the extent of NATO's intervention and the scope of the UN mandate would color the views of China and other countries toward the idea of intervening in the next humanitarian crisis of the Arab Spring.

Syria

In mid-March 2011, just a month after the uprising in Libya began, large-scale public demonstrations against the regime of President Bashar al-Assad spread across Syria. Assad deployed government forces almost immediately, and the crackdown was brutal: military forces opened fire on demonstrators, and heavy tanks laid siege to towns where anti-government sentiment ran strong.[293]

With the shadow of NATO's recent intervention in Libya looming large and the scope of that action facing mounting criticism from China, Russia, and the Arab League, early efforts by Western states on the Security Council to issue a formal statement condemning the Syrian regime for its violence against civilians were stymied by Russia and China.[294] When the Council finally took up the issue in late April 2011, China said very little of substance and noted only that the matter was of "deep concern."[295] According to reports, both China and Russia resisted the issuance of even a press statement condemning Syria out of fear "that it could be a prelude to a similarly aggressive intervention" as the one that took place in Libya.[296]

291 *See* Brian Spegele, "China Takes New Tack in Libya Vote," *Wall Street Journal*, 20 March 2011 (noting that "China's rare acquiescence moved it further away from its long-standing foreign policy based on non-intervention").

292 *See* Colin Moynihan, "Libya's U.N. Diplomats Break with Qaddafi," *New York Times*, 21 February 2011.

293 Liz Sly, "Global Condemnation, But No Action, Against Bloody Syria Crackdown," *Washington Post*, 26 April 2011; Liz Sly, "Syrian Troops Open Fire on Protesters; Dozens Feared Dead," *Washington Post*, 3 June 2011.

294 Neil MacFarquhar, "Push in U.N. for Criticism of Syria Is Rejected," *New York Times*, 28 April 2011; Dan Bilefsky, "New Move to Condemn Syria in U.N.," *New York Times*, 9 June 2011.

295 U.N. SCOR, 66th Sess., 6524th mtg. at p. 7, U.N. Doc. S/PV.6524 (27 April 2011).

296 Bilefsky, *supra* note 294; Neil MacFarquhar, "Syria Tries to Defend Its Record to United Nations," *New York Times*, 27 April 2011 (reporting that China and Russia were "firmly opposed" to even "the mildest of statements criticizing Syria").

In light of these concerns, the Council's first statement on Syria, issued in August 2011, was relatively mild and did not single out the Assad regime for condemnation but rather "call[ed] for an immediate end to all violence and urge[d] all sides to act with utmost restraint, and to refrain from reprisals, including attacks against state institutions."[297]

However, with violence escalating and reports of massacres by Assad's forces becoming all too frequent, Western member states sought tougher action against Syria by introducing three draft Security Council resolutions. All three were vetoed by China and Russia, demonstrating the chasm between the West on the one hand and China and Russia on the other regarding how to address the humanitarian crisis. The first draft was introduced in October 2011 and "strongly condemned the continued grave and systematic human rights violations and the use of force against civilians by the Syrian authorities," demanding "an immediate end to all violence."[298] In order to satisfy Beijing and Moscow, it made no reference to sanctions.[299]

Despite its lack of teeth, and despite reaffirming the Council's "strong commitment to the sovereignty, independence, territorial integrity and national unity of Syria," the draft met Chinese and Russian vetoes.[300] This was China's first veto of a draft resolution condemning a government for its attacks against civilians—an especially significant event considering China's usual practice of abstaining on such votes. Notably, in its explanation of its vote, China made no mention of Libya and instead stuck to its traditional talking points regarding noninterference, respect for sovereignty, and its preference for resolving crises "through political dialogue."[301] Nonetheless, subsequent statements in the Security Council demonstrate that China's displeasure with the scope of NATO's intervention in Libya played a crucial role in its veto.[302] Russia's post-veto

297 "Statement by the President of the Security Council," U.N. Doc. S/PRST/2011/16 (3 August 2011).

298 France, Germany, Portugal and the United Kingdom of Great Britain and Northern Ireland: Draft Resolution, U.N. Doc. S/2011/612 (4 October 2011).

299 Id.; Colum Lynch, "Russia, China Veto Syria Resolution at the United Nations," *Washington Post*, 4 October 2011; Neil MacFarquhar, "U.N. Resolution on Syria Blocked by Russia and China," *New York Times*, 5 October 2011.

300 U.N. SCOR, 66th Sess., 6627th mtg. at p. 5, U.N. Doc. S/PV.6627 (4 October 2012). Brazil, India, Lebanon and South Africa abstained from the vote. Id. at p. 2.

301 Id. at p. 5.

302 *See* U.N. SCOR, 67th Sess., 6705th mtg. at p. 14, U.N. Doc. S/PV.6705 (19 January 2012) (stating that the international rule of law "does not allow for arbitrary distortions or extensive interpretations of the contents of resolutions, even less the option of action beyond the mandate provided in such resolutions"); U.N. SCOR, 67th Sess., 6710th mtg. at p. 25, U.N. Doc. S/PV.6710 (31 January 2012) (stating that China "firmly oppose[d] the use of force to

statement was more direct and forceful, deploring the fact that its "proposals for wording on the non-acceptability of foreign military intervention were not taken into account" and noting that this could "only put us on our guard" in light of "the Libyan experience."[303] Pressure from Russia is reported to have been a significant influence on China's vote.[304]

The second draft resolution was introduced in early February 2012 on the heels of the Arab League's promulgation of a plan to address the spiraling violence in Syria. This time, China and Russia exercised their vetoes against 13 votes in favor of the resolution.[305] Once again, the draft reaffirmed the Council's "strong commitment to the sovereignty, independence, unity and territorial integrity of Syria" and emphasized "its intention to resolve the current political crisis in Syria peacefully."[306] In an attempt to ameliorate Chinese and Russian concerns that the resolution could be used to justify intervention in Syria, it also expressly stated "that nothing in this resolution authorizes measures under Article 42 of the Charter," also dropping language calling for a voluntary arms embargo and sanctions.[307] Moreover, it sought to mute criticism that the Council was taking sides by condemning all violence, regardless of the perpetrators.[308]

---

resolve the Syrian issue, as well as practices, such as forcibly pushing for regime change, that violate the purposes and principles of the United Nations Charter and the basic norms that govern international relations").

303 U.N. SCOR, 66th Sess., 6627th mtg. at p. 4, U.N. Doc. S/PV.6627 (4 October 2012).

304 *See* Neil MacFarquhar, "With Rare Double U.N. Veto on Syria, Russia and China Try to Shield Friend," *New York Times*, 6 October 2011.

305 Bahrain, Colombia, Egypt, France, Germany, Jordan, Kuwait, Libya, Morocco, Oman, Portugal, Qatar, Saudi Arabia, Togo, Tunisia, Turkey, United Arab Emirates, United Kingdom of Great Britain and Northern Ireland and United States of America: Draft Resolution, U.N. Doc. S/2012/77 (4 February 2012). See Anthony Shadid, "Fear of Civil War Mounts in Syria as Crisis Deepens," *New York Times*, 15 January 2012.

306 Bahrain, Colombia, Egypt, France, Germany, Jordan, Kuwait, Libya, Morocco, Oman, Portugal, Qatar, Saudi Arabia, Togo, Tunisia, Turkey, United Arab Emirates, United Kingdom of Great Britain and Northern Ireland and United States of America: Draft Resolution, U.N. Doc. S/2012/77 (4 February 2012).

307 Neil MacFarquhar, "U.N. Tentatively Backs a Plan for Syria," *New York Times*, 3 February 2012. The draft also stated that the Council "[f]ully supports" the Arab League's proposal for a political transition, having removed an explicit reference to the elements of that proposal from an earlier draft due to Russian opposition and further amended it to say that the process would be "Syrian-led." Neil MacFarquhar, "U.N. Tentatively Backs a Plan for Syria," *New York Times*, 3 February 2012.

308 Colum Lynch and Alice Fordham, "Russia, China Veto U.N. Resolution on Syria," *Washington Post*, 4 February 2012 (stating that the draft resolution had been "significantly watered down" to win China's and Russia's support).

Still, the draft met the double veto, despite indications in the lead-up to the vote that China and Russia might support the draft resolution.[309] As in October, China's remarks were relatively subdued, with its rhetoric very similar to that used when abstaining from votes on earlier intervention-related Security Council resolutions.[310] However, as with the October 2011 vote, subsequent statements indicated that China sought to avoid a repeat of Libya, where a Chapter VII resolution predicated on the protection of civilians authorized an intervention that effectively led to regime change.[311] Russian pressure to veto again appeared to be a significant factor in China's vote.[312] In its statement, Russia more forcefully inveighed against supporters of the draft, asserting that they had "undermined any possibility of a political settlement, calling for regime change, encouraging the opposition towards power, indulging in provocation and nurturing the armed struggle."[313]

---

[309] Id.; Neil MacFarquhar, "At U.N., Pressure Is on Russia for Refusal to Condemn Syria," *New York Times*, 1 February 2012.

[310] U.N. SCOR, 67th Sess., 6711th mtg. at p. 9, U.N. Doc. S/PV.6711 (4 February 2012) (cautioning that "the sovereignty, independence and territorial integrity of Syria should be fully respected" and stating that the Security Council's actions "should comply with the purposes and principles of the Charter of the United Nations").

[311] *See* Keith B. Richburg, "'Trust Deficit' Cited by China," *Washington Post*, 9 February 2012 (reporting that China's vice foreign minister in charge of U.S. affairs stated in no uncertain terms that it, the veto, reflected Beijing's concerns that the Western countries might use a Council resolution to justify regime change and citing China's "principled position" that "in international relations, one should not wantonly resort to the use of force for purposes of regime change"). *See also* U.N. GAOR, 66th Sess., 95th plen. mtg. at p. 19, U.N. Doc. A/66/PV.95 (13 February 2012) (stating that "countries should refrain from resort to use or threat of force" and that they should not "push [for] regime change"); U.N. SCOR, 67th Sess., 6790th mtg. at p. 28, U.N. Doc. S/PV.6790 (25 June 2012) (emphasizing that countries should not "arbitrarily interpret" Council resolutions and that "no actions overstepping Council mandates should be allowed," stating that military intervention "often proves counterproductive," and criticizing the "practice of selectivity and double standards" in intervening); U.N. SCOR, 67th Sess., 6734th mtg. at p. 19, U.N. Doc. S/PV.6734 (12 March 2012) ("China is against any attempt by external forces to engage in military intervention or push for regime change. Sanctions or the threat thereof are not conducive to a proper solution to these problems. ... Security Council resolutions must be strictly and comprehensively implemented. No party is to interpret them in any way it wants, let alone take action that exceeds Council mandates. ... China is against any interference in internal affairs in the name of humanitarianism. ... No external parties should engage in military intervention in Syria or push for regime change.").

[312] *See* U.N. SCOR, 67th Sess., 6711th mtg. at p. 10, U.N. Doc. S/PV.6711 (4 February 2012) (noting that China had supported amendments proposed by Russia and stating that "[i]t is regrettable that these reasonable concerns were not taken into account" given that the Council was "seriously divided over the issue").

[313] Id. at p. 9. Russia was also reportedly upset that draft resolution unrealistically demanded that Syrian forces withdraw to their barracks. Neil MacFarquhar, "Russia and China Block U.N. Action on Crisis in Syria," *New York Times*, 5 February 2012.

With violence continuing to escalate in Syria,[314] the Security Council issued a statement in March unanimously endorsing the peace plan put forward by the joint UN and Arab League envoy, Kofi Annan. In order to secure unanimity, there was no condemnation of the Syrian Government, no specific timetable for political transition, and only a very weak threat of future action if Syria failed to comply with the plan.[315] China (and Russia) also voted in favor of Security Council Resolutions 2042 and 2043, which called for the implementation of Annan's six-point proposal to end the violence, authorized an advance team of 30 observers, and established a UN Supervision Mission in Syria (UNSMIS) of up to 300 observers.[316] Neither resolution, however, included sanctions if Syria failed to implement Annan's plan.[317] China and Russia also supported a unanimous Security Council statement in late May 2012 that condemned the killing of civilians in Houla and demanding that Syrian government forces cease the use of heavy weapons in population centers and return to their barracks.[318]

China's support for UNSMIS and the May 2012 Council statement, however, did not prevent it for vetoing the next draft resolution on Syria that was put to a Council vote on July 19, even in the face of mounting civilian casualties.[319] The May 2012 draft resolution invoked Chapter VII, demanded the Syrian government's immediate implementation of Annan's peace plan, reiterated its demand that Syrian forces cease use of heavy weapons

[314] Neil MacFarquhar, "Syria Resumes Shelling of Homs," *New York Times*, 15 February 2012; Alan Cowell and Steven Lee Myers, "U.N. Panel Accuses Syrian Government of Crimes Against Humanity," *New York Times*, 24 February 2012; Ann Barnard, "Massacre Is Reported in Homs, Raising Pressure for Intervention in Syria," *New York Times*, 13 March 2012.

[315] Colum Lynch, "Syrian Peace Plan: U.N. Security Council Endorses Kofi Annan's Proposal," *Washington Post*, 21 March 2012.

[316] S.C. Res. 2042, U.N. Doc. S/RES/2042 (14 April 2012); S.C. Res. 2043, U.N. Doc. S/RES/2043 (21 April 2012). *See also* U.N. SCOR, 67th Sess., 6751st mtg. at p. 2, U.N. Doc. S/PV.6751 (14 April 2012); U.N. SCOR, 67th Sess., 6756th mtg. at p. 2, U.N. Doc. S/PV.6756 (21 April 2012).

[317] The threat of sanctions if Syria failed to comply with Annan's plan was removed from an earlier draft of Resolution 2043 in a compromise with Russia. Neil MacFarquhar, "Security Council Approves More Monitors of Cease-Fire in Syria," *New York Times*, 22 April 2012.

[318] "Security Council Press Statement on Attacks in Syria," U.N. Doc. SC/10658 (27 May 2012) (also reaffirming the Council's "strong commitment to the sovereignty, independence, unity and territorial integrity of Syria, and to the purposes and principles of the Charter").

[319] Rick Gladstone and Annie Lowrey, "Amid Reports of a New Massacre, Nations Seek to Step Up Pressure on Syria," *New York Times*, 7 June 2012; Neil MacFarquhar, "Cease-Fire in Syria Exposes the Heavy Price of Just Buying Time," *New York Times*, 29 April 2012. In addition to China's and Russia's veto, Pakistan and South Africa abstained.

against population centers and withdraw to their barracks, and decided that if Syria did not comply with the latter demand within ten days that the Council would immediately impose measures under Article 41 of the Charter (i.e., measures not involving the use of armed force).[320]

China's explanation of its third veto of a Syria resolution was its most forceful of the three. While explaining that Beijing was "deeply concerned" about the violence, China stated that the draft was "seriously flawed" and "unbalanced" because it "put pressure on only one party."[321] China also voiced its traditional refrain that "sovereign equality and non-interference in the internal affairs of other countries are the basic norms governing inter-State relations enshrined in the [UN] Charter."[322] However, China went further and bluntly criticized the sponsoring countries for "fail[ing] to show any political will or cooperativeness [and] adopting a rigid and arrogant approach to the reasonable basic concerns of other concerned countries and refusing to make revisions," characterizing the setting of preconditions to an extension of the mandate of UNSMIS as an "old trick" and noting that the sponsors "have shown only arrogance, not sincerity, during the consultations."[323]

While China's vetoes marked a significant departure from its prior practice of abstaining on Security Council resolutions addressing humanitarian crises, it is not clear that they necessarily signal a new, more assertive Chinese posture against intervention going forward. Because China exercised its veto in tandem with Russia, it had more than a modicum of cover in the face of strong condemnation by the international community.[324] It is one thing for China to veto with Russia taking the lead, as the rhetoric and media reports suggest was the case, but it is quite another for China to risk the opprobrium and international isolation that would attend taking such a position on its own.[325] The salience of the events of the Arab Spring

---

320 France, Germany, Portugal, United Kingdom of Great Britain and Northern Ireland and the United States of America: Draft Resolution, U.N. Doc. S/2012/538 (19 July 2012).

321 U.N. SCOR, 67th Sess., 6810th mtg. at p. 13, U.N. Doc. S/PV.6810 (18 July 2012).

322 Id.

323 Id. at p. 14.

324 Keith B. Richburg, "China Remains Hands-Off in Syria," *Washington Post*, 21 July 2012. *See also* Colum Lynch, "Russia, China Veto U.N. Sanctions Resolution on Syria," *Washington Post*, 19 July 2012; Rick Gladstone, "Friction at U.N. as Russia and China Veto Another Resolution on Syria Sanctions," *New York Times*, 20 July 2012; Andrew E. Kramer, "Russia Warns It Will Not Back Britain on Syria Sanctions," *New York Times*, 17 July 2012.

325 *See* Neil MacFarquhar, "All Eyes on Russia as Syria Cease-Fire Deadline Passes," *New York Times*, 12 April 2012 (reporting that "China is basically considered to be following Russia's lead"); Jane Perlez, "Putin Arrives in China, Seeking Stronger Ties," *New York Times*, 6 June 2012.

to China's vetoes also should not be underestimated, given that Beijing was nervous about a similar uprising erupting within its borders. China likely took a stronger position on noninterference in Syria as a result. Future humanitarian crises at other times or in other areas of the world may not be similarly freighted with domestic significance. Moreover, Libya had taught China a lesson about the perils of acquiescing in an intervention-related resolution and its limited ability to control implementation, particularly by Western countries who might have different views on the scope of language authorizing intervention to protect civilians.[326] On the other hand, deadlock in the Council risks creating an opening for Western states to take action independent of the United Nations, an outcome that China is certain to dislike as much if not more than a disagreement over the mandate of a Council-authorized intervention.

Analysis: Continuity and Change in Chinese Attitudes Toward Humanitarian Intervention

The story that emerges from the cases above is one of China grappling with a much-changed post-Cold War world—as well as its own rapidly evolving position within that world—as it sought to define and redefine its approach to core international legal principles, such as state sovereignty and nonintervention. From its founding in 1949 until the late 1980s, few events led the PRC to reexamine its largely anti-interventionist stance. It was only with the Security Council's adoption of a more activist agenda in the 1990s that China was forced to develop and articulate a more nuanced policy toward humanitarian intervention.[327] During this period, the contours of China's position grew clearer as Beijing confronted concrete humanitarian crises and decided whether to support, acquiesce in, or oppose outside intervention to ameliorate the suffering.

[326] *See* U.N. SCOR, 67th Sess., 6826th mtg. at p. 33, U.N. Doc. S/PV.6826 (30 August 2012) ("We should especially guard against and oppose any act of interference in Syria's internal affairs or military intervention under the pretext of humanitarianism. ... China opposes any externally imposed solution aimed at forcing a regime change."); U.N. GAOR, 66th Sess., 125th plen. mtg. at p. 5, U.N. Doc. A/66/PV.125 (3 August 2012) (stating that "China opposes any measures aimed at forcing regime change" and characterizing China's position as "a consistent and responsible attitude," further stating that it was safeguarding "the principles of sovereign equality and non-interference in the internal affairs of other States," as well as the interests of "small and medium-sized countries").

[327] Allen Carlson, "Helping to Keep the Peace (Albeit Reluctantly): China's Recent Stance on Sovereignty and Multilateral Intervention," *Pacific Affairs*, vol. 77, no. 1, Spring 2004, pp. 9–27, at pp. 11–13.

Two lines of interpretation have arisen regarding China's record on humanitarian intervention in the 1990s and 2000s. The first claims that China's position on sovereignty and intervention since the end of the Cold War has proved inflexible and unyielding.[328] Commentators adopting this view often reduce China's position on humanitarian intervention to labels such as "anti-interventionist" or "strict sovereignist."[329]

The second line of interpretation is typified by the scholarship of Allen Carlson, who credits China with a much-changed position on humanitarian intervention since the end of the Cold War and concludes that "many Chinese elites have now come to accept the general legitimacy of multilateral intervention to resolve particularly prominent humanitarian crises."[330] Indeed, Carlson argues that even in the immediate aftermath of NATO's intervention in Kosovo, "Chinese policy circles ... basically accepted the legitimacy of human rights and humanitarian intervention."[331] It is important to note that Carlson's analysis relies heavily on the work of Chinese foreign policy analysts and scholars rather than on official government statements, and his conclusion relates to the former group, not the latter.[332] In contrast, this chapter focuses on China's official statements and acts in order to discern patterns of state practice and *opinio juris*. Although international law recognizes the work of eminent publicists as evidence of emerging legal norms,[333] such scholarship

328 See, e.g., Olivier Corten, "Human Rights and Collective Security: Is There an Emerging Right of Humanitarian Intervention?", in *Human Rights, Intervention, and the Use of Force*, *supra* note 183, pp. 87–138, at pp. 133–134 ("Some, like China, stick to an extremely restrictive interpretation [of sovereignty and noninterference], according to which even dramatic humanitarian situations in a civil war context cannot be termed a threat to peace within the meaning of Chapter VII of the Charter."); Feigenbaum, *supra* note 179, at p. 32 ("China's stance on sovereignty [during the 1990s] remained rigid in rhetoric and almost always inflexible in practice.").

329 Others take the view "that China is opposed to international intervention simply because, itself a gross violator of human rights, it wishes to perpetuate its authoritarian rule and, by defending national sovereignty, hopes to shield itself from international criticism." Jia Qingguo, "China," in Watanabe Koji (ed.), *Humanitarian Intervention: The Evolving Asian Debate* (Washington, DC: Brookings Institution Press, 2003), pp. 19–32, at p. 20 ("[S]uch an understanding fails to capture the complexity of the problem.").

330 Carlson, *supra* note 327, at pp. 24–25.

331 Carlson, *supra* note 179, at p. 176.

332 See, e.g., Carlson, *supra* note 327, at pp. 11, 18 ("In other words, while the official Chinese discourse was designed to delegitimize such normative change in the international arena, some foreign policy elites were increasingly convinced of, and perhaps even internalized, these new norms."). For a similar but more extensive analysis by Carlson that relies predominantly on Chinese scholarship rather than official PRC statements, see Carlson, *supra* note 179, at pp 146–183.

333 Statute of the International Court of Justice, art. 38(1), June 26, 1945, 33 U.N.T.S. 993; *Restatement (Third) of Foreign Relations* § 103(2) (1986).

cannot be said to constitute *opinio juris* and is insufficient, particularly in light of Beijing's persistent statements to the contrary, to demonstrate China's acceptance of the legitimacy of a right of humanitarian intervention under international law.[334]

Although it would be wrong to conclude that China has recognized a right of humanitarian intervention, it would be equally mistaken to conclude that China's position on humanitarian intervention has demonstrated little or no flexibility since the end of the Cold War.[335] To be sure, China's official rhetoric has been laced with statements defending sovereignty and the principles of noninterference and nonintervention. Since the end of the Cold War, China has argued variously that humanitarian intervention causes more harm than good,[336] that it promotes the interests of the intervening state rather than the target state's population,[337] and that it violates the UN Charter and general principles of international law.[338]

Yet, China has also acquiesced in or actively supported a number of humanitarian interventions in the last two decades, including the Iraqi no-fly zones, Haiti, Somalia, Bosnia, East Timor, and Libya. Moreover, China has shown greater flexibility on the principle of noninterference through its willingness to use its political leverage with Khartoum to secure Sudan's consent to deploy a hybrid UN–AU peacekeeping force in Darfur.[339] Additionally, China has demonstrated a significant shift in its position on sovereignty by accepting the basic tenets of the R2P, even if Beijing has proved reluctant to allow the concept to harden into a norm of international law and has prevented its implementation by resisting the promulgation of criteria that would trigger application of the R2P.[340]

Because China has not always objected to humanitarian intervention in practice, it is useful to reexamine the conditions under which China is willing to countenance such interventions. The cases analyzed above

---

334 See Chesterman, *supra* note 3, at pp. 210–215 (discussing the 1999 NATO campaign in Kosovo, and noting China's opposition to such intervention as a violation of the UN Charter).

335 See, e.g., Carlson, *supra* note 327, at p. 10 ("[T]he conventional wisdom about Chinese intransigence on intervention (and sovereignty) is inaccurate. On the contrary, a subtle yet significant change in the Chinese stance on these issues has taken place during the last fifteen years.").

336 Gill and Reilly, *supra* note 27, at p. 46.

337 See, e.g., *supra* note 189 and accompanying text.

338 See, e.g., *supra* notes 145–147, 151 and accompanying text.

339 Lynch, *supra* note 268.

340 See *supra* notes 212, 216–217, 235 and accompanying text.

indicate two baseline conditions. First, China invariably insists that any international intervention in response to a humanitarian crisis is solely the province of the Security Council and that the legality of any intervention depends on authorization by the Security Council, after a determination that the situation constitutes a threat to international peace and security.[341] To some, this condition suggests Beijing's opposition to the idea of humanitarian intervention. However, this conclusion overlooks the distinction between a unilateral right and a multilateral right of humanitarian intervention. China's position is best understood as rejecting claims to a unilateral right of humanitarian intervention while, in practice, acquiescing to the exercise of a multilateral right through the Security Council. Here, one can see an evolution in China's willingness to accept the Security Council's expanded conception of what constitutes a threat to international peace and security under Article 39 of Chapter VII of the Charter. Moreover, China has shown a greater willingness to authorize the use of force for humanitarian objectives under the auspices of UN peacekeeping missions.

China's insistence on the Security Council's primacy in authorizing humanitarian interventions was most apparent in Beijing's harsh condemnation of the illegality of NATO's 1999 intervention in Kosovo.[342] This baseline condition continues to shape China's interaction with the concept of the R2P, particularly regarding the question of with whom the residual R2P resides after national authorities prove unwilling or unable to prevent or end mass atrocities or gross violations of human rights.[343] This insistence on the primacy of the Security Council in responding to

---

341 Studies of China's attitudes toward UN peacekeeping operations since 1989 identify the same two preconditions for Chinese support and participation: Security Council authorization and host state consent. *See* Gill and Reilly, *supra* note 27, at p. 44 (noting a possible third precondition, "the *a priori* achievement of a political settlement before sending troops"); *see also* Fravel, *supra* note 27, at pp. 1115–1119 (discussing China's bases for supporting or opposing various peacekeeping operations); Stefan Stähle, "China's Shifting Attitude Toward United Nations Peacekeeping Operations," *China Quarterly*, vol. 195, September 2008, pp. 631–655, at p. 645 ("China was obviously willing to condone [peacekeeping operations] as long as two conditions could be met: authorization by the [Security Council] and consent of the parties concerned."); Pang, *supra* note 27 (discussing Beijing policymakers" increasingly flexible view of principles of state sovereignty and noninterference in the context of UN peacekeeping operations).

342 *See supra* notes 144–147 and accompanying text.

343 China's apparent acquiescence in the unilateral establishment of the northern and southern no-fly zones in Iraq in 1992–93 is best viewed in the context of Beijing's efforts to break out of its post-Tiananmen diplomatic isolation and not as acceptance of a unilateral right to intervene in another state's affairs for humanitarian purposes. *See* Carlson, *supra* note 327, at p. 13.

humanitarian crises is unsurprising. China's adoption of such a position safeguards its interests by allowing it to retain control over any outcome by way of its status as a permanent, veto-wielding Security Council member, as in the case of Syria.[344] At the same time, however, China's position carries political risks. By insisting that the Security Council is the sole legitimate actor in this arena, China risks focusing attention on its position anytime it obstructs Security Council action, with attendant consequences for China's international image and reputation. Darfur is a case in point.[345]

China's second requirement for supporting humanitarian intervention is consent of the host state or the parties to the conflict. The prerequisite of consent essentially derives from China's insistence that respect for sovereignty and the principle of noninterference is fundamental to international law. China's expressions of this position can be found in its statements in the cases of Rwanda,[346] the enlargement of UNPROFOR's mandate in Bosnia,[347] NATO's intervention in Kosovo,[348] the intervention in East Timor,[349] Darfur,[350] and, most recently, Syria.

In spite of its strong rhetoric, China has demonstrated flexibility on its requirement of consent. For example, China voted in favor of enforcement resolutions that expanded UNPROFOR's mandate in Bosnia to include the establishment of "safe areas" and authorized the use of force to protect civilians in physical danger.[351] In these cases, the conflicting parties' consent to UNPROFOR's enlarged mandate was unclear, eroding, or nonexistent.[352] Additionally, the case of Somalia demonstrates an

---

344 U.N. Charter arts. 23, 27 (providing that all resolutions must be adopted by the concurring vote of all permanent members of the Security Council, which includes China, effectively giving the permanent members a veto over the adoption of any resolution).

345 *See supra* notes 267–273 and accompanying text.

346 *See supra* text accompanying note 103.

347 *See* U.N. SCOR, 47th Sess., 3114th mtg., *supra* note 117, at p. 12 (abstaining on Resolution 776, in part because "enlarging the mandate of UNPROFOR has not received the express consent of the parties concerned in Bosnia and Herzegovina"); *supra* text accompanying notes 126–127.

348 *See* U.N. SCOR, 53d Sess., 3937th mtg., *supra* note 144, at p. 14 (arguing that action should "be completed through full consultation and cooperation with the Federal Republic of Yugoslavia Serbian Government").

349 *See* U.N. SCOR, 54th Sess., 4043d mtg., *supra* note 172, at p. 13 ("The deployment of any peacekeeping force should be at the request of the Indonesian Government … .").

350 *See* U.N. SCOR, 61st Sess., 5434th mtg., *supra* note 253, at p. 7 ("[T]he consent and cooperation of the Sudanese Government are prerequisites for the deployment of a United Nations operation.").

351 *See supra* note 120 and accompanying text.

352 *See supra* notes 109–112 and accompanying text.

important exception to Beijing's requirement of consent, albeit a limited exception because host state consent proved impossible to secure due to Somalia's lack of an effective, functioning government.[353]

In general, the cases examined above demonstrate that, except in narrow circumstances involving a failed state with no effective government, China is likely to continue to insist on host state consent to any humanitarian intervention. However, as indicated by Beijing's diplomacy on East Timor and Darfur, China may prove more willing in the future to use its economic and diplomatic leverage to secure host state consent to intervention, thereby blurring China's position on noninterference.[354]

China's two baselines for humanitarian intervention place it in direct opposition to those who claim a right of unilateral humanitarian intervention.[355] Indeed, Beijing's consistent position on these two preconditions to intervention discredits the argument that a "norm" of unilateral humanitarian intervention has emerged since the end of the Cold War. It also means that such a norm is unlikely to emerge any time soon, as China is likely to continue to be a persistent objector to any claim of such a unilateral right.

China's position does not place it in the minority regarding the status of humanitarian intervention under international law, although its position as a permanent member of the Security Council perhaps endows Beijing's views with greater visibility and weight than those of other objectors. If anything, China's opposition to claims of a right of unilateral intervention reflects the sentiment of much of the international community, especially the developing world.[356]

Moreover, China's position does not place it on the wrong side of the "evolving norm" of the R2P, the discussion of which has largely supplanted efforts to promote a right of humanitarian intervention since NATO's

353 Chesterman, *supra* note 3, at p. 142.

354 *See supra* notes 181, 266–272 and accompanying text.

355 *See supra* notes 136–138 and accompanying text.

356 For example, China was not alone in condemning the assertions of a unilateral right of humanitarian intervention at the turn of the century. In addition to China, the following states condemned claims of a unilateral right to humanitarian intervention in the wake of NATO's intervention in Kosovo: Algeria, Barbados, Belarus, Cyprus, Colombia, Costa Rica, Cuba, Egypt, Ecuador, India, Indonesia, Iraq, Jordan, Libya, Laos, Malaysia, Mexico, Mongolia, Namibia, North Korea, Norway, Peru, the Philippines, Qatar, Russia, Singapore, South Africa, Syria, Venezuela, and Vietnam. Corten, *supra* note 328, at p. 124. Additionally, other states did not condemn the idea of humanitarian intervention outright but rather insisted that any intervention should be authorized by the UN Security Council. These states included Brazil, Gambia, Iran, Jamaica, Liechtenstein, Mali, Moldova, Pakistan, Sierra Leone, South Korea, and Tunisia. Id. at 124–125.

intervention in Kosovo in 1999.[357] As noted above, Beijing has adopted some of the rhetoric of the R2P as well as its basic tenets, including the idea that the R2P resides primarily with national governments and secondarily with the international community.[358] This is a significant change in China's position, as Beijing formerly endorsed a more absolutist conception of sovereignty and resisted attempts to make sovereignty conditional on a state's internal situation.[359]

Additionally, China's view that the international community's residual responsibilities can be exercised only through the Security Council is reflected in the work of both the High-Level Panel[360] and the 2005 World Summit Outcome document.[361] This, of course, remains contested territory, and it remains unclear whether Security Council inaction opens the door to action by individual member states, as it might with respect to Syria. Moreover, there are signs that China is reticent to further engage with the concept of the R2P, and Beijing continues to resist efforts to flesh out clear criteria for when and how the Security Council should act if individual states fail to live up to their responsibilities.[362]

As the cases make clear, it is too simplistic to view China as opposed to any and all humanitarian intervention per se. Rather, China has opposed the emergence of a right to unilateral humanitarian intervention and instead has sought to channel any intervention through the Security Council after obtaining the target state's consent. Notably, as shown in this chapter, China has chosen not to block certain humanitarian interventions by the United Nations (with Syria the exception), and it has endorsed others. This pattern suggests that China's insistence on Security Council authorization is not merely an extension of its earlier advocacy of strict conceptions of sovereignty and nonintervention; it appears that Beijing also seeks to retain influence over when, where, and how such

---

357 *See* Bellamy, *supra* note 193, at p. 152 (noting divided opinion among states on the validity of the R2P); Gareth Evans, President, International Crisis Group and Co-Chair of the ICISS, "The Responsibility to Protect: Rethinking Humanitarian Intervention," Address to the American Society of International Law's Panel on "Rethinking Collective Action," 98th Annual Meeting, 1 April 2004, http://www.gevans.org/speeches/speech103.html, accessed 28 October 2012 (noting the ongoing debate on the R2P); *see also* Evans, *supra* note 182, at pp. 714–715 (discussing the process by which the R2P gained acceptance); *supra* Part V.A (providing a general overview of the R2P).

358 *See supra* notes 212, 216–217, 235 and accompanying text.

359 *See supra* notes 19–32 and accompanying text.

360 *See* High-Level Panel on Threats, Challenges and Change, *supra* note 206, ¶ 203.

361 *See* 2005 World Summit Outcome, *supra* note 221, ¶ 139.

362 *See supra* Part V.A.

interventions take place, which has allowed it, along with Russia, to block UN action on Syria. However, as noted above, China has shown greater flexibility on the principle of noninterference in practice, especially in Darfur.[363]

In order to understand the development of Chinese attitudes toward humanitarian intervention since the end of the Cold War, it is helpful to consider the determinants of China's position, which may help to predict future developments in its position. These determinants can be grouped into four categories: historical factors, ideological factors, domestic political factors, and international systemic factors.[364]

The first two categories of determinants are, to a large degree, related. First, China's position on sovereignty and intervention has been significantly shaped by its historical experience during its "century of humiliation"—the period from roughly 1839 to 1949 that was characterized by repeated invasions of foreign armies, bullying by imperialist states, and infringements on sovereignty through unequal treaties.[365] The PRC's adoption of a strict anti-interventionist stance upon its founding in 1949 reflected the sense that China could prevent a recurrence of past humiliations only through a strong defense of sovereignty.[366] One can observe the continuing salience of China's historical experience in the September 1999

---

363 U.N. SCOR, 59th Sess., 5040th mtg., *supra* note 249, at p. 4.

364 For a similar typology, see Jia, *supra* note 329, at p. 25 ("China's stance on international intervention is based on four factors: the nature of the existing international system; China's experience with the outside world in modern times; its international status; and its domestic politics.").

365 *See* Gill and Reilly, *supra* note 27, at p. 42.

> China's adherence to strict Westphalian norms of state sovereignty derives from its traumatic entry into international society during the tumultuous late imperial period, roughly extending from the first Opium War in 1839 to the fall of the last dynasty in 1912. From its earliest years in the 1920s, the Chinese Communist Party used its defense of China's sovereignty to buttress its nationalist credentials and advance its broader state-building project.

Id.; Carlson, *supra* note 327, at p. 11 ("[T]he shadow of the past loss of Chinese sovereignty during the "century of humiliation" caused elites to be particularly leery of humanitarian intervention and to weight their policy decisions and internal debates toward the defence of a conventional interpretation of sovereignty."); Jia, *supra* note 329, at pp. 26–27 ("If, under the existing international system, China asserts its national sovereignty, it is in part because of its historical experience in foreign relations in modern times that has made doing so imperative.").

366 Jia, *supra* note 329, at pp. 27–28.

General Assembly statement of Chinese Ambassador Tang Jiaxuan, in which he declared that the idea of humanitarian intervention is merely a pretext for power politics and warned that its embrace would entail the triumph of "might is right," ultimately leading to a new era of "gunboat diplomacy" that would allow strong countries to impose their will on the weak.[367] To a significant degree, the Chinese Communist Party incorporated this historical experience into its founding ideology, which was partially premised on nationalistic credentials gained by standing up to foreign intervention in the 1930s and 1940s.[368]

Second, an ideological mistrust of Western motivations—a legacy of historical experience as well as Communism's opposition to Western imperialism—continues to color Chinese attitudes toward humanitarian intervention, albeit to a lesser degree than in the past. One can observe the continuing salience of this ideology in Chinese claims that humanitarian intervention is a pretextual tool of imperialism and hegemony, cynically manipulated by self-interested great powers.[369]

Third, certain characteristics of China's domestic political system influence Beijing's position on humanitarian intervention. Michael Davis, for example, suggests that China's one-party, non-democratic political system "is fundamentally at odds, both in principle and practically, with the sovereignty deprecating features of a substantial humanitarian intervention regime."[370] According to this theory, as long as China remains non-democratic, it will continue to obstruct the development of a norm of humanitarian intervention and will resist any erosion of the principles of nonintervention and noninterference.[371] Domestic political reform, however, may increase China's engagement with the concept and make Beijing

---

[367] U.N. GAOR, 54th Sess., 8th plen. mtg. at p. 16, U.N. Doc. A/54/PV.8 (22 September 1999) ("The history of China and other developing countries shows the sovereignty of a country is the prerequisite for and the basis of the human rights that the people of that country can enjoy.").

[368] *See* Edward Friedman, *National Identity and Democratic Prospects in Socialist China* (Armonk, NY: M.E. Sharpe, 1995), pp. 117–118 ("This grand narrative of patriotic history is given its modern origin in 1839, with a failed popular defense against Britain's barbaric attempt to force civilized Chinese to buy British opium.").

[369] Carlson makes the interesting point that such ideological or historical heuristics have led the Chinese to overstate the implications of international interventions elsewhere in the world for China's own sovereignty. Carlson, *supra* note 327, at p. 16 ("In other words, the loss or gain of sovereign rights by other actors was always seen through this prism of China's own sovereignty in a way that often overemphasized the possible implications of intervention elsewhere for China's own sovereignty claims.").

[370] Davis, *supra* note 2, at p. 249.

[371] Davis concludes:

more accommodating to the development of a right of humanitarian intervention as an international legal norm.[372]

Furthermore, the Chinese Communist Party's focus on economic development and growth as a critical source of legitimacy may influence China's position on humanitarian intervention. Although the opposite claim can also be made, intervention for humanitarian purposes could destabilize target countries or regions and thereby jeopardize Chinese investments and China's economic growth. Shades of these concerns are evident in China's argument that intervention should avoid aggravating conflicts and, thus, should be a last resort.[373]

In addition to regime type and domestic political objectives, the PRC's multiethnic character also may influence Beijing's attitudes toward humanitarian intervention.[374] The Chinese state consists of close to sixty nationalities, several of which, including Tibetans and Uighurs, have demanded greater autonomy and even independence.[375] China's multiethnic character makes it especially sensitive to issues of national sovereignty and intervention—without a strong stand on these principles, Beijing risks emboldening certain of its own populations to foment a conflict or crisis that could justify outside intervention. One can observe these concerns in China's fear that intervention in Bosnia and Kosovo would lead to a slippery slope of increased interference in the internal affairs of other multiethnic states.[376]

Similarly, the PRC's long-standing goal of reunifying Taiwan with the mainland makes Beijing wary of outside interference in its relations across

---

> [T]his, at most, points to a sustained nonintervention principle with limited exceptions on an ad hoc basis .... It is doubtful that China would agree to formal standards for such limited exceptions but, faced with continuing humanitarian crises, may permit such to arise from practice. It has already to a limited extent tolerated such practice.

Id.

372 Id. at pp. 248–251.

373 See, e.g., U.N. SCOR, 60th Sess., 5153d mtg, *supra* note 249, at p. 5 (cautioning that ratcheting up pressure on the Sudanese government "could end up further complicating the situation and making it even more difficult to resolve").

374 See Davis, *supra* note 2, at p. 242 ("China's current status as an authoritarian unitary state with several restless peripheral communities clearly shapes China's present resistance to humanitarian intervention.").

375 Amanda Lilly, "A Guide to China's Ethnic Groups," *Washington Post*, 8 July 2009; *see generally* Morris Rossabi (ed.), *Governing China's Multiethnic Frontiers* (Seattle, WA: University of Washington Press, 2004) (discussing the status of minority groups in China).

376 See *supra* notes 121, 143.

the Taiwan Straits.[377] A strong stand on sovereignty and nonintervention serves Beijing's purposes here too. One can observe the salience of the PRC's goal of reunification in China's special sensitivity to NATO's intervention in Kosovo,[378] which spoke most directly to its sensitivities about its own "breakaway province," Taiwan. While future humanitarian crises may not always involve questions of secession and independence, the PRC may nonetheless view the establishment of a norm of humanitarian intervention as a further slide down a slippery slope toward greater interference in what it perceives to be its internal affairs. China's sensitivities about interference in Syria following the Libyan intervention reflect such concerns.

Finally, both the nature of the international system and China's place within it influence Beijing's attitudes toward humanitarian intervention. At least until recently, China's status as a weaker power—first in a bipolar, Cold War world, and then in a largely unipolar one after the Soviet Union's collapse—made an absolutist stance on sovereignty and nonintervention useful for preventing China from becoming a target of intervention or interference itself. China's historical positioning of itself as a defender of developing countries' rights also plays a role in Beijing's attitudes toward humanitarian intervention.[379]

In contrast, China's present status as a rising great power works in the opposite direction. Given China's status as a permanent member of the Security Council and its growing military and economic power, it is arguably irrational for Beijing to fear foreign intervention outside of the context of Taiwan. Additionally, China's growing power and increasing global integration are likely to lead to more expansive views of its national interests. The extent to which China's economic and political interests are increasingly affected by instability abroad potentially could change Beijing's calculus on the utility of a strict anti-interventionist stance.[380]

---

[377] *See* Feigenbaum, *supra* note 179, at p. 41 ("China insists on an orthodox approach to sovereignty on a global scale for fear of the precedent any change would set with respect to Taiwan.").

[378] *See supra* note 142.

[379] *See* Jia, *supra* note 329, at p. 21 (noting that China's position reflects the fact that humanitarian intervention "more often than not serves the interests of the strong and damages the sovereign rights and interests of weaker states, reflecting Western domination of world affairs").

[380] *See* Gill and Reilly, *supra* note 27, at p. 46 ("China frequently justifies its resistance to humanitarian intervention with the argument that such interventions might foster domestic turbulence, civil wars, and even regional conflict."); *see also* Feigenbaum, *supra* note 179, at pp. 32–33 (noting that China has become "uncharacteristically flexible in recent years on

Furthermore, China's growing desire to be recognized as a great power and responsible international actor means that image and reputational concerns will influence Beijing's position on humanitarian intervention to a much greater extent.[381] This, combined with China's greater participation and enmeshment in multilateral institutions and sovereignty-limiting regimes, might accelerate the diffusion of norms regarding humanitarian intervention. Such norm diffusion already appears to have begun, as demonstrated by China's acceptance of the basic tenets of the R2P.[382] As a result, China's increasing participation in UN peacekeeping operations and more active international role may create a feedback loop that shapes China's worldview, with the result being that the Chinese government may no longer consider it conscionable or politically possible to fail to act in the face of mass atrocities or genocide, although the case of Syria is providing a test of this theory.[383]

Conclusion

The direction in which—and the extent to which—Chinese attitudes toward humanitarian intervention continue to evolve will depend on the relative salience of the various determinants identified above in future

certain aspects of political sovereignty," but that "these subtleties are utterly lacking on topics concerning Taiwan").

381 *See* Carlson, *supra* note 327, at p. 14 (attributing change in Chinese attitudes toward intervention to "broader reputational and image concerns that shifted and evolved over the course of" the 1990s).

382 *See supra* notes 212, 216–217, 235 and accompanying text.

383 *See* Carlson, *supra* note 179, at pp. 148, 183 ("[I]nternational norms on human rights and sovereign authority and on the transgression of conventional sovereign boundaries gained a foothold in China's foreign policy establishment through its long-term involvement in argumentative human rights discourses."); Evans, *supra* note 183, at p. 73 ("[T]here are also grounds for believing that, as China's participation and stature in global institutions grows, and as its governance becomes increasingly sophisticated, its leaders simply will not see the commission of mass atrocity crimes as a remotely permissible option."); Kleine-Ahlbrandt, *supra* note 270, at p. 2 (arguing that the West's heightened expectations for China's global role have motivated significant changes in the PRC's foreign policy in recent years and shifted debates in Beijing "from how to defend the principle of noninterference to the conditions under which intervention is justified"). For more theoretical treatments of the process of norm diffusion and socialization in the area of human rights and humanitarian intervention, see Finnemore, *supra* note 5, at pp. 52–84; Martha Finnemore, "Constructing Norms of Humanitarian Intervention," in Peter J. Katzenstein (ed.), *The Culture of National Security: Norms and Identity in World Politics* (New York: Columbia University Press, 1996), p. 153; Martha Finnemore and Kathryn Sikkink, "International Norm Dynamics and Political Change," *International Organization*, vol. 52, no. 4, Autumn 1998, pp. 887–917, at pp. 894–909.

humanitarian crises, as well as how those determinants interact with each other in the specific contexts of future humanitarian crises. Recent trends suggest that, while historical experience will continue to influence China's position on intervention, the influence of ideology will decrease.

Government statements redolent with historical and ideological referents reached a fever pitch immediately after NATO's intervention in Kosovo, particularly following the bombing of the Chinese embassy in Belgrade.[384] This indicates that historical and ideological determinants are likely to prove most salient when China feels most threatened or slighted by a proposed or actual intervention, including situations in which nationalist sentiments run high. But on the whole, the cases above demonstrate a trend toward pragmatism and away from ideology in China's position on humanitarian intervention. For example, China's stance on Darfur reflected a decidedly pragmatic focus on its economic and political self-interest and less of a concern about the legal and precedential effect of interference and humanitarian intervention in Sudan. In other words, with respect to Darfur, China acted more like a great power—with concrete material and reputational interests at stake—than an ideological obstructionist.

Furthermore, despite China's historical insecurities, its rising political, economic, and military power should make the PRC more confident that it can resist intervention in its own affairs and, perhaps, more willing to embrace the development of the law of humanitarian intervention. Additionally, to the extent that future humanitarian crises look sufficiently dissimilar to situations the PRC perceives as challenges to its own sovereignty, such as those of Taiwan or Tibet, China may be less likely to fear that intervention elsewhere might lead to interference at home. To the extent such humanitarian crises increase China's willingness to contemplate humanitarian intervention may also increase as its ability to project military power abroad grows. Finally, China's growing participation in UN peacekeeping operations and increasing integration in multilateral security and economic institutions are likely to force Beijing to grapple with the responsibilities attendant to its great-power status, including the future shape and legal status of concepts like the R2P.

At present, however, there is no reason to expect China to relax its status as a "persistent objector" to claims of a right of unilateral humanitarian intervention. A strong presumption against intervention continues to be

---

384 *See supra* note 368–369 and accompanying text.

China's default position, as demonstrated in the case of Syria. Still, China's willingness to support multilateral interventions upon Security Council approval and target state consent—as well as its willingness to apply significant diplomatic pressure to secure that consent—suggests, despite Beijing's recent vetoes of draft resolutions on Syria, that China may continue to liberalize its position on the role of the United Nations in intervening to end mass atrocities or gross violations of human rights. Over the course of the coming decade, it should become apparent whether Syria represents a turning point or whether longer-term trends will prevail.

CHAPTER SIX

THE PARADOX OF NON-USE OF "USE OF FORCE" OPTION IN JAPAN'S FOREIGN AND SECURITY POLICY CONSENSUS

Toshiya Hoshino

Introduction

The foreign and security policies of post-World War II Japan are governed by three key legal instruments, namely, the Constitution of Japan (1947), the Japan-United States Security Treaty (1951, revised in 1960), and the Charter of the United Nations (1945. Japan joined the UN in 1956).[1] To mark a clear discontinuity from the previous Imperialist and military-led authoritarian governance structure, those Japanese political leaders who took the helm of government affairs in the aftermath of war made a conscious choice when it promulgated, concluded and acceded to the respective document with one common underlying goal in their mind: the self-imposed strict limitation to, and preferably the non-use of, the use of military force in the future conduct of its international affairs. It was and continues to be 'the Gordian knot' to the Japanese political system.

In retrospect, the idea was pragmatic as much as practical. Practically speaking, there was no choice but to remain a non-military power, as Tokyo, after the total surrender from the war it launched in the Pacific and in East Asia, was completely disarmed and placed under the occupation by the United States-led Allied Powers for six and a half years (August 1945 to April 1952). As we see below, the no-war Constitution was drafted during this period, although Japan subsequently took the steps to "rearm" itself, pushed by the policy change on the part of the U.S. to place Japan firmly in the Western camp as Cold War tension with the Soviet bloc escalated, which was most notably demonstrated by the outbreak of

---

[1] Basing its foreign and security policies on these three documents, Japan announced the "Three Principles of Japanese Diplomacy" in its first *Diplomatic Bluebook* published in 1957. They were "the UN-Centrism", "the cooperation with the (Western) liberal countries" and "A membership in Asia". Gaimusho (Ministry of Foreign Affairs), *Wagagaiko no kinkyo* (The Recent Developments of Our Diplomatic Activities), September 1957, pp. 7–8.

the Korean War (1950–1953). It is against this background that Japan established the Japan Defense Agency and the Self-Defense Forces (SDFs) in 1954. At the same time, however, from a pragmatic standpoint, Tokyo explored the way to keep the prolife of the SDFs as "modest" as possible, which not only helped Japan looked non-aggressive but also allowed it to concentrate most of its efforts to economic recovery. This is the idea of the Yoshida doctrine, the politico-strategic dictum of light defense burden in favor of fast-track economic development, named after Prime Minister Shigeru Yoshida, who set the basic course of the post-War Japan's foreign and security policies by signing the Security Treaty with Washington.

Contrary to its sense of uneasiness to use its military, however, Japan was heavily dependent on the resources, personnel, equipment and facilities, of the SDFs. It was particularly evident in the wake of the Great East Japan Earthquake of March 11, 2011. On that fatal day, the massive magnitude 9.0 earthquake hit the Pacific Ocean-side of *Tohoku* (north-eastern) region of Japan's mainland, which caused the most destructive tsunami ever measured in Japan. The disaster claimed the lives of about 19,000 and displaced hundreds of thousands of people. It damaged many cities and even hit the Fukushima Daiichi Nuclear Power Plant, which caused widespread radioactive contamination. To counter these multiple challenges, the government of Japan mobilized its ground, maritime, and air SDFs immediately. The SDFs' largest ever operation, involving 100,000 personnel, helped by the U.S. forces under the *Tomodachi* (friend in Japanese) Operation, played a critical role in this major disaster relief and humanitarian assistance activities. In a sense, it is a totally unexpected turn of events to find the most sophisticated weapons and most diligently trained troops were used not for the military defense of Japan but to conduct a major operation of humanitarian nature. It certainly helped change the image of the SDFs in Japan and vindicated its *reason d'etre*. In fact, the approval rating for the SDFs jumped to 97.7% according to an opinion poll conducted by the Cabinet Office of Japan in January 2012.[2]

Although the use of SDFs' capabilities for disaster relief and humanitarian assistance is not considered the most traditional nor main role of the military, the efficient mobility of the SDFs and the smooth Japan-U.S. operational coordination demonstrated in the post-3.11 phase did send the

---

[2] *Jieitai·Boei Mondai ni Kansuru Yoronchosa* (Opinion Poll related to the SDFs and Defense Issues), January 2012. Cabinet Office of Japan. http://www8.cao.go.jp/survey/h23/h23-bouei/index.html.

concrete signal to the region about the readiness of the Japan-U.S. security alliance. In fact, the close Japan-U.S. ties, and the deterrence power embedded in the alliance, are deemed crucial in the second decades of the 21st century as the rise of military power of China, now the second largest economy surpassing Japan, becomes more prominent. Also, the situation of North Korea, the most secret authoritarian state in northeast Asia, grows into a more unpredictable stage under the new leadership, among others. Now the significance of the East Asia and the Pacific in global strategic environment is increasing more than ever. So Washington announced a plan to "rebalance" its defense and military, to focus more on this region.[3]

This is where Japan stands today. The deployment of the SDFs, and particularly the use of its military capabilities, remains a contentious question in Japan all through its post-World War II history. It is a paradox of Japan, in which the government and people do understand the need and utility of their military strength to maintain peace and stability (with the clear consensus to exclude war and the aggressive use of force options) while they share a fundamental sense of uneasiness in even possessing it. As a result, Japan has established a legally, morally and politically bound military and has gone through the often turbulent post-War years without firing a shot in an actual theater of operation. This chapter will analyze the background thinking and practice behind Japan's persistent stance of non-use of the "use of force" option.

Meaning of "Peace" in Peace Constitution

What defines the current Constitution of Japan, the "Peace Constitution," largely derives from Article 9. This widely recognized "renunciation of war" clause has served as a key foundation, and a principal constraint, to the people of Japan—legal, political and moral—as they discuss any matter that might involve the role of the Japanese military, SDFs.

The origin of this Constitution was unusual because it was drafted not by the Japanese government but by the team led by the Supreme Commander of Allied Powers, General Douglas MacArthur, who occupied Japan as a part of its demilitarization and democratization of this

[3] Remarks by President Obama to the Australian Parliament, November 17, 2011. Please see also, Hillary Clinton, "America's Pacific Century," *Foreign Policy*, November 2011.

defeated former Imperial state. The GHQ (General Headquarters), so the occupation authority was called, declined any draft prepared by the Japanese government. In that sense, the GHQ was literally imposing the draft Constitution. Nonetheless, this U.S.-made text was accepted by the government and people of Japan probably for two reasons among others. One is the fact that the draft was clear enough to maintain the Emperor in the system of the new post-War Japan, though status of the Emperor was rather abstractly described as "the symbol" of the state and of the unity of the people of Japan. The other is the spirit of Article 9 and its clear sense of commitment to peace as defined in terms of non-military, non-use of force and no war.

The full 2-part article is read as follows:

> ARTICLE 9 Aspiring sincerely to an international peace based on justice and order, the Japanese people forever renounce war as a sovereign right of the nation and the threat or use of force as means of settling international disputes. (2) To accomplish the aim of the preceding paragraph, land, sea, and air forces, as well as other war potential, will never be maintained. The right of belligerency of the state will not be recognized.

While the non-use or the non-threat of use of force commitment is included in Article 2–4 of the Charter of the United Nations, the Japanese constitution goes further to the renunciation of war as a sovereign right forever. For those people who suffered the total defeat after huge loss of lives and properties, together with the deep sense of remorse to the militarist past, it was likely that the text was not considered the deprivation of the part of its sovereign right but the safeguard for Japan not repeating its past mistake. The second part of Article 9, therefore, can be seen as another guarantee for Japan not to engage in any future aggressive action as it stipulates that any "land, sea and air forces, as well as other war potential, will never be maintained." This is, in a way, the genesis of the uniquely Japanese sentiment of equating "peace" primarily with the non-military, non-use of force and the no-war option.

It is an irony in history if we find that this most unique part of the Peace Constitution became obsolete as a disarmed Japan moved to change its policies as early as three years after the constitution became effective in 1947. The outbreak of the Korean War on the Korean Peninsula in June 1950 immediately placed Japan in the Cold War context. The result was the "rearmament" of Japan and the establishment of the National Police Reserve in August 1950, which was later reinstituted to the National Safety Forces in October 1952. These initiatives were not necessarily from the

Japanese side but rather pushed by the U.S. side.[4] But there was no doubt that the process would help quicken the process of terminating the state of war between Japan and the world. So Prime Minister Shigeru Yoshida made the calculations and accepted the idea. Subsequently, Japan was invited to sign the San Francisco Peace Treaty with the U.S. and other Western countries in September 8, 1951 at the grandiose Opera House in this city by the Bay. And later in the day, Yoshida moved to the Presidio Army Base by the side of the Golden Gate Bridge to sign the Japan-U.S. Security Treaty. The two treaties helped justify the early end of the Occupation and bringing Tokyo back to the international community (for the Western bloc, for that matter) as an independent sovereign state.

Based on the Security Treaty, Japan agreed to make two new policy choices: One was to host the American bases on its soil even after the Occupation period was over in exchange for the U.S. support to the defense of Japan and the other was the formal establishment of Ground, Maritime and Air Self-Defense Forces in July 1954, replacing the previously formed National Safety Forces. While these steps were considered important from a strategic perspective, it nonetheless worried the Japanese as they feared the new military might compromise their definition of peace as non-military, non-use of force and no-war commitments. It was for this reason that the SDFs were carefully characterized and distinguished from the "land, sea, and air forces, as well as other war potential" possession of which was banned by the Peace Constitution. As the name represented, the Self-Defense Forces, under the Basic Policy on National Defense document of May 1957, were only allowed to build up "by steps within the limit necessary for self-defense in accordance with national strength and situation."[5] The UN Charter does not deny the use of force to exercise the right of individual and collective self-defense of the Member States. Japan was not yet allowed to join the UN, but the Charter ensured the international consensus on the legality of the self-defense nature of the military.

[4] Through the detailed study of diplomatic documents of the U.S. and the UK, Professor Shibayama explained the U.S.'s clear strategic intention to make Japan the "stop line" from future Soviet invasion so as to avoid the Third World War. The UK reluctantly but shrewdly followed the U.S. lead, but, according to Shibayama's work, London expected the defense pact between Japan and the U.S. would serve as a "shield" to defend the Britain's interests in the Far East and the Pacific region. Please see, Futoshi Shibayama, *Nihon Saigunbiheno Michi - 1945~1954* (*The Road to Japan's Remilitarization: 1945–1954*), Minerva Shobo, 2010.

[5] The Basic Policy on National Defense was adopted by the Japan's National Defense Council and the Cabinet on May 20, 1957. This more than fifty-five year-old document remained unchanged at the time of writing.

Here, Japan found room to secure its commitment to peace while meeting the U.S. expectation. But peace can take many forms for many requirements. The following sections will review the ways that the government of Japan approached the issue of the use of force in the past seven decades.

Developments in Japan's Pursuit of Non-use of Force Commitment

There are certain developments in Japan's post-World War II policy orientations, particularly its use and deployment of the SDFs composed of the Ground Self-Defense Force, the Maritime Self-Defense Force and the Air Self-Defense Force. It is true that Japan's commitment to the Peace Constitution continues to be the foundation of its overall national policies and the alliance with the United States continues to be considered the cornerstone of its foreign and security policies. And Tokyo, after its accession to this world body in 1956, generally placed high priority on obtaining the United Nations endorsement to justify the SDFs' operations, whenever they were involved in the actions to maintain international peace. It should be noted, however, that the nature of peace and security issues that Japan and the world confront has become more diverse and multifaceted since the end of the Cold War.

In the Asia-Pacific region, there are five sets of issues that affect peace and stability among the countries. First and foremost, the historical legacies of Japan's colonialism still casts a heavy shadow particularly in the relationships with Japan's neighbors: China, South Korea and North Korea.

Second, there is the traditional rivalry among regional countries, including military-to-military competition and territorial disputes. These are essentially modern issues in nature, addressing the sovereign rights of the parties involved. During the Cold War, issues were framed in the East vs. West context. But those unresolved matters were carried over to the 21st century. Those issues include the tensions between the two sides of the Taiwan Strait and between the two Koreas on the Peninsula. China's recent assertive maritime policies and the series of North Korean provocative actions (from the dispatch of spy ships to the launch of ballistic missiles, nuclear tests, and the artillery shelling of a South Korean island, to list a few.)

Third is the other type of sovereign issues regarding fragile states. In the absence of the patron countries after the Cold War, the situation of these weak but sovereign states deteriorated to a condition of absolute poverty, corruption, and poor governance structure, coupled frequently with violent armed conflict.[6] Afghanistan under the Taliban regime hosted Al-Qaeda terrorist groups and Somalia could not control piracy. Other examples include Somalia, the Democratic Republic of Congo, Afghanistan, and Iraq. Ordinary people in these countries are faced with "human security" challenges, with the threat to their fundamental freedom to live in a dignified manner.

Fourth is the non-traditional type of threats caused by non-state actors among others. The 9/11 terrorist attacks on U.S. soil began this post-modern era of globalization and asymmetrical conflict. Fear is further multiplied with weapons of mass destruction, such as nuclear, biological and chemical arsenals. The post-modern security threats also go beyond traditional land, sea and air space to include cyber space.

Finally, the fifth consideration includes those security challenges caused primarily by natural disasters which seemed to have become more intense because of the climate change.

For Japan, the past 20 years have proved to be more challenging than the Cold War period for its conduct of foreign and security policies. The real dilemma is the increase of the need for Japan to take proactive positions to deal with the matters that affect international peace and security, while not crossing the threshold of the non-use of military means commitment. The first shock wave came in the wake of the Gulf Crisis/War of 1990–91 which was triggered by the Iraq's aggression to Kuwait. Because of the conspicuous absence of its physical participation in the coalition against Iraq, and in spite of its huge amount of financial contributions (US$13 billion), Japan was exposed to severe international criticism. This traumatic experience led political leaders to openly pursue options to send Japanese personnel, preferably uniformed contingents, to troubled regions. Subsequently, the so-called International Peace Cooperation Law (or the PKO Law) was enacted in June 1992, by the determined efforts by the then-ruling Liberal Democratic Party government, overcoming a tough opposition and delaying tactics of the left-wing opposition parties, which constantly ran an ideological campaign about the possibility of Japan's revival of militarism if they were to send overseas even a machine gun. Tokyo then quickly dispatched the SDF units to join the UN peacekeeping missions both in Cambodia and in Mozambique later that year. That was the beginning of Japan's proactive use of the SDFs overseas. Since then,

[6] Those countries tend to be ranked high in the annual list of countries based on the Failed States Index, put together by The Fund for Peace. Please see http://www.fundforpeace.org.

the SDFs have undertaken a total of 14 UN-mandated peacekeeping missions in the Middle East, Central America, Asia and Africa (as of March 2013).

Since then, the legal and administrative mechanisms have become more open for the SDFs to operate overseas. The acceptance of Japan's general public to involvement in UNPKO was also growing. Partly encouraged by these positive reactions to its activities, and partly obliged to respond to the series of real security crises with global scope, Tokyo explored various measures to enact new laws, generally with the endorsement of the UN, to justify SDFs proactive missions. In this regard, and in addition to Japan's involvement in UNPKOs, we can identify two additional set of SDFs activities to address two issues out of the five above questions.

One is related to the traditional national and regional security balance-of-power issues, most vividly reflected in the political developments on the Korean Peninsula and the cross-strait China-Taiwan relations, which necessitated the upgrading of Japan-U.S. defense cooperation. The other is more global in nature and pertained to the maintenance of international peace and security, such as the international responses to the situations in Iraq, Afghanistan and Somalia, for example. In order to deal with the latter set of issues, Tokyo enacted new laws which enabled Japan to send SDFs abroad to actively conduct specific missions; namely, the Anti-Terrorism Special Measures Law (2001), which authorized the dispatch of Japanese Maritime SDF's vessels to the Indian Ocean to supply fuel to the Coalition vessels; the Iraq Reconstruction Assistance Special Measures Law (2004), pertaining to the activities of the Ground SDFs in southern Iraqi city of Samawah for humanitarian and reconstruction missions and the Anti-Piracy Measures Law (2009), escorting the vessels off the Coast of Somalia and in the Gulf of Aden as a part of international efforts to counter piracy issues.[7]

The government of Japan stressed that these missions did not infringe upon the Constitutional restraints. No combat missions were involved. Both in Iraq and in Afghanistan, no Japanese SDF were expected to operate in a combat zone. Weapons could be carried (and could be used for defensive purposes) but this was clearly distinguished from the use of force. It has also been stressed that the missions are conducted by Japanese

[7] In order to promptly respond to the issue which is taking place half the globe away the Maritime SDF initially conducted the escort operation in March 2009 in accordance with the "maritime security operation" as stipulated in Article 82 of the Self-Defense Law until the Anti-Piracy Law passed the National Diet in June that year.

troops for the purpose of enhancing international (and not national) peace and security. However limited it might be, what Japanese SDFs have been doing can be viewed as a contribution to the "collective security" system broadly defined. In this connection, it should be pointed out that the government always made sure to obtain the authorization from the UN as a prerequisite of Japan's involvement in every overseas mission.

Japan's participation in the humanitarian and reconstruction mission in Iraq may deserve special attention because Japanese troops acted as a part of the coalition force particularly after sovereignty was transferred to the local Iraqi transitional government. Since it was the first Japanese participation in the multinational force operating in an unstable foreign land, Tokyo took extra care to maneuver diplomatically at the UN Security Council, mainly through the U.S., in order to incorporate the specific mandate of humanitarian aid and reconstruction in the resolution so that the government of Japan could stress the legitimacy of SDF activities in the field.[8] This sort of diplomatic effort was deemed necessary particularly because the U.S. engaged in the Iraq War of 2003 without the clear UN authorization. Then-Prime Minister Junichiro Koizumi expressed his strong support for President Bush's decisions while he patiently persuaded his U.S. counterpart to obtain the endorsement at the Security Council to garner wider international acceptance. Ultimately, President Bush did not bend his unilateralist posture of always placing U.S. decisions over those of the UN.

In retrospect, the changing nature and evolution of the mission and capabilities of Japan's foreign and security policies can be characterized by the transformation from its own individual security (self-defense only) in the period immediately after the end of World War II to a collective but non-military security during much of the 1960s to the 1980s, under the Japan-U.S. alliance, to a collective *and* military (but *non*-combat and *non*-use of force) security in the post-Cold War and post-9/11 era. Japan's use of SDFs is always considered sensitive. Every effort is made to avoid both actual and appearance of "*i'ttaika*（一体化）", or the integration of Japan's

[8] U.N. Doc. S/RES/1546 (2004), 8 June 2004. Japan, through the U.S., made sure that the resolution included the Member States' role in the areas of "humanitarian and reconstruction assistance." Please see the Operative Paragraph 15 of the resolution; it says that the Security Council "(*R*)*equests* Member States and international and regional organizations to contribute assistance to the multinational force, including military forces, as agreed with the Government of Iraq, to help meet the needs of the Iraqi people for security and stability, humanitarian and reconstruction assistance, and to support the efforts of UNAMI."

actions with the direct use of military (combat) forces by other states. As a result, the successive administrations in Tokyo have taken extra care to do two things; one is obtain UN authorizations to all the actions that Japan undertakes to meet the domestic legal requirements and the other is to keep a distance from the actual heavy military (offensive) actions and, if it is needed, to support international military actions. To this end, Japan concentrates its efforts on logistics outside of combat areas, so as to avoid any "*i'ttaika*" from offensive missions.

New Consensus on "Peace Enforcement" and "Comprehensive Collective Security" in International Stage

While the U.S.-led military operation in Iraq, with its contested legitimacy and legality questions, is widely discussed, there is an important step forward in the discourse and consensus over the use of force question on the international stage. There is an increasing recognition, on the part of the international community, that the enforcement actions (including the use of military force) can be taken legitimately if they were intended to achieve "the maintenance of international peace and security." These are the enforcement actions, of course as the last resort, for public and peaceful purposes (as against narrow, national and antagonistic), and endorsed by the Security Council resolutions under Chapter VII of the UN Charter. On my own count, these broadly defined international "peace enforcement" actions now undertaken are categorized in the following five contexts; namely; 1) counter-aggression (the original conception of "collective security"); 2) humanitarian rescue (the exercise of "the Responsibility to Protect" idea); 3) stabilization (as in the mission of the Australia-led "INTERFET: The International Force for East Timor" to quell the humanitarian and security crisis in Timor Leste in 1999–2000 to pave the ground for the UNPKO); 4) counter-terrorism (as seen in the NATO-led activities of the ISAF (International Security Assistance Force) in Afghanistan); and 5) counter-proliferation (as demonstrated, though in an ill-fated way, by the U.S.-U.K.-led multinational force in Iraq).[9] These actions are not always free from criticisms. But they represent the new and growing consensus on both the needs and the utility of the use of force to respond to a variety of security challenges of global implications.

---

[9] Please see Toshiya Hoshino, "Gunji-kainyu (Military Intervention)" in Ryo Oshiba, Kiichi Fujiwara, Tetsuya Yamada eds., *Heiwa Seisaku* (*Peace Policies*),Yuhikaku, 2006.

In one respect, this broadening of international recognition of collective enforcement actions for peaceful purposes encouraged Japan to be more open to the use of force question. But it never changed Japan's own style of prudent and constraining use of the SDFs abroad. Their actions are continually bound by the non-combat, rear area, humanitarian and logistical activities, to support various "peace enforcement" missions. Having discussed that, however, it is of use to revisit the traditional conception of "collective security" to redefine it in a more comprehensive sense. This redefinition moves beyond the original understanding of collective action to countering military emergencies of the victim states, to incorporating more actions in the socio-economic and humanitarian areas, to helping relieve the dire situations of the government and people on the ground. And this broadening of the ideas of collective security can open the horizon for Japan to play a more active role, both with the SDFs or without, in concert with other states.

In fact, this new perspective is rightly introduced in the 2004 report of the High-level Panel of Threats, Challenges and Change, organized by then-UN Secretary-General Kofi Annan.[10] By bringing these two directions (on one hand, the growing consensus on the utility of "peace enforcement" and the introduction of the "comprehensive collective security" concept on the other), it would be legitimate for Japan to employ its foreign and security policy tools, military and non-military, more creatively. The next section will review Japan's salient policy initiatives that demonstrate the recent trends of its international cooperation.

Japan's Policy Tools in the Areas of International Peace and Security

For many years, the term "collective security" has had an unpopular connotation for the people of Japan. The reason is the term's militaristic implications, which recognize military actions and the use of force even for the legitimate purpose of responding to aggressors. It is easy to find Japan's

---

[10] The United Nations, *A More Secure World: Our Shared Responsibility – Report of the High-level Panel on Threats, Challenges and Change*, 2 December, 2004. U.N. Doc. A/59/565. The report identified six clusters of threats, namely economic and social threats (including poverty, infectious diseases and environmental degradation), inter-state conflict, internal conflict (including civil war, genocide and other large-scale atrocities), nuclear, radioactive, chemical and biological weapons, terrorism and transnational organized crime. These threats require international collective actions, combining military force, when necessary, and all the non-military measures, whenever possible.

remorse over, and its strong desire to distance itself from, the militarist and aggressive past. As a result, Japan's post-World War II pacifist sentiment has created a unique atmosphere in Japan to take overly cautious, and even negative, views of the military establishment and its actions.

As seen at the outset of this chapter, the Constitution of 1947, particularly Article 9 states that "(a)spiring sincerely to an international peace based on justice and order, the Japanese people forever renounce war as a sovereign right of the nation and the threat or use of force as means of settling international disputes". The second paragraph of the same article says that "(i)n order to accomplish the aim of the preceding paragraph, land, sea, and air forces, as well as other war potential, will never be maintained". This wording has made it very difficult to justify the status of its military, namely the Ground, Maritime, and Air Self-Defense Forces of Japan. The official government explanation stresses the exclusive defensive nature of the mission of these forces as opposed to full-fledged armed forces. But this sort of interpretation did not prevent the leftist parties and activists from questioning the government's position, together with their criticism against the Japan-U.S. security alliance that, they said, could entrap Japan in unwanted wars.

In recent years, however, those critical and ideological sentiments, which were rather loudly expressed during the Cold War period by left wingers, were replaced by a more "realistic" sense of security, mainly driven by the series of threats originating from North Korea and China. The Pyongyang government's repeated launches of long-range Taepodong missiles and nuclear testings coupled with its involvement in the a number of cases of abduction of Japanese nationals, and the infiltration by its spy ships, are among the explicit examples that exacerbated the Japanese sense of insecurity regarding this dictatorial state. Moreover, China's rise and its rapid pace of military modernization without much transparency concerns many Japanese, together with the series of disputes over many bilateral political issues, regarding territory and resources in the East China Sea.

Although delicate diplomatic matters still remain, and there is a stalemate over concentrations of U.S. military in Okinawa island, the overall public understanding of the utility of the Japan-U.S. alliance is high. Indeed, today, the security alliance is generally considered a prerequisite when discussing both the defense posture and policies of Japan. There is no question that the recent rising political tensions surrounding Japan–the assertive move of the Chinese navy in the East China Sea as well as the surge of Beijing's defense budget, the ever mysterious moves of North

Korea, the return of Putin's powerful presidency in Russia, and the unusually high tension over Japan and Korea over history issues, etc. – all provided an opportunity for many Japanese to be conscious about the positive-side of the alliance with the U.S.

Against these realistic security policy backgrounds, how has Japan developed its policies towards international diplomacy, as opposed to more national, peace and security arena? There are three key policy areas: 1) the SDF's "dynamic defense force" posture; 2) human security; and 3) Official Development Assistance (ODA) with a focus on peacebuilding of the post-conflict countries beyond the traditional scope of socio-economic development. Though many of the policy tools, both military (if not combat) capabilities and non-military assets, hitherto taken under these three areas are yet to be coordinated, they are indeed interconnected, and they have a potential to contribute effectively to the "comprehensive collective security" in many parts of the world.

First, on the SDFs' "dynamic defense force" posturing, Japan announced its policy shift in the 2010 review of the National Defense Program Guidelines (NDPG) and introduced the concept of "dynamic defense force" in place of the previous "basic defense force" concept, to "proactively perform various types of operations" with "readiness, mobility, flexibility, sustainability, and versatility." The SDFs are "reinforced by advanced technology based on the latest trends in the levels of military technology and intelligence capabilities."[11] The change was obviously prompted by the increasing tension in the area that surrounds Japan. So the dynamic defense was planned to enhance "interoperability" with the American military to be more agile in time of crisis. The use of force, outside of the pure defense of Japan, is not anticipated even with this update and upgrade of the force posture of Japan.

Second, Japan has been actively promoting the idea of "human security" mainly in terms of coping with human suffering that easily transcends national borders. While the term "human security" has been around for a while, Japan promotes a unique perspective, as described by Prime Minister Keizo Obuchi who said in his Hanoi speech in December 1998, that "human security" is "a concept that takes a comprehensive view of all threats to human survival, life and dignity and stresses the need to respond to such threats."[12] In this speech, Obuchi announced Japan's

[11] Part 2. Chapter 2, Section 2, The Ministry of Defense, *Defense of Japan 2012*.

[12] Keizo Obuchi, "Toward the Creation of A Bright Future for Asia", Policy Speech by Prime Minister at the Lecture Program hosted by the Institute for International Relations.

decision to finance the establishment of the "Human Security Trust Fund" under the UN auspices to provide support not just for recovery from the economic crisis that Asian countries had experienced in 1997–98 but also for more medium-to-longer-term problems.

The concept of human security has subsequently been refined and elaborated through the works of the Commission on Human Security, jointly headed by Sadako Ogata, former UN High Commissioner for Refugees and Nobel Prize winning economist, Amartya Sen.[13] The bottom line of the commission report was to focus on "protection" and "empowerment" of people under extremely harsh situations by ensuring their 'freedom from fear' and 'freedom from want'. The idea of focusing on human "freedoms" has largely affected and guided the overall discourse of UN reform as evidenced in the title of the Secretary-General's report of March 2005, *In Larger Freedom*, in which the needs were identified to promote "freedom from want" (development), "freedom from fear" (peace and security) and "freedom to live in dignity" (human rights).[14] Here, although it is not directly mentioned, is the basic idea of "human security" that enabled the integrative approach of bringing together three policy areas (peace and security, development, and human rights).

The language of "human security", which takes people as the referent of security (as opposed to national governments) has not necessarily been well-received by many Member States of the UN as it could undermine their basic adherence to sovereign rights. In this regard, it was an important step forward to note that world leaders agreed, with the active persuasion of Japan, to incorporate a paragraph on human security in the World Summit Outcome Document.[15] This was the first time that the term was explicitly written into an official UN document. It recognized that "all individuals, in particular vulnerable people, are entitled to freedom from fear and freedom from want, with an equal opportunity to enjoy all their rights and fully develop their potential", and the Member States pledged to "commit ourselves to discussion and defining the notion of human security in the General Assembly." The introduction of the concept of 'human

Hanoi, Vietnam, December 16, 1998. Please see also, Toshiya Hoshino, "Ningen no Anzenhosho to Nihon no Kokusai Seisaku (Human Security and Japan's International Policy)", *Kokusai Anzenhosho* (*International Security*), Vol. 30, No. 3 (2002).

[13] Commission on Human Security, *Human Security Now* (New York: Commission on Human Security, 2003).

[14] U.N. Doc. A/59/2005, *In larger freedom: towards development, security and human rights for all – Report of the Secretary-General*, 21 March 2005.

[15] U.N. Doc. A/RES/60/1, 2005 *World Summit Outcome*, 24 October 2005, para. 143.

security' will have other implications that help expand the scope of the concept of collective security, which primarily dealt with national security challenges in a collective manner (namely, collective *national* security), to include actions to tackle human security challenges by collective means (namely, collective *human* security). This sort of conceptual expansion will certainly provide more room for Japan to utilize its resources.

Third, Japan's ODA policy has to be put into perspective in this context. As is widely known, Japan considers its ODA a prime tool of international contribution. A certain set of approaches has been identified as the Japanese way of extending ODA that stresses self-help efforts and local initiatives of the recipient countries. This approach has then been adopted in the international arena as a 'new development strategy', an effort to combine the ownership of the developing world and the partnership of the developed world to comprehensively pursue development assistance and market-oriented economies.

Probably one of the key challenges for Japan to increase the effectiveness of its ODA was to utilize it not just for social and economic development but for broader stability and peace in recipient counties. It was 1992 when Japan formulated the ODA Charter to take into account the post-Cold War international situation and the government's new policy priorities. Then, as noted above, in 1998, Japan introduced the concept of "human security" in ODA policy in its response to the Asian financial crisis. Next came an attempt to connect its development assistance with other policy objectives such as conflict prevention, emergency humanitarian assistance, and post-conflict recovery and reconstruction. The "Action from Japan on Conflict and Development" document was released in July 2000, marking a new willingness on the part of the Japanese government to overcome the traditional policy divides between development and conflict management. It was an element of policy innovation that Japan put forward when it hosted the G8 Summit meetings in Kyūshū and Okinawa. This approach was subsequently incorporated in the concept of "peace consolidation and nation-building", a policy idea that Koizumi stressed at his speech in Sydney in May 2002.[16] This speech was instrumental in the process of revising the ODA Charter, and the new Charter, released in 2003, included "peacebuilding" as one of the formal priorities together with poverty reduction, sustainable development, and addressing global issues.

---

[16] Junichiro Koizumi, "Japan and Australia: Toward a Creative Partnership", Speech by Prime Minister in Sydney, Australia, May 1, 2002.

In fact, the policy area of supporting post-conflict countries in their process of peacebuilding has been one of Japan's most actively engaged in, on the ground from Cambodia, Sri Lanka, Timor Leste to Afghanistan and Iraq, as well as in the UN headquarters in New York, as an active member of the Security Council (when elected as the Non-Permanent Member) and of the Peacebuilding Commission (PBC), among others. In fact, Japan assumed the position of the Chair of the PBC from June 2007 to December 2008, leading the discussion to explore how best the international community can promote local peacebuilding efforts. The PBC is a small organ in the enormous UN system. Nonetheless, it has a unique position to link the Security Council and the General Assembly, the UN's Headquarters in New York and local field, and the all relevant stakeholders on the ground and the international community, as described in the founding resolutions.[17] As the founding member as well as the former Chair, Japan has a responsibility to make this commission develop. The PBC is supporting six country-specific efforts at the time of this writing, namely, Burundi, Sierra Leone, Guinea, Guinea Bissau, Liberia, and the Central African Republic, by accumulating the best practices and mobilizing material resources to effectively facilitate the local peacebuilding efforts.[18] In this regard, it is useful to highlight that Japan, under the DPJ-government, has continued stressing its role in these joint local and international peacebuilding efforts. As a significant step, Japan hosted a public debate, and Mr. Katsuya Okada, for the first time as the Foreign Minister of Japan, chaired a Security Council debate on post-conflict peacebuilding on 16 April 2010.[19] The event inspired those involved in the peacebuilding the importance of providing hope for the future. In this way, Japan continues to facilitate international joint collaborations in this policy area while

---

[17] The resolutions say, "The Commission was established "(a) to bring together all relevant actors to marshal resources and to advise on and propose integrated strategies for post-conflict peacebuilding and recovery; (b) to focus attention on the reconstruction and institution-building efforts necessary for recovery from conflict and to support the development of integrated strategies in order to lay the foundation for sustainable development; (c) to provide recommendations and information to improve the coordination of all relevant actors with and outside the United Nations, to develop best practices, to help to ensure predictable financing for early recovery activities and to extend the period of attention given by the international community to post-conflict recovery." This work formula has a certain universal relevance in formulating and implementing a country-specific peacebuilding strategy. U.N. Docs. A/60/180 and S/RES/1645 (2005), both adopted 20 December 2005.

[18] Toshiya Hoshino, "Peacebuilding & Human Security in Fragile States", *Japan Spotlight*, November/December 2009, pp. 18–19.

[19] U.N. Doc. S/PV.6299 and its resumption, 16 April 2010.

extending bilateral support to the post-conflict counties in Asia, Africa and Latin America, which are struggling to consolidate the foundation for peace.

With regard to the past practice of Japan's ODA policies, it is useful to recognize its renewed focus in Africa as most vividly shown in the Tokyo International Conference on African Development (TICAD) project. Japan is going to host its fifth conferences in June 2013 and mark the 20th anniversary since its first meeting in 1993. TICAD is an attempt of Japan to promote high-level dialogue between Japan and African countries. This will include and development institutions such as the United Nations, respecting the importance of "African ownership" and extending international support as the "partner." Africa is troubled by poverty, conflict and environmental and natural disasters. But it does have the potential to become the last continent of golden opportunity. If properly planned, the TICAD process can be an effective tool to deal with development, human security, post-conflict peacebuilding and the response to environmental change, all at the same time with the policy leadership of Japan. It is to be hoped that this process would push up the performance of the participating African countries in their achievement of the UN Millennium Development Goals (MDGs).

Fortunately, Japan's ODA to Africa is revamped with the political commitment attached to the TICAD process to double it from 900 million (the average disbursement of Japanese ODA directed to Africa between 2003 and 2007) to 1.8 billion dollars by 2012.[20] But the overall trend of ODA's budget is declining in Japan, pushed by the huge deficit and the additional financial burden to recover from the Great East Japan disaster. But considering the fact that Japan's stability and economic health are largely interconnected to those of the rest of the world, an urgent political will needs to be demonstrated to reverse this trend and encourage the more dynamic use of ODA.

Having seen the policy developments of Japan in the above three areas, namely, SDFs' "dynamic defense force" posture, human security, and ODA with a renewed peacebuilding focus, it seems that the basic "tools", both military and non-military, exist in Japan. No doubt, all of these initiatives are made within the framework of the Peace Constitution. But as seen from above, while "dynamic defense force" is conceived to work more closely with the American forces to substantiate the bilateral alliance in

20 Ministry of Foreign Affairs of Japan, *ODA White Paper 2010*. http://www.mofa.go.jp/policy/oda/white/2010/html/honbun/b1/s2_3_1.html#chu1.

the face of intractable regional challenges, it does not give proper attention to the international peace cooperation areas in which the SDFs can also play useful roles. On the contrary, Japan's focus on human security and the ODA do pay sufficient consideration to the global agenda of MDGs, post-conflict peacebuilding, the climate change, and disaster relief and humanitarian assistance. All of these issues are discussed under the auspices of the United Nations, but not so much thought is given to how to join forces between Tokyo and Washington to bring peace and stability in fragile countries in Africa and elsewhere (with probably one clear exception of the anti-piracy operation near Somalia and in the Gulf of Aden). Going back to the original trinity of the Peace Constitution, the Japan-U.S. Security Alliance, and the United Nations Charter, it is useful to explore the creative way for Japan to play a constructive role not just in the East Asia and the Pacific, but also on the global stage.

In tense fields in Sudan, in Syria, or in Haiti, or in Timor-Leste, there is always a risk of Japanese SDF personnel in the field being caught in a situation where they would have to use weapons (not full scale military force, per se). It is valuable for the Japanese SDFs to avoid any "use of force" option, believing that peace means non-military, non-use of force, and no war. But in order to escape from any over-reaction to any future use of force, which is most certainly for a peaceful purpose, Japan may wish to build a more sober view of its non-use of "use of force" option in the world.

Conclusion: Toward a 'Normal Country'?

Heiwa (平和) means peace in Japanese. It implies that the true tranquility (平) comes only when it is founded on harmony or concord (和). The Japanese has learned a hard lesson by disrupting the "tranquility" and "harmony" of the region significantly through military conquest, only to find tragedy for all, including themselves. The experience was sufficient enough to motivate the people of Japan to recall the long forgotten image of Japan as "the Land of *Wa* (harmony)," so the country was called in ancient time, and the old lesson in Article 1 of Prince Shotoku's 17-Article Constitution (604), which said, "Harmony is to be valued, and an avoidance of wanton opposition to be honored." There is no way to prove it, but there seems to be a deep-rooted tendency among the Japanese to value harmony. And this value might have played a role when they chose to define peace in terms of non-military, non-use of force and no-war in the immediate aftermath of the War.

But a subsequent twist of history pressured Japan to modify its own foreign and security policies as envisioned in the Peace Constitution of 1947 and to engage in remilitarization (i.e., the establishment of the Self-Defense Forces), the alliance with the United States, and the admission to the United Nations, among others. As it became a major economic power, Japan began to realize the growing international expectations to play more proactive role in international diplomacy, development, and security, particularly after its conspicuous "physical" absence (beyond the financial contributions) in the international response to the Gulf Crisis/War of 1990–91. Since then, Japan began to send its SDFs overseas for various missions, from UN peacekeeping, humanitarian assistance, post-conflict reconstruction, disaster relief to the rear area, logistical support to anti-terrorist mission from outside of the combat zone, all backed by domestic laws enacted within the framework of the Constitution and under the United Nations authorization or request. These multiple layers of precautions and safeguards have certainly made Japan's move slower. But at the same time, these were the reflections of Tokyo's efforts to be more innovative in fulfilling its internationally expected role within the self-imposed constitutional constraints, if not untying 'the Gordian Knot.'

It is easy to dismiss Japan's way as abnormal. In fact, there has been a discussion in Japan to make it a more "normal" country. This issue was raised by Mr. Ichiro Ozawa, the political maverick who wrote *Blueprint for A New Japan* in 1993 as the old, left-right political order was beginning to crumble.

In Ozawa's Blueprint, the definition of a 'normal country' had two features: "First, it is a nation that willingly shoulders those responsibilities in the international community. It does not refuse such burdens on account of domestic political difficulties. Nor does it take action unwillingly as a result of 'international pressure'. A second requirement for a 'normal' nation is that it cooperates fully with other nations in their efforts to build prosperous stable lives for their people."[21]

There are some criticisms that the 'normal country' concept is a conservative's justification to revise the constitution and even to enable Japan to use force to settle international disputes.[22] It is true that the idea of "normalcy" opened a new avenue of discourse about to what degree Japan

[21] Ichiro Ozawa, *Nihon kaizokeikaku* (Blueprint for a New Japan) (Tokyo: Kodansha, 1993), pp. 94–95.

[22] See for example. Sun Dongmin, "Japan Wants Rearmament," December 6, 2002, English *People's Daily* Online, http://english.peopledaily.com.cn/200212/06/print20021206_108053.html.

should be both ready and capable to do more than before. In effect, it raised the concern, both inside and outside of Japan, whether Japan is finally untying the 'Gordian knot'.

Breaking out of the Cold War ideological mold that limited the scope of Japan's security debate, followed by the response to severe criticisms over the "too little, too late" participation in international joint efforts to meet common threats in the Gulf region, as well as the rising needs to meet both the modern/traditional security challenges in East Asia and the post-modern/non-traditional threats in global scale, it would have been a policy failure and negligence of significant scale if Japan simply followed the framework created in the 1950s and 1960s. Looking from the 'normal country' perspective, Japan, including the SDFs, has normalized to a significant degree. The knot was certainly loosened, if not untied, because the process is taking place within two boundaries; one is the basic non-military, non-use of force, no-war commitment, as discussed in this Chapter, and the other is the overall level of Japanese public toleration and acceptance.

The key is of course to find a balance between Japan's own commitment to pacifism and the appropriate level of an internationally legitimate role in the field of peace and security. One clue to solve this paradox might be seen in the redefinition of the principle of collective security in favor of a more comprehensive approach beyond its traditional, military-oriented one.

In fact, no term is more symbolic than "collective security" to portray the transformation of the status of Japan on the international stage from the aggressive user of force, that is, one of the target states of the World War II collective security mechanism of the "United Nations" (the Allied Powers), to a peace-loving and even a major peace-contributing member of the post-World War II universal inter-governmental organization for collective security, the United Nations. But today, considering the multi-faceted background (economic, political, social and cultural) of international security challenges as manifested in various conflicts and incidents around the world, a military-alone collective response is no longer viable and more comprehensive approaches are required. If this is the case, we can reasonably assume that the policy tools that Japan has been accumulating over the years have roles to play in contributing to a "comprehensive collective security" approach, employing the military tools (certainly not for a combat purpose) and other socio-economic and humanitarian tools. The new emphasis on "human security" perspective to protect and empower people in vulnerable situations explains the direction that Japan pursues to make collective security comprehensive beyond its simple protection of state sovereignty and regime security. Starting from the realization of its past failures, there exists an important consensus, among the government and people of Japan, to resist an aggressive "use of military force" option to the maximum degree. But also realizing the need of comprehensive responses to complicated contemporary security challenges, it can be said that the Japanese are exploring the balance to harmonize the pro-active but non-aggressive use of military tools on one side, and the innovative non-military tools on the other side, to pursue peace nested in tranquility and harmony among the stakeholders involved.

CHAPTER SEVEN

"THE CRIME OF AGGRESSION" AND JAPAN*

Madoka Futamura

Introduction

Since the end of the First World War, the international community has been trying to criminalise aggression. This required the dual task of defining an act of aggression and then establishing legal mechanisms to prosecute individuals responsible for the act. The two tasks need to be completed in order to institutionalise the crime of aggression. In 1998, the International Criminal Court (ICC) was finally established through the adoption of the Rome Statute. This was historic both in the context of international law and international peace and security, but it was also a revolutionary step for a long-term international attempt to criminalise aggression. Article 5 of the ICC statute includes "the crime of aggression' in one of its subject jurisdictions, together with war crimes, crimes against humanity, and genocide. As it was included in the ICC jurisdiction, the definition of aggression is now on the table as an issue of international criminal law, because the ICC cannot exercise jurisdiction over the crime until the definition of aggression, including the conditions for the exercise of jurisdiction by the Court, is clarified.[1] Under the Review Conference of the Rome Statute held in Kampala between 31 May and 11 June 2010, this was one of the crucial issues to be discussed. The amendments to the Rome Statute and to the Elements of Crimes concerning the crime of aggression were finally adopted, which was regarded as an "historic achievement" or "diplomatic miracle".[2]

* In this chapter, the Japanese names, except for those authors who publish in English, are cited with the family name first then the first name, following Japanese convention.

1 Article 5, 2 of the ICC statute.

2 For Resolutions and Declarations adopted by the Review Conference, see http://www.icc-cpi.int/iccdocs/asp_docs/ASP9/OR/RC-11-Part.II-ENG.pdf, accessed on 3 September 2010. For the general overview, see for example, Claus Kreß and Leonie von Holtzendorff, "The Kampala Compromise on the Crime of Aggression", *Journal of International Criminal Justice* 8 (2010), pp. 1179–1217. One of the key achievements in Kampala is that the amendments allow the ICC to exercise jurisdiction on the crime of aggression without a prior determination by the Security Council regarding the existence of an act of aggression.

Japan ratified the Rome Statute and became a member state of the ICC in July 2007. Although the Japanese government acknowledged the role of the ICC and expressed its support for the development of international criminal justice from the early stage,[3] it took nine years for the country to become a member of the ICC following its establishment. Indeed, originally, the Japanese attitude towards the ICC was seen as not very clear.[4] As for the criminalisation of aggression, Japan has also been, until recently, rather passive. Of course, not a few states would be cautious about the criminalisation of aggression because of its implication for state sovereignty. At the same time, Japan, like Germany, has gone through a peculiar experience of having its wartime leaders, right after the Second World War, prosecuted and punished under the International Military Tribunal for the Far East (the Tokyo Trial) for "crimes against peace", namely the crime of aggression.

The Japanese attitude towards the international attempt to ciminalise aggression is suspected by some as to have been influenced by Japan's experience with the Tokyo Trial,[5] in which the validity of crimes against peace as a legal concept was fiercely debated by the defendants.[6] The linkage between the past experience of the war, the Trial, and the post war policy on the criminalisation of aggression is not necessarily obvious, as the Japanese government has rarely expressed such a linkage explicitly. With this in mind, this chapter surveys Japan's attitude towards the international attempt on the criminalisation of aggression, dating back to the post-First World War, and points out some key elements to understand its attitude, examining whether and how Japan's experience in the Second World War (so-called Asian-Pacific War) and the Tokyo Trial has had any impact.

---

[3] Masaki Yasushi, "Nihon to Kokusaikeijisaibansho [Japan and the ICC]," in Murase Shinya and Kō Keiko (eds), *Kokusaikeijisaibansho: Mottomo Jūdaina Kokusaihanzai wo Sabaku* [The International Criminal Court: Prosecuting the Most Serious International Crimes] (Tokyo: Tōshindō, 2008), p. 325.

[4] For example, Philipp Osten "Kokusaikeijisaibanshokitei to Kokunairippō: Doitsu 'Kokusaikeihōten' sōanwo sozaitoshite," *Juristo*, No.1207 (2001), p. 132.

[5] See for example Benjamin B. Ferencz, *Defining International Aggression, the Search for World Peace: A Documentary History and Analysis* (Oceana Publications, 1975), vol. 2, p. 44; Yamagami Shingo, "Kokusaikeijisaibansho he no wagakunino kameito kokusaishakaini okeru hōnoshihaino shinten [The Accession of Japan to the International Criminal Court and the Progress of Rule of Law in the International Community]," *Hōgaku Shinpō*, 116 (2009), p. 776.

[6] The defense motion on the jurisdiction of the Tribunal: *Transcripts*, 119–215. See also Neil Boister and Robert Cryer, *The Tokyo International Military Tribunal: A Reappraisal* (Oxford University Press, 2008), pp. 115–153.

Post-First World War and the Envisaged Trial of the German Kaiser

The well-known Nuremberg and Tokyo Trials are not the first international attempts to prosecute state leaders for the responsibility of war. In the aftermath of the First World War, the victor of the war discussed prosecuting and punishing the German Kaiser, Wilhelm II, for the responsibility for the origin of the war.[7] Japan was involved in this process as a victor of the war.

The issue of war responsibility and punishment was raised at the Preliminary Peace Conference on 18 January 1919, and the Conference decided on 25 January to create a commission to inquire into the responsibilities relating to the war.[8] Japan was a member of the commission as one of the five "Great Powers," together with the United States, Britain, France and Italy.[9] The Commission on the Responsibility of the Authors of the War and on Enforcement of Penalties was expected to inquire into and report on the issues, such as the responsibility of the authors of the war; the facts of the breaches of the laws and customs of war; the degree of personal responsibility including those highly placed; and the constitution and procedure of an appropriate tribunal.[10] On the authors of an aggression, the Commission determined that the responsibility for the origin of the World War, as well as the violations of neutrality and of frontiers, rested first on Germany and Austria, secondly on Turkey and Bulgaria.[11] However, while admitting criminal responsibility of individuals, including those in high position of these countries, for offences against the laws and customs of war that concern conduct during the war,[12] the Commission took a position that "a war of aggression may not be considered as an act

---

[7] For details, see James F. Willis, *Prologue to Nuremberg: The Politics and Diplomacy of Punishing War Criminals of the First World War* (Westport, Conn.; London: Greenwood Press, 1982); Gary Jonathan Bass, *Stay the Hand of Vengeance: The Politics of War Crimes Tribunals* (Princeton, N.J: Princeton University Press, 2000), pp. 58–105; Kirsten Sellars, "Delegitimizing Aggression: First Steps and False Starts after the First World War," *Journal of International Criminal Justice*, vol. 10, 2012, pp. 7–40.

[8] Commission on the Responsibility of the Authors of the War and on Enforcement of Penalties, Report Presented to the Preliminary Peace Conference, March 29, 1919 [reprinted in *The American Journal of International Law*, vol. 14, no. 1, 1920, pp. 95–154; (*The Commission's Report* hereafter)], p. 95.

[9] The commission composed of fifteen individuals, two each from five Great Powers and one each from Belgium, Greece, Poland, Romania and Serbia.

[10] *The Commission's Report*, p. 95.

[11] Ibid., p. 98.

[12] Ibid., p. 117.

directly contrary to positive law, or one which can be successfully brought before a tribunal such as the Commission is authorized to consider under its terms of reference."[13] The Commission's conclusion was:

> no criminal charge can be made against the responsible authorities or individuals (and notably the ex-Kaiser) on the special head of these breaches of neutrality, but the gravity of these gross outrages upon the law of nations and international good faith is such that the Commission thinks they should be the subject of a formal condemnation by the Conference.[14]

Based on the Commission's report, the Peace Treaty of Versailles in 1919 had to give up using the term, "a crime of aggression." Instead, its Article 227 noted: "The Allied and Associated Powers publicly arraign William II of Hohenzollern, formerly German Emperor, for *a supreme offence against international morality and the sanctity of treaties*" (emphasis added).[15] As Gary Bass states, "This dubious wording allowed a trial for aggression, but relied less on codified law and more on substantive justice as seen by the Allies, whose definition of justice was hardly universally shared."[16] Prosecuting and punishing the Kaiser, as noted in the Treaty, was not realised due to the Netherlands' refusal to relinquish him.

The report was signed by all the members but witnessed strong reservations from the United States and Japan.[17] Japan, as did the U.S., issued the memorandum of reservations, in which it questioned "whether international law recognizes a penal law as applicable to those who are guilty" and expressed hesitation in indicting high-ranking individuals for the ground of negative criminality, i.e., abstained from preventing, putting an end to or repressing criminal acts. The Japanese delegates also raised "whether it can be admitted as a principle of the law of nations that a high tribunal constituted by belligerents can, after a war is over, try an individual belonging to the opposite side, who may be presumed to be guilty of a crime against the laws and customs of war."[18] In other words, Japan questioned

---

[13] Ibid., p. 118. The Commission expressed that any inquiry into the authorship of the war would be more appropriately done by historians and statesmen than by a tribunal, and even stated: "Any tribunal ... might hardly be a good court to discuss and deal decisively with such a subject as the authorship of the war." Ibid., p. 119.

[14] Ibid., p. 120.

[15] Article 227 of the Treaty of Versailles, 28 June 1919.

[16] Bass, *Stay*, p. 76.

[17] The memorandum of reservations presented by the U.S. is available in *The Commission's Report*, pp. 127–151.

[18] Reservations by the Japanese Delegation, April 4, 1919 (Annex III), Ibid., pp. 151–2. It also stated: "it seems to us important to consider the consequences which would be created in the history of international law by the prosecution for breaches of the laws

the appropriateness of unilateral prosecution after the war, the concept of individual criminal responsibility under international law, and the concept of the negative criminality, all of which later became fiercely questioned by the defendants at the Tokyo Trial.[19]

Post-Second World War and the Tokyo Trial

The Nuremberg Trial and the Tokyo Trial established after the Second World War criminalised aggression under international law and set up a precedent for prosecuting and punishing individuals, including those high-ranking individuals, for the responsibility of such a crime. Unlike after the First World War, this time Japan found itself on the side of being prosecuted.

The Tokyo Trial was established on 19 January 1946 by the Allied powers after Japan's defeat in the Asian-Pacific War, and was composed of eleven judges and eleven prosecutors; one each from countries such as Australia, Canada, China, France, India, The Netherlands, New Zealand, The Philippines, The Soviet Union, the United Kingdom and the United States.[20] Twenty-eight individuals were indicted, many of who were military officers and members of wartime cabinets. The Trial aimed to prosecute and punish Japanese wartime leaders for crimes against peace, as well as, war crimes and crimes against humanity conducted in the Asia-Pacific during the war.[21] A sentence was handed down on 12 November 1948 to 25 defendants, excluding two who died during the proceedings and one removed from the proceedings due to mental health. All were found

---

and customs of war of enemy heads of states before a tribunal constituted by the opposite party."

[19] See also Sellars, "Delegitimizing," pp. 12–13. He points out that "in order to avoid the establishment of precedents that would affect the Emperor Meiji or his descendents, [the Japanese delegates] requested the elimination of references to heads of state in the majority report." Ibid.

[20] For the detail of the Tokyo Trial, see for example: Boister and Cryer, *The Tokyo*; Yuma Totani, *The Tokyo War Crimes Trial: The Pursuit of Justice in the Wake of World War II* (Harvard University Press, 2008); Awaya, Kentarō, *Tōkyō Saiban heno Michi* [The road to the Tokyo Trial], in two volumes (Tokyo: Kōdansha, 2006); Higurashi, Yoshinobu, *Tōkyō Saiban* [The Tokyo Trial] (Tokyo: Kōdansha, 2008).

[21] Article 5 of the Charter of International Military Tribunal for the Far East. Fifty-five counts of the indictment were separated into three groups under headings of "crimes against peace" (Group I: Counts 1 to 36); murder (Group II: Counts 37 to 52); and conventional war crimes and crimes against humanity (Group III: Counts 53 to 55). Responsibility for maltreatment of prisoners of war (POWs) and atrocities such as the "Nanjing Massacre" were also judged. See Totani, *Tokyo*.

guilty, and seven were sentenced to death. Japan has accepted the Tokyo Trial judgment through the 1951 San Francisco Peace Treaty.[22]

The focus of the Tokyo Trial was on crimes against peace, that is, the crime of aggression (on which the argument hereafter would concentrate). Article 5 of the Charter of the Tokyo Trial noted that war criminals tried and punished by the Tribunal were to be those who "are charged with offenses which include Crimes against Peace." In other words, no defendant who was responsible for crimes against humanity or war crimes was prosecuted unless they were also responsible for crimes against peace. This is one major difference from the Nuremberg Trial which did not have such a condition. The Prosecution was also well aware that their focus was on crimes against peace and tried to prove the aggressive nature of Japan's war and the existence of conspiracy in its wartime policy. An opening statement of the prosecution highlighted that the primary purpose of the Tokyo Trial was to criminalize aggression and prevent and deter future aggressive war.[23] The prosecution developed the case that the accused participated in the formulation or execution of conspiracy to wage wars of aggression to secure domination of East Asia, the Pacific and Indian Oceans and ultimately the world.[24] It resorted to the doctrine of conspiracy in order to "avoid the difficulties of establishing individual responsibility for action in extensive, complex, fluid and opaque decision-making processes."[25]

Crimes against peace was a controversial concept even at the time, and the Defense Section, which consisted of Japanese as well as American lawyers, fiercely fought over "the validity" of these crimes, the legal aspect of the concept, as well as its applicability to the defendants.[26] It challenged the validity of crimes against peace by pointing out that the General Treaty for the Renunciation of War 1928, the so-called Kellogg-Briand Pact, which Japan had signed, did not criminalise aggressive war and thus these crimes were newly created by the Allies; therefore the Charter of the Tokyo Trial was *ex post facto* law. The Defense also emphasised a self-defensive

---

22 Article 11 of the Treaty of Peace with Japan (San Francisco Peace Treaty), September 8, 1951.

23 *Transcripts*, 387–8. The Transcripts of the Tokyo Trial are available at R. John Pritchard (ed.), *The Tokyo Major War Crimes Trial: The Complete Transcripts of the Proceedings of the International Military Tribunal for the Far East*, in 124 volumes (Edwin Mellen Press).

24 *Transcripts*.

25 Neil Boister, "The Application of Collective and Comprehensive Criminal Responsibility for Aggression at the Tokyo International Military Tribunal: The Measure of the Crime of Aggression?," *Journal of International Criminal Justice*, vol. 8, 2010, p. 431.

26 See Boister and Cryer, *Tokyo*, pp. 115–153.

aspect of the war Japan was fighting, and furthermore challenged the validity of individual criminal responsibility, especially of senior officers, for crimes of aggression.[27]

The judges of the Tokyo Trial declined the Defense case. The Tribunal affirmed the validity of crimes against peace, stating that those who planned and waged a war of aggression were criminal, simply quoting the Nuremberg judgment given in October 1946 saying:

> the solemn renunciation of war as an instrument of national policy necessarily involves the proposition that such a war is illegal in international law; and that those who plan and wage such a war, with its inevitable and terrible consequences, are committing a crime in so doing.[28]

The judgement generally supported the case of the prosecution and concluded that since 1928 there was, in Japanese policy, a criminal conspiracy to wage wars of aggression in order to dominate the Asia-Pacific politically, military and economically, and this judgement defined the conspirators as the military and their supporters.[29] All but one defendant were found guilty of at least one count falling under crimes against peace. Yet, despite the heavy emphasis on crimes against peace, no one was sentenced to death under the Trial for this crime alone.

At the Tokyo Trial, a total of five separate opinions were submitted, in which some reservations about crimes against peace were raised. Justice Roling believed that a war of aggression was not criminal, and was against the application of conspiracy to the defendant. Judge Bernard questioned if there was criminal desire among the Japanese leaders to secure domination of East Asia.[30] Most famously, the Indian Justice Radhabinod Pal concluded that all defendants were not guilty of any charges, denying crimes against peace as a legal concept and questioning the superior responsibility of the defendants for atrocities committed on the ground.

The Tokyo Trial and its judgement were welcomed by Japanese intellectuals at the time.[31] Especially, the validity of crimes against peace and prosecuting Japanese wartime leaders for this count were positively regarded by legal scholars. Yokota Kisaburō, for example, emphasised that the primary importance of the Tokyo judgment was its clarification that it

---

[27] See *Transcripts*, 119–215, for the argument developed under the defense motion on the jurisdiction of the Tribunal.

[28] *Transcripts*, 48, 437–8.

[29] *Transcripts*, 49, 765–9.

[30] Boister, "Appreciation," p. 430.

[31] See Totani, *Tokyo*, pp. 190–217.

was not a state that resorts to the right of self-defense but international judicial organisations that were entitled to make the final decision whether a claim to such a right is acceptable. He expected that the impact of such a judgement would make any treaty banning war and use of force more effective and meaningful and contribute to the implementation of international law in future.[32]

Among the Japanese people at the time, the Tokyo Trial was generally accepted, though not enthusiastically. The Japanese accepted that it was an inevitable result of defeat on the one hand, and with a strong anger and distrust towards wartime leaders after the war on the other.[33] However, the Tokyo Trial was, and still is, seen by many as "victor's justice" that applied "new" criminal concepts of crimes against peace and crimes against humanity retroactively and did so only to the vanquished unilaterally. Such a view has been raised by right-wing politicians who strongly deny the Tokyo Trial and its judgment and enthusiastically promote Pal's opinion instead.[34] Even among those who accepted the Trial, there has been a rather cynical view that "the Tokyo Trial is a victor's justice, nothing more."[35] Aided by several inherent problems, including not indicting the Emperor, the Tokyo Trial has become a rather controversial and difficult issue for the Japanese people to frankly face.[36]

The Tokyo Trial showed the Japanese the criminality of war of aggression and its legal consequence, and thus potentially had something to share with post-war Japan's pacifist and anti-militarist culture. However, it has far from become a symbolic milestone for the criminalisation of aggression, as the Trial itself remained almost absent from the Japanese public discourse until the late 1970s.[37] In fact, when we see a postwar Japanese discourse on a war of aggression, especially in terms of Japan's own war, the Tokyo Trial's impact would be rather negative. The conservative and right-wing thinkers, who emphasise the self-defensive aspect of the Japan's war and even justify its causes, strongly attack the Tokyo Trial

---

[32] Yokota Kisaburō, "Tōkyo hanketsu to jieiken," *Kokusaihō Gaikō Zasshi*, vol. 48, no. 2 (1949), pp. 1–20.

[33] Madoka Futamura, *War Crimes Tribunals and Transitional Justice: The Tokyo Trial and the Nuremberg Legacy* (Routledge, 2008), pp. 68–72.

[34] Ibid., pp. 93–99. See also Totani, *Tokyo*, pp. 218–245; John Dower, *Embracing Defeat: Japan in the Aftermath of World War II* (London: Penguin Books, 2000), pp. 461–469.

[35] Futamura, *War*, pp. 102–4.

[36] On the taboo and silence over the Tokyo Trial, see ibid., pp. 107–11.

[37] Chihiro Hosoya et al. (eds), *The Tokyo War Crimes Trial: An International Symposium* (Tokyo: Kodansha; New York, N.Y.: Distributed in the U.S. by Kodansha International through Harper & Row, 1986), p. 123.

for unjustly and unilaterally deciding that Japan fought a war of aggression.[38] In other words, the shortcoming of the Tokyo Trial is used to deny the validity of the Tokyo judgment that Japan fought a war of aggression. Surrounded by ideological and political debates on the historical perception of the past, the Tokyo Trial became a controversial topic in Japan on the one hand, and remained within the Japanese as a taboo and national trauma on the other. The Tokyo Trial came to be re-examined more openly and constructively only after 2005.[39] It was not the Tokyo Trial but Article 9 of the new constitution, which states that "the Japanese people forever renounce war as a sovereign right of the nation and the threat or use of force as means of settling international disputes," that has been strongly associated with Japan's post-war pacifist culture and renouncement of any type of wars.

Post-World War II Attempt to Define Aggression

With the precedent of the Nuremberg and Tokyo Trials and the concept of crimes against peace established there, the international community thereafter paved the way towards codifying and institutionalising the crime of aggression. On 11 December 1946, the United Nations General Assembly adopted a resolution affirming the principles of international law as recognized by the Charter of the Nuremberg Tribunal and the judgment of the Tribunal.[40] States at the time did agree that an act of aggression is a crime under international law.[41] However, the Nuremberg and Tokyo Trials did not define aggression *per se*. The international community soon realised the need for a definition of aggression, and the General Assembly attempted to achieve the agreed definition in 1950, 1954 and 1957. However, none of these attempts were successful in reaching an international agreement.

---

[38] See Futamura, *War*, pp. 93–99.

[39] See Madoka Futamura, "Japanese Societal Attitudes towards the Tokyo Trial: A Contemporary Perspective" in Yuki Tanaka, Tim McCormack and Gerry Simpson (eds.), *Beyond Victors' Justice? The Tokyo War Crimes Trial Revisited* (Leiden, The Netherlands: Martinus Nijhoff Publishers, 2011).

[40] General Assembly Resolution 95 (I): "Affirmation of the Principles of International Law Recognized by the Charter of the Nuremberg Tribunal," 11 December 1946, A/RES/95 (I).

[41] Principle VI of the General Assembly Resolution 95 (I) states that "Crimes against peace' is (i) Planning, preparation, initiation or waging of a war of aggression or a war in violation of international treaties, agreements or assurances; (ii) Participation in a common plan or conspiracy for the accomplishment of any of the acts mentioned under (i).

In 1967, responding to the request from the Soviet Union, the General Assembly again adopted a resolution and established the Special Committee on the Question of Defining Aggression.[42] This was the fourth attempt at the United Nations, and, this time, after seven years of discussion, the Committee finally came up with an agreed definition in 1974. Japan participated in this process as one of 35 member countries of the Committee.

The first session of the Special Committee was held in 1968 but could not agree on anything because of political recrimination between the blocs of the Soviet Union and the United States under the Cold War context. When the Soviet Union proposed the Committee to meet again the following year, Japan joined Australia, France, Italy, Norway, Turkey, the UK, and the U.S. to abstain from the proposal, expressing scepticism about the attempt as a whole.[43] However, these countries gathered again in the 1969 session and submitted the so-called Six-power draft proposal to counter the Soviet draft proposal and the Thirteen-power draft proposal which had been submitted earlier.[44] Japan was a member of the six-power, together with Australia, Canada, Italy, the UK, and the U.S.. Following discussions in the Committee up to 1974 were developed through comparing, contrasting, and adjusting these three proposals.

Japan's position during the sessions therefore was in tune with the other five countries. At the same time, Japan participated in discussions and made several points based on its own. First is on the issue of evidentiary value of the first strike and other circumstances. The Japanese delegation stated: "It had repeatedly emphasized the importance of striking a proper balance between the question of priority—the objective element—and the question of intent—the subjective element."[45] It was very cautious about the "priority principle," which focuses on the fact of the first strike, and instead emphasised the need also to take the intent into consideration when defining aggression. However, Japan in the end accepted the final agreed draft without explicit reference to intention, taking a position that the question of intent was what the Security Council takes into consideration when they determine an act of aggression.[46] Japan did see the definition as a guideline for the UN Security Council, which has an authority under the UN Charter to decide the existence of aggression.

---

42 General Assembly Resolution 2330, A/RES/2330(XXII), 18 December 1967.
43 Ferencz, *Defining*, pp. 9–10.
44 Twenty-Fourth Session, Supp. No. 20, A/7260 (1969).
45 Twenty-Ninth Session, Supp. No. 19, A/9619 (1974), p. 16.
46 Ibid.

Second, Japan was keen to differentiate "a war of aggression" and "an act of aggression" which was not part of a war, in order to restrict the legal consequences for individuals. The delegation stated that "an act of aggression which was not part of a war of aggression gave rise only to State responsibility and that the question of individual responsibility for an act of aggression should be left for future study."[47] In fact, Japan was not alone in taking such a position. The UK also objected to a reference merely to "aggression" without restricting it to "aggressive war." This was due to the concern that "there be a war before there could be personal criminal responsibility," which was supported also by the U.S..[48] Benjamin Ferencz critically analyzed this position and stated that this "may have minimized the value of deterrence,"[49] which was one of the aims expressed by the General Assembly on establishing the Special Committee to define aggression.[50] At the same time, as to the Japanese position, Ferencz made the following statement:

> It was perhaps to be expected that the Japanese, some of whose leaders had suffered the consequences of a broad interpretation of personal responsibility for crimes against peace, would favor a restrictive view of criminal liability.[51]

Of course, as Ferencz himself admitted, Japan did not articulate such motivation in taking its position. Also it was not necessarily clear whether the Japanese position came from being a close ally of the U.S. and the West under the Cold War or from having had a historical experience of the Tokyo Trial. Still, it is noteworthy that Japan's past made an international legal scholar speculate about its cautious attitude, and as is seen below, he would not be entirely wrong to highlight the linkage between the past and the current policy on the international criminal law.

And third, Ambassador Iguchi Takeo, representing the Japanese delegation, stated at the concluding stage of the session in 1974: "Personally, he would have been in favour of including a reference to the importance of

47 Ibid.

48 Ferencz, *Defining*, p. 43.

49 Ibid., p. 44. Ferencz argues that this position "might lead to the conclusion that any government leader could engage his country in any hostilities but would be immune from criminal prosecution by simply declaring that a state of war did not exist."

50 General Assembly Resolution 2330 (XXII) stated: "there is a widespread conviction that a definition of aggression would have considerable importance for the maintenance of international peace and for the adoption of effective measures under the Charter for preventing acts of aggression."

51 Ferencz, *Defining*, p. 44.

utilizing the available means of achieving pacific settlement of disputes."[52] This statement accurately reflected postwar Japan's stance under Article 9 of the Constitution, renouncing war and the threat or use of force as means of settling international disputes. Emphasising the means for peaceful settlement of disputes is important for deterring a war of aggression; however it is less direct than the criminalisation of aggression, to which Japan, just like other states, held a cautious position. Here, it is interesting to note the gap between Japan's commitment to the pacifist ethos of the Constitution and its cautious stance for the criminalisation of aggression. In 1974, the General Assembly finally adopted a consensus definition of aggression. Article 1 states that "Aggression is the use of armed force by a State against the sovereignty, territorial integrity or political independence of another State, or in any other manner inconsistent with the Charter of the United Nations."[53] However, the definition was not very useful for an actual international prosecution. Mary Ellen O'Connell and Mirakmal Niyazmatov point out that during the debate on whether to use "aggression" or "a war of aggression," the focus was on the consequences for states of committing aggression.[54] Yoram Dinstein concludes: "the General Assembly largely deemphasized the criminal aspect of its formulation, and brought to the fore the political dimension."[55] Indeed, many of the member states, including Japan, expected the definition to serve as a guideline for the Security Council, not for an international court to prosecute and punish individuals for this crime. This is why, when the ICC was established in 1998 and finally included the crime of aggression in its subject jurisdiction, the international community again faced the need to tackle the definition of the crime.

The ICC and the Crime of Aggression

During the Cold War, the definition of aggression strongly influenced the draft statute of a permanent international criminal court—the lack of the

[52] A/9619 (1974), p. 16.

[53] General Assembly Resolution 3314 (XXIX), 14 December 1974. Article 3 lists examples, while Article 4 notes that "the Security Council may determine that other acts constitute aggression under the provisions of the Charter."

[54] Mary Ellen O'Connell and Mirakmal Niyazmatov, "What is Aggression?: Comparing the Jus ad Bellum and the ICC Statute," *Journal of International Criminal Justice*, vol. 10, 2012, pp. 195–198. Article 5 (2) in the end included the two terms of "a war of aggression" and "aggression."

[55] Yoram Dinstein, *War, Aggression, and Self-Defence*, 3rd ed. (New York: Cambridge University Press, 2001), p. 115.

former was one of the hindrances to the creation of the court at the time.[56] In the post-Cold War, it became opposite: when the creation of the ICC gained its momentum in the 1990s, the definition of aggression was also brought back to the international arena—this time within the context of prosecuting and punishing individuals responsible for the crime. The establishment of the ICC made the international community face the issue of the definition, as well as the conditions for the exercise of jurisdiction by the Court. In this sense, in order to examine Japan's attitude to the emerging crime of aggression, it would be useful first to see Japan's position towards the ICC.

The Japanese government's position towards the ICC has been consistently positive. It participated actively in discussions of a preparatory committee for the draft statute of the ICC during 1996 and 1998, and Owada Hisashi, who was the Head of the Japanese Delegation to the UN Diplomatic Conference on the Establishment of an International Criminal Court in 1998, emphasised that Japan has contributed to the adoption of the Rome Statute by adjusting different opinions among states.[57] Japan also continued to participate in sessions of the Assembly of States Party as an observer, including in the Special Working Group on the Crime of Aggression, which presented in 2009 draft amendments including definition of the "crime" and the "act" of aggression (draft article 8 bis) and conditions for the exercise of jurisdiction (draft article 15 bis).[58] This proposal became the basis of the discussion in Kampala.

However, Japan became a member of the ICC only in July 2007, as the 105th state. One of the major challenges for Japan's accession to the Rome Statute was said to have been the need to harmonize domestic laws with the Statute. Japan could not ratify 1977 two Protocols additional to the Geneva Conventions of 1949 until 2004, when the Law Concerning the

---

56 See M.C. Bassiouni, "Historical Survey: 1919–1998," in M.C. Bassiouni compiled, *The Statute of the International Criminal Court: A Documentary History* (New York: Transnational Publishers, Inc., 1998), pp. 11–15.

57 Owada, Hisashi, "Kokusaikeijisaibansho Setsuritsuno Igito Mondaiten," *Kokusaihō Gaikō Zasshi*, vol. 98, no. 5, pp. 29–30. For example, Owada emphasises that the delegation contributed to the inclusion of Article 124 in the Statute.

58 Report of the Special Working Group on the Crime of Aggression, ICC-ASP/7/SWGCA/2, 20 February 2009. In Kampala, the group's proposal on the definition of the crime of aggression and elements of crimes, which were based on the 1974 General Assembly Resolution, was adopted as it is. For the work of the Special Working Group on the Crime of Aggression, see Stefan Barriga, Wolfgang Danspeckgruber, Christian Wenaweser, *The Princeton Process on the Crime of Aggression: Materials of the Special Working Group on the Crime of Aggression, 2003–2009* (Lynne Rienner, 2009).

Punishment of Grave Breaches of International Humanitarian Law (PGB Law) was adopted by the Japanese Diet. The adoption of the PGB law finally created in the Japanese legal system a basis for prosecuting and punishing grave breaches in the Additional Protocols, and thus led to the Japanese accession to the two Protocols in August 2004. This development finally enabled the country to become a member of the ICC.

An important question here is why the PGB Law was not adopted much earlier. Yachi Shōtarō pointed out the fact that the harmonisation of domestic law and the Geneva Conventions had been understood in relation to the Emergency Legislation on National Security, which deals with situations including an armed attack against Japan. Such legislation, as Yachi states, had been seen as a taboo under the political and social climate in post-war Japan, taking a pacifist stance under Article 9 of the constitution.[59] Indeed, the Legislation was regarded as politically sensitive and faced strong opposition from leftist parties, such as the Japanese Socialist Party and the Japanese Communist Party, which considered its enacting as paving the way to the country's remilitarization and enabling the Japanese Self-Defense Force (JSDF) to participate in war-fighting activities. As Jens Meierhenrich and Keiko Ko point out, "no legislation was supposed to be adopted that in any way—directly or indirectly—was linked to the phenomenon of war".[60]

A sense of taboo surrounding the Emergency Legislation, as well as international humanitarian law, came to be softened only in the 1990s, when Japan started to seek a more active role in international peace cooperation and started to pass domestic laws for the country's participation in peace operations abroad.[61] Since then, International Peace Cooperation Law, the Anti-Terrorism Special Measures Law, and the Law Concerning Special Measures on Humanitarian and Reconstruction Assistance in Iraq were adopted. In 2007, international peace cooperation activities were given the status of a primary mission of the JSDF, and the Self-Defense Forces Law was amended accordingly.[62] It is under such a development

[59] Yachi, Shōtarō, "Nihonniokeru Kokusai Jōyaku no Jisshi [Implementing International Treaties in Japan]," 100 *Kokusaihō Gaikō Zasshi* (2001), p. 10.

[60] Jens Meierhenrich and Keiko Ko, "How Do States Join the International Criminal Court? The Implementation of the Rome Statute in Japan," *Journal of International Criminal Justice*, vol. 7, 2009, p. 239, p. 253. See also Akira Mayama, "Japan's New Emergency Legislation and International Humanitarian Law," 47 *Japanese Annual of International Law*, vol. 47, 2004, pp. 69–70.

[61] Meierhenrich and Ko, "How," p. 239; Mayama, "Japan's," p. 70.

[62] See *Defense of Japan 2007* (Annual White Paper), Chapter 3, Section 2: http://www.mod.go.jp/e/publ/w_paper/pdf/2007/29Part2_Chap3_Sec2.pdf, accessed on 13 May 2010.

that the PGB Law was finally adopted in 2004, two Additional Protocols to the 1949 Geneva Conventions were ratified accordingly, and the path to becoming a member state of the ICC was legally opened.

Of course, the PGB Law did not solve all issues, and further adjustment of domestic laws took some more years to be completed.[63] Some MPs supporting the ICC criticised the government by pointing out that domestic laws alone could not explain the slow process of the accession, and questioned if the government had been taking into consideration the United States' position on the ICC.[64] On the part of the Japanese government, it repeatedly highlighted the amount of Japan's financial obligation to the ICC, in addition to domestic law, as one of the major challenges for speeding up its accession to the Rome Statute. Based on the adoption of the UN scale of assessment, it was estimated in 2006 that Japan's share of expenses for the ICC would amount to about three billion yen, about 28% of its overall expense.[65]

Although it took nine years to become a member, Japan was expressing the willingness to contribute to the activities of the ICC even before the accession to the Rome Statute. It emphasized that its becoming a state party to the ICC would have a positive impact on other Asian countries, many of which still have not joined the ICC, and thus would reinforce the universality of the ICC.[66] In addition, an active support of the ICC was seen as crucial in terms of fostering Japanese diplomacy vis-à-vis African countries and in the field of human rights and humanitarian activities.[67] Furthermore, prior to its submission of the instrument of accession to the Rome Statute, the Japanese government had nominated, as a candidate for a by-election of ICC judges, Ms. Saiga Fumiko, Ambassador in Charge of Human Rights and Member of the Committee on the Elimination of All Forms of Discrimination against Women. She was elected in November 2007 and became the first Asian female judge at the ICC.

With all these active stances, Japan's attitude towards the definition of aggression in relation to the ICC statute remained unclear and rather passive. Being asked about the Japanese stance, the government under the

63 For details, see Meierhenrich and Ko, "How"; Mayama Akira, "Kokusaikeijisaibansho no Taishōhanzai to Kokunaitekitaiō [The Municipal Response to the Crimes that Fall Within the Jurisdiction of the ICC]," 79 *Hōritsujihō* (2007), pp. 31–36.

64 Record of the LDP's voluntary's study sessions on the ICC on 15 December 2005 and 14 March 2006. Available at: http://blog.goo.ne.jp/jnicc_org_tk_06/e/fae9e45b212b35e132c8190d426d332d, accessed on 10 May 2010.

65 Masaki, "Nihon," pp. 327–330.

66 Ibid., p. 336.

67 Ibid., p. 345.

Liberal Democratic Party (LDP) responded in April 2007 by stating that they had no clear policy on the matter. Yet, they emphasised their willingness to actively participate in the discussion once they became the formal state party to the ICC.[68]

Indeed, once having become the member state, Japan became more outspoken on the crime of aggression. During the 2010 Review Conference, Special envoy of the Government of Japan, Komatsu Ichirō, emphasized that the country considered it important for the ICC to become able to exercise its jurisdiction over the crime of aggression. Significantly, he clearly mentioned that there is "a historical" in Japan's position:

> Japanese nationals were convicted of crime against peace and of war crimes by the International Military Tribunal for the Far East. Japan solemnly accepted its judgments by virtue of the San Francisco Peace Treaty. As a country with an ingrained memory of the history and lessons learned therefrom, Japan firmly believes that ICC should be able to exercise its jurisdiction over the crime of aggression.[69]

Here, the positive significance of the country's experience of the Tokyo Trial was publicly stated by the Japanese envoy at the Review Conference. This is an important remark clearly connecting Japan's experience in the Tokyo Trial to its stance on the criminalization of aggression, which in the past was not clearly made. At the same time, Japan expressed its firm legalistic stance emphasizing that "international criminal tribunals should not be operated on the basis of *ex post facto* law."[70] This stance may also reflect a bitter lesson that Japan learned from the Tokyo Trial.

Several reasons can be pointed out for such a statement to be made in 2010. Japan's self-awareness as a member of the ICC after 2007 would be one of the major reasons. At the same time, the change of the administration from that of the LDP to the Democratic Party of Japan (DPJ) might have had a certain impact on the government's attitude towards the crime of aggression. The LDP is a conservative party which was originally less enthusiastic about the ICC than the DPJ, who had been raising "early accession" of the Rome Statute in its manifesto. What is more, since 2005 the active re-examination of and public discourse on the Tokyo Trial

[68] Heisei 19-nen, 4-gatsu 26-nichi, Sangiin Gaikō Bōei Iinkaikaigiroku, Dai Hachigō, 26 April 2007, p. 6.

[69] Statement by H.E. Mr. Ichiro Komatsu, Special Envoy of the Government of Japan, Ambassador Extraordinary and Plenipotentiary of Japan, At the Review Conference of the Rome Statute of the ICC, 4 June 2010, Kampala: http://www.mofa.go.jp/policy/i_crime/icc/pdfs/statement_1006.pdf, accessed on 16 July 2010.

[70] Ibid.

started to emerge, led by the media and academics, who tried to overcome traditional taboo, go beyond ideological debates surrounding the issue, and learn constructive lessons out of it.[71] This trend may have enabled the governments' official to more directly refer to the Tokyo Trial in the context of the ICC and the crime of aggression.

At Kampala, Japan consistently stated the importance of "creating and fostering an International Criminal Court that can truly function effectively on the basis of total confidence of the international community" and, for this reason, emphasized that any decision should be adopted by consensus, not by vote, and the legal integrity of the amendment procedure should be secured.[72] From this perspective, Japan expressed on the final day of the conference its disappointment and "serious doubts regarding the legality of the amendment procedures contained in the amendments," though it did not stand in the way of adoption.[73] Indeed, as Mauro Politi argues, "the final text reflects the delicate compromise reached and, for this very reason, is quite ambiguous and convoluted on various points," which he thinks should be scrutinized carefully in order to examine whether the amendments really meet the demand for the effective prosecution and punishment of the crime of aggression.[74]

Background of Japan's Attitude towards the Crime of Aggression

Prosecuting and punishing those responsible individuals for the crime of aggression directly challenge the core of state sovereignty. In that sense, Japan's sometime cautious position towards the criminalisation of aggression would not be unique. At the same time, there are several elements related to its past history that need to be taken into consideration when analysing Japan's position on this issue.

---

71 Futamura, "Japanese," pp. 49–52.

72 Statement by Japan (11 June 2010) (before adoption): http://www.mofa.go.jp/policy/i_crime/icc/pdfs/before_adoption_1006.pdf, accessed on 16 July 2010. See also Okano Masataka, "Kokusaikeijisaibansho Romakiteikentōkaigino Kekkanitsuite," *Kokusaihō Gaikō Zasshi*, vol. 109, no. 2, 2010, pp. 80–82.

73 Statement by Japan (11 June 2010) (after adoption): http://www.mofa.go.jp/policy/i_crime/icc/pdfs/after_adoption_1006.pdf, accessed on 16 July 2010. For the analysis of the Japanese argument, see Kreß and Holtzendorff, "Kampala."

74 Mauro Politi, "The ICC and the Crime of Aggression: A Dream that Came Through and the Reality Ahead," *Journal of International Criminal Justice*, vol. 10, 2012, p. 272. See also Mayama Akira, "Kokusaikeijisaibanshokitei Kentōkaigisaitakuno Shinryakuhanzaikanrenkitei," *Kokusaihō Gaikō Zasshi*, vol. 109, no. 4, 2011, pp. 1–33.

First is Japan's postwar pacifist attitude. Having gone through the war and defeat, Japan had a bitter experience both as perpetrators, as well as victims, of war and war crimes.[75] In post-war Japan, there emerged a culture of pacifism and anti-militarism, through the demilitarisation and democratisation process, as well as through the new constitution embracing Article 9. Article 9 and its pacifist orientation have strongly influenced post-war Japanese foreign policy. The spirit of Article 9 has been also internalised in the Japanese people's mentality and created people's cautious attitude towards any possibility of JSDF taking a part in war conduct. Such an attitude has been pressuring the government via leftist political parties. At the same time, as Meierhenrich and Ko analyse, it also came to hinder Japan's engagement with international humanitarian law, because it is a law on the conduct of war. On signing the San Francisco Peace Treaty in 1951, Japan has declared its intention for accessions to the 1949 Geneva Conventions, and Japan became party to them in 1953. However, Japan could not adopt the 1977 additional protocols until 2004 for reasons examined above. International humanitarian law aims to "humanize" existing armed conflict, which itself is an important approach to war and peace. However, within the post-war Japanese context, it was seen as incompatible with the renouncing of war. It is ironic that Japan's pacifist and anti-militarist stance prevented it, until recently, from actively committing itself to international humanitarian law. It is even more ironic that it had consequently deterred the country from becoming member of the ICC earlier.

Second, a passive attitude towards the issue of laws and wars could be observed also within the Japanese academics until the late 1970s. Fujita Hisakazu underscores that since the end of the Second World War up until a certain time, there was an absence of substantial research on the 1949 Geneva Conventions, as well as on the laws of war in general. This, according to Fujita, is noteworthy compared with the post-WWI era when such research was conducted by academics at the time.[76] This may be partly to do with the pacifist social and political atmosphere mentioned above, which may have distanced many researchers from the issue of war and law. At the same time, Fujita analyses that this absence is interrelated to the fact that Japanese academics, after WWII, failed to conduct all-inclusive research evaluating Japan's act in the Asia-Pacific War from

[75] For Japan's experience in war and defeat, see Dower, *Embracing*.

[76] Fujita Hisakazu, "Nihonniokeru Sensōhō Kenkyu no Ayumi [The Evolution of Study on the Laws of War in Japan during the Century]," *Kokusaihō Gaikōu Zasshi*, vol. 94, no. 4 & 5, p. 81.

international legal perspectives;[77] such a task required them to face the criminality of Japan's war and war conduct. Indeed, the legal status of the use of force and the criminalization of aggression were not enthusiastically researched by Japanese legal scholars up until a certain time,[78] except for some legal scholars who examined the Tokyo Trial right after its judgment. According to Fujita, the study on international humanitarian law in Japan started to develop after the Additional Protocols to the Geneva Conventions were adopted in 1977.[79] The slow development of the study on these topics by Japanese academics is one element that needs to be taken into consideration when examining Japan's stance on the criminalisation of aggression.

Then, one might question to what extent Japan's attitude towards the ICC and the crime of aggression was influenced by its experience with the Tokyo Trial, in which Japan had a bitter experience of their wartime leaders being prosecuted for alleged crimes against peace. Philipp Osten, a German legal scholar based in Japan, pointed out that the experience of the Nuremberg Trial had an impact on post-war German attitude towards international criminal law. He stated that the German refusal of the Trial at the early stage of the postwar era made the country sceptical about international criminal law as a whole. Accordingly, the body of international criminal law did not develop in the country during the Cold War.[80] It is only after the Cold War, according to Osten, when the country faced a need to prosecute and punish political crimes committed in East Germany that the German courts started to take international criminal law into consideration. This was the first step that gradually made Germany into one of the most active supporters of the ICC.[81] Osten argues that this attitude contrasts with that of post-war Germany. If Nuremberg had a certain impact on the way post-war Germany approached the issue of international criminal justice, post-war Japan's stance would not be totally free from its experience in the Tokyo Trial. The "negative" impact, from the perspective of international criminal justice, of the international trial may be even bigger in Japan than Germany, which has been facing and digesting

77 Ibid.

78 Exceptions are: Onuma Yasuaki, *Sensōsekininron Josetsu: "Heiwanitaisurutsumi"no Keiseikateiniokeru Ideorogiseito Kōsokusei* (Tokyo: Tōkyo Daigaku Shuppan, 1975); Miyoshi, Masahiro, "Kokusairengō niyoru Shinryakuno Teigi," *Juristo*, no. 584 (1975); Takahashi Michitoshi, "Shinryakunoteiginikansuru Kokuren-iinnkaianno Seiritsu," *Kokusaimondai*, vol. 176 and 177 (1974).

79 Fujita, "Nihonniokeru," p. 83.

80 Osten, "Kokusai," pp. 127–8.

81 Ibid.

the Nuremberg lessons more actively than Japan concerning the Tokyo Trial.[82] What is more, unlike post-war Germany, Japan did not prosecute its war criminals in its domestic courts after the completion of the international trial.

Just as Ferencz did, some of Japanese scholars themselves pointed out that the experience of the Tokyo Trial may have negatively impacted on Japan's approach to the ICC and international criminal justice. Yamagami Shingo stated that the international criminal court immediately reminds the Japanese of the Tokyo Trial, the pros and cons of which have been debated within society.[83] More specifically, Niikura Osamu pointed out that the issue of the crime of aggression would require Japan to face its collective trauma, imprinted in postwar Japan.[84] That is why he emphasises that the ICC is a good opportunity for the former Axis Power to overcome its "negative legacy" and that this is important for Japan to overcome "the Tokyo Trial shock".[85]

In that sense, the stance of the Japanese delegation at the 2010 Review Conference referring to the Tokyo Trial to support the criminalisation of aggression is noteworthy. It may show that Japan has started to face its own experience in war and trial in relation to the development of international humanitarian law and international criminal justice. Indeed, having their wartime leaders prosecuted and punished for crimes against peace, Japan is in a strong position to contribute to the criminalisation of aggression; it can support the process while pointing out, from its own experience, any legal and institutional shortcomings of the crime of aggression and its political, as well as, normative, consequences to follow.

---

[82] See for example, Ian Buruma, *The Wages of Guilt: Memories of War in Germany and Japan* (Phoenix, 1994), pp. 160–162.

[83] Yamagami, "Kokusaikeijisaibansho," p. 776.

[84] Niikura, Osamu, "Kokusaikeijisaibanshokiteino Hijunto Kokunaihōseibino Kadai," *Hōritsujihō*, vol. 79, no. 4, p. 28.

[85] Ibid., p. 26.

CHAPTER EIGHT

QUESTIONING THE LEGALITY AND LEGITIMACY OF A PREVENTIVE STRIKE BY THE U.S. TO DISARM NORTH KOREA OF NUCLEAR WEAPONS*

Dan Ernst

This chapter addresses the following central question: Does the United States of America have legal or moral justification for taking preventive (as distinguished from preemptive) military action against North Korea (DPRK) for the sake of disarming it of nuclear weapons? To be clear, this is not to ask whether such an action is prudent—such an attack was judged imprudent by the Clinton administration in the 1990s even before the DPRK successfully tested nuclear weapons.[1] Yet, concluding that a preventive strike is imprudent is different from saying that it is morally unjustified or illegal. Contemporary scholars looking into questions of legal authorization for preventive or preemptive military action primarily look to the United Nations Charter and its interpretation by the International Court of Justice.[2] Contemporary scholars thinking about the moral justification of the decision to use armed force (*jus ad bellum*) also

---

* This work was supported by an Intramural Research Grant of Ewha University (grant no. 2008-2153-1)

[1] U.S. Defense Secretary Perry determined that such a preventive action was possible but would likely lead to 1 million deaths: "Such an attack was very likely to incite the North Koreans to launch a military attack on South Korea. Even though the North Koreans would surely lose this second Korean War, they could cause hundreds of thousands, perhaps millions, of casualties before being defeated." Quoted in Lyle J. Goldstein, *Preventive attack and Weapons of Mass Destruction* (Stanford University Press, 2006), p. 135.

[2] Specifically, Articles 51 and 42 of the UN Charter, and *Military and Paramilitary Activities in and Against Nicaragua*, International Court of Justice, 1986. *See* Ian Brownlie, *International Law and the Use of Force by States* (Oxford: Clarendon Press, 1963); Ian Brownlie, *Basic Documents in International Law, 6th edition* (Oxford University Press, 2009); Alex Bellamy, *Just Wars: from Cicero to Iraq* (Cambridge: Polity Press, 2006); Mary Ellen O'Connell, "The Myth of Preemptive Self-Defense," *American Society of International Law: Task Force on Terrorism* (August 2002); Michael Bothe, "Terrorism and the Legality of Pre-emptive Force," *European Journal of International Law*, vol. 14, 2003, pp. 227–240; Asa Kasher, "Operation Cast Lead and the Ethics of Just War," *Azure, vol. 30*, 2009; Karl P. Mueller, et al., *Striking First: Preemptive and Preventive Attack in U.S. National Security Policy* (Santa Monica, CA: RAND Air Force Project, 2006).

look to the history of the "just war" tradition initiated by Augustine and Aquinas, carried into the 17th Century by Suárez, and Grotius, and recently experiencing a renaissance exemplified by the work of Ramsey and Walzer.[3] This tradition commonly identifies six criteria for evaluating the decision to use force: legitimate authority, just cause, right intention, last resort, proportionality, and its having a reasonable chance of success.[4] Each of these principles is thought to provide necessary conditions for evaluating the use of military force as just. This chapter will follow these trends in analyzing the legality and morality of inter-state military action, concluding that the U.S. currently has no legal authorization to launch a preventive strike to disarm the DPRK, but that a convincing argument can be made that such an action would meet all but the criteria of legality for just war.

Part One: International Law Regarding Preventive Strike by U.S. against the DPRK

Legality of Anticipatory Military Action in general under the UN Charter

In assessing the legality of one state's using military strikes against another state, we note that in Article 2(4) of the United Nations Charter all signatories mutually agree to "refrain in their international relations from the threat or use of force."[5] Yet if this pledge is broken, and if one state does engage in the use of force against another, then Article 51 of the Charter

[3] Nicholas Rengger, "On the Just War Tradition in the Twenty-First Century," *International Affairs*, vol. 78, 2002, p. 354; *See* Michael Walzer, *Just and Unjust Wars*, 3rd ed. (NY: Basic Books, 2000); *See Also* Paul Ramsey, *The Just War: Force and Political Responsibility* (Lanham, MD: University Press of America, 1983).

[4] Although writers commonly identify as many as nine criteria of just war (*See* Kasher 2009), arguably, such criteria can be reduced to the core principles identified by Augustine and expounded by Thomas Aquinas. *See* Rengger, 2002, p. 358: "over time the *jus ad bellum* had coalesced around a set of seven principles: in rough order of priority, just cause, right authority, right intention, proportionality of ends, last resort, reasonable hope of success and the aim of peace. The *jus in bello*, meanwhile, had come to revolve around two central principles: proportionality of means and non-combatant immunity." *See Also* J. von Elbe, "The Evolution of the Concept of the Just War in International Law," *American Journal of International Law*, vol. 33, 1939, p. 669; Gregory Reichberg, "Preventative War in Classical Just War Theory," *Journal of the History of International Law*, vol 9, 2007, pp. 5–34; Alex Bellamy, *Just Wars: from Cicero to Iraq* (Cambridge: Polity Press, 2006); Bruno Coppieters and Nick Fotion eds. *Moral Constraints on War: Principles and Cases* (Lanham, MD: Lexington Books, 2002); Brendan Howe, "Conflicting Normative Dimensions of Justification: The Gulf War," *Just War in Comparative Perspective*, Paul Robinson ed. (Ashgate, 2003).

[5] UN Charter, Article 2 paragraph 4.

recognizes the legality of military actions taken by states in their own defense. Additionally, Article 42 authorizes the Security Council to "take such action by air, sea, or land forces as may be necessary to maintain or restore international peace and security."[6] Notice that Article 42 authorizes the Security Council to use military force in response to *threats* made by one state against another, even *before* the threatening state actually launches an attack.[7] Article 51, on the other hand, is notable in its stipulation that military action in self-defense is authorized "if an armed attack occurs."[8] This disparity in the treatment of anticipatory defense, legal if initiated by the UN Security Council and illegal if taken by the state being threatened, is in need of justification. Such a justification could not rely on a condemnation of anticipatory self-defense *per se*. However, this distinction could rely on a practical prediction that states are poor judges of the necessity of anticipation when their own defense is threatened. We will return to discussion of the morality (legitimacy) of anticipatory self-defense in Part Two of this chapter, here in Part One, we begin by examining the legality of anticipatory self-defense.

In order to assess the legality of a military strike by the United States on the DPRK at this time we begin with a look at Article 51. The language of Article 51 reads as follows:

> Nothing in the present Charter shall impair the inherent right of individual or collective self-defence if an armed attack occurs against a Member of the United Nations.[9]

There are three key phrases in this language which require clarification: "self-defense," "armed attack," and "if an armed attack occurs." We will revisit the concept in more detail, but to begin discussion, I will treat

---

6 Ibid. Chapter VII, Article 42.

7 Karl P. Mueller, et al., *Striking First: Preemptive and Preventive Attack in U.S. National Security Policy* (Santa Monica, CA: RAND Air Force Project, 2006), pp. 51–52: "[T]he U.N. Charter implicitly grants the Security Council the right to authorize an anticipatory attack: It permits the Security Council to authorize force in response to a threat to the peace where there has not yet been a breach of the peace or an act of aggression. In addition, the Security Council can authorize force to *maintain* peace and security. If peace and security are to be maintained, as opposed to restored, then peace has not yet been breached." *Cf.* T.D. Gill, "The Temporal Dimension of Self-Defence: Anticipation, Pre-emption, Prevention and Immediacy," *Journal of Conflict and Security Law*, vol. 11, 2006, pp. 362–369: "Legal opinion is in wide agreement that the only clearly recognized exceptions to the prohibition [Article 2(4)] are those which the Charter sets forth—the maintenance of collective security by or through Security Council mandate and self-defence."

8 UN Charter, VII, Article 51.

9 Ibid.

"self-defense" as referring to military actions intending to thwart enemy attempts to destroy one's state. Such actions can be distinguished from military acts whose aim is to gain territory, resources, or dominance, and military actions whose aim is to achieve humanitarian goals. To be succinct: the term "self-defense" refers to the aim of the acting state to thwart attempts to destroy it.

The second term we must define clearly is "armed attack." The term has been interpreted by the International Court of Justice to be a threshold concept. That is to say, only "sufficiently grave" uses of force are considered "armed attacks" for legal purposes.[10] One line of reasoning for taking the phrase "armed attack" to be a threshold concept is the nexus it shares with "self-defense" in Article 51. Self-defense, as just mentioned above, has to do with being motivated to thwart attempts to destroy one's state. It is the dire situation of saving one's state from destruction that is being referred to in Article 51, not actions aimed at deterring provocation, and not military action intending to punish theft or other misdeeds.[11]

Third, it is important to distinguish between several understandings of the phrase "if an armed attack occurs." The phrase could be taken to refer to a time after an enemy has landed a blow; and it could refer to a time after which an attack has been launched but is still on its way to landing. Either of these interpretations is compatible with what have come to be referred to as "restrictionist" readings of Article 51. "Restrictionists" read the phrase, "if an armed attack occurs," as meaning "*only* if an armed attack occurs."[12] Even by strict "restrictionist" legal standards, a state need not wait to suffer the first blow of an enemy before launching a self-defensive strike. If the enemy has launched an attack, then a state may

---

[10] *Case concerning Military and Paramilitary Activities in and against Nicaragua*, 1986 (Nicaragua v. U.S.) ICJ Rep. 14, par. 191, 195; *Case concerning Oil Platforms*, 2003 (Islamic Republic of Iran v. U.S.) ICJ Rep. par. 61–64, 72.

[11] There are eminent legal scholars who oppose treating "armed attack" as a threshold concept. According to Christopher Greenwood, for example, the distinction between the use of force and armed attack is "regrettable," the distinction is, considered "rather thin" by Malcolm Shaw, and utterly rejected as "misguided" by Sir Michael Wood. See Responses to Chatham House Questionnaire Re: "Principles of International Law on the Use of Force by States in Self-Defence," ed. Elizabeth Wilmshurst (Chatham House, Oct. 2005).

[12] Yoram Dinstein, *War Aggression and Self-Defence, 5th edition* (Cambridge University Press, 2012), p. 196: "the use of the phrase "armed attack" in Article 51 is not inadvertent… The choice of words in Article 51 is deliberatively restrictive. The exercise of the right to self-defense, in compliance with the article, is confined to a response to an armed attack." *See also* Dinstein p. 198: "What is the point in stating the obvious (i.e., that an armed attack gives rise to the right of self-defence), while omitting reference to the ambiguous conditions of preventive war?"

send out its own military to intercept the enemy.[13] Furthermore, a state taking self-defensive action before the enemy has landed a blow (yet after an enemy attack has been launched) need not be limited to interception—the self-defensive action may be as strong as is sufficient to convince the enemy to cease trying to destroy one's state. On the other hand, military responses to an enemy attack that has landed must aim at self-defense, not retaliation, punishment or deterrence. Thus, even if one has been hit by an enemy strike, this does not legally entitle one to hit back unless one's state is threatened with destruction.

A second group of legal scholars, the "Counter-Restrictionists," read the phrase, "if an armed attack occurs," as merely listing one among several possible scenarios when state action in self-defense is a recognized right. A situation where an armed attack is imminent, for example, is conceptually distinct from a situation where an armed has occurred—an armed attack is imminent even before it has been launched—yet, self-defensive anticipation when an enemy attack is imminent is legal according to "counter-restrictionists." An attack is considered "imminent" when it is certain that the enemy intends to attack, and that time is running out to neutralize the coming blow.[14] Less formally, an attack is imminent when the enemy is about to attack (i.e., *before* the attack occurs). Military action aiming at self-defense in anticipation of an imminent attack is referred to as a "preemptive" strike;[15] and this chapter will demonstrate that there is currently an acceptance of the legality of preemptive strikes.[16]

---

[13] This interpretation of "occurs" conforms with the common sense that, for example, a strike by the U.S. to intercept the Japanese on their way to Pearl Harbor in 1941 should be considered legal. Cf. M.N. Shaw, *International Law* (4th ed. 1997), p. 790; M.M. Whiteman, *Digest of International Law*, V, (1965), p. 867.

[14] *Cf.* Karl P. Mueller, et al., *Striking First: Preemptive and Preventive Attack in U.S. National Security Policy* (Santa Monica, CA: RAND Air Force Project, 2006), p. 7: "when facing an imminent threat of attack against which preemption might be useful, leaders face intense time pressure when making decisions about whether or not to strike first." *Cf.* Gill, pp. 362–3: "The term "preemptive self-defence" will be used here to denote the exercise of self-defence in relation to manifest threats of armed attack that are in progress or at the point of being launched."

[15] The U.S. Department of Defense defines preemptive attack as follws: "preemptive attack [is] initiated on the basis of incontrovertible evidence that an enemy attack is imminent" Joint Chiefs of Staff, *Department of Defense Dictionary of Military and Associated Terms*, Washington, D.C.: Joint Chiefs of Staff, (2004), p. 415.

[16] The legality of preemption is demonstrated by the validation by the ICJ of Daniel Webster's language in the *Caroline* incident, the deference this language is given in UN General Assembly debates, and the UN Security Council's reaction to the post-WWII paradigmatic case of preemption, Israel's strike in 1967 on Egyptian forces in the Sinai desert.

The "restrictionist" reading of Article 51 must reject the legality of preemptive military strikes. Since today preemption is considered legal (this will be demonstrated below), the then "restrictionist" reading of Article 51 must be rejected. We must read the phrase, "if an armed attack occurs" as listing one among several scenarios where self-defense is a recognized right. Article 51 should be understood as authorizing the use of force in self-defense if an armed attack occurs, and also if an armed attack is imminent—that is, inevitable and in the near future (barring a military action to neutralize it). Part One of this chapter asks whether current law and state practice warrants adding "preventive" self-defense—action to thwart an enemy's arming himself—to the list of scenarios when armed self-defense is authorized, and specifically whether it does so in the case of a U.S. preventive attack on the DPRK; Part Two asks whether such a strike *should* be authorized.

Distinguishing Preventive And Preemptive Strikes

The terms "preventive" military action and "preemptive" military action are conceptually distinct. Both are military strikes taken before an enemy has launched an attack, and both aim at using force to thwart an attempt by the enemy to destroy one's state, thus both can be subsumed under the category of "anticipatory self-defense." Yet the two can be distinguished as separate types of anticipatory self-defense. A strike is termed "preemptive" when it attempts to thwart an imminent enemy attack; and a strike is termed "preventive" when it attempts to thwart an enemy's acquiring the capacity to attack. Despite this seemingly clear conceptual distinction, it is often difficult to achieve consensus on labeling any particular instance of anticipatory attack as "preventive" or "preemptive".[17] I will argue that this is not just the result of self-serving rhetoric and politicians" lies. Rather, the lack of consensus on identifying particular instances is due to a conceptual problem. The two concepts are distinguished by two distinct

---

Authorities confirming the thesis that preemption is legal include Chatham House respondents (op. cit. note 8), and Anthony Clark Arend, "International Law and the Preemptive Use of Military Force," *The Washington Quarterly*, vol 24, p. 89 ("traditional international law required there to be 'an imminent danger of attack' before preemption would be permissible").

[17] *Cf.* Francois Heisbourg, "A Work in Progress: The Bush Doctrine and Its Consequences," *The Washington Quarterly*, vol. 24, p. 78*ff* ("For example, the Israeli attack in 1981 against the Osirak reactor...has been indiscriminately portrayed as preventive and/or preemptive... Conversely, the Six-Day War of 1967 was, in the purest sense, a preemptive attack...based on "an imminent threat"... [yet] the June 1967 war is more often than not portrayed as an act of prevention.").

factual scenarios, and yet they are meant to differentiate between legitimate and illegitimate anticipatory actions. The distinguishing fact does not always amount to a decisive normative consideration; we will see in Part Two that the same moral considerations justifying preemptive strikes may be present in some instances of preventive action.

The problem of rhetorical and conceptual slippage between "preemption" and "prevention" is notably evident in the September 2002 U.S. National Security Strategy. The subsequent U.S. National Security Strategy of 2006 perpetuates this conceptual muddle when it explicitly asserts "the place of preemption in our national security strategy remains the same."[18] President Obama's U.S. National Security Strategy of 2010 does little to clear up the controversies surrounding anticipatory self-defense,[19] and thus implicitly perpetuates the Bush-era understanding of "preemption" and "prevention".[20]

In the NSS 2002, the term "preemptive" is used to refer to military action many legal scholars would not recognize as fitting that definition, slipping between the use of "imminent danger" and "sufficient threat" as a criterion for distinguishing preemption.

> For centuries, international law recognized that nations need not suffer an attack before they can lawfully take action to defend themselves against

---

[18] *The National Security Strategy of the United States of America* (2006), p. 23.

[19] *See* Christine Gray, "President Obama's 2010 U.S. National Security Strategy," 10 *Chinese JIL* (2011), p. 50 ("In the 2006 USNSS, [Bush] asserted that "The place of preemption in our national security strategy remains the same," and said that "To forestall or prevent such hostile acts by our adversaries, the United States will, if necessary, act preemptively in exercising our inherent right of self-defence." However, Obama makes almost no mention of self-defense in the 2010 USNSS. ... It is possible to interpret [this omission] in various ways. Firstly, the omission of any mention of pre-emption means that Obama has abandoned this controversial doctrine. Or, secondly, the omission of any mention means that the position remains what it had been under President Bush. Or, thirdly, the position is left deliberately open. The statement earlier in the 2010 USNSS that "Force will sometimes be necessary to confront threats" leaves the matter unclear.")

[20] Arguably, President Obama's vague and contradictory language relating to anticipatory self-defense has added to the conceptual muddle. *See* Christian Henderson, "The 2010 United States National Security Strategy and the Obama Doctrine of "Necessary Force"," *Journal of Conflict & Security Law*, vol. 15, p. 414 ("[W]hilst Obama went on to recall "the so-called Bush doctrine" and noted that "[t]he preventive use of force—in anticipation of potential threats that may not be imminent—is a different matter", he also, and rather confusingly, was clear that "[s]ometimes, the preventive use of force may be necessary." However, Obama gave no indications of what conditions might make it "necessary" or indeed the types of threats being referred to and what his interpretation of "imminence" was. Given a somewhat veiled criticism of pre-emptive force, or preventive force as Obama described it, and the national security policy of his predecessor, whilst at the same time making it clear that it would be resorted to when "necessary", it is arguable that this was the first signs of a broader and more vague Obama doctrine of "necessary force" emerging.").

> forces that present an imminent danger of attack. Legal scholars and international jurists often conditioned the legitimacy of preemption on the existence of an imminent threat...The United States has long maintained the option of preemptive actions to counter a sufficient threat to our national security. The greater the threat, the greater is the risk of inaction—and the more compelling the case for taking anticipatory action to defend ourselves, even if uncertainty remains as to the time and place of the enemy's attack. To forestall or prevent such hostile acts by our adversaries, the United States will, if necessary, act preemptively.[21]

The first and second sentences in the quote use "preemptive" in accord with the definition suggested earlier, i.e., referring to a situation where "an imminent danger of attack" exists. But the next sentences link preemption to a "sufficient threat" rather than an imminent attack. The fourth and fifth sentences speak of preemption when "uncertainty remains as to the time and place of the enemy's attack," and this notion seems to be a self contradiction. "Preemptive" attacks are defined as those launched when an enemy's attack is "imminent," and an attack's being "imminent" suggests that *there is* certainty about the time and place of attack. If we are uncertain as to the time and place of the enemy's attack, it is contrary to common usage to refer to his attack as being imminent. Common usage of the word, "imminent," implies that a prediction is being made of the highest possible certainty that an event will occur in the near future. In brief, there are two things implied in the common usage of the term: (1) the certainty of the event predicted, and (2) that the event will occur a short time into the future.

Furthermore, the NSS 2002 was made public very soon before the U.S. launched an attack to destroy Saddam Hussein's nascent nuclear weapons program. The 2003 attack to destroy Saddam's nuclear weapons program seems a clear case of "preventive" war, which (according to our rough definition above) aims to thwart an enemy's acquiring the *capability* of launching an attack. Many commentators have taken the Bush administration to task for this conflation, often suggesting motives of purposeful obfuscation and disingenuous attempts at rhetorical persuasion. Yet using the term may have been neither mendacious nor careless. It seems that the NSS 2002 is using the term "imminent" in a manner other than that suggested by common usage. And indeed the NSS (2002) suggests we update our understanding of "imminence."

---

[21] *The National Security Strategy of the United States of America* (2002), p. 15. *Available at* http://georgewbush-whitehouse.archives.gov/nsc/nss/2002/nss.pdf.

> We must adapt the concept of imminent threat to the capabilities and objectives of today's adversaries. Rogue states and terrorists do not seek to attack us using conventional means. They know such attacks would fail. Instead, they rely on acts of terror and, potentially, the use of weapons of mass destruction—weapons that can be easily concealed, delivered covertly, and used without warning.[22]

I would like to suggest another explanation to the confusion. In Part Two of this chapter, I will argue that the reason for the conflation and the difficulty in applying the terms "prevention" and "preemption" is that the factual distinction between the two concepts does not live up to the promise of separating them into two distinct normative concepts. The normative concepts justifying military action swim between the two categories of anticipatory self-defense. Leaving aside the normative evaluation, we will distinguish "preemption" by the factual distinction that an enemy's attack is imminent, where "imminent" entails certainty that an event will occur shortly.

Legality in the Specific Case of a U.S. strike on DPRK

As mentioned earlier, under the United Nations Charter a military attack is explicitly authorized in two instances. In this section we will examine whether these explicit instances apply to an attack by the U.S. on the DPRK. First of all, military force is authorized by "the inherent right of self-defense" acknowledged in Article 51, "if an armed attack occurs against a member of the United Nations;"[23] and secondly, it is authorized when the Security Council determines to "take such action by air, sea, or land forces as may be necessary to maintain or restore international peace and security."[24]

When it comes to the question of a state's using force legally—that is, in accordance with its obligation to abide by pledges made in signing the UN Charter—we remember that Article 51 acts as an exception to the blanket prohibition on a state's use of force articulated in Article 2(4) of the Charter.[25]

---

22 NSS (2002), p. 15.

23 Article 51: Nothing in the present Charter shall impair the inherent right of individual or collective self-defense if an armed attack occurs against a Member of the United Nations...

24 Article 42: [T]he Security Council ... may take such action by air, sea, or land forces as may be necessary to maintain or restore international peace and security.

25 "The point of departure of the legal debate is uncontroversial: the prohibition of the use of force is a valid norm of customary international law and is enshrined in the Charter

> Article 2(4): All members shall refrain in their international relations from the threat or use of force against the territorial integrity or political independence of any state, or in any other manner inconsistent with the Purposes of the United Nations.

Use of Force in Response to Threats

Article 51 authorizes the use of armed forces in self-defense "if an armed attack occurs." Legal use of force, it is stipulated, must be motivated by "self-defense;" but it is also stipulated that such force is used "if an armed attack occurs." At this time, it seems that no armed attack has occurred by the DPRK against the United States. There have been threats of nuclear attack,[26] and issuing "threats of force" is a violation of Article 2(4) of the UN Charter, but no attack has been launched. Article 51 claims that the UN charter is not intended to obstruct a state's use of force in self-defense in situations when "an armed attack occurs," it makes no mention of situations when "a threat has been issued." Thus, *prima facie*, Article 51 does not seem to commit the UN to accept as legal a claim by the U.S. to a right to attack the DPRK because of the threats issued.

> Even declarations of war, if it is evident to all that they are unaccompanied by deeds, are not enough. The notion that mere… "bellicose utterances" as such may justify self-defense within the framework of Article 51, has no foundation.[27]

Use of Force in Defense of Allies

However, there have been uses of force by the DPRK against South Korea. If those incidents constitute an "armed attack," then Article 51 may authorize the U.S. to counter-attack by invoking a right to "collective self-defense." In the *Case Concerning Military and Paramilitary Activities in and against Nicaragua* (1986),[28] the International Court of Justice acknowledged that under Article 51, there is an established right to collective self-defense. Although the court acknowledged a right to collective self-defense, a right to use force in such a situation requires that the state

---

of the United Nations. Thus, any specific use of force can be lawful only if it can be based on an exception to this rule…" Michael Bothe, "Terrorism and the Legality of Pre-emptive Force," 14 *European Journal of International Law*, vol. 14, 2003, p. 228.

[26] Jae-Soon Chan, "North Korea Threatens to Wipe Out the U.S. 'Once and For All'," *Huffington Post*, 24 June, 2009.

[27] Dinstein, p. 200.

[28] *Case Concerning Military and Paramilitary Activities in and against Nicaragua* (1986), "Summaries of Judgments, Advisory Opinions and Orders," ICJ Rep. 14.

suffering illegal armed attack issues a request for help from the country acting in "collective" self-defense.

> Whether self-defence be individual or collective, it can only be exercised in response to an "armed attack"...the Court finds that... there is no rule permitting the exercise of collective self-defence in the absence of a request by the State which is a victim of the alleged attack, this being additional to the requirement that the State in question should have declared itself to have been attacked.[29]

Indeed recently, on May 20, 2010,[30] after confirmation by an international investigation, South Korea has publicly declared that it was attacked by the DPRK. Two months earlier, on March 26, 2010, a South Korean Navy Ship, the *Cheonan,* sank, resulting in the death of 46 ROK sailors. Investigation revealed that the *Cheonan* was struck by a DPRK torpedo.[31] In addition to publicly declaring itself to have been attacked, South Korea requested that the United States participate in joint anti-submarine naval exercises that would be announced as a direct response to the *Cheonan's* sinking.[32] President Obama has agreed to the request, authorizing the joint naval maneuvers "to ensure readiness and to deter future aggression" by North Korea.[33] President Obama's statement as well as the nature of the joint exercise,[34] make it clear that the U.S. interprets the request for help issued by South Korea as a request to increase the ROK's abilities to intercept future attacks rather than a request to help eliminate the DPRK's abilities to attack. Supporting the interpretation of South Korea's request for help as limited to increasing its own naval capabilities is the fact that the Republic of Korea has announced its intention to take the matter to the UN Security Council. Thus, even though South Korea has declared that it has suffered an attack, and has made a request for U.S. help, the evident nature of that request makes it untenable for the U.S. to claim a legal right

---

29 Ibid. 6.

30 "Irrefutable Evidence Implicates North Korea, Says Lee Myung-bak", *Chosun blog,* 20 May 2010. *See Also,* Jean H. Lee, *Associated Press*, "North Korea Threatens "all-out war" Denies South's Claim that the North Torpedoed a Warship," 20 May 2010. *See Also,* "Korea: Seoul: the Sinking of *Cheonan* Violates the Armistice between North and South Korea," *Speronews,* 21 May 2010.

31 "Investigation Result on the Sinking of ROKS Cheonan," *ROK Ministry of National Defense*, 20 May 2010.

32 "U.S.-S. Korean Exercises May Be Postponed, But Planning Continues," *ChosunIlbo*, 17 June 2010.

33 Peter Grier, "Pentagon Dials up Pressure on North Korea for Cheonan Sinking," *Christian Science Monitor*, 24 May 2010.

34 Ibid.

to "collective" self-defense authorizing unilateral U.S. military action against the DPRK at this time. Article 51 does not seem to authorize an attack by the U.S. on the DPRK. However, this conclusion does not tackle our question of the legality of preemptive or preventive strikes.

The Legality of Preemptive Strikes

Not only is there debate and difficulty in distinguishing an action as preemptive, but there is still debate about whether preemptive (let alone preventive) strikes are legal under Article 51 of the UN charter.[35]

> Article 51: Nothing in the present Charter shall impair the inherent right of individual or collective self-defense if an armed attack occurs against a Member of the United Nations.

"Restrictionist" scholars such as Mary Ellen O'Connell claim, "Preemptive self-defense, however, is clearly unlawful under international law. Armed attack in self-defense is permitted only against armed attack."[36] By contrast, "counter-restrictionsist" scholars such as Alex Bellamy claim to "demonstrate that states and scholars are prepared to make judgments about the legitimacy [legality] of pre-emption on a case-by-case basis."[37] In support of the "restrictionist" position, we see that Article 51 does explicitly stipulate that the UN acknowledges a state's right to self-defense "if an armed attack occurs." The stipulation that "an armed attack occurs" suggests that preemption is illegal even when an attack is imminent. But there is a decisive consideration that stands conclusively in opposition to the "restrictionist" position. That is, the acceptance of language used in the *Caroline* incident[38] to mark off a class of legitimate preemptive strikes by the International Military Tribunal at Nuremberg in 1946,[39] and the International Court of Justice in 1986.[40]

---

[35] "The ambiguous place of pre-emptive self-defence in Article 51 of the UN Charter gave rise to a debate between restrictionists, who called for a literal interpretation (ruling out pre-emption), and counter-restrictionists, who argued that the UN Charter did not replace the customary right of pre-emption." Alex Bellamy, *Just Wars: from Cicero to Iraq* (Malden, MA: Polity Press, 2006), p. 158. See also Oscar Schachter, "The Rights of States to Use Armed Force," *Michigan Law Review*, vol. 82, 1984.

[36] Mary Ellen O'Connell, "The Myth of Preemptive Self-Defense, *American Society of International Law: Task Force on Terrorism*, August 2002, p. 2.

[37] Bellamy p. 161.

[38] Letter of Webster to Fox, 24 April 1841, 29 *British and Foreign State Papers* (1840–41). An examination of Webster's language and reasoning will follow in later sections of this chapter.

[39] *International Military Tribunal*, vol. 1, pp. 171, 207.

[40] *Case Concerning Military and Paramilitary Activities in and against Nicaragua* (1986), ICJ Rep 14.

There might be difficulty in determining whether any particular incident meets the criteria for legitimate preemption outlined in the *Caroline* case. However, contrary to the lack of consensus amongst commentators cited above, the IMT's and the ICJ's accepting the relevance of Webster's language in the *Caroline* incident makes it is clear that the legal regime made operational by the UN Charter accepts as legal the use of preemptive force before an armed attack has occurred. Thus, the question of whether any preemptive strike whatsoever is presumptively illegitimate under our post WWII inter-state legal regime should be foreclosed: there is at least some class of preemptive strikes which are legitimate under the UN Charter.

Legality of Preventive Strikes

As mentioned earlier, an argument can be made that since Article 51 uses the conditional ("if") rather than the bi-conditional ("if and only if"), the language "if an armed attack occurs" merely lists one example when the right to self-defense can be invoked to authorize military action. This is to say: Article 51 does not imply that military action is authorized "*only* if an armed attack occurs."[41] In the ICJ's *Nicaragua* case, this is the reading Judge Schwebel takes in his Dissenting Opinion.[42] Schwebel's reading is lent credence by what we saw earlier—the acceptance as legal preemptive strikes conforming to the *Caroline* criteria. Thus we already see one addition to the list of conditions stated in Article 51—force is legal not only if an armed attack occurs, but also if the armed attack is imminent. This raises the possibility that there are further conditions that authorize force, and that an examination of legal opinion and state practice might reveal such additional conditions.

Lending support to such speculation is the fact that in Article 51 the UN member states pledge that the UN will not interfere in a state's "inherent right to self-defense." It makes little sense to qualify a pledge not to interfere in a state's "inherent right" with a condition that this pledge holds only if an armed attack occurs, and otherwise the UN *will interfere* in this inherent right. If the UN Charter acknowledges a preexisting right to use

41 This reading is supported by D.W. Bowett, *Self-Defense in International Law* (NY: Praeger, 1958), pp. 187–192; M.S. McDougal and F.P. Feliciano, *Law and Minimum World Public Order* (New Haven: Yale University Press, 1961), pp. 232–41; J. Stone, *Aggression and World Order* (Berkeley: University of California Press, 1958), p. 44.

42 *Case Concerning Military and Paramilitary Activities in and against Nicaragua* (Merits), [1986] ICJ Rep. 14, p. 347.

force in self-defense, as the phrase "inherent right" indicates, then a reasonable interpretation must conclude that this right is acknowledged whenever enemy actions put the very existence of a state in jeopardy (e.g., blockade, diversion of rivers essential to a state's fresh water supply, or other actions that jeopardize a nation's survival even in the absence of armed attack). This reasoning lends credence to the speculation that military actions responding to enemy actions threatening the survival of a state (even if not an armed attack) may be legal under Article 51.

The necessary criterion for legality of military action which Article 51 provides is then the stipulation that the action be motivated by self-defense. This opens the possibility that Article 51 legitimizes state use of force in *preventive* strikes, so long as they are motivated by self-defense. It is perhaps the openness of the language of Article 51 to this line of speculation that leads Professor Henkin to regret the Charter's use of "inherent right/ *droitenaturelle*," and write that the argument that an "inherent right" exists independently of armed attack is "unfounded, its reasoning is fallacious, its doctrine pernicious."[43] Nevertheless, language acknowledging an inherent right to self-defense was inserted in this important document, and we will follow up on the speculation that prevention is legal—beginning with a look at the *Caroline* criteria for legal anticipation.

Prevention and the Caroline Criteria: Immediacy, Necessity, Proportionality

Guidelines for assessing whether a military operation is an act of legal anticipation have been found in the correspondence of U.S. Secretary Daniel Webster with British envoys concerning the destruction of the American steamship *Caroline* by British soldiers.[44] Webster wrote that for the British anticipatory action to be considered legitimate, it was required to:

> Show a necessity of self-defense, instant, overwhelming, leaving no choice of means, and no moment for deliberation… [And] since the act is justified by the necessity of self-defense, [it] must be limited by that necessity, and kept clearly within it.[45]

43 According to Louis Henkin, *How Nations Behave*, 2nd ed. (1979), p. 141.

44 See Bellamy, pp. 161–163; Dinstein, pp. 197–198, 267, 272–274; Bothe, p. 231.

45 Letter of Webster to Fox, 24 April 1841, 29 *British and Foreign State Papers* (1840–41) p. 1129, p. 1138.

Webster's words have been taken[46] as articulating reliable criteria—necessity, proportionality, and immediacy—for establishing the legality of self-defensive anticipation by the International Military Tribunal at Nuremberg (1946)[47] and the ICJ in the *Nicaragua* case. Webster's language is taken as articulating three *necessary* criteria required to establish the legality of military action. Thus "immediacy" is required for a strike to be legal. The "immediacy" clause—stipulating that the use of force is "instant...leaving...no moment for deliberation" –at first blush, seems to single out preemption for legal acceptance. Since preemption is thought of as a category of actions entirely distinct from prevention, this seems to rule out prevention as a class of legal military actions. The logic of assuming mutual exclusivity means that if we determine a criterion for preemption, we can simply say that prevention is not that. Yet, preemption is defined as a response to "imminent" enemy attack; and "immediacy" is not the same thing as "immanence." To say that "immediacy" obtains is to say that there is no moment for deliberation, and it is necessary to act instantly. When we say an attack is "imminent," we are focused on describing the enemy's action; when we use the term "immediacy" we are focused on describing the actions of the state being threatened.

It is true that when an enemy attack is imminent, then usually there is no moment for deliberation, and it is necessary that the state threatened act instantly (immediately). However, there might be other scenarios, other than when an enemy attack is imminent, where one must act instantly and there is no moment for deliberation. The paradigmatic example of preventive strike in the post-WWII era can be described as such a scenario. That is to say, the clearest contemporary case of "preventive" strike (Israel's 1981 attack on Osirak) was a situation where "immediacy" was obtained. If this is true, then the "immediacy" clause of the Caroline Criteria does not rule out preventive attack from legality.

What distinguishes preventive attacks, we will remember from earlier, is that they mean to destroy an enemy's capability of attacking—paradigmatically, the enemy's attempts to arm itself. The paradigmatic case of prevention in the post-WWII era is the example of Israel's 1981 destruction of the Osirak nuclear reactor in Iraq.[48] In this case, there was

---

[46] R.Y. Jennings and A. Watts (eds.), *Oppenheim's International Law*, vol. 1, 9th edition (Longman Harlow, 1992), p. 420.

[47] International Military Tribunal, vol. 1, pp. 171, 207.

[48] Dan Reiter, "Preventive Attacks against Nuclear, Biological and Chemical Weapons Programs: the track record," Working Paper, Ridgway Working Group on Preemptive and Preventive Military Intervention; Karl P. Mueller, et al., *Striking First: Preemptive and*

an "immediate" necessity to strike Iraq's reactor, since the WMD program was about to reach the point of no-return. The window of opportunity for anticipatory self-defense was closing.[49] Yet, an attack by Iraq on Israel was not "imminent"—that is, no one predicted that an attack was certain to occur in the near future. Thus, the criterion of "immediacy" obtained despite the fact that no attack by an enemy was "imminent".

Concern for the specific case of an anticipatory strike on the DPRK by the U.S. must then raise the question whether "immediacy" obtains with respect to a U.S. strike. Although before the DPRK had an operational atomic weapon it could have been argued along the same lines made with respect to the Osirak strike that "immediacy" obtained, now that the DPRK is in possession of nuclear weapons this argument for claiming "immediacy" is no longer tenable. Nor does it seem to be the case that the DPRK is about to achieve some strategic change such as moving an atomic weapon to Cuba or some territory within striking distance.[50] The circumstances currently surrounding the relations between the DPRK and the U.S. do not seem to be plausibly characterized as a moment when some important strategic shift is about to occur, thereby putting the U.S. in a time-constrained crisis where there is no moment for deliberation and making it necessary that the U.S. act instantly. In the absence of an alternative argument that "immediacy" obtains at this moment, since the reasoning relating to the *Caroline* incident requires that all three criteria (immediacy, necessity, and proportionality) obtain to establish the legality of a strike, it cannot be argued that the reasoning of the *Caroline* incident supports the legality of a U.S. strike on the DPRK at this time.

Preventive Attack in U.S. National Security Policy (Santa Monica, CA: RAND Air Force Project, 2006); William W. Keller and Gordon R. Mitchell, "Preemption, Prevention, Prevarication," *Hitting First: Preventive Force in U.S. Security Strategy*, ed. Keller & Mitchell (U. Pittsburgh Press, 2006).

[49] Walter B. Slocombe, U.S. Under Secretary of Defense for Policy (1994–2001), writes of the decision to invade Iraq in similar terms: "If waiting for "imminence" means waiting until it is no longer possible to act effectively, then the victim is left no alternative to suffering the first blow. So interpreted, the "right" [to anticipatory self-defense] would be illusory." Walter B. Slocombe, "Force, Preemption and Legitimacy," *Survival*, vol. 45, 2003, p. 125.

[50] The DPRK has, however, been linked to proliferation of nuclear weapons in Syria and Iran. Actions taken by Iran, Syria and the DPRK to proliferate nuclear weapons have been countered with the use of force over the last several years, including: aerial bombardment of Syria's al-Kibarnuclear facilities in 2007, sabotage of Iranian nuclear facilities at Natanz and Bushehr in 2010, and killing of Iranian nuclear scientists in 2011. The legality of these uses of preventive force is ambiguous, while they have not been condemned by the Security Council, neither have they been endorsed by the Security Council (nor have the parties responsible admitted their responsibility).

The further questions relating to the "necessity" and "proportionality" of a preventive U.S. strike on the DPRK will be taken up in Part Two of this chapter, where discussion of the moral evaluation of preventive action is explored.

UN Security Council Authorization of Preventive Strikes

Regardless of whether Article 51 legalizes a state's unilateral decision to take preventative military action, Chapter VII, Article 42, of the UN charter *does* authorize preventative military action taken by the Security Council. The UN Security Council is authorized to act in response to "threats" not merely "armed attacks." Article 42 speaks of actions "necessary to maintain" peace and security, not merely actions necessary to restore peace once it has been breached. When the Security Council determines that preventative military action is necessary to maintain international security, the Charter legitimates such action. This is to say, the UN Charter recognizes the justice of some military actions against a state even before that state launches an armed attack. Clearly, the UN Charter establishes the legality of preventive strikes authorized by the Security Council. In Part Two, we will examine whether the *justice* of such strikes is limited to those authorized by the Security Council—i.e., whether the moral status of such a strike is undermined when a state rather than the Security Council decides to take preventive action.

UN Security Council Authorization: Specific Case of U.S. strike on DPRK

There have been numerous Security Council Resolutions passed over the last ten years in regards to the DPRK's nuclear capabilities and activities. Resolution 825 (1993), called the DPRK to return to the Non-Proliferation Treaty and allow IAEA inspectors back into the country. Resolution 1695 (2006) condemned the DPRK for launching missiles capable of bearing nuclear, chemical, or biological weapons.[51] Resolution 1718 (2006) was passed under Chapter VII, Article 41, authorizing states to use means short of armed force to punish and put pressure on the DPRK.[52] Resolution 1874

[51] The UN Security Council "*Condemns* the multiple launches by the DPRK of ballistic missiles on 5 July 2006." S/RES/1695 (2006), UN Security Council Resolution, 1695 (2006).

[52] SC/8853; UNSC public information regarding UNSC Resolution 1718 (2006): "Acting under Chapter VII of the United Nations Charter, but barring automatic military enforcement of its demands under the Charter's Article 41, the Council unanimously adopted resolution 1718 (2006), which prevents a range of goods from entering or leaving the Democratic People's Republic of Korea and imposes an asset freeze and travel ban on persons related to the nuclear-weapon programme."

(2009) once again authorized states to act against the DPRK under Chapter VII, Article 41.[53] However, since it is Article 41 (and not Article 42) that is invoked in Resolutions 1874 and 1718, the Security Council has authorized measures *not involving the use of armed force* to give effect to its decisions. A strike by the U.S. against the DPRK would not be able to claim UN Security Council authorization for such action.

Summary: No Clear Legal Authorization for U.S. Strike on DPRK

To conclude the first part of the chapter, we have an answer to the question of whether the UN Charter currently authorizes military action by the U.S. against the DPRK. The answer is, No. First of all, since the UN has yet to authorize such an action under Chapter VII, Article 42 of the Charter, there is no Security Council authorization for such an attack. Secondly, under a "restrictionist" interpretation of Article 51 as authorizing military action *only* if an armed attack has already occurred, and since it is clear that an armed attack on the U.S. by the DPRK has not occurred, the U.S. cannot claim a right to simple self-defense. Furthermore, a right to "collective self-defense" is also beyond the claims the U.S. can make since (even if the sinking of the *Cheonan* is "sufficiently grave"[54] as to constitute an armed attack) the request by the ROK for help to increase its own capacity to thwart attacks cannot be reasonably interpreted as a request for help to prevent the DPRK's capacity to attack. But even if emphasis is placed on Article 51's acknowledgment of an "inherent right to self-defense" rather than the condition, "if an armed attack occurs," when we look to legal authorization for self-defensive anticipation by the U.S. against the DPRK's nuclear capabilities, we find that there no evidence that an attack is "imminent," thus no argument that such an attack is a legal act of "preemption," and that there is no evidence that "immediacy" obtains, thus no argument that such an attack would conform to the *Caroline* criteria for

---

[53] UNSC Resolution 1874 (2009): "Acting under Chapter VII of the Charter of the United Nations, and taking measures under its Article 41".

[54] In the *Nicaragua* case, the ICJ treats "armed attack" as a threshold concept, finding that not all illegal uses of armed force rise to the level of armed attack. "[It is] necessary to distinguish the most grave forms of the use of force (those constituting an armed attack) from other less grave forms." (Bothe, p. 101). It should also be noted that there are legal scholars who contend that treating "armed attack" as a threshold concept is a mistake. "Any requirement that a use of force must attain a certain gravity and that frontier incidents, for example are excluded is relevant only in so far as the minor nature of an attack is prima facie evidence of absence of intention to attack or honest mistake." (Wilmshurst, p. 6).

legal anticipation. We must conclude that an attack by the U.S. on the DPRK at this time would not be accepted as legal.

Now, since it is said that each of the criteria of just war provide necessary criteria for establishing the justice of a military action, and legality is one of the conditions, we might end the discussion here. There is no legal authorization for military action under the UN charter. Yet, this is an argument concluding that the law, as it is right now, does not authorize military action by the U.S. against the DPRK. It is not an argument for the claim that this is what the law should be. The argument that a preventive military attack is morally justified, despite the fact that it is not currently authorized by law, is a first step towards arguing that the law should change. It is to this argument that the remainder of the chapter addresses itself.

Part Two: Is There Moral Justification for Preventive Attack on the DPRK by U.S.?

First Moral Standard: Is the Strike Legal?

Though this chapter is separated into two parts—an examination of the legality of preventive attack, and an application of just war principles to preventive strikes—the two parts are intimately related. The first principle identified by just war theorists for evaluating the morality of a decision to use force asks whether the war is legal. This question is usefully divided into two: the question of external legitimacy, and the question of internal legitimacy. In our contemporary context, the first, external, question asks whether the UN Charter, ICJ, and UNSC authorize such a strike, this was dealt with in the first part of the chapter; the second, internal, question asks, "Was the military action initiated in a lawful manner by decision makers authorized by the state's constitution to take such action in the name of the state?" This criterion has a long history in the thinking about just war. Thomas Aquinas makes it the first of his three fundamental rules: "A war, in order to be just, must (1) be waged under the authority of a prince as the responsible leader of a nation, not by a private individual; the latter may apply to a tribunal for the defense of his rights."[55]

The reason for such a rule is clear, and the decision to use armed force has serious consequences for all members of a state that takes such an

[55] Von Elbe, p. 669. The other two criteria are that the war has a just cause, and that combat is aimed at the right intention.

action. Thus, for such a decision to be just, it must be made only if authorized by a legitimate representative of the citizenry. Of course, in the specific case we are considering, the question, "Was the military action initiated in a lawful manner?" cannot be answered before an actual military action by the U.S. is taken against the DPRK. If there is such a strike, then we will be able to answer whether it was initiated in accord with U.S. law or if some rogue part of the U.S. government or military initiated the action without legal authorization.

Second and Third Moral Standards: Does the Strike Aim at a Just Goal, and Is the Action Motivated by the Right Intention?

A second fundamental standard for evaluating the moral justification of military action is whether or not there is a just cause for the action.[56] Related to this standard is the further stipulation that just action be motivated by the right desires.[57] Although answers as to what constitutes a justified aim for launching war have changed over the millennia, in the post-WWII era, amongst contemporary state leaders and amongst those who can command national armies, neither a nation's material interest, nor the spread of a preferred economic, political or cultural way of life provide morally acceptable goals of military action. Furthermore, revenge, punishment, or the vindication of a nation's honor do not provide morally acceptable motivations. Self-defense is the only uncontroversially acceptable goal and motivation of a state's military action in order for it to be considered morally justified.[58]

Given the intentional threats made by the DPRK of nuclear attack against the U.S. (including missile launches[59] and public speeches[60]) the U.S. government could claim that the DPRK's acquiring nuclear weapons is threatening to the U.S. population. Furthermore, there is evidence that

---

[56] St. Thomas Aquinas made "just cause" one of his three criteria for determining that a war is just. Though answers to what constitutes a justifiable aim have changed over the millennia, in the just war tradition, this criteria of "just aim" is canonical.

[57] *See* Von Elbe. *See Also,* Gregory Reichberg, "Preventative War in Classical Just War Theory," *Journal of the History of International Law*, vol. 9, 2007, pp. 5–34.

[58] See Von Elbe, pp. 665–688. *See also* Reichberg, pp. 5–34; Kasher; Walzer (2000); Ramsey (1983); Bellamy; Bruno Coppieters and Nick Fotion eds. *Moral Constraints on War: Principles and Cases* (Lanham, MD: Lexington Books, 2002); Brendan Howe, "Conflicting Normative Dimensions of Justification: The Gulf War," *Just War in Comparative Perspective*, Paul Robinson ed. (Ashgate, 2003).

[59] "North Korea plans missile launch towards Hawaii on Independence Day," *Daily Mail* (UK), June 19, 2009.

[60] "N. Korea Threatens To "Wipe Out" U.S.," *CBS News*, June 24, 2009.

North Korea has been secretly providing nuclear weapons related technology to states hostile to the U.S. and states known to transfer weapons to non-state terrorist armies. Most notably, North Korea has been accused of helping to build an undeclared nuclear reactor in Syria,[61] share nuclear weapons knowledge with Iran,[62] and recently had a shipment of missiles on their way to the Middle East interdicted in Thailand. The U.S. could plausibly claim that a military action taken to disarm the DPRK of its nuclear weapons, would be aimed at nothing other than thwarting a nuclear attack on the U.S.—that is, such a strike would not aim at material gain or the goal of liberating North Koreans from an oppressive political system, and would not be motivated by a desire for revenge, national honor, or punishment. Yet, even if the aim and motivation of a military action is indeed self-defense, the question of whether or not a particular military action is *necessary* for attaining that goal is a separable question, and that "necessity" seems to be a large part of what justifies a military action according to the Just War tradition.[63]

The Complex "Necessity" Standard

A key condition for determining whether a war is just is given by the proposition that justified military action must be necessary. This proposition can be parsed into three separate criteria: the criteria of "last resort," "proportionality", and "reasonable chance of success." Indicating that a military action is a "last resort" is to say that there are no means other than military force available to achieve one's aim. Michael Walzer reformulates this criteria as follows: "*Last resort.* A state may resort to war only if it has exhausted all plausible, peaceful alternatives to resolving the conflict in question, in particular, diplomatic negotiation."[64] In the context of anticipatory self-defense, this is equivalent to the counter-factual claim, "Were it not for our military action, the enemy would have struck a destructive blow against our state." Indicating that an action is "proportional" is to say that the particular tactics chosen were limited to only those necessary for achieving one's goal. Even if a military operation has a just aim, it can be

[61] "N. Koreans Taped At Syrian Reactor," Robin Wright, *Washington Post,* 24 April 2008.

[62] "N. Korea Helping Iran with Nuclear Testing," Con Coughlin, *Telegraph/UK,* 24 Jan 2007.

[63] *See* Bruno Coppieters and Nick Fotion, eds., *Moral Constraints on War: Principles and Cases* (Landham, Md: Lexington, 2002).

[64] Quoted in Brian Orend, "Michael Walzer on Resorting to Force," *Canadian Journal of Political Science/Revue Canadienne de Science Politique*, vol. 33, September 2000, p. 525.

criticized as unjust if it uses means beyond those which are required to achieving this aim. And finally, an action may be criticized as an "unnecessary" waste of lives and property if it was known beforehand that the operation had no chance for success. This last criterion is referred to as the "reasonable chances of success" criterion.

If a military action is to be evaluated as just, it must be shown that the action taken is necessary. This can be understood as saying that once a just aim has been established, the specific tactics used must fit that aim. A military strike must use only that amount of force required to achieve a just goal. Another way of putting this is that the use of force must be "proportional."[65] In fact, this interpretation of the proposition, "justified military action must be necessary," is suggested by Webster's correspondence concerning the *Caroline* case.

> Since the act is justified by the necessity of self-defense, [it] must be limited by that necessity, and kept clearly within it.[66]

The scope of the military action taken must fit the goal of self-defense. If self-defense is the sole goal of a military action, then the tactics and technicalities of the action will reflect this. That is to say, the goal will limit the scope of the action taken. In the case we are examining, the military action would have to be limited to the minimum force needed to thwart a nuclear attack on the U.S.

At this point in time, the minimum force needed to thwart such an attack has likely increased substantially from a few years ago. Before the DPRK managed to build nuclear weapons, it seemed likely that thwarting a DPRK nuclear attack could be achieved by destroying the means the DPRK needed to build such weapons.[67] The destruction of the DPRK's nuclear weapons-making facilities might have been able to be achieved with less than an invasion, perhaps by bombing from air or ships. Now that the DPRK is in possession of such weapons, in addition to destroying the nuclear weapons-making facilities, disarming the DPRK of nuclear weapons will require finding those weapons and destroying (or confiscating) them. It is likely that this additional objective will require additional use of military force. Nevertheless, whatever military forces are used, they must reflect the goal which in this case is the elimination of a threat of

65 *See* Judith Gail Gardam, *Necessity, Proportionality and the Use of Force by States* (Cambridge University Press, 2004).

66 Webster to Fox, *British and Foreign State Papers*, vol. 29, pp. 1840–41, 129, 1138.

67 "South Korea Stopped US Strike on North Korea: Former President," *AFP*, 24 May 2000.

nuclear attack. If that goal is likely to be achieved without regime change or military occupation, then action of such a broad scope would be unjust.

On the flip side of this calculation: if it is likely that *whatever the scope* of military force one uses, the "just aim" will not be achieved, and then taking military action is unjust. If the United States unleashes the maximum amount of force available to it, and is still unlikely to thwart a nuclear attack by the DPRK, then it is immoral to waste the lives and property of those involved in such a fruitless military action. This is referred to as the "chances of success" principle. If a military action has no chance for successfully achieving a just goal, such an action is an "unnecessary" waste of lives and property; it must not be taken.

In thinking about the case at hand, however, it seems unlikely that the total military might available to the United States is still insufficient to achieve the goal of eliminating the DPRK's nuclear weapons.[68] The U.S. has made public announcements that its military and "Allies [are] ready to remove NK Nukes,"[69] as recently as March 2010, and as far back as the beginning of the crisis when Clinton Administration Defense Secretary William Perry publicly announced that such a preventive action was possible (though likely lead to 1 million deaths).[70] Given the massive force known to be available to the U.S. military (including hydrogen bombs many times more powerful than those dropped on Hiroshima) it is not the case that a military action by the U.S. to eliminate the DPRK's nuclear weapons could be deemed unjust because it is a futile, mission impossible.

Directly above, we saw that the "reasonable chances of success" criterion can be understood as an interpretation of the proposition that "justified military action must be necessary." But this criterion may also be seen as a corollary to the principle that war must have a just cause. If the only aim recognized as just is self-defense, and it is known that a war has no possibility of achieving self-defense, then it cannot be a just war. Its aim must be something other than self-defense, perhaps honor or revenge. When non-military means of self-defense are ineffective, and it can be

68 *Cf.* Joel Witt, Daniel B. Poneman, and Robert L. Gallucci, *Going Critical: The First North Korea Nuclear Crisis* (Washington, DC: Brookings Institution, 2004), p. 104*ff.*

69 Jung Sung-ki, "Allies Ready to Remove NK Nukes," *The Korea Times*, 12 March 2010.

70 "Such an attack was very likely to incite the North Koreans to launch a military attack on South Korea. Even though the North Koreans would surely lose this second Korean War, they could cause hundreds of thousands, perhaps millions, of casualties before being defeated." Quoted in Lyle J. Goldstein, *Preventive Attack and Weapons of Mass Destruction* (Stanford University Press, 2006), p. 135.

predicted that military means will also be ineffective, there can be a temptation to nevertheless embark on military action (if only for the symbolic effect). This type of futile "fighting the honorable fight" is judged immoral and the "possibility of success" rules out the justice of launching such a military operation.[71]

Earlier, we derived the criterion of "proportionality" from consideration of "necessity," yet there is another way that we can understand the standard of "proportionality." It might be the case that the amount of force needed to achieve a just goal is so overwhelming that it overshadows (i.e., seems "disproportionate" to) the threat being eliminated. So for example, imagine that the DPRK has developed a new missile that can reach the United States and intends to use it to attack the U.S. But this missile carries an explosive load equivalent to a child's fire-cracker. The danger to U.S. citizens may be real, but the amount of force needed to find and destroy this missile is likely to be disproportionate to the benefits of thwarting the attack. To put numbers to this, let's assume that the DPRK missile threatens 100 people's lives, and that achieving the military objective of eliminating the missile requires an invasion likely to result in one hundred thousand deaths. In such a case, launching a military action is thought to be unjust. This type of calculation for the sake of evaluating the moral justification for a military action is also referred to as the principle of "proportionality".

Under this understanding of the "proportionality" standard, in order to evaluate the justice of a military strike to eliminate the DPRK's nuclear threat we would have to know the expected casualties of the military strike and compare those numbers to the number of casualties that would result from a DPRK nuclear weapons attack. Without such technical details, it is difficult to make the evaluation, however it is not *prima facie* impossible that such a military action would be "proportionate" since a nuclear weapon threatens a great many people. In short, the enormous potential for damage held by nuclear weapons (threatening hundreds of thousands of deaths) makes it conceivable that even a large-scale military action would be "proportional."

In recent years, the term "proportionality" has come into frequent use by journalists and political commentators on contemporary military actions. In these contexts, often the term has been used mistakenly.[72]

---

[71] *Cf.* Kasher.

[72] Allan Richarz, "In Defense of Israel's Disproportionate Response in Gaza," *Christian Science Monitor*, 9 January 2009; "Sarkozy: Israel Has a Right to Protect itself: They Must Be

In the tradition of just-war theory, "proportionality" in military action has nothing to do with returning like damage for like. After all, military action, if it is to be deemed just, must be aimed at self-defense; it is not retributive. As mentioned earlier, in the contemporary milieu there is only one goal that is recognized as justifying a state's sovereign decision to use of armed force: self-defense. Just military actions are intended to achieve self-defense once non-military means have proven ineffective through tactics likely to succeed, narrowly tailored to eliminate threats, and unlikely to cause damage vastly greater than the damage being threatened by the enemy.

In the case at hand, asking whether military action is necessary (understood as a last resort) is to ask: "Are there means of thwarting attack on the U.S. DPRK nuclear weapons other than a U.S. military strike?" Before the DPRK's public testing of nuclear weapons in 2006 and then again in 2009, it was widely thought that there were means short of military action which could achieve this; it was thought that the DPRK could be convinced through bilateral negotiations with the U.S. (the 1994 Agreed Framework)[73] or through multilateral negotiations (the Six-Party Talks)[74] to agree not to develop such weapons. It is now clear that this prediction was incorrect. The negotiations did not convince the DPRK not to develop nuclear weapons.[75]

Nevertheless, even though non-military means were ineffective in preventing the DPRK from acquiring nuclear weapons, before a military action to eliminate those weapons would be evaluated as justified under the "last resort" criterion, the U.S. would still have to answer whether there is certainty of the intention to attack, and whether means other than military action could change the intention of the DPRK to attack. Perhaps circumstances could be changed that will make the possession of nuclear weapons by the DPRK non-threatening, or perhaps the willingness of the DPRK to voluntarily disarm its weapons and weapon-making facilities

---

appropriate and proportional," *Jerusalem Post*, 3 May 2007; Lionel Beehuer, "Did Israel use disproportionate force?" *Huffington Post*, 31 December 2008; "Stanford Students Protest Israeli Military Strikes," *Paloaltoonline*, 9 January 2009.

[73] *See* Daniel Poneman, "The History of the 1994 Agreed Framework," History News Network, *available at*, http://hnn.us/articles/31633.html. *See Also* Daniel B. Poneman, Joel S. Wit and Robert L. Gallucci, *Going Critical The First North Korean Nuclear Crisis* (Brookings Institution Press, 2004).

[74] *See*, Full text of 6-party talks joint statement 2005-09-19, *available at*, http://www.chinadaily.com.cn/english/doc/2005-09/19/content_479150.htm. *See Also*, John S. Park, "Inside Multilateralism: The Six-Party Talks," 28 *The Washington Quarterly*, p. 89.

[75] Justin McCurry and Tania Branigan, "North Korea tests nuclear weapon as powerful as Hiroshima bomb," *The Guardian*, http://www.guardian.co.uk, 25 May 2009.

may change. It could be argued that in general, until an actual attack is launched, there is always a chance that a would-be attacker will reconsider. Negotiation, economic sanctions, diplomatic pressure, or creating deterrence through a credible mechanism for counter-strike might yet change the enemy's professed intention. In the specific case of the DPRK, such measures, it is hoped, will change DPRK's will to possess nuclear weapons or its intention to attack the United States with them.

In the context of anticipatory self-defense, the claim that military action is a last resort is equivalent to asserting the counter-factual proposition, "Were it not for military action, we will be struck by an enemy attack." Such counter-factual assertions leave one with difficult problems in trying to verify their truth. It is unclear whether one could ever know with certainty that it is impossible to change an enemy's intention to attack. This is where the matter of "imminence" comes into the discussion. There has been a tradition of assessing the "necessity" of military action by determining that the timing of an enemy attack is "imminent"—that is, waiting until the attack is about to occur. The "imminence" of an enemy attack is a good indication of the "necessity" of anticipatory strike since the time constraint eliminates all other alternatives. When alternatives are unavailable, an attack by the threatened party is considered as fulfilling the "necessity" criterion. An imminent enemy attack is a reliable indication that alternatives are unavailable, since changing the will of a would-be attacker generally takes more time than is now left before the enemy strike is predicted to occur. When it becomes clear that there is no chance that alternative means could be effective in the time left before an attack, then there is proof that the use of force by the threatened party is a last resort. However, "imminence" of an enemy attack is but one indication that alternatives are no longer available. There may be other reliable indicators that alternatives to anticipation are unavailable.

One reason for waiting until the attack is about to occur, is that generally, there are visible preparations an enemy must take right before launching an attack. Thus, in these last minute preparations, the enemy tips his hand and we have reasonable evidence for believing that "if we do not use military force, we will be struck by an enemy attack." Thus, one way of understanding the moral grounding of the "imminence" criterion is that the risk involved in waiting to launch an anticipatory strike is thought to be outweighed by the chance of avoiding war. This formula suggests that rational moral judgment requires that the chance of avoiding war must be assessed and weighed against the consequences of absorbing the first strike of an attacker.

Both of these reasons for waiting until an attack is imminent are questionable in the DPRK case. The first reason is undermined if attack is launched in stealth by non-state terrorists. Such attacks provide no warning. The DPRK's history of nuclear proliferation to Syria[76] and Iran[77] (which arm and employ non-state terrorist armies) makes DPRK's nuclear weapons particularly threatening. And secondly, when the first strike is presumed to be a nuclear strike, the consequences of absorbing the attack are so devastating that there is a case to be made that the risk involved makes it unreasonable to wait until the attack is imminent. This reasoning explains the use of the criterion "sufficient threat" in the discussion of anticipatory self-defense we saw earlier in the NSS 2002.

> The United States has long maintained the option of preemptive action to counter a sufficient threat to our national security. The greater the threat, the greater is the risk of inaction—and the more compelling the case for taking anticipatory action to defend ourselves...Given the goals of rogue states and terrorists, ...the magnitude of potential harm that could be caused by our adversaries' choice of weapons, ... We cannot let our enemies strike first."[78]

The down-side of using "imminence" as the indicator that alternatives to force are unavailable to thwart an enemy attack is that waiting until such a moment entails a risk that the attacker will get off his first strike before one can thwart it. In Webster's words, anticipatory self-defense is considered justifiable when one can "show a necessity of self-defense, instant, overwhelming, leaving no choice of means, and no moment for deliberation." Stating that there is "no choice of means" is equivalent to saying, "the use of force is necessary;" what Webster's words add is that action must be taken "instantly," that a critical moment has been reached where there is "no moment for deliberation." At such a time of crisis, where "immediate" action is called for, there is no longer time to let negotiations, sanctions, diplomatic moves, demonstrations of strength, etc. effect a change in the intention of the attacker to strike.

---

[76] "Syria Conducted Nuclear Experiments: IAEA Document," *AFP*, 31 May 2010.

[77] Con Coughlin, "N Korea Helping Iran with Nuclear Testing," *Telegraph.co.uk*, 24 Jan 2007.

[78] *The National Security Strategy of the United States* (2002), p. 15; *See also* L. Feinstien and A.M. Slaughter, "A Duty to Prevent," *Foreign Affairs*, vol. 83, 2004, pp. 147–9: In the case of threats of WMD attack, waiting for a moment of imminence "is usually impractical because suspected facilities are often difficult to spot or hit...this is not to suggest that the use of [preemptive] force should be discounted as ineffective but that the most effective action is preventive."

A recent Chatham House study surveyed a group of eminent legal scholars on the legal concept of imminence, summarizing their consensus as follows:

> The [legal] concept of "imminence" reflects the *Caroline* formulation of "instant, overwhelming, leaving no choice of means, and no moment for deliberation". In the context of contemporary threats imminence cannot be construed by reference to a temporal criterion only...There must exist a circumstance of irreversible emergency. Whether the attack is "imminent" depends upon the nature of the threat and the possibility of dealing effectively with it at any given stage. The criterion of imminence requires that it is believed that any further delay in countering the intended attack will result in the inability of the defending state effectively to defend itself against the attack. In this sense, necessity will determine imminence: it must be necessary to act before it is too late.[79]

As discussed earlier, Webster's "immediacy" criterion characterizes the action of the state acting in self-defense, while the word "imminence" makes reference to the enemy attack. To say that something is "imminent" is to say that one believes that something is certain to occur in the near future. In the context of the reasoning surrounding the *Caroline* incident, "immediacy," also has to do with time, but it has no necessary relation to predicting whether something will happen. Rather, "immediacy" is an assertion that the threatened party felt it necessary to strike *now*. Explanation of why the threatened party felt it necessary to strike now might include evidence that an enemy attack was certain to occur in the near future, but there might be other explanations. Since "preemptive" strikes have traditionally referred to legal anticipations, and taken "imminence" as their defining characteristic, the Chatham House scholars quoted above suggest treating the legal term "imminence" as referring to the concept of "immediacy" used in the reasoning surrounding the *Caroline* incident.

In line with the Chatham House scholars' and Webster's focus on the actions of the state striking in self-defense, a recent RAND/U.S. Air Force study suggests that "preemptive" attacks can be distinguished by "the need to decide quickly whether to attack or absorb a potential blow."[80] This also fits with Lawrence Freedman's characterization that, "preemption is a ... desperate strategy employed in a crisis."[81] Under this interpretation,

---

[79] Wilmshurst, pp. 8–9.

[80] Karl P. Mueller, et al., *Striking First: Preemptive and Preventive Attack in U.S. National Security Policy* (Santa Monica, CA: RAND Air Force Project, 2006), p. 21.

[81] Lawrence Freedman, "Prevention, Not Preemption," *The Washington Quarterly*, vol. 26, p. 107.

"preemption" (and this term is meant to indicate a class of just military actions) is characterized by a severe time constraint on the defending state's decision process. This characterization is in marked contrast with the definition of "preemption" as characterized by the imminence of an enemy attack. "Immediacy" rather than "imminence" is taken to be a proper articulation of the just war tradition's moral standard of "last resort." Thus there is a disconnect between the traditional definition of "preemption," which requires establishing the fact of an enemy attack's being imminent, and the just war tradition's moral standard, requiring that a threatened state's action is a "last resort."

Returning to the criteria of the just war tradition, remember that it is "necessity" (understood as a strike's being a last resort) which holds moral weight. "Imminence" of an enemy attack is merely a reliable indicator of "necessity"—that no other means of thwarting the enemy attack are available. Whereas the "imminence" criterion is by definition a function of time,[82] "necessity" is not *a priori* a function of time. That military action is a last resort to avoiding an attack is a matter of all other means to achieving this goal being ineffective. The time-bound nature of the "imminence" criterion adds an element of risk that makes it an inappropriate standard in the case of a threat of nuclear attack. Given this consideration, there is reason to pick a different criterion for establishing that non-military means are unavailable. The prediction that non-military means will be ineffective in thwarting an attack need not rely on the evidence that time constraints make those means ineffective. It can be argued that non-military means will be ineffective by demonstrating that non-military means were attempted in good faith, given a reasonable amount of time to work, and have proven ineffective.

Attempts to prevent the DPRK from attaining nuclear weapons and taking actions to prevent the DPRK from proliferating nuclear weapons have included non-military means such as deliberations,[83] sanctions,[84] diplomatic condemnations,[85] and interdiction of ships suspected of smuggling

---

82 *The National Security Strategy of the United States* (2002) suggests we "adapt the concept of imminent threat to the capabilities and objectives of today's adversaries." Though the word "imminent" is kept, the suggested criteria to determine "imminence" are (1) intention to harm, and (2) capability to harm; the criterion of time is excised from the suggested definition.

83 Bilateral deliberations between the U.S. and the DPRK occurred during the Clinton Administration, Multilateral deliberations between the U.S., Russia, China, Japan, South Korea, and the DPRK have been ongoing since 2003.

84 UNSC Resolution 1874 (2009), Res. 1718 (2006).

85 "North Korean Nuclear Blast Draws Global Condemnation: China, Russia Decry Ally," Blaine Harden, *Washington Post*, 26 May, 2009.

nuclear weapons technology.[86] These means have been ineffective in preventing the DPRK from acquiring nuclear weapons (as evidenced by their weapons tests of 2006 and 2009), and have been ineffective in preventing the DPRK from proliferating nuclear weapons technology (as evidenced by the discovery of a secret nuclear reactor in Syria built with North Korean help).[87]

Conclusion

We have been considering established principles of *jus ad bellum*, i.e., standards for evaluating whether the decision to launch a military action is just. In summary, we articulated several important tests for determining whether a decision to launch military action can be condemned as unjust. They are as follows: (1) if the military action is not for the sake of self-defense, (2) if there are other means of achieving self-defense, (3) if the targets include more than what is required for self-defense, (4) if there is no possibility for achieving the objectives necessary for self-defense, (5) if the means required to achieve the objectives necessary for self-defense will likely cause damage vastly greater than the damage being threatened by the enemy. We also saw that the "imminence" test is not an independent moral criterion. Rather, it is merely a means of establishing that condition (2) obtains. We argued that such a means of establishing "last resort"—that is, waiting until an enemy attack is imminent—is inappropriate to cases of nuclear threat from regimes that arm non-state terrorist armies. Along the way, we have seen that a hypothetical attack by the U.S. on the DPRK in order to eliminate its nuclear weapons could be conceived as complying with these five tests for justification. Such an attack could be justified as aimed at self-defense since it is aims to thwart the intention of the DPRK to destroy the state by nuclear attack. Deliberations, diplomacy, sanctions and other means short of armed force have proven ineffective to achieving an elimination of the threat. It is possible to conceive of an attack that is limited to achieving only those objectives necessary to eliminating the DPRK's nuclear threat. There does seem to be sufficient force available to the U.S. to achieve the goal of eliminating the threat. And finally, considering the magnitude of the threat, we cannot pre-judge military action taken by the U.S. as "disproportionate" to the threat. Finally, we

86 "U.S. Weighs Intercepting North Korean Shipments," David E. Sanger, *New York Times*, 7 June, 2009.

87 "Official: Syrian Nuclear Reactor Was Weeks from Functioning," *Fox News*, 24 April 2008.

must conclude that the criteria of just war considered in this paper do not rule out the justice of a preventative strike by the United States on the DPRK aimed at eliminating its nuclear weapons.

However, there is an important question that our discussion thus far has left unanswered: The question of whether the law (the UN Charter) should change. We saw that the UN Charter recognizes the justice of some military actions against a state even before that state launches an armed attack. The UN Charter reserves legitimacy to those preventative military actions which are authorized by the Security Council. The analysis of Section Two seems to indicate that the justice of a preventative strike is conditioned by criteria which might be met independently of whether the Security Council judges that those criteria are met. The question of whether a change in the law (the UN Charter) should reflect this is, I believe, a matter of prudence. That is, it is an open question whether the Security Council is a more reliable judge of the necessity of preventative action than individual states are. The UN Charter means to take out of the hands of parties to a dispute the authorization to decide when preventative military action is necessary, and this seems like a prudent approach since states (like people) are thought to be poor judges of disputes to which they are a party. To properly assess whether the Security Council is a better judge of the necessity of preventative action than states, however, would require an empirical study not an argument about principles of justice. Such an empirical study is a task for another day.

BIBLIOGRAPHY

"A Hopeful Wind of Change," *Economist*, 12 May 2007.

"China "Stands against Use of Force to Solve Int'l Disputes'," *China Daily*, 7 April, 2011.

"China Criticizes Japan over Talk of Preemptive Strike on N. Korea," Yonhap News Agency, 13 July 2006.

"China Presses Sudan Over Darfur," *New York Times*, 12 June 2008.

"China: Nation to Send Police to E. Timor," *China Daily*, 17 September 1999.

"Chinese Diplomats Criticize Myanmar's New Capital" *The New York Times* 23 May 2007.

"Chinese President Meets French Counterpart, Saying Force Is No Solution to Libyan Issue," *Xinhua*, 30 March 2011.

"Humanitarian and Security Situations in Western Sudan Reach New Lows, UN Agency Says," *UN News Service*, 5 December 2003.

"Investigation Result on the Sinking of ROKS Cheonan," *ROK Ministry of National Defense*, 20 May 2010.

"Iraq 'No-Fly Zone' China 'Concerned'," *Xinhua Gen. Overseas News Service*, 31 August 1992.

"Korea: Seoul: the Sinking of *Cheonan* Violates the Armistice between North and South Korea," *Speronews*, 21 May 2010.

"N Korea Threatens US with First Strike", *The Guardian*, 6 February 2003.

"N. Korea Threatens To 'Wipe Out' U.S.," *CBS News*, June 24, 2009.

"North Korea Plans Missile Launch towards Hawaii on Independence Day," *Daily Mail* (UK), June 19, 2009.

"Official: Syrian Nuclear Reactor Was Weeks From Functioning," *Fox News*, 24 April 2008.

"S. Korea, U.S. Practice Stabilizing N. Korea in Civil War," *Chosun Ilbo*, 6 April 2012.

"Sarkozy: Israel Has a Right to Protect itself: They Must be Appropriate and Proportional," *Jerusalem Post*, 3 May 2007.

"Seoul Overhauls N. Korea Contingency Plan", *Chosun Ilbo*, 14 January 2010.

"South Korea Stopped US Strike on North Korea: Former President," *AFP*, 24 May 2000.

"Spokesman on U.S. Warplane Shooting Down Iraqi Fighter," *Xinhua General Overseas News Service*, 28 December 1992.

"Stanford Students Protest Israeli Military Strikes," *Paloaltoonline*, 9 January 2009.

"Sudan: Envoy Warns of Ethnic Cleansing as Security Council Calls for Ceasefire," *UN News Service*, 2 April 2004.

"Syria Conducted Nuclear Experiments: IAEA document," *AFP*, 31 May 2010.

"Too Few, Too Late?," *Economist*, 21 April 2007, p. 52.

"U.S. Weighs Intercepting North Korean Shipments," David E. Sanger, *New York Times*, 7 June, 2009.

"U.S.-S. Korean Exercises May Be Postponed, But Planning Continues," *ChosunIlbo*, 17 June 2010.

Acharya, Amitav, "Will Asia's Past Be Its Future?", *International Security*, vol. 28, no. 3, 2003, pp. 149–164.

Adelmann, Jonathan R., and Chih-yu: *Symbolic War: The Chinese Use of Force. 1840–1980* (Taipei, 1993).

Akira Mayama, "Japan's New Emergency Legislation and International Humanitarian Law", *Japanese Annual of International Law*, vol. 47, 2004, pp. 69–70.

Albright, Madeleine, "The End of Intervention" *The New York Times*, 11 June 2008.

Al-Rhodan, Khalid R., "A Critique of the China Threat Theory: A Systematic Analysis", *Asian Perspective*, vol. 31, no. 2, 2007, pp. 41–66.

Alston, P., and E. MacDonald, *Human Rights, Intervention, and the Use of Force* (Oxford: Oxford University Press 2008).

Alvarez, José E., "The Schizophrenias of R2P," in Philip Alston and Euan Macdonald (eds.), *Human Rights, Intervention, and the Use of Force* (Oxford: Oxford University Press, 2008), pp. 275–284.

Amnesty International, *Kosovo: the Evidence* (London: Amnesty, 1998).

Aoi, C., "Beyond 'Activism-Lite'?: Issues in Japanese Participation in Peace Operations", *Journal of International Peacekeeping*, vol. 13, nos. 1–2, 2009, pp. 72–100.

Arend, Anthony Clark, "International Law and the Preemptive Use of Military Force," *The Washington Quarterly*, vol. 24, p. 89.

Awaya, Kentarō, *Tōkyō Saiban heno Michi* [The Road to the Tokyo Trial], in two volumes (Tokyo: Kōdansha, 2006).

Bae, C., "Island Sovereignties of East Asia: A Comparative Colonial Legacy" in Northeast Asian History Foundation, *Territorial Issues in Europe and in East Asia: Colonialism, War Occupation, and Conflict Resolution* (Seoul, 2009).

Barnard, Ann, "Massacre Is Reported in Homs, Raising Pressure for Intervention in Syria," *New York Times*, 13 March 2012.

Barriga, S., and L. Grover, "A Historic Breakthrough on the Crime of Aggression", *AJIL*, vol. 105, 2011, pp. 517–533.

Barriga, Stefan, Wolfgang Danspeckgruber, Christian Wenaweser, *The Princeton Process on the Crime of Aggression: Materials of the Special Working Group on the Crime of Aggression, 2003–2009* (Lynne Rienner, 2009).

Bass, Gary J., *Freedom's Battle: The Origins of Humanitarian Intervention* (New York: Alfred A. Knopf, 2008), pp. 5–8.

Bass, Gary Jonathan, *Stay the Hand of Vengeance: The Politics of War Crimes Tribunals* (Princeton, N.J: Princeton University Press, 2000), pp. 58–105.

Bassiouni, M.C., *Crimes against Humanity in International Criminal Law* (Kluwer Law International, The Hague, 1999), p. 152.

Bassiouni, M.C., "Historical survey: 1919–1998", in M.C. Bassiouni compiled, *The Statute of the International Criminal Court: A Documentary History* (New York: Transnational Publishers, Inc., 1998), pp. 11–15.

Bechtol Jr., B.E., "The Implications of the Cheonan Sinking", *International Journal of Korean Unification Studies*, vol. 19, no. 2, 2010, pp. 1–40.

Beehuer, Lionel, "Did Israel Use Disproportionate Force?" *Huffington Post*, 31 December 2008.

Bell, Daniel A., "Just War and Confucianism. Implications for the Contemporary World" in Bell, Daniel A. (ed.), *Confucian Political Ethics* (Princeton 2007), pp. 226–257.

Bellamy, Alex J., *Just Wars: From Cicero to Iraq* (Polity Press, Cambridge, 2006).

Bellamy, Alex J., "Responsibility to Protect or Trojan Horse? The Crisis in Darfur and Humanitarian Intervention," *Ethics and International Affairs*, vol. 19, no. 2, September 2005, pp. 31–54.

Bellamy, Alex J., *Responsibility to Protect: The Global Effort to End Mass Atrocities* (Malden, MA: Polity Press, 2009).

Bellamy, Alex J., "Whither the Responsibility to Protect? Humanitarian Intervention and the 2005 World Summit," *Ethics and International Affairs*, vol. 20, no. 2, Summer 2006, pp. 143–169.

Bellamy, Alex J., and Paul Williams, *Understanding Peacekeeping* (Malden, MA: Polity Press, 2d ed., 2010), pp. 193–202.

Bellamy, Alex J., and Sarah E. Davies, "The Responsibility to Protect in the Asia-Pacific Region", *Security Dialogue* vol. 40, no. 6, pp. 547–574, p. 553.

Benett, B.W., and J. Lind, "The Collapse of North Korea: Military Missions and Requirements", *International Security*, vol. 36, vol. 2, 2011, pp. 84–119.

Bernstein, Richard, and Ross H. Munro, "China 1: The Coming Conflict with America", *Foreign Affairs*, vol. 76, no. 2, 1997, pp. 18–32.

Billioud, Sébastian, "Confucianism, 'Cultural Tradition', and Official Discourse in China at the start of the New Century", *China Perspectives*, vol. 69, no. 3, 2007, pp. 50–65.

Black, L., "Debating Japan's Intervention to Tackle Piracy in the Gulf of Aden: beyond Mainstream Paradigms", *International Relations of the Asia-Pacific*, volume 12, 2012, pp. 259–285.
Blix, H.P., *Hirohito and the Making of Modern Japan* (New York: Perennial, 2001).
Bobbitt, P., *The Shield of Achilles. War, Peace and the Course of History* (London: Allan Lane, The Penguin Press, 2002).
Boister, N., and R. Cryer, *Documents on the Tokyo International Military Tribunal* (Oxford: Oxford University Press, 2008).
Boister, Neil, "The Application of Collective and Comprehensive Criminal Responsibility for Aggression at the Tokyo International Military Tribunal: The Measure of the Crime of Aggression?", *Journal of International Criminal Justice* vol. 8, 2010, p. 431.
Booth, William, and James Rupert, "Exodus Swells, Straining Capacity of Refugee Camps," *Washington Post*, 18 April 1999.
Bothe, M., "Terrorism and the Legality of Pre-emptive Force", *EJIL*, vol. 14, 2003, pp. 227–240.
Boutros-Ghali, Boutros, *The United Nations and Rwanda 1993–1996* (New York: UN, 1996).
Bowett, D.W., *Self-Defense in International Law* (New York: Praeger, 1958), pp. 187–192.
Briant, Pierre, *Histoire de l"empire Perse. De Cyrus à Alexander* (Paris, 1996).
Bronner, Ethan, and David E. Sanger, "No-Flight Zone in Libya Backed by Arab League," *New York Times*, 13 March 2011.
Brownlie, Ian, *International Law and the Use for Force by States* (Oxford: Oxford University Press, 1963).
Brownlie, Ian, *Basic Documents in International Law, 6th edition* (Oxford: Oxford University Press, 2009).
Brownlie, Ian, *Principles of Public International Law* (Oxford: Oxford University Press, 7th ed., 2008).
Bruno Coppieters and Nick Fotion (eds.), *Moral Constraints on War: Principles and Cases* (Lanham, MD: Lexington Books, 2002).
Buckley, Chris, "China Seizes on Libya for Propaganda War Against West," *Reuters*, 23 March 2011.
Bumiller, Elisabeth, and David D. Kirkpatrick, "Allied Airstrikes Pound Libyan Ground Forces," *New York Times*, 23 March 2011.
Burles, Mark, and Abram N. Shulsky: *Patterns in China's Use of Force. Evidence from History and Doctrinal Writings*, Washington 2000, Appendix, pp. 79–95.
Burns, John F., "Serbs Intensify Sarajevo Attack; U.N. Fears A Final All-Out Push," *New York Times*, 23 March 1993.
Burns, John F., "Vicious "Ethnic Cleansing" Infects Croat-Muslim Villages in Bosnia," *New York Times*, 21 April 1993.
Buruma, I., *The Wages of Guilt. Memories of War in Germany and Japan* (Phoenix, London, 2002).
Bush, M., *Our Chancellor* (New York: Scribner and Sons, Vol. 1, 1884).
Buzan, Barry, *People, States and Fear: an Agenda for International Security in the Post-cold War Era*, 2nd edition (New York, 1991).
Byers, Michael, *War Law: Understanding International Law and Armed Conflict* (London: Atlantic Books, 2005).
Callahan, William A., "Chinese Visions of World Order: Post-hegemonic or a New Hegemony?", *International Studies Review*, vol. 10, 2008, p. 752.
Canadian Commission on Intervention and State Sovereignty, *The Responsibility to Protect* (2001), accessible at http://www.iciss.ca/report-en.asp.
Carlson, Allen, "Helping to Keep the Peace (Albeit Reluctantly): China's Recent Stance on Sovereignty and Multilateral Intervention," *Pacific Affairs*, vol. 77, no. 1, Spring 2004, pp. 9–27.
Carlson, Allen, *Unifying China, Integrating with the World: Securing Chinese Sovereignty in the Reform Era* (Stanford, CA: Stanford University Press, 2005).

Cassese, A., and B.V.A. Röling, *The Tokyo Trial and Beyond* (Polity Press, Cambridge, 1993).

Center for U.S.-Korea Policy (report written by S.-W. Byun), "North Korea Contingency Planning and U.S.-ROK Cooperation", September 2009, available at http://asiafoundation.org/resources/pdfs/DPRKContingencyCUSKP0908.pdf.

Chan, Jae-Soon, "North Korea Threatens to Wipe Out the U.S. 'Once and For All'," *Huffington Post*, 24 June, 2009.

Chan, Joseph, "Territorial boundaries and Confucianism", in Daniel A. Bell (ed.), *Confucian-Political Ethics* (Princeton, NJ: Princeton University Press, 2008).

Chan, P.C.W., "The Legal Status of Taiwan and the Legality of the Use of Force in a Cross Taiwan Strait Conflict", *Chinese Journal of International Law*, vol. 8, 2009, pp. 455–492.

Chanda, Nyan, "Globalization and International Politics in Asia" in Shambaugh, David and Michael Yahuda (eds) *International relations of Asia* (Plymouth: Rowman & Littlefield 2008).

Chen Yali, "China: No Violence in East Timor," *China Daily*, 10 September 1999.

Chesterman, Simon, *Just War or Just Peace?: Humanitarian Intervention and International Law* (New York: Oxford University Press, 2001).

Chihiro Hosoya et al. (eds), *The Tokyo War Crimes Trial: An International Symposium* (Tokyo: Kodansha; New York, N.Y.: Distributed in the U.S. by Kodansha International through Harper & Row, 1986).

Chinen, M.A., "Article 9 of the Constitution of Japan and the Use of Procedural and Substantive Heuristics for Consensus", *Michigan Journal of International Law*, vol. 27, no. 1, 2006, pp. 56–114.

Christensen, Thomas J., "Chinese Realpolitik", *Foreign Affairs*, vol. 75, no. 5, 1996, pp. 37–52.

Christensen, Thomas J., "Fostering Stability or Creating a Monster? The Rise of China and U.S. policy toward East Asia", *International Security*, vol. 31, no. 1, 2006, p. 81.

Christensen, Thomas J., "Posing Problems without Catching Up. China's Rise and Challenges for U.S. Security Policy", *International Security*, vol. 25, no. 4, 2001, pp. 5–40.

Christie, Kenneth, and Denny Roy, "The Politics of Human Rights in East Asia" (London: Pluto Press 2001) p. 5.

Chu, Shulong, "China, Asia and Issues of Sovereignty and Intervention" *Pugwash Occasional Papers*, Vol. 2, No. 1, January 2001, p. 1.

Chung, Chien-peng, "Confronting Terrorism and Other Evils in China: All Quiet on the Western Front?", *The China and Eurasia Forum Quarterly*, vol. 4, no. 2, 2006, pp. 75–87.

Chung, I.S., *Korean Questions in the United Nations* (Seoul National University Press, Seoul, 2002).

Claude, I., *Power and International Relations* (Random House, New York, 1962).

Clausewitz, C. von, *On War* (1832), Anatol Rapoport (ed.) (Penguin, Baltimore, 1968).

Clausewitz, C. von, *On War* (1832), translated and edited by M. Howard and P. Paret (Princeton University Press, Princeton, 1976).

Clinton, Bill, "President Clinton Apologizes", in "Text of President Clinton's Address to Genocide Survivors at the Airport in Kigali, Rwanda" (The Associated Press, 25 March 1998).

Cockayne, James, and David M. Malone, "The Security Council and the 1991 and 2003 Wars in Iraq," in Vaughan Lowe, Adam Roberts, Jennifer Welsh, and Dominik Zaum (eds.), *The United Nations Security Council and War* (Oxford: Oxford University Press, 2010), pp. 384–405.

Cockayne, James, and David M. Malone, "Creeping Unilateralism: How Operation Provide Comfort and the No-Fly Zones in 1991 and 1992 Paved the Way for the Iraq Crisis of 2003," *Security Dialogue*, vol. 37, no. 1, March 2006, pp. 123–141.

Cohen, Jerome Alan, "China and Intervention: Theory and Practice," *University of Pennsylvania Law Review*, vol. 121, no. 3, January 1973, pp. 471–505.

Cohen, Roberta, "Talking Human Rights With North Korea" *The Washington Post*, 29 August 2004.

Commission on Human Security, *Human Security Now* (New York: Commission on Human Security, 2003).
Commission on the Responsibility of the Authors of the War and on Enforcement of Penalties, Report Presented to the Preliminary Peace Conference, March 29, 1919. Reprinted in *The American Journal of International Law*, Vol. 14, No. 1 (1920), pp. 95–154.
Confucius, *Analects of Confucius* (Beijing, 1994).
Cooper, Helene, "Darfur Collides with Olympics, and China Yields," *New York Times*, 13 April 2007.
Coppieters, Bruno, and Nick Fotion, eds., *Moral Constraints on War: Principles and Cases* (Landham, Md: Lexington, 2002).
Corten, O., "The Controversies over the Customary Prohibition on the Use of Force: A Methodological Debate", *EJIl*, vol. 16, no. 5, 2006, pp. 803–822.
Coughlin, Con, "N Korea Helping Iran with Nuclear Testing," Telegraph/UK, 24 Jan 2007.
Cowell, Alan, and Steven Lee Myers, "U.N. Panel Accuses Syrian Government of Crimes Against Humanity," *New York Times*, 24 February 2012.
Creel, Herlee G., *The Origins of Statecraft in China (vol. 1) The Western Chou Empire* (Taipei, 1970).
Crossette, Barbara, "Annan Warns Indonesians that Inaction May Lead to Criminal Charges," *New York Times*, 11 September 1999.
Crossette, Barbara, "As Support for Intervention Grows, Indonesia Persuades U.N. to Delay Evacuation of Mission," *New York Times*, 9 September 1999.
Crossette, Barbara, "Security Council Presses Indonesia to Restore Order," *New York Times*, 6 September 1999.
Crossette, Barbara, "U.N. Says a Quarter of East Timorese Have Fled," *New York Times*, 8 September 1999.
Crossette, Barbara, "U.N. Says Jakarta's Opposition to Peacekeepers Is Weakening," *New York Times*, 12 September 1999.
Cumings, B., *The Korean War. A History* (Modern Library, 2010).
Davida, Kellogg E., "Jus post Bellum: The Importance of War Crime Trials", *Parameters*, vol. 32, no. 3, 2002, pp. 87–99.
Davis, Michael C., "The Reluctant Intervenor: The UN Security Council, China's Worldview, and Humanitarian Intervention" in Michael C. Davis, Wolfgang Dietrich, Bettina Scholden, and Dieter Sepp (eds.), *International Intervention in the Post-Cold War World* (Armonk, NY: M.E. Sharpe, 2004), pp. 241–253.
Dean, Jason, "China's Vote on Libya Signals Possible Shift," *Wall Street Journal*, 28 February 2011.
Delbrück, J., "Effektivität des Gewaltverbots. Bedarf es einer Modifikation der Reichweite des Art. 2(4) UN Charta", *Die Friedens-Warte*, vol. 74, 1999, pp. 139–185.
Dinstein, Yoram, *Aggression and Self-Defence, 3rd ed.* (Cambridge: Cambridge University Press, 2001).
Dinstein, Yoram, *War, Aggression and Self-Defence, 4th ed.* (Cambridge: Cambridge University Press, 2005).
Dinstein, Yoram, *War Aggression and Self-Defence, 5th ed.* (Cambridge: Cambridge University Press, 2012).
Dower, John, *Embracing Defeat: Japan in the Aftermath of World War II* (London: Penguin Books, 2000).
Doyle, Michael W., and Nicholas Sambanis, *Making War and Building Peace: United Nations Peace Operations* (Princeton, NJ: Princeton University Press, 2006).
Dunne, Tim, and Nick Wheeler (eds.) *Human Rights in Global Politics* (Cambridge: Cambridge University Press, 1999).
East Asia Foundation and the Jeju Peace Institute (eds.), *The 5th Jeju Peace Forum: Shaping New Regional Governance in East Asia. A Common Vision for Mutual Benefit and Common Prosperity*, vol. I & III (ORUEM Publishing House, 2010).
Economy, Elizabeth C., "Leadership Gap in China," *Washington Post*, December 1, 2008.

Einsiedel, Sebastian von, and David M. Malone, "Haiti," in David M. Malone (ed.), *The UN Security Council: From the Cold War to the 21st Century* (Boulder, CO: Lynne Rienner Publishers, 2004), pp. 467–482, at p. 467.

Elbe, J. von, "The Evolution of the Concept of the Just War in International Law," *American Journal of International Law*, vol. 33, 1939, p. 669.

Elliott, K.A., "Responding to North Korean Provications: Limitations Sanctions", *International Journal of Korean Unification Studies*, vol. 19, no. 2, 2010, pp. 41–60.

Evans, Gareth, "From Humanitarian Intervention to the Responsibility to Protect," *Wisconsin International Law Journal*, vol. 24, no. 3, 2006, pp. 703–722.

Evans, Gareth, "Time for an Aid Invasion?" *The Age* 19 May 2008.

Evans, Gareth, *The Responsibility to Protect: Ending Mass Atrocity Crimes Once and For All* (Washington, DC: The Brookings Institution, 2008), pp. 38–50.

Fahim, Kareem, and David D. Kirkpatrick, "Qaddafi Orders Brutal Crackdown as Revolt Grows," *New York Times*, 23 February 2011.

Fairbank, John K., "Introduction: Varieties of the Chinese Military Experience", in Frank A. Kiermann & John K. Fairbank (eds.), *Chinese Ways in Warfare* (Cambridge, Mass., 1974), pp. 1–26.

Fairbank, John K., *The Chinese World Order: Traditional China's Foreign Relations* (Cambridge, Mass.: Harvard University Press, 1968).

Falk, R., "What Future for the UN Charter System of War Prevention?", *AJIL*, vol. 97, 2003, pp. 590–598.

Falk, R., *The Costs of War. International Law, the UN, and the World Order after Iraq* (New York: Routledge, 2008).

Feigenbaum, Evan A., "China's Challenge to *Pax Americana*," *Washington Quarterly*, vol. 24, no. 3, Summer 2001, pp. 31–43.

Feinstien, L., and A.M. Slaughter, "A Duty to Prevent," *Foreign Affairs*, vol. 83, 2004, pp. 147–9.

Ferencz, Benjamin B., *Defining International Aggression, the Search for World Peace: A Documentary History and Analysis* (Oceana Publications, 1975), Vol. 2, p. 44.

Findlay, Trevor, "The New Peacekeepers and the New Peacekeeping," in Trevor Findlay (ed.), *Challenges for the New Peacekeepers* (Oxford: Oxford University Press/SIPRI, 1996), pp. 1–31.

Finnemore, Martha, "Constructing Norms of Humanitarian Intervention," in Peter J. Katzenstein (ed.), *The Culture of National Security: Norms and Identity in World Politics* (New York: Columbia University Press, 1996).

Finnemore, Martha, "Military Intervention" in Lepgold and Weiss, *Collective Conflict Management and Changing World Politics*, (Albany: State University of New York Press, 1998).

Finnemore, Martha, *The Purpose of Intervention: Changing Beliefs About the Use of Force* (Ithaca, NY: Cornell University Press, 2003).

Finnemore, Martha, and Kathryn Sikkink, "International Norm Dynamics and Political Change," *International Organization*, vol. 52, no. 4, Autumn 1998, pp. 887–917.

Fisher, L., "The Korean War: On What Legal Basis Did Truman Act?", *AJIL*, vol. 89, 1995, pp. 21–39.

Franck, T., "Who Killed Art. 2(4)? Or: Changing Norms Governing the Use of Force by States", *AJIL*, vol. 64, 1970, pp. 809–837.

Franck, T., *Recourse to Force. State Action against Threats and Armed Attacks* (Cambridge: Cambridge University Press, 2003).

Fravel, M. Taylor, "China's Attitude Toward U.N. Peacekeeping Operations Since 1989," *Asian Survey*, vol. 36, no. 11, November 1996, pp. 1102–1121, at pp. 1103–1104.

Frederking, Brian, *The United States and the Security Council: Collective Security Since the Cold War* (New York: Routledge, 2007).

Freedman, Lawrence, "Prevention, Not Preemption," *The Washington Quarterly*, vol 26, p. 107.

Frei, Matt, "Robin Cook's Moral Crusade Enrages Asia's Fiercest Tiger" *The Daily Telegraph* 7 September 1997.

French, Howard W., "Chinese Leader to Visit Sudan for Talks on Darfur Conflict," *New York Times*, 25 January 2007.

Friedberg, Aaron L., "Ripe for Rivalry? Prospect for Peace in a Multipolar Asia", *International Security*, vol. 18, 1993, pp. 5–33.

Friedberg, Aaron L., "The Future of U.S.-China Relations. Is Conflict Inevitable?", *International Security*, vol. 30, no. 2, 2005, pp. 7–45.

Friedman, Edward, *National Identity and Democratic Prospects in Socialist China* (Armonk, NY: M.E. Sharpe, 1995).

Friedrich, J., *Yalu. An den Ufern des dritten Weltkriegs* (*Propyläen*, Berlin, 2007).

Fujita Hisakazu, "Nihonniokeru Sensōhō Kenkyu no Ayumi" ["The Evolution of Study on the Laws of War in Japan during the Century"], 96 *Kokusaihō Gaikōu Zasshi*.

Futamura, M., "Memory of War Crimes and War: Japanese Historical Consciousness and the Tokyo Trial" in J. Macleod, *Defeat and Memory. Cultural Histories of Military Defeat in the Modern Era* (Hampshire, UK: Palgrave Macmillan, 2008), pp. 137–153.

Futoshi Shibayama, *Nihon SaigunbihenoMichi—1945~1954* (*The Road to Japan's Remilitarization: 1945–1954*), Minerva Shobo, 2010.

Gardam, Judith Gail, *Necessity, Proportionality and the Use of Force by States* (Cambridge: Cambridge University Press, 2004).

Gardner, R.N., "Neither Bush Nor the 'Jurisprudes'", *AJIL*, vol. 97, 2003, pp. 585–590.

Garwood-Gowers, Andrew, "China and the "the Responsibility to Protect": The Implications of the Lybian Intervention", *Asian Journal of International Law*, vol. 2, issue 2, 2012, pp. 375–393.

Gill, Bates, and C.-H. Huang, "China's Expanding Role in Peacekeeping, Prospects and Policy Implications", *SIPRI Policy Paper*, 25 November 2009.

Gill, Bates, and James Reilly, "Sovereignty, Intervention and Peacekeeping: The View from Beijing", *Survival*, vol. 42, no. 3, 2000. pp. 41–59.

Gill, Bates, and Yanzhong Huang: "Sources and Limits of Chinese 'Soft Power'", *Survival*, vol. 48, no. 2, 2006, pp. 17–36.

Gill, T.D., "The Temporal Dimension of Self-Defence: Anticipation, Pre-emption, Prevention and Immediacy," *Journal of Conflict and Security Law*, vol. 11, 2006, pp. 361–369.

Gill, T.D., and D. Fleck (eds.), *The Handbook of the International Law of Military Operations* (Oxford: Oxford University Press, 2010).

Gladstone, Rick, "Friction at U.N. as Russia and China Veto Another Resolution on Syria Sanctions," *New York Times*, 20 July 2012.

Gladstone, Rick, and Annie Lowrey, "Amid Reports of a New Massacre, Nations Seek to Step Up Pressure on Syria," *New York Times*, 7 June 2012.

Glennon, M.J., "The Blank-Prose Crime of Aggression", *The Yale Journal of International Law*, vol. 35, 2010, pp. 71–114.

Glennon, M.J., *Limits of Law, Prerogatives of Power. Interventionism after Kosovo* (New York: Palgrave Macmillan, 2001).

Godehardt, Nadine, and E. MacDonald, "The Same, Only Different: Just War Theory, International Law, and Traditional Chinese Thought", 2004–09–02, paper presented at the annual meeting of the American Political Science Association, accessible at http://www.allacademic.com/meta/p61063_index.html.

Goldstein, Lyle J., *Preventive attack and Weapons of Mass Destruction* (Stanford University Press, 2006), p. 135.

Gong Yuzheng (宫玉振), 文化流变与中国传统兵家的形态更替 ("Cultural Transformation and the Substitution of the Chinese Traditional Military Theory"), 军事历史研究 (*Military Historical Record*), no. 1, 2000, pp. 172–180.

Goodrich, L.M., *Korea: A Study of U.S. Policy in the United Nations* (Council on Foreign Relations, New York, 1956).

Goodman, Ryan, "Humanitarian Intervention and Pretexts for War," *American Journal of International Law*, vol. 100, no. 1, January 2006, pp. 107–141.

Gourevitch, Phillip, *We Wish to Inform You that Tomorrow We Will Be Killed with Our Families: Stories From Rwanda* (New York: Picador, 1998).

Graff, D.A., "The Chinese Concept of Righteous War" in H.M. Hensel, ed. *The Prism of Just War. Asian and Western Perspectives on the Legitimate Use of Military Force* (Surrey: Ashgate, 2010), pp. 195–216.

Gray, C., *International Law and the Use of Force* (Oxford: Oxford University Press, 3rd edition, 2008).

Gray, Christine, "From Unity to Polarization: International Law and the Use of Force Against Iraq," *European Journal of International Law*, vol. 13, no. 1, 2002, pp. 1–19.

Gray, Christine, "President Obama's 2010 U.S. National Security Strategy," 10 *Chinese JIL* (2011).

Gray, Christine, "The Use of Force and the International Legal Order," in Malcolm D. Evans (ed.), *International Law* (Oxford: Oxford University Press, 2d ed., 2006), pp. 589–620.

Greenwood, C., "The Concept of War in Modern International Law", *ICLQ*, vol. 36, 1987, pp. 283–306.

Greenwood, C., "Humanitarian Intervention: the Case of Kosovo", *Finnish Yearbook of International Law*, vol. 10, 2002, pp. 145–175.

Greenwood, C., "International Law and the NATO Intervention in Kosovo," *International and Comparative Law Quarterly*, vol. 49, no. 4, October 2000, pp. 926–934.

Greenwood, C., "International Law and the Pre-emptive Use of Force: Afghanistan, Al-Quaida, and Iraq", *San Diego Journal of International Law*, vol. 4, 2003, pp. 7–37.

Grier, Peter, "Pentagon Dials up Pressure on North Korea for Cheonan Sinking," *Christian Science Monitor*, 24 May 2010.

Gross, L., "Voting in the Security Council: Abstention from Voting in the Security Council: Abstention from Voting and Absence from Meeting", *Yale Law Journal*, vol. 60, 1951, pp. 209–257.

Grotius, H., *De Jure Belli ac Pacis* (1625).

Grünigen, Marianne von, "Neutrality and Peace-Keeping," in *United Nations Peace-Keeping*, (Alphen aan den Rijn, The Netherlands: Sithoff & Noordhoff, 1978), pp. 125–153.

Halderman, J.W., "Legal Basis for United Nations Armed Forces", *AJIL*, vol. 56, 1962, pp. 971–996.

Haley, J.O., "Waging War: Japan's Constitutional Constraints", *Constitutional Forum*, vo. 14, issue 2, 2005, pp. 18–34.

Hall, W.E., *A Treatise on International Law* (A.P. Higgins, ed., 8th ed. 1924).

Han, Feizi, *Die Kunst der Staatsführung. Die Schriften des Meisters Han Fei* (transl. by Wilmar Mögling, Leipzig, 1994).

Harden, Blaine, "North Korean Nuclear Blast Draws Global Condemnation: China, Russia Decry Ally," *Washington Post*, 26 May, 2009.

Harris, John F., and John Mintz, "U.S. Warplanes Patrol Wider "No-Fly" Zone," *Washington Post*, 5 September 1996.

Heisbourg, Francois, "A Work in Progress: The Bush Doctrine and Its Consequences," *The Washington Quarterly*, vol. 24.

Henderson, Christian, "The 2010 United States National Security Strategy and the Obama Doctrine of "Necessary Force"," *Journal of Conflict & Security Law*, vol. 15.

Henkin, L., "The Reports of the Death of Art. 2(4) Are Greatly Exaggerated", *AJIL*, vol. 65, 1971.

Henkin, Louis, "Kosovo and the Law of "Humanitarian Intervention,"" *American Journal of International Law*, vol. 93, no. 4, October 1999, pp. 824–828.

Hensel H.M. (ed.), *The Prism of Just War. Asian and Western Perspectives on the Legitimate Use of Military Force* (Surrey: Ashgate, 2010).

Higgins, Rosalyn, "A General Assessment of United Nations Peace-Keeping," in Antonio Cassese (ed.), *United Nations Peace-Keeping* (Alphen aan den Rijn, The Netherlands: Sijthoff & Noordhoff, 1978), pp. 1–14.

Higurashi, Yoshinobu, *Tōkyō Saiban* [The Tokyo Trial] (Tokyo: Kōdansha, 2008).

Hilaire, Max, *United Nations Law and the Security Council* (Burlington, VT: Ashgate, 2005).

Hilpold, P., "Humanitarian Intervention: Is There a Need for a Legal Reappraisal", *EJIL*, vol. 12, 2001, pp. 437–467.

Hobbes, Thomas, *Leviathan: Oder Stoff, Form und Gewalt eines kirchlichen und bürgerlichen Staates* (edited by Irene Fetscher, Frankfurt am Main, 2006 [1651]).

Holzgrefe, J.L., "The Humanitarian Intervention Debate" in J.L. Holzgrefe, R.O. Keohane, *Humanitarian Intervention. Ethical, Legal, and Political Dilemmas* (Cambridge University Press, Cambridge, 2003), pp. 15–52.

Howe, Brendan, "Conflicting Normative Dimensions of Justification: The Gulf War," in Paul Robinson, ed., *Just War in Comparative Perspective* (Ashgate, 2003).

Hsü, Leonard S., *The Political Philosophy of Confucianism. An Interpretation of the Social and Political Ideas of Confucius, his Forerunners, and his early Disciples* (London/ Dublin/New York, 1932), p. 73.

Hummrich, M., *Der völkerrechtliche Straftatbestand der Aggression* (Nomos, Baden-Baden, 2001).

Ichiro Ozawa, *Nihon kaizokeikaku* (Blueprint for a New Japan) (Tokyo: Kodansha, 1993), pp. 94–95.

International Commission on Intervention and State Sovereignty [ICISS], *The Responsibility to Protect: Research, Bibliography, Background* (Ottawa, Canada: International Development Research Centre, 2001), pp. 391–394.

Israel, F.L., *Major Peace Treaties of Modern History, 1648–1967* (Vol. VI, Chelsea House Publishers, 1967).

Jacobs, Andrew, "China Urges Quick End to Airstrikes in Libya," *New York Times*, 22 March 2011.

Jacobs, Andrew, and Jonathan Ansfield, "In China, Security Muffles Calls for Change," *New York Times*, 28 February 2011.

Jacques, Martin, *When China Rules the World. The Rise of the Middle Kingdom and the End of the Western world* (London, Penguin, 2009).

Jang, D.-J., Y.-H. Byun, and K.-H. Song, "Human Rights Problems in North Korea: Humanitarian Intervention or Humanitarian Assistance?", paper presented at the annual meeting of the American Political Science Association, 30 August 2007, available at http://www.allacademic.com/meta/p210862_index.html.

Jennings, R.Y., and A. Watts (eds.), *Oppenheim's International Law*, vol. 1, 9th edition (Longman Harlow, 1992) p. 420.

Jia Qingguo, "China," in Watanabe Koji (ed.), *Humanitarian Intervention: The Evolving Asian Debate* (Washington, DC: Brookings Institution Press, 2003), pp. 19–32.

Jiangyu Wang, "China and the Universal Human Rights Standards," *Syracuse Journal of International Law and Commerce*, vol. 29, no. 1, Fall 2001, pp. 135–158, at pp. 146–147.

Johnston, Alastair I., "China as a Status Quo Power?", *International Security*, vol. 27, no. 4, 2003, pp. 5–56.

Johnston, Alastair I., "Cultural Realism and Strategy in Maoist China" in Peter J. Katzenstein (ed.), *The Culture of National Security: Norms and Identity in Word Politics* (New York, 1996).

Johnston, Alastair I., "Thinking about Strategic Culture", *International Security*, vol. 19, no. 4, 1995, pp. 32–64.

Johnston, Alastair I., *Cultural Realism. Strategic Culture and Grand Strategy in Chinese History* (Princeton, 1995).

Joint Chiefs of Staff, *Department of Defense Dictionary of Military and Associated Terms*, Washington, D.C.: Joint Chiefs of Staff, (2004).

Jung Sung-ki, "Allies Ready to Remove NK Nukes," *The Korea Times*, 12 March 2010.

Kadelbach, S., "Staatenverantwortlichkeit für Angriffskriege und Verbrechen gegen die Menschlichkeit" in Berichte der Deutschen Gesellschaft für Völkerrecht, *Entschädigung nach bewaffneten Konflikte. Die Konstitutionalisierung der Welthandelsordnung* (Heidelberg: C.F. Müeller, 2001), pp. 63–105.

Kang, David, *China Rising. Peace, Power, and Order in East Asia* (New York, 2007).

Kang, David, "Hierarchy, Balancing and Empirical Puzzles in Asian International Relations", *International Security*, vol. 28, 2003.

Kang, David, "The Theoretical Roots of Hierarchy in International Relations", *Australian Journal of International Affairs*, vol. 58, 2004.

Kasher, Asa, "Operation Cast Lead and the Ethics of Just War," *Azure, vol. 30*, 2009.

Kegley Jr., Charles W., "International Peacemaking and Peacekeeping: The Morality of Multilateral Measures" *Ethics & International Affairs*, vol. 10, issue 1, pp. 25–45.

Keller, William W., and Gordon R. Mitchell, "Preemption, Prevention, Prevarication," *Hitting First: Preventive Force in U.S. Security Strategy*, ed. Keller & Mitchell (University of Pittsburgh Press, 2006).

Kelsen, H., *Law and Peace in International Relations* (Cambridge, Mass.: Harvard University Press, 1948).

Khong, C.O., "Asian Values: The Debate Revisited" *"Asian Values" and Democracy in Asia* Proceedings of a Conference Held on 28 March 1997 at Hamamatsu, Shizuoka, Japan available at http://www.unu.edu/unupress/asian-values.html#DEBATE.

Kim, D.J., "The North Korean Nuclear Issue and the United Nations", *The Korean Journal of Defense Analysis*, vol. 23, no. 2, 2011, pp. 289–302.

Kim, J.S., and B. Howe, "Pre-emption against Pyongyang: Is a Military First Strike on the Korean Peninsula Legal?", *Journal of Korean Law*, vol. 4, no. 1, 2004, pp. 123–154.

Kim, S. (ed.), *The International Relations of Northeast Asia* (Lanham: Roman Littlefield Publishers, 2004).

Kim, Y.S., "The Korean Implementing Legislation on the ICC Statute", *Chinese Journal of International Law*, 2011, pp. 161–170.

Kirkpatrick, David D., Steven Erlanger, and Elisabeth Bumiller, "Allies Open Air Assault on Qaddafi's Forces in Libya," *New York Times*, 19 March 2011.

Kivimäki, T., "The Long Peace of ASEAN", *Journal of Peace Research*, vol. 38, no. 1, 2001, pp. 5–25.

Kleine-Ahlbrandt, Stephanie, and Andrew Small, "China's New Dictatorship Diplomacy: Is Beijing Parting with Pariahs?," *Foreign Affairs*, vol. 87, no. 1, January/February 2008, pp. 38–56.

Koechler, Hans (ed.), *The Use of Force in International Relations* (Vienna: Progress Organization Studies in International Relations XXIX, 2006).

Koji, M., "Japan" in W. Koji, *Humanitarian Intervention: The Evolving Asian Debate* (Japan Center for International Exchange, Tokyo, 2003), pp. 11–18.

Korman, S., *The Right of Conquest. The Acquisition of Territory by Force in International Law and Practice* (Oxford: Clarendon Press, 2003).

Köster, Hermann (trans.), Hsün-Tzu (Kaldenkirchen: Steyer Verlag, 1967).

Kozaryn, Linda D., "NATO Orders Air Strikes to End 'Humanitarian Catastrophe,'" *American Forces Press Service*, 24 March 1999.

Kramer, Andrew E., "Russia Warns It Will Not Back Britain on Syria Sanctions," *New York Times*, 17 July 2012.

Kreß, C., "Time for Decision: Some Thoughts on the Immediate Future of the Crime of Aggression: A Reply to Andreas Paulus", *EJIL*, vol. 20, no. 4, 2010, pp. 1129–1146.

Kreß, C., and Leonie von Holtzendorff, "The Kampala Compromise on the Crime of Aggression", *Journal of International Criminal Justice*, vol. 8, 2010, pp. 1179–1217.

Krushchev, N., *The Glasnost Tapes* (Strobe Talbot (ed.), Little Brown, 1990).

Kyo Arai, Akira Mayama and Osamu Yoshida, "Japan's Accession to the ICC Statute and the ICC Cooperation Law", *The Japanese Yearbook of International Law*, vol. 51, 2008, pp. 359–383.

Lam, Willy, "Socialism with a Harmonious Face: Hu Jintao's Plan for Reform", *China Brief*, vol. 4, no. 20, 2004, pp. 5–7.

Landler, Mark, "The Fate of East Timor: The Indonesian View; Jakarta Military Is Taking Central Role in Crisis," *New York Times*, 10 September 1999.

Lauterpacht, E., "The Legal Irrelevance of the State of War", *ASIL Proc.*, vol. 62, 1968.

League of Nations Official Journal, Special Supplement, no. 101, 1932, pp. 87–88.

Leclerc-Gagné E., and M. Byers, "A Question of Intent: The Crime of Aggression and Unilateral Humanitarian Intervention", *Case Western Reserve Journal of International Law*, vol. 41, nos. 2–3, 2009, pp. 379–390.

Lee, C.-J., *China and Korea: Dynamic Relations* (Stanford, CA: Hoover Press, 1996).

Lee, Jean H., "North Korea Threatens "all-out war" Denies South's Claim that the North Torpedoed a Warship," *Associated Press*, 20 May 2010.

Lepgold, Joseph, and Thomas Weiss, *Collective Conflict Management and Changing World Politics*, (Albany: SUNY Press 1998).

Letter of Webster to Fox, 24 April 1841, 29 *British and Foreign State Papers* (1840–41).

Lewis, Mark E., "The Just War in Early China" in B. Torkel (ed.), *The Ethics of War in Asian Civilizations* (London/New York, 2006), pp. 185–200.

Lewis, Mark E., *Sanctioned Violence in Early China* (Albany, New York, 1990).

Lillich, R., "Forcible Self-help by States to Protect Human Rights", *Iowa Journal of International Law Review*, vol. 53, 1967/1968, pp. 325–351.

Lilly, Amanda, "A Guide to China's Ethnic Groups," *Washington Post*, 8 July 2009.

Lintott, Andrew, *Imperium Romanum. Politics and administration* (London/New York, 1993).

Lippman, Thomas W., "Yugoslavs Begin Kosovo Retreat," *Washington Post*, 11 June 1999.

Littman, QC, Mark, *Kosovo: Law & Diplomacy* (London: Centre for Policy Studies, 1999).

Lobel, Jules, and Michael Ratner, "Bypassing the Security Council: Ambiguous Authorizations to Use Force, Cease-Fires and the Iraqi Inspection Regime," *American Journal of International Law*, vol. 93, no. 1, January 1999, pp. 124–154.

Lou Chunhao (楼春豪), 进攻性现实主义"中国威胁论"的实质 ("The Essence of the Offensive Realism View on the „China Threat Debate""), 国际关系学院研9i,生部 (*Journal of University of International Relations*), no. 3, 2006, pp. 14–18.

Lu Jianping and Wang Zhixiang, "China's Attitude towards the ICC", *Journal of International Criminal Justice*, vol. 3, no. 3, 2005, pp. 608–620.

Luard, E., *A History of the United Nations, Vol. 1: The Years of Western Domination 1945–1955* (St. Martin's Press, New York, 1982), pp. 228–274.

Luo Jianbo (罗建波), 构建中国崛起的对外文化战略 ("Establishing an External Cultural Strategy Currently Rising in China"), 现代国际关系 (*Contemporary International Relations*), no. 3, 2006, p. 36.

Lynch, Colum, "China Filling Void Left by West in U.N. Peacekeeping," *Washington Post*, 24 November 2006.

Lynch, Colum, "Russia, China Veto Syria Resolution at the United Nations," *Washington Post*, 4 October 2011.

Lynch, Colum, "Russia, China Veto U.N. Sanctions Resolution on Syria," *Washington Post*, 19 July 2012.

Lynch, Colum, "Syrian Peace Plan: U.N. Security Council Endorses Kofi Annan's Proposal," *Washington Post*, 21 March 2012.

Lynch, Colum, and Alice Fordham, Russia, "China Veto U.N. Resolution on Syria," *Washington Post*, 4 February 2012.

Lynn, H.G., *Bipolar Orders. The Two Koreas since 1989* (London/New York: Zed Books, 2007).

MacFarquhar, Neil, "All Eyes on Russia as Syria Cease-Fire Deadline Passes," *New York Times*, 12 April 2012.

MacFarquhar, Neil, "At U.N., Pressure Is on Russia for Refusal to Condemn Syria," *New York Times*, 1 February 2012.

MacFarquhar, Neil, "Cease-Fire in Syria Exposes the Heavy Price of Just Buying Time," *New York Times*, 29 April 2012.

MacFarquhar, Neil, "Push in U.N. for Criticism of Syria Is Rejected," *New York Times*, 28 April 2011; Dan Bilefsky, "New Move to Condemn Syria in U.N.," *New York Times*, 9 June 2011.

MacFarquhar, Neil, "Russia and China Block U.N. Action on Crisis in Syria," *New York Times*, 5 February 2012.

MacFarquhar, Neil, "Security Council Approves More Monitors of Cease-Fire in Syria," *New York Times*, 22 April 2012.

MacFarquhar, Neil, "Syria Resumes Shelling of Homs," *New York Times*, 15 February 2012.

MacFarquhar, Neil, "Syria Tries to Defend Its Record to United Nations," *New York Times*, 27 April 2011.

MacFarquhar, Neil, "U.N. Resolution on Syria Blocked by Russia and China," *New York Times*, 5 October 2011.

MacFarquhar, Neil, "U.N. Tentatively Backs a Plan for Syria," *New York Times*, 3 February 2012.

MacFarquhar, Neil, "With Rare Double U.N. Veto on Syria, Russia and China Try to Shield Friend," *New York Times*, 6 October 2011.

Madoka Futamura, "Japanese Societal Attitudes towards the Tokyo Trial: A Contemporary Perspective" in Yuki Tanaka, Tim McCormack and Gerry Simpson (eds.), *Beyond Victors" Justice? The Tokyo War Crimes Trial Revisited* (Leiden, The Netherlands: Martinus Nijhoff Publishers, 2011).

Madoka Futamura, *War Crimes Tribunals and Transitional Justice: The Tokyo Trial and the Nuremberg Legacy* (Routledge, 2008).

Mahbubani, Kishore, *The New Asian Hemisphere: the Irresistible Shift of Global Power to the East* (New York: Public Affairs, 2008).

Malone, K.J., "Preemptive Strikes and the Nuclear Crisis: Legal and Political Limitations on the Use of Force", *Pacific Rim Law & Policy Journal*, vol. 12, no. 3, 2003, pp. 807–834.

Marauhn, T., "The Debate about a Revolution in Military Affairs – A Comment in the Light of Public International Law", *Die Friedens-Warte*, vol. 77, 2002, pp. 411–435.

Martin, C., "Binding the Dogs of War: Japan and the Constitutionalizing of *Jus ad Bellum*", *U. Pa. J. Int'l.*, vol. 30, 2008, pp. 267–357.

Masaki Yasushi, "Nihon to Kokusaikeijisaibansho [Japan and the ICC]", in Murase Shinya and Kō Keiko (eds), *Kokusaikeijisaibansho: Mottomo Jūdaina Kokusaihanzai wo Sabaku* [The International Criminal Court: Prosecuting the Most Serious International Crimes] (Tokyo: Tōshindō, 2008), p. 325.

Matheson, Michael J, *Council Unbound: The Growth of UN Decision Making on Conflict and Postconflict Issues after the Cold War* (Washington: United States Institute for Peace, 2006).

Matheson, Michael J., "Justification for the NATO Air Campaign in Kosovo," *Proceedings of the Annual Meeting of the American Society of International Law*, vol. 94, April 2000.

Mayama Akira, "Kokusaikeijisaibansho no Taishōhanzai to Kokunaitekitaiō [The Municipal Response to the Crimes that Fall Within the Jurisdiction of the ICC]", 79 *Hōritsujihō* (2007), pp. 31–36.

Mayama Akira, "Kokusaikeijisaibanshokitei Kentōkaigisaitakuno Shinryakuhanzaikan-renkitei", *Kokusaihō Gaikō Zasshi*, vol. 109, no. 4, 2011, pp. 1–33.

McDougal, M.S., and F.P. Feliciano, *Law and Minimum World Public Order* (New Haven: Yale University Press, 1961), pp. 232–241.

McDougal, M.S., and R. Gardner, "The Veto and the Charter: An Interpretation for Survival", *Yale Law Journal*, vol. 60, 1951, pp. 285–292.

McDougall, C., "When Law and Reality Clash - The Imperative of Compromise in the Context of the Accumulated Evil of the Whole: Conditions for the Excercise of the International Criminal Court's Jurisdiction over the Crime of Aggression", *International Criminal Law Review*, vol. 7, no. 2–3, 2007, pp. 277–333.

Mearsheimer, John, *The Tragedy of Great Power Politics* (New York, 2001).

Medeiros, Evan, and Taylor Fravel, China's New Diplomacy, *Foreign Affairs*, vol. 82, no. 6, 2003, pp. 22–35.

Meer, S. van der, "North Korea after Kim Jong Il: Four Scenarios", *Strategic Insights*, vol. 8, issue 5, 2009.

Meierhenrich, Jens, and Keiko Ko, "How Do States Join the International Criminal Court? The Implementation of the Rome Statute in Japan", *Journal of International Criminal Justice*, vol. 7, 2009, p. 239, p. 253.

Meng, S.M., *The Tsungli Yamen: Its Organization and Functions*. (Cambridge, Mass.: Harvard University Press, 1970).

Mengzi (孟子), 陈成国 (Chen Chengguo): 四书五经 (*Four Books and Five Classics*), (Hunan Changshao, 2002).

Michishita, N., *North Korea's Military-Diplomatic Campaigns, 1966–2008* (Routledge, London, New York, 2010).

Minear, R.H., *Victor's Justice. The Tokyo War Crimes Trial* (University of Michigan, Ann Arbour, 2001).

Miyoshi, Masahiro, "Kokusairengō niyoru Shinryakuno Teigi", *Juristo*, No. 584 (1975).

Mon, C.J. Le, "International Law and North Korean Nuclear Testing", *ASIL Insight*, 19 October 2006, http://www.asil.org/insights061020.cfm.

Morris, Nicholas, "Humanitarian Intervention in the Balkans," in Jennifer M. Welsh, ed., *Humanitarian Intervention and International Relations* (New York: Oxford University Press, 2004).

Moynihan, Colin, "Libya's U.N. Diplomats Break with Qaddafi," *New York Times*, 21 February 2011.

Mueller, Karl P., et al., *Striking First: Preemptive and Preventive Attack in U.S. National Security Policy* (Santa Monica, CA: RAND Air Force Project, 2006).

Muenkler, Herfried, *Imperien: die Logik der Weltherrschaft – vom Alten Rom bis zu den Vereinigten Staaten* (Hamburg, 2007).

Murphy, S.D., "Criminalizing Humanitarian Intervention", *Case Western Reserve Journal of International Law*, vol. 41, nos. 2–3, 2009, pp. 341–377.

Murphy, S.D., "Protean Jus ad Bellum", *Berkeley Journal of International Law*, vol. 27, 2009, pp. 22–52.

Mydans, Seth, "In East Timor, Decisive Vote for a Break from Indonesia," *New York Times*, 4 September 1999.

Mydans, Seth, "Indonesia Invites a U.N. Force to Timor," *New York Times*, 13 September 1999.

Mydans, Seth, "Indonesia Says No to Timor Peacekeepers," *New York Times*, 9 September 1999.

Mydans, Seth, "Jakarta Concedes a Loss of Control Over Timor Forces," *New York Times*, 12 September 1999.

Mydans, Seth, "Militias Raise Tensions After Timor Votes," *New York Times*, 1 September 1999.

Mydans, Seth, "Timorese Flee as Militias Seem to Gain Upper Hand," *New York Times*, 3 September 1999.

Mydans, Seth, "Violence as East Timor Awaits Vote Count," *New York Times*, 2 September 1999.

Nau, Henry R., *At Home Abroad: Identity and Power in American Foreign Policy* (Ithaca: Cornell University Press, 2002).

Neff, S.C., *War and the Law of Nations. A General History* (Cambridge: Cambridge University Press, 2005).

Neuffer, Elizabeth, *The Key to My Meighbor's House: Seeking Justice in Bosnia and Rwanda* (London: Bloomsbury 2002).

Ni Lexiong (倪乐雄), 孔子与战争 ("Confucius and War"), 军事历史研91, (*Military Historical Record*), no. 4, 1999, pp. 93–104.

Niikura, Osamu, "Kokusaikeijisaibanshokiteino Hijunto Kokunaihōseibino Kadai", *Hōritsujihō*, vol. 79, no. 4.

O'Connell, Mary Ellen, *International Law and the Use of Force* (Foundation Press, New York, 2005).

O'Connell, Mary Ellen, "The Myth of Preemptive Self-Defense," *American Society of International Law: Task Force on Terrorism* (August 2002).

O'Connell, Mary Ellen, and Mirakmal Niyazmatov, "What is Aggression?: Comparing the Jus ad Bellum and the ICC Statute", *Journal of International Criminal Justice* 10 (2012), pp. 195–198.

Oberdorfer, D., *The Two Koreas: A Contemporary History* (Basic Books, 2001).

Okano Masataka, "Kokusaikeijisaibansho Romakiteikentōkaigino Kekkanitsuite", *Kokusaihō Gaikō Zasshi*, vol. 109, no. 2, 2010, pp. 80–82.

Onuma Yasuaki, *Sensōsekininron Josetsu:"Heiwanitaisurutsumi"no Keiseikateiniokeru Ideorogiseito Kōsokusei* (Tokyo: Tōkyo Daigaku Shuppan, 1975).

Orend, Brian, "Jus Post Bellum", *Journal of Social Philosophy*, vol. 31, no. 1, 2000, pp. 117–137.

Orend, Brian, "Michael Walzer on Resorting to Force," *Canadian Journal of Political Science/ Revue Canadienne De Science Politique*, vol. 33, September 2000.

Orend, Brian, *The Morality of War* (Ontario, 2006).

Osten, Philipp, *Der Tokioter Kriegsverbrecherprozess und die japanische Rechtswissenschaft* (BWV, Berlin, 2003).

Osten, Philipp, "Kokusaikeijisaibanshokitei to Kokunairippō: Doitsu "Kokusaikeihōten" sōanwo sozaitoshite", *Juristo*, no. 1207 (2001).

Owada, Hisashi, "Kokusaikeijisaibansho Setsuritsuno Igito Mondaiten", *Kokusaihō Gaikō Zasshi*, vol. 98, no. 5, pp. 29–30.

Owens, Patricia, "IR Theory in Practice Case Study: The 1999 Kosovo Crisis" in *Oxford web support material*, Section 1, p. 4 (Oxford: Oxford University Press 2005).

Pak, Y., *Korea and the United Nations* (The Hague: Kluwer Law International, 2000).

Pang Zhongying, "China's Changing Attitude to UN Peacekeeping," *International Peacekeeping*, vol. 12, no. 1, Spring 2005, pp. 87–104.

Paulus, A., "Second Thoughts on the Crime of Aggression", *EJIL*, vol. 20, no. 4, 2010, pp. 1117–1128.

Paust, J.J., "Self-Defense Targeting of Non-State Actors and Permissibility of U.S. Drones in Pakistan", *Journal of Transnational Law and Policy*, vol. 19, 2010, pp. 237–280.

Perlez, Jane, "Putin Arrives in China, Seeking Stronger Ties," *New York Times*, 6 June 2012.

Picigallo, P.R., *The Japanese on Trial. Allied War Crimes Operations in the East 1945–1951* (University of Texas Press, Austin and London, 1979), pp. 158–173.

Pin Sun, *Military Methods* (transl. by Ralph D. Sawyer with Mei-chün Sawyer, Boulder/San Francisco/Oxford, 1995).

Pinkston, D.A., and K. Sakurai, "Japan Debates Preparing for Future Preemptive Strikes against North Korea", *The Korean Journal of Defense Analysis*, vol. 18, no. 4, 2006, pp. 95–121.

Polgreen, Lydia, "China, in New Role, Uses Ties to Press Sudan on Troubled Darfur," *New York Times*, 23 February 2008.

Polgreen, Lydia, and Warren Hoge, "Sudan Relents on Peacekeepers in Darfur," *New York Times*, 13 June 2007.

Politi, Mauro, "The ICC and the Crime of Aggression: A Dream that Came Through and the Reality Ahead", *Journal of International Criminal Justice* 10 (2012).

Poneman, Daniel B., Joel S. Wit and Robert L. Gallucci, *Going Critical The First North Korean Nuclear Crisis* (Brookings Institution Press, 2004).

Popovski, V., G.M. Reichberg, N. Turner (eds.), *World Religions and Norms of War* (Tokyo: United Nations University, 2009).

Power, Samantha, "Bystanders to Genocide: Why the United States Let the Rwandan Tragedy Happen," *Atlantic Monthly*, September 2001.

Power, Samantha, "Dying in Darfur: Can the Ethnic Cleansing in Sudan Be Stopped?," *New Yorker*, 30 August 2004, pp. 56–73.

Power, Samantha, *A Problem From Hell: America and the Age of Genocide* (New York: HarperCollins Publishers, 2003), pp. 329–389.

Pritchard, R. John (ed.), The Tokyo Major War Crimes Trial: The Complete Transcripts of the Proceedings of the International Military Tribunal for the Far East, in 124 volumes (Edwin Mellen Press).

Przetacznik, F., *The Philosophical and Legal Concept of War* (The Edwin Mellen Press, Lewiston, 1994).

Ramsey, Paul, *The Just War: Force and Political Responsibility* (Lanham, MD: University Press of America, 1983).

Rawls, John, 1987 "The Idea of an Overlapping Consensus", *Oxford Journal of Legal Studies*, vol. VII, no. 1. spring 1987, pp. 1–27.

Reichberg, Gregory, "Preventative War in Classical Just War Theory," *Journal of the History of International Law*, vol. 9, 2007, pp. 5–34.

Reisman, W. Michael, "Assesing Claims to Revise the Laws of War", *AJIL*, vol. 97, 2003, pp. 82–90.

Reisman, W. Michael, "Hollow Victory: Humanitarian Intervention and Protection of Minorities," *Proceedings of the Annual Meeting of the American Society of International Law*, vol. 91, April 1997, pp. 431–437.

Reisman, W. Michael, "Sovereignty and Human Rights in Contemporary International Law", *AJIL*, vol. 84, 1990, pp. 866–876.

Reiter, Dan, "Preventive Attacks against Nuclear, Biological and Chemical Weapons Programs: the Track Record," Working Paper, Ridgway Working Group on Preemptive and Preventive Military Intervention.

Rengger, Nicholas, "On the Just War Tradition in the Twenty-First Century," *International Affairs*, vol. 78, 2002.

Report to the President from Justice Robert H. Jackson, Chief of Counsel for the United States in the Prosecution of Axis War Criminals, AJIL (Supplement: Official Documents (July 1945)), vol. 39, 1945, pp. 178–90.

Richarz, Allan, "In Defense of Israel's Disproportionate Response in Gaza," *Christian Science Monitor*, 9 January 2009.

Richburg, Keith B., "'Trust Deficit' Cited by China," *Washington Post*, 9 February 2012.

Richburg, Keith B., "China Remains Hands-Off in Syria," *Washington Post*, 21 July 2012.

Rifaat, M., *International Aggression* (Almqvist & Wiksell International, Stockholm, 1979), pp. 7–11.

Robinson, T., "The Sino-Soviet Border Dispute: Background, Development, and the March 1969 Clashes", *The American Political Science Review*, vol. 66, no. 4, 1972, pp. 1175–1202.

Roscher, B., "The "Renunciation of War as an Instrument of National Policy"", *Journal of the History of International Law*, vol. 4, no. 2, 2002, pp. 293–309.

Roscini, M., "Threats of Armed Force and Contemporary International Law", *NILR*, vol. 54, 2007, pp. 229–277.

Ross, Robert, and Feng Zhu, *China's Ascent. Power, Security, and the Future of International Politics* (Ithaca: Cornell University Press, 2008).

Rossabi, Morris (ed.), *Governing China's Multiethnic Frontiers* (Seattle, WA: University of Washington Press, 2004).

Roy, Denny, "Hegemon on the Horizon? China's Threat to East Asian Security", *International Security*, vol. 19, no. 1, 1994, pp. 149–168.

Rupert, James, "Refugees Report Roadside Slaughter," *Washington Post*, 29 April 1999.

Saito, H., "A Japanese View of the Manchurian Situation", *Annals of the American Academy of Political and Social Science*, vol. 165, 1933, pp. 159–166.

Sang Donghui (桑东辉), 也谈春秋战国时期的诸侯国是否为主权国家. 以《墨子》为例,以国际法为视角 ("From the Perspective of International Law Using Mozi as an Example: The Renewed Discussion about whether the Feudal States of the Chunqiu and Warring States Period Represent Sovereign States or not"), 国际政治研究 (*Studies of International Politics*), no. 2, 2006, pp. 137–149.

Sanger, David E., "Indonesia Is Warned It Could Lose Western Aid," *New York Times*, 8 September 1999.

Sawyer, Ralph D., *The Seven Military Classics of Ancient China* (transl. by Ralph D. Sawyer with Mei-chün Sawyer, Boulder/San Francisco/Oxford, 1993).
Schachter, Oscar, "The Rights of States to Use Armed Force," *Michigan Law Review,* vol. 82, 1984.
Scheffer, D., "State Parties Approve New Crimes for International Criminal Court", *ASIL Insight*, vol. 14, issue 16, 2010.
Schindler, D., "Der Kriegszustand im Völkerrecht der Gegenwart" in *Festschrift v. Heydte* (Duncker & Humblot, Berlin, 1977), pp. 555–576.
Schmitt, M.N., "Computer Network Attack and the Use of Force in International Law: Thoughts on a Normative Framework", (1999) *Columbia Journal of Transnational Law*, vol. 37, 1999, pp. 885–937.
Scobell, Andrew, "The Chinese Cult of Defense", *Issues & Studies*, vol. 37, no. 5, 2001, pp. 100–127.
Scobell, Andrew, *China's Use of Military Force. Beyond the Great Wall and the Long March* (Cambridge, 2003).
Segal, Gerald, "Does China Matter?", *Foreign Affairs*, vol. 78, no. 5, 1999, pp. 24–36.
Sellars, Kirsten, "Delegitimizing Aggression: First Steps and False Starts after the First World War", *Journal of International Criminal Justice* 10 (2012), pp. 7–40.
Shabas, W.A., "Origins of the Criminalization of Aggression: How Crimes against Peace Became the "Supreme International Crime" in M. Politi, G. Nesta (eds.), *The International Criminal Court and the Crime of Aggression* (Aldershot, UK: Ashgate, 2004).
Shadid, Anthony, "Fear of Civil War Mounts in Syria as Crisis Deepens," *New York Times*, 15 January 2012.
Shaeffer, Sheldon, "Foreword" in Zhou Nan-Zhao and Bob Teasdale (eds.) *Teaching Asia-Pacific Core Values of Peace and Harmony* (Bangkok: UNESCO, 2004).
Shambaugh, David, "China Engages Asia. Reshaping the Regional Order", *International Security*, vol. 29, no. 3, May 2004, pp. 64–99.
Shambaugh, David, "International Relations in Asia: The Two-Level Game" in Shambaugh, David and Michael Yahuda (eds.), *International Relations of Asia* (Plymouth: Rowman & Littlefield 2008).
Sharma, S.P., "The India-China Border Dispute: An Indian Perspective", *AJIL*, vol. 59, no. 1, 1965, pp. 16–47.
Shaw, Malcolm N., *International Law* (Cambridge University Press, Cambridge, 4th ed. 1997), p. 790.
Shaw, Malcolm N., *International Law*, 6th ed. (Cambridge: Cambridge University Press, 2008).
Sheen, S.H., "U.S. Contingency Plan for North Korea's Regime Collapse", *IIRI Working Paper Series* 10, October 2011.
Shenon, Philip, "President Asserts Jakarta Must Act or Admit Troops," *New York Times*, 10 September 1999.
Sherwood, J.T., "An Examination of the Legal Justifications Presented by Japan before the League of Nations in Defense of Her Actions Concerning the Mukden Incident, the Occupation of Manchuria and the Creation of Manchukuo", *Military Law & Law of War Review*, vol. 16, 1977, pp. 204–243.
Shi Yinhong (时殷弘), 关于战争与和平的伦理传统: 西方与中国 ("Theoretical Tradition of War and Peace. China and the West"), 世界经济与政治 (*World Economics and Politics*), no. 10, 1999.
Shirk, Susan L., *China: Fragile Superpower* (Oxford: Oxford University Press, 2008).
Simei Qing, *From Allies to Enemies: Visions of Modernity, Identity, and U.S.–China Diplomacy, 1945–1960* (Cambridge, MA: Harvard University Press, 2007), p. 254.
Simma, B., *The Charter of the United Nations. A Commentary, 2nd ed.* (Oxford: Oxford University Press, 2002).
Slaughter, A.-M., and Lee Feinstein, "A Duty to Prevent", *Foreign Affairs*, vol. 83, 2004.
Slocombe, Walter B., "Force, Preemption and Legitimacy," *Survival,* vol. 45, 2003.

Sly, Liz, "Syrian Troops Open Fire on Protesters; Dozens Feared Dead," *Washington Post*, 3 June 2011.

Sly, Liz, "Global Condemnation, But No Action, Against Bloody Syria Crackdown," *Washington Post*, 26 April 2011.

Smith, R. Jeffrey, "New Wave of Kosovo Exiles Tells of Atrocities by Serbs," *Washington Post*, 15 April 1999.

Smith, R. Jeffrey, and William Booth, "Yugoslavia Steps Up Expulsions," *Washington Post*, 17 April 1999.

Snyder, S., and S.-W. Byun, "Cheonan and Yeonpyeong. The Northeast Asian Response to North Korea's Provocations", *RUSI Journal*, vol. 156, no. 2, 2011, pp. 74–81.

Solana, Javier, "NATO's Success in Kosovo," *Foreign Affairs*, vol. 78, no. 6, November/December 1999, pp. 114–120.

Solera, O., *Defining the Crime of Aggression* (Cameron May, London, 2007).

Son, K-Y., "From a Garrison State to a Humanitarian Power?: Security Identities, Constitutive Norms and South Korea's Overseas Troop Dispatches", *The Korean Journal of Defence Analysis*, vol. 23, no. 4, 2011, pp. 557–573.

Special Proclamation: Establishment of an International Military Tribunal for the Far East annexed to the *Judgement of the International Military Tribunal for the Far East*, Annex No. A-4, Art. 1.

Spegele, Brian, "China Takes New Tack in Libya Vote," *Wall Street Journal*, 20 March 2011.

Spence, Jonathan D., *The Search for Modern China* (New York: W.W. Norton & Co., 1999).

Ståhle, Stefan, "China's Shifting Attitude Toward United Nations Peacekeeping Operations," *China Quarterly*, vol. 195, September 2008, pp. 631–655.

Stahn, Carsten, "Responsibility to Protect: Political Rhetoric or Emerging Legal Norm?," *American Journal of International Law*, vol. 101, no. 1, January 2007, pp. 99–120.

Stone, J., *Aggression and World Order* (Berkeley: University of California Press, 1958).

Stromseth, Jane E., "Iraq's Repression of Its Civilian Population: Collective Responses and Civilian Challenges" in Lori Fisler Damrosch (ed.), *Enforcing Restraint: Collective Intervention in Internal Conflicts* (New York: Council on Foreign Relations Press, 1993), pp. 77–117.

Stromseth, J.E. "Law and Force after Iraq: A Transitional Moment", *AJIL*, vol. 97, 2003, pp. 628–642.

Stueck, W., "The United Nations, the Security Council, and the Korean War" in V. Lowe, et al. (eds.), *The United Nations Security Council and War: The Evolution of Thought and Practice since 1945* (Oxford University Press, 2008), pp. 265–279.

Stürchler, N., *The Threat of Force in International Law* (Cambridge University Press, Cambridge, 2007).

Subedi, S.P., "The Concept in Hinduism of "Just War"", *Journal of Conflict and Security Law*, vol. 8, no. 2, 2003, pp. 339–361.

Sudetic, Chuck, "Serbian Forces Said to Overrun Muslim Villages," *New York Times*, 3 June 1993.

Suisheng Zhao, *Power Competition in East Asia: from the Old Chinese World Order to Post-cold War Regional Multipolarity* (London, 1997), p. 8.

Sun Tsu, *Wahrhaft siegt, wer nicht kämpft* (transl. by Ingrid Fischer-Schreiber, Freiburg 1990).

Sun Tzu, *The Art of War* (transl. by. Samuel B. Griffith, Oxford, 1963).

Sunga, Lyal S., "The Role of Humanitarian Intervention in International Peace and Security: Guarantee or Threat?" in Hans Koechler (ed.), *The Use of Force in International Relations International* (Vienna: Progress Organization Studies in International Relations XXIX, 2006).

Swaine, Michael D., and Ashley J. Tellis, *Interpreting China's Grand Strategy. Past, Present, and Future* (Project Air Force RAND, Santa Monica, 2000), p. 45.

Takahashi Michitoshi, "Shinryakunoteiginikansuru Kokuren-iinnkaianno Seiritsu", *Kokusaimondai*, vol. 176 and 177 (1974).

Teitt, Sarah, "The Responsibility to Protect and China's Peacekeeping Policy", *International Peacekeeping*, vol. 18, no. 3, pp. 298–312.
Tesón, Fernando, *Humanitarian Intervention: An Inquiry into Law and Morality* (Ardsley, NY: Transnational Publishers, 1997).
Thomas, Daniel C., *The Helsinki Effect* (Princeton: Princeton University Press, 2001).
Tiejun Zhang, *Reconstruction the Great Wall. Chinese Security Strategy in the Early 21st Century* (Goteborg, 2003).
Tiewa, L., "Marching for a More Open, Confident and Responsible Great Power: Explaining China's Involvement in UN Peacekeeping Operations", *Journal of International Peacekeeping*, vol. 13, nos. 1–2, 2009, pp. 101–130.
Tingyang Zhao, "A Political World Philosophy in terms of All-under-heaven (Tian-xia)", *Diogenes*, vol. 56, no. 5, 2009, pp. 9–10.
Tønnesson, S., "What Is It that Explains the East Asian Peace since 1979? A Call for a Research Agenda?", *Asian Perspective*, vol. 33, no. 1, 2009, pp. 111–136.
Toshiya Hoshino, "Gunji-kainyu (Military Intervention)" in Ryo Oshiba, Kiichi Fujiwara, Tetsuya Yamada eds., *Heiwa Seisaku (Peace Policies)*, Yuhikaku, 2006.
Toshiya Hoshino, "Ningen no Anzenhosho to Nihon no Kokusai Seisaku (Human Security and Japan's International Policy)", *Kokusai Anzenhosho (International Security)*, vol. 30, no. 3, 2002.
Toshiya Hoshino, "Peacebuilding & Human Security in Fragile States", *Japan Spotlight*, November/December 2009, pp. 18–19.
Totani Yuma, *Tōkyō Saiban: Dainijitaisengono Hōto Seigino Tsuikyū* (Tokyo: Misuzu Shobō, 2008), which is the Japanese translation of her *The Tokyo War Crimes Trial*.
Traub, James, "The World According to China," *New York Times Magazine*, 3 September 2006, p. 27.
Tumarnidze, S., *Status of the De Facto State in Public International Law. A Legal Appraisal of the Principle of Effectiveness* (2010), pp. 109–131 accessible at http://www.sub.uni-hamburg.de/opus/volltexte/2010/4686/pdf/Doktorarbeit.pdf.
Turner, Karen, "War, Punishment and The Law of Nature in Early Chinese Concepts of the State", *Harvard Journal of Asiatic Studies*, vol. 53, no. 2, 1993, pp. 285–324.
Turns, D., "The Stimson Doctrine of Non-Recognition: Its Historical Genesis and Influence on Contemporary International Law," *Chinese Journal of International Law*, vol. 2, no. 1, 2003, pp. 105–143.
UNESCO Director-General, Mr. Koichi Matsuura cited in "Preface" in Zhou Nan-Zhao and Bob Teasdale eds *Teaching Asia-Pacific Core Values of Peace and Harmony*, p. vii.
United Nations Development Programme [UNDP], *Human Development Report 1994* (New York: Oxford University Press, 1994), p. 22.
Vattel, E. de, *Le Droit des Gens* (Lodres, 1758).
Waltz, Kenneth N., *Man, the state and war. A Theoretical Analysis* (New York, 2001 [1959]).
Walzer, Michael, *Arguing about War* (New Haven/London: Yale University Press, 2004).
Walzer, Michael, *Just and Unjust War* (New York: Basic Books, 1977).
Walzer, Michael, *Just and Unjust Wars*, 2nd ed. (New York: Basic Books, 1992).
Walzer, Michael, *Just and Unjust Wars*, 3rd ed. (New York: Basic Books, 2000).
Walzer, Michael, "The Moral Standing of States: A Response to Four Critics" in Charles Beitz et al (eds.) *International Ethics*, (Princeton: Princeton University Press, 1985) p. 218.
Walzer, Michael, *On Toleration* (New Haven: Yale University Press 1997) p. 21.
Walzer, Michael, *Spheres of Justice: A Defence of Pluralism & Equality* (New York: Basic Books, 1983).
Wang Lianbin (王联斌), 中华武德文化研9i,论纲 ("Theory Outline of the Chinese Military Virtue Culture Research"), 军事历史研9i, (*Military Historical Record*) no. 4, 2005, pp. 150–159.
Wang, Edward, "History, Space, and Ethnicity: The Chinese Worldview," *Journal of World History*, vol. 10, no. 2, 1999, pp. 285–305.
Weber, Max, *Gesammelte Werke zur Wissenschaftslehre* (Tübingen: J.C.B. Mohr, 1922), p. 191.

Weisburd, A.M., *Use of Force. The Practice of States since World War II* (Penn State Press, 1997), pp. 261–264, 268–269, 272–273 and 281–284.

Wellens, K., "The UN Security Council and the New Threats to the Peace. Back to the Future", *JCSL*, vol. 8, 2003, pp. 15–70.

Welsh, Jennifer M., "Implementing the Responsibility to Protect: Where Expectations Meet Reality," *Ethics and International Affairs*, vol. 24, no. 4, Winter 2010, pp. 415–430.

Welsh, Jennifer M., "Introduction" in Jennifer M. Welsh (ed.), *Humanitarian Intervention and International Relations* (New York: Oxford University Press, 2004).

Welsh, Jennifer M., "The Security Council and Humanitarian Intervention" in Vaughan Lowe, Adam Roberts, Jennifer Welsh, and Dominik Zaum (eds.), *The United Nations Security Council and War: The Evolution of Thought and Practice Since 1945* (New York: Oxford University Press, 2008), pp. 535–562.

Wenhua Shan, "Redefining the Chinese Concept of Sovereignty" in Gungwu Wang & Yongnian Zheng (eds.): *China and the New International Order.* (London: Routledge, 2008).

Wheeler, N.J., *Saving Strangers: Humanitarian Intervention in International Society* (Oxford: Oxford University Press, 2000).

Whitehead, Laurence (ed.), *The International Dimensions of Democratization: Europe and the Americas* (Oxford University Press, New York, 1996).

M.M. Whiteman, *Digest of International Law*, V, (1965), p. 867.

Williams, Daniel, "Brutal Conditions Enveloping Kosovo," *Washington Post*, 27 March 1999.

Williams, Daniel, "Yugoslavs Yield to NATO Terms," *Washington Post*, 4 June 1999.

Williams, Daniel, and William Drozdiak, "NATO Peace Force Hastens Into Kosovo," *Washington Post*, 12 June 1999.

Williams, Paul D., "Military Responses to Mass Killing: The African Union Mission in Sudan," *International Peacekeeping*, vol. 13, no. 2, June 2006, pp. 168–183.

Willis, James F., *Prologue to Nuremberg: The Politics and Diplomacy of Punishing War Criminals of the First World War* (Westport, Conn.; London: Greenwood Press, 1982).

Wines, Michael, "U.S. and Allies Say Flight Ban in Iraq Will Start Today," *New York Times*, 27 August 1992.

Wisnumurti, Nugroho, "The United Nations and Peace Enforcement: Prescription for Disorder or Path Towards a New World Order?," *Brown Journal of World Affairs*, vol. 3, Winter/Spring 1996, pp. 67–76.

Withnana, R., *Power, Politics, Law: International Law and State Behaviour during International Crisis* (Leiden/Boston: Martinus Nijhoff Publishers, 2008).

Witt, Joel, Daniel B. Poneman, and Robert L. Gallucci, *Going Critical: The First North Korea Nuclear Crisis* (Washington, DC: Brookings Institution, 2004), p. 104*ff.*

Wright, Q., "The Stimson Note of January 7, 1932", *AJIL*, vol. 26, 1932, pp. 342–348.

Wright, Robin, "N. Koreans Taped At Syrian Reactor," *Washington Post*, 24 April 2008.

Wu Zengyu (吴征宇), 正义战争理论的当代意义论析 ("Contemporary Meaning of the Just War Theory"), 现代国际关系 (*Contemporary International Relations*), no. 8, 2004, pp. 12–17.

Xi Mi, "China: Positive Gesture Made," *China Daily*, 15 September 1999.

Yachi, Shōtarō, "Nihonniokeru Kokusai Jōyaku no Jisshi" ["Implementing International Treaties in Japan"], 100 *Kokusaihō Gaikō Zasshi* (2001).

Yamagami Shingo, "Kokusaikeijisaibansho he no wagakunino kameito kokusaishakaini okeru hōnoshihaino shinten [The Accession of Japan to the International Criminal Court and the Progress of Rule of Law in the International Community]", *Hōgaku Shinpō*, 116 (2009).

Yang Shang, *The Book of Lord Shang. A Classic of the Chinese School of Law* (transl. by Duyvendak, London, 1928).

Yang, Sung Chul, *The North and South Korean Political Systems - A Comparative Analysis*, revised ed., (Seoul: Hollym 1999).

Yao Youzhi (姚有志)/马德宝 (Ma Debao),《孙子兵法》与当代中国主流战争理论 ("Sun Zi's Art of War and Mainstream Contemporary Chinese Theories of War"), 中国军事科学 (*China Military Science*), no. 6, 2004, pp. 9–16.

Yardley, Jim, "China Defends Sudan Policy and Criticizes Olympics Tie-In," *New York Times*, 8 March 2008.

Yearbook of the United Nations, 1950.

Yokota Kisaburō, "Tōkyo hanketsu to jieiken", *Kokusaihō Gaikō Zasshi*, vol. 48, no. 2, 1949, pp. 1–20.

Yongjin Zhang, "China's Entry into International Society: Beyond the Standard of Civilization", *Review of International Studies*, vol. 17, 1991.

Yongjin Zhang: "System, Empire and State in Chinese International Relations", *Review of International Studies*, vol. 27, 2001.

Yu Zemin (于泽民), 两千年军事思想的沟通. 中国古典战略今用 (*The Understanding of 2000 Years Chinese Military Thought. The Present Usage of Classical Chinese Strategy*), (Beijing, 2006).

Yuma Totani, *The Tokyo War Crimes Trial: The Pursuit of Justice in the Wake of World War II* (Cambridge: Harvard University Press, 2008).

Zakaria, Fareed, *The Post-American World* (London: Penguin, 2009).

Zhang Lu (张露): 中西正义战争思想比较分析 ("A Comparison of Chinese and Western Just War Thought"), 现代国际关系 (*Contemporary International Relations*), no. 4, 2005, pp. 15–20.

Zhao Tingyang (赵汀阳), 怀世界研究. 作为第一哲学的政治哲学 ("Investigations of the Bad World: Political Philosophy as First Philosophy"), (Beijing: Zhongguo Renmindaxue Chubanshe, 2009), pp. 82–87.

Zheng, Yongniang, and Keat Tok Sow, "Harmonious Society and Harmonious World: China's Policy Discourse under Hu Jintao", *Briefing Series* (University of Nottingham, 2007).

Zhou Zhenfu (周振甫), 古代战纪选 (*A Selection of Classical War Records*), (Nanjing, 2005).

Zhu Zhijiang (朱之江), 论道德视角下的战争 ("Discussion about War from a Moral Viewpoint"), 军事历史研究(*Military Historical Research*), Nr. 1, 2005, pp. 142–152.

Zuo Gaoshan (左高山), 正义的战争与战争的正义. 关于战争伦理的反思 ("Just War and Justice of War. About the Recollection of War Morality"), 伦理学研究 (*Studies in Ethics*), no. 6, 2005, pp. 43–48.

INDEX

1994 Agreed Framework 257
2001 Declaration on Establishment of
  Shanghai Cooperation Organisation 45
9/11 terrorist attacks 197, 199

Afghanistan 35, 113, 197, 198, 200, 206
  Al-Qaeda terrorist groups 197
  Taliban regime 197
  United Nations Assistance Mission in
    Afghanistan (UNAMA) 35
African Union (AU) 62, 162–164, 168, 170
Agenda for Peace (1992) 57
Aggression 3, 5–41, 48, 49, 51, 81, 92, 95–97,
  102, 125, 213–32, 243
  Crime of crimes 3
  Criminalization of 3
  Definition of 23
  Prevention of 26
  Prohibition of 2
  Resist or reverse an act of 48
  UN General Assembly resolution 3314
    (XXXIX) (1974) 23–4
Aggression, crime of 213–32
  ICC 224–9
  Japan's attitude towards 229–32
Aggression, definition 221–4
  Consensus on definition 224
  Six-power draft 222
  Special Committee on the Question of
    Defining Aggression 222
  Thirteen-power draft 222
Albright, Madeleine (former US Secretary
  of State) 60, 68
Allied Powers 19, 191, 193, 210, 217
Amartya Sen (Nobel Economics Prize
  Laureate) 57, 204
Anarchy 102
Anti-Secession Law (2005) (China re
  Taiwan) 32, 82
Antung 15
Aquinas, St. Thomas 7, 234, 251
Arab Spring 170, 175
Arbritration 11, 12
ARF 104
Argentina 14
ASEAN Way 37, 45
ASEAN+3 104
Asia 1, 2, 8, 43, 45, 64, 66, 70–72, 103,
  106, 207
Asian values 2, 37, 44, 46, 47, 52, 55, 59, 60,
  65, 71
Asia-Pacific region 72, 103, 196, 217, 219
Asia-Pacific War 2, 31, 214
Assembly of State Parties 25
Assembly of States Party 225
Association of Southeast Asian Nations
  (ASEAN) 45, 59–62, 72
Atomic bombs 18
Augustine 234
Aung San Suu Kyi 60
Australia 18, 55, 60, 217, 222
Austria 215
Authoritarian regimes 62–65, 69–71, 104,
  191, 193
Axis of Evil 34

Balance of power 9, 10, 17, 104, 107, 108
Bali Treaty of Amity and Cooperation in
  Southeast Asia (a976) 45
Ban Ki-moon (former Korean Foreign
  Minister; current UN Secretary
  General) 58
Bangkok Declaration 44
Bangkok 44
Bangladesh 69
Bay Bridge 195
Beijing 37, 62, 77, 79, 113, 118, 119, 123–125,
  127–129, 131, 134–136, 143, 147, 149, 153,
  154, 156, 157, 159–161, 163–166, 168, 171,
  175, 176, 178, 179, 181, 182, 184ff., 202
Bellum iustum 7
Bellum legale 13
Bolivia 14
Bosnia 66, 68, 69, 118, 125, 136–41, 178,
  180, 185
  Bosnia and Herzegovina 138
  Chapter VII 139
  Dubrovnik 138
  Federal Republic of Yugoslavia
    (FYR) 136–7
  Implementation Force (IFOR) 141
  Mission creep 137
  No-fly zone 140
  Prevlaka Peninsula 138

Sarajevo 136–138
Srebrenica 137
UN Protected Areas (UNPAs) 137
UN Protection Force (UNPROFOR) 136–140, 180
Yugoslav republic of Croatia 137
Bougainville 60
Boutros Boutros-Ghali, UN Secretary-General 52, 53, 57, 67
Boxer Rebellion 8
Britain 17, 215
British Commonwealth 21
British Empire 110
Brookings-SAIS Project on Internal Displacement 64
Brunei 55
Buddhism 44
Bulgaria 215
Burma Lawyers' Council 60–1
Burma 18, 43, 60, 61
Burma/Myanmar 43
Burundi 206
Bush, President 34, 199, 239, 240

Cairo Declaration 19
Cambodia 36, 55, 67, 69, 149, 197, 206
Cambodia, mission to (UNTAC) 66
Canada 217, 222
Canadian Commission on Intervention and State Sovereignty 8
Caroline formula/incident (1837) 34, 244–248, 250, 254, 260
Central African Republic 206
Chaco War (1932–35) 17
Chatham House 260
Cheonan 38, 39, 243, 250
China
Ascent as a threat 76
Century of shame and humiliation 110
Constitution 123
Criminal law 85
Cult of Defense 85, 86
Cutural moralists 79–81
Earthquake 43
Five Principles of Peaceful Coexistence 123
Foreign policy 3, 31, 75, 77–79, 103, 105, 106, 108, 109–10, 113, 115, 123, 177
Determining principles 75
Harmonious society (*hexie shehui*) 75, 79, 95, 109, 114, 115
Harmonious world (*hexie shijie*) 75, 79, 103–115
Japanese occupation 110
Just war theory 6, 78, 84, 88
Mandate of heaven 78, 80, 90, 99
Peace rhetoric 79
Peaceful rise 76, 77
Permanent Member of UN Security Council 3, 30, 31, 62, 118, 181, 186
Political order in traditional 78
Position on humanitarian intervention 3, 117–89
Reform and opening program 124
Seat at UN and Security Council (1971) 124
Song dynasty 82
Spring and Autumn Period 78, 89
Tiananmen Square 125, 127, 168
Tianxia 78, 90–92, 94, 99–101, 111, 111, 116
Warring States Period 6, 78, 89, 93, 108
Zero-sum politics 84
China Insitute of International Studies (Beijing) 153
China-Taiwan relations 198
Chinese Communist Party 184, 185
Chinese embassy bombing in Belgrade 188
Chinese philosophy 6, 78, 87, 89, 98
Christian theologians and philosophers 7
Clinton, Bill (former US President) 62, 68, 233, 255
Cohen, Roberta 64
Cold War 1, 8, 66, 69, 118, 122, 147, 151, 152, 177, 178, 181, 183, 186, 191, 194, 196, 202, 210, 222–224, 231
Collective conflict management 67
Collective security 1, 5, 9, 12, 17, 25, 26, 63, 199, 200–201, 203, 205, 210, 211
Comfort women 38
Commission on Enforcement of Penalties 215
Commission on Human Security (CHS) 57, 204
Commission on the Responsibility of the Authors of the War 215
Common man (*xiao ren*) 99
Communists 6, 7
Communitarians 46, 66, 70–72
Comprehensive Security Treaty Organization (CSTO) 113
Concert of Europe 10
Conference on Security and Cooperation in Europe (CSCE) 63
Confucianism 6, 44, 70, 71, 78, 80, 82ff., 88, 90–94, 96, 102
Emperor (Son of Heaven) (*Tianzi*) 90

Humanity (*ren*) 93
Mandate of Heaven (*tianming*) 90
Men living uder heaven (*tianxia*) 90
Mengzi 92
Punitive expedition 92–3
Righteousness (*yi*) 93
Rites (*li*) 90
Traditional conventions (*li*) 93
Virtues (*de*) 90
Confucius 6, 78, 92, 93, 98
Congress of Vienna 10
Convention on the Prevention and Punishment of the Crime of Genocide 50, 51
Cook, Robin (former British Foreign Secretary) 59
Corfu Channel Case 49
Covenants on Civil and Political Rights and Economic, Social and Cultural Rights (1966) 50
Crimes against humanity 54
Cuba 248
Cult of offensive 86
Cyber space 197
Cyclone Nargis 60, 73

Darfur 62, 118, 122, 150, 161–7, 178, 180, 181, 183, 188
African Union Mission in Sudan (AMIS) 163
al-bashir, Sudanese President Omar Hassan 166
Chad 165
Darfur Peace Agreement 164
Egeland, Jan 161
Genocide Olympics (2008 Beijing Olympics) 166
Government of National Unity 165
Janjaweed militia 161, 162
Khartoum 161–167, 178
Li Zhaoxing, China's Foreign Minister 164
Liu Guijin (Chinese special envoy to Darfur) 166
N'djamena Ceasefire Agreement 164
Resolution 1556 162
Resolution 1706 165
Resolution 1769 166
UN Assistance Mission in Darfur (UNAMID) 166
UN Mission in Sudan (UNMIS) 164
UN-AU peacekeeping force 166
Wang Guangya 166
Western Sudan 161
Zhai Jun, Chinese Assistant Foreign Minister 166
Zhang Yishan 162
Defensive warfare 81, 88, 95–8, 102
Actively defend 97
Art of war 96
Attack the strategy 97
Deception 97
Espionage 97
Foreknowledge 97
Orthodox tactics 98
Stratagems 97
Sunzi 96
Unorthodox tactics 98
Democratic Republic of Congo 197
Deng Xiaoping 113, 124
Dezhi 99
Diaoyutai Islands 37
Disenfranchisement of women 71
Disorder (*Luan*) 100, 102
DMZ (Korea) 33
Dokdo/Takeshima 37
Draft Treaty on Mutual Assistance 13
Duty towards citizens 70

East Asia 2, 18
East Germany 231
East Pakistan, see Bangladesh
East Sea, naming of 38
East Timor 59, 60, 118, 125, 147–50, 178, 180, 181
International Force in East Timor (INTERFET) 149, 200
Jakarta 148–150
Ramos-Horta, President Jose 60
UN Mission for East Timor (UNAMET) 147, 148
UN Transitional Administration in East Timor (UNTAET) 149
East Turkestan Islamic Movement (ETIM) 112
El Salvador 14
Elements of Crimes 213
Endemic corruption 65
Enlightenment 44
Environment 65
Environmental hazard 56, 207
Ethiopia, Invasion by Italy (1935) 17
Ethnic cleansing 54, 137, 139, 141, 155, 158, 159, 162
Europe 7, 10, 17, 60, 107, 108, 111, 146
Europe-ASEAN Meeting (ASEM) (2009) 60
Evans, Gareth 60

Family of Nations 111
Federal Republic of Yugoslavia 69, 136–7, 141, 145
Ferrero-Waldner, Benita (EU External Relations Commissioner) 61
Fiji 60
Finland, Invasion by Soviet Union (1939) 17
France 10, 14, 17, 21, 126, 142, 215, 217, 222
Freedom from fear 57, 58, 204
Freedom from want 57, 58, 204
Freedom to live in dignity 197, 204

Gambari, Ibrahim 62
Garment, U.S. Ambassador leonard 64
Gates, Robert (U.S. Defense Secretary) 60
General Treaty for the Renunciation of War (1928), see Kellogg-Briand Pact
Geneva Conventions 51, 226, 227, 230, 231
Genocide 2, 8, 22, 51, 54, 58, 67, 68, 119, 122, 124, 125, 134, 135, 155, 158, 159, 167, 187, 213
German war criminals 18
Germany 11, 14, 17, 142, 168, 214, 215, 231, 232
Golan Heights 36
Gorbachev 63
Gray, Colin 69
Great Britain 14
Great East Japan Earthquake 192
  Fukushima Daiichi Nuclear Power Plant 192
  Tohoku 192
  Tomodachi Operation 192
Great Powers 16, 215
  China 77, 111, 117, 118, 184, 186–188
  European 10
Grotius 234
Guinea Bissau 206
Guinea 206
Gulf Crisis 197, 209
Gulf of Aden 198, 208
Gulf War (1990) 52, 118, 197, 207, 209

Haiti 118, 125, 131–4, 178, 208
  Aristide, Jean-Bertrand 131, 132
  Government of 131, 132
  Organization of American States 132
Han-Chinese 112
Hanoi 60, 203
Harmony 6, 45, 72, 73, 76, 77, 80, 92, 95, 98, 99, 101, 108, 115, 208, 211
  He (Chinese) 72, 101
  Sang-saeng (Korean) 72
  Wa (Japanese) 72
Helsinki effect 64
Helsinki Final Act (1975) 63
Hierarchical tradition in Asia 106
High-level Panel on Threats, Challenges and Change (HLP) 155, 201
High-Level Panel 182
Hiroshima 18, 255
Hisaichi, Field Marshall 21
Hmong repatriation 43
Holocaust 51
Holy war 6
Hong-Kong 18
Hu Jintao 159, 166
Human Rights Clinic (Harvard Law School) 60
Human rights violations 2, 55, 171
Human security and development 56–8
Human Security Now (2003) 57
Human Security Trust Fund 204
Human security 3, 43, 45, 47, 55–8, 60, 71–73, 197, 203–205, 207, 208, 210
  Non-state centric threats to 47
  State centric view of 47
Humanitarian crisis 117, 122, 125, 127, 131, 136, 143, 148, 150, 156–158, 161, 165, 167, 170, 171, 175–177, 179, 180, 186, 188
Humanitarian intervention 1–3, 24, 27, 33, 34, 41, 43–73, 78, 117–89
  Chinese attitudes toward 176–87
    Anti-interventionist 177
    Determinants of 122, 183
    Domestic political factors 183
    Gunboat diplomacy 184
    Hegemony 184
    Historical factors 183
    Ideological factors 183
    Imperialism 184
    International systemic factors 183
    Might is right 184
    Mistrust of West 184
    Sovereignty, strict 177
    Unilateral 181
  China's position on 122
  China's post-Cold War attitudes to 122
  International law, and 119–22
  Multilateral 118
  Sovereignty as responsibility 121
Hussein, Saddam 126, 240

Iguchi Takeo (Japanese Ambassador) 223
Inaction guilt 68
Incheon 29
India 52, 61, 66, 145, 168, 217
Indian Ocean 47, 198, 218
Individualism 44, 46

Indonesia 55, 147, 148
International Commission on Intervention and State Sovereignty (ICISS) 53, 54, 56, 153–155
  Criteria for military intervention 154
  Responsibility to Protect, The 53, 154
International Court of Justice (IJC) 18, 41, 49, 51, 233, 236, 242, 244
International Criminal Court (ICC) 3, 5, 23, 25, 61, 167, 168, 213, 214, 224ff.
  Crime of aggression 22, 224–9
  Crimes against humanity 22
  Genocide 22
  Jurisdiction 22, 24
  War crimes 22
International Crisis Group 60
International law 1, 2, 5, 7, 10, 12, 14, 15, 18, 24, 26, 33, 34, 41, 46, 48–50, 52, 54, 61, 68, 71, 73, 88, 112, 117ff., 126, 142, 144–146, 150, 153, 161, 169, 177, 178, 180, 181, 213, 216, 217, 219, 221, 239, 244
International Military Tribunal (IMT) (Nuremberg) 18, 19, 244, 247
International Military Tribunal for the Far East (IMTFE) 19, 52, 215, 228
International Peace Cooperation Law (PKO Law) 197, 226
International relations (IR) 1–3, 5, 9, 16, 26, 48, 50, 55, 77, 107, 117, 128, 133, 144–146, 152, 153, 234, 242
International Security Assistance Force (ISAF) 200
Iraq 8, 32, 197
  Invasion of Kuwait 32
  Samawah 198
Iraq War (2003) 31, 88, 199, 200
  No-fly zones (NFZ) 31, 126–9
Islam 44
Israel attack on Osirak 247, 248
Italy 14, 17, 215, 222
Ius ad bellum 7

Jackson, Robert M. (American Chief Prosecutor) 19
Jackson, U.S. Supreme Court Justice Robert 51
Japan 3
  Abduction by North Korea 202
  Aggressor state 3
  American bases in 195
  Annexation of Korea 9
  Anti-militarist culture 220
  Anti-Piracy Measures Law (2009) 198
  Anti-Terrorism Special Measures Law (2001) 198, 226
  Anti-Terrorism Special Measures Law 226
  Basic Defense Force 203
  Blueprint for a New Japan (1993) 209
  Cabinet Office of Japan 192
  Chinese navy in East China Sea 202
  Cold War tension 191
  Constitution of (1947) 191
  Democratic Party of Japan (DPJ) 197, 228
  Diplomacy re Africa 227
  Emergency Legislation on National Security 226
  Empire 9, 16, 18
  G8 Summits (Kyushu, Okinawa) 205
  Gordian knot 191
  Harmony or concord 208
  Heiwa (peace) 208
  Human security discourse 55
  Human Security Trust Fund 204
  ICC, share of expenses for 227
  Ichiro Ozawa 209
  International Peace Cooperation Law 226
  Iraq Reconstruction Assistance Special measures Law (2004) 198
  Japan Defense Agency 192
  Japanese Communist Party 226
  Japanese Socialist Party 226
  Japan-United States Security Treaty (1951) 191, 192, 195
  Japan-US Alliance 193, 202, 208
  Japan-US Security Alliance 193
  Junichiro Koizumi (former Prime Minister) 199
  Keizo Obuchi, Prime Minister 203
  Key policy arenas 203
    Dynamic defense force 203
    Human security 203
    Official Development Assistance (ODA) 203
  Land of *Wa* (harmony) 208
  Law Concerning Special Measures on Humanitarian and Reconstruction Assistance in Iraq 226
  Liberal Democratic Party (LDP) 197, 228
  Member of UN 191
  National Constitution 35
  National Defense Program Guidelines (NDPG) (2010) 203
  National Reserve Force 194
  National Safety Forces 194, 195

Normal country 209
Occupation 191, 194, 195
ODA Charter 205
ODA policy 203, 205, 207, 208
Okinawa, US military in 202, 205
Pacifist culture 220
Pacifist state 3
Peace Constitution 193–6, 202, 207–209, 224
Promoter of human security 3
Putin 203
Sadako Ogata (former UN High Commissioner for Refugees) 204
Self-Defense Forces (JSDF) 36, 192, 193, 195–199, 201–203, 207–210, 226, 230
Shigeru Yoshida, Prime Minister 192, 195
Shotoku, Prince, 17-Article Constitution (604) 208
Soviet bloc 191
UNKPO involvement 198
Western camp, in 191
Yoshida doctrine 192
Japan's colonialism 196
Japanese Diet 226
Japanese history books 38
Japanese Self-Defence Force (JSDF) 36, 226
Japanese war criminals 18–19, 21, 52
Japan-US Security Alliance 193, 202, 208
Japan-US Security Treaty 195
Jiang Yu (Chinese spokesperson) 37
Jus ad bellum 14, 84, 87, 88, 94, 233, 262
Jus contra bellum 14
Jus in bello 7, 87, 88, 94
Just War 2, 3, 6–9, 50, 75–115, 234, 251, 253, 255, 257, 261, 263
Three conditions for 7
Authority of prince (*autoritas principis*) 7
Just cause (*causa justa*) 7
Righteous intention (*intentio recta*) 7

Kampala 3, 23, 225, 229
Katsuya Okada (Japanese Foreign Minister) 206
Kellogg-Briand Pact 14, 15, 17, 20, 26, 48, 218
Khmer Rouge 45
Kim Dae Jung, President 38
Kim Jong Il 34
Kissinger, Henry 69
Kleptocracies 70
Kofi Annan, UN Secretary-General 53, 58, 151, 174, 201
Komatsu Ichirō (Special Envoy of the Government of Japan) 228
Konoe, Prince 21
Korea 8, 9, 28–30
Korea, sovereign State of 29
Korean Peninsula 3, 37
Korean War 27–30, 32, 33, 192, 194
Kosovo 8, 31, 36, 68, 69, 71, 118, 125, 141–7, 150, 153, 177, 179, 180, 182, 185, 186, 188
Albanian 141, 143
Federal Republic of Yugoslavia (FYR) 141
G-77 146
Kosovo Force (KFOR) 142
Milošević, Slobodan 141–2
NATO 144–7
Rambouillet Accord 141
Serbia 143
Serbian 140, 141, 143
Kouchner, Bernard (French Foreign Minister) 60
Kuomintang 29, 30, 124
Kuwait 32, 36, 126, 127, 197
Kyrgyz crises 112

Lao Tzu 6
Laos 43, 55
Law Concerning the Punishment of Grave Breaches of International Humanitarian Law (PGB Law; 2004) 226
League of Nations 1, 5, 12, 15–18, 48, 50, 111
Committee of Nineteen 16
Council 12
Covenant 12
Illegal war 17
Legal war 17
Resolutions of Assembly 14
Sanctions 13
Sub-Committee of Far Eastern Advisory Committee 17
League of Nations Resolutions 14, 16
Resolution 4 13
Legal regulations on recourse to war 12–13
Li Baodong (Chinese permanent representative) 31
Liberal states 59–65
Liberia 206
Libya 31, 114, 118, 122, 150, 167–173, 176, 178, 186
Anti-Qaddafi forces 168
Arab League 168
International Criminal Court (ICC) 167
Muammar el-Qaddafi 167, 168, 170
No-fly zone (NFZ) 31, 168

Pro-Qaddafi forces 168, 169
Resolution 1970 167
Resolution 1973 168
Tripoli 169
Locarno Pact 14
London Agreement 19
Lytton Commission 16

MacArthur, General Douglas 19, 52, 193
Special Proclamation 19
Supreme Commander for the Allied Powers (SCAP) 19
Madeleine's War 68
Malaysia 43, 55, 59, 66
Malik, Jakob (Soviet Delegate to Security Council) 29
Manchukuo 16, 17
Manchuria 15–18
Manchurian Crisis 15, 16
Mao Zedong 6, 29, 86, 112
Mencius 78
Middle Ages 7
Military action 3, 4, 23, 28, 31, 41, 50, 94, 119, 127, 133, 142, 200, 201, 233ff., 245–247, 249ff., 261–263
Atrocities 119
Crimes against humanity 119
Genocide 119
Humanitarian catastrophes 119
Military intervention 27, 48, 55, 66, 68, 102, 123, 126, 136, 141, 142, 154, 155, 161, 172
Millennium Declaration 53
Millennium report 53
Millennium Summit 53
Minxin 99, 101
Mo Ti 6
Mogadishu 67, 129
Mohamad, Dr. Mahatir (Malaysia prime minister) 59
Mohism 6
Moscow Declaration 19
Moscow 63, 171
Mozambique 36, 197
Mukhden 15
Multi-ethnic PRC 185

Nagasaki 18
Napoleonic Wars 10
Nauru 60
Nazi war criminals 51
Nepal 36
Netherlands 21, 216, 217
New Preachers 70
New Zealand 55, 217
NGOs 66, 68, 70
Nicaragua case 41, 242, 245, 247
Nicaragua v. US 49
Non-Aggression Treaty (1937) (USSR and China) 14
Nonintervention 1, 114, 118, 123, 134, 154, 155, 176, 178, 182, 184, 186
East Asia 43
Northeast Asian policy stances 2
North East project (China) 38
North Korea (Democratic People's Republic of Korea, DPRK) 3
Abduction of Japanese nationals 202
Attack on South Korean island 4, 196
Attack on South Korean naval vessel 4
Biological weapons 249
Brinksmanship 4
Chemical weapons 249
Inflammatory rhetoric 4
Iran, nuclear weapons knowledge 253
Missile launch 249, 252
Missile tests 36, 38, 196, 256
Non-Proliferation Treaty 249
IAEA inspectors 249
Resolution 825 249
Nuclear attack 253–256, 261
Nuclear tests 36, 38, 61, 196, 202
Nuclear threat 256, 262
Nuclear weapons 233, 248, 249, 253, 254
Nuclear weapons program 3, 4
Nuclear weapons proliferation prevention 261
Deliberations 261
Diplomatic condemnation 261
Interdiction of ships 261
Non-military means 261
Sanctions 261
Provocative actions 196
Pyongyang 4, 202
Regional security 3
Sabre rattling 4
Satellite launch 39
Spy ships 196, 202
Syrian nuclear reactor 253
Taepodong missile 202
Threat to neighbors 3
US preventive strike 233–63
Armed attack occurs 235
Armed attack 235
Authorization of 249
Caroline criteria 246–9
Counter-Restrictionists 237
Defense of allies 242–4
Deterrence 237

Imminent threat 239, 241
International law 234–51
Legal authorization 234, 250
Legality of 241, 245–6
Nicaragua case 245
Preemptive strike 237–41, 244–5
Punishment 237
Response to threats 242
Restrictionists 236
Retaliation 237
Schwebel, Judge 245
Self-defense 235, 238, 241
Sufficient threat 239
UN Charter 234–8
Webster, U.S.Secretary of State Daniel 246
US preventive strike moral justification 251–62
Anticipatory self-defense 258
Disproportionat force 256
External legitimacy 251
Honor of nation 252
Internal legitimacy 251 moral standards 252–3
Just goal 254
Last resort 253
Legality 251–2
Necessity standard 253–62
Proportionality 253, 256
Reasonable chance of success 253–255
Revenge 252, punishment 252
Self-defense 257
Sufficient threat 259
Threats 252
Waste of lives and property 255
North Korean Human Rights Act 64
North Korean Peninsula 78, 113
Northeast Asia, alternative communal heritage 2, 59
Northeast Asian perspectives 1
Norway 222
Nullun crimen sine lege, nulla poena sine lege (no crime without law, without law no punishment) 20
Nuremberg Charter 19, 20
Art. 6(a) 19
Planning and waging aggressive war 20

Obama, President 239, 243
Opium War, First 110
Opium Wars 8, 111
Order (*Zhi*) 100
Osh 112
Osirak nuclear reactor (Iran) 247, 248
Owada Hisashi 225

Pacific Ocean 192, 218
Pacific War 18
Pacific 191
Pact of Paris, see Briand-Kellogg Pact
Pal, Radhabinod, Indian Judge 21, 219
Pamunjon 30
Papua New Guinea 60
Paquete Habana Case 49
Parabellum paradigm 82, 105, 106
Paracel Islands 32
Peace enforcement actions 200
Counter-aggression 200
Counter-proliferation 200
Counter-terrorism 200
Humanitarian rescue 200
Stabilization 200
Peace Treaty of Versailles 11–12, 216
Peaceful coexistence 45, 112
Five principles of 31, 123
Peacekeepers 35, 36, 62, 68, 149, 166
Pearl Harbor 18
Perry, William (former Defense Secretary) 255
Philippines 18, 29, 43, 52, 55, 56, 66, 217
Philosophical attempts to regulate war 1–3, 6
Pitsuwan, ASEAN Secretary-General Dr. Surin, (former Thai Foreign Minister) 59, 72
Pol Pot 45
Post-Cold War 65, 69, 117ff., 147, 176, 199, 205, 225
Post-World War I 214, 215
Post-World War II 191, 193, 196, 202, 210, 217, 221
Potsdam Declaration 19
Power politics in disguise 46, 184
Predatory democracies 70
Presidential Decision Directive (PDD) 25, 67
Presidio Army Base 195
Prohibition of aggression, history of 2, 5–18, 26, 41
Prohibition of the use of force 1, 5–41, 48
Protocol for the Pacific Settlement of International Disputes 13
Psychological warfare 81
Public health 65
Public services 65
Pueblo (US intelligence gathering ship) 33

Qian Qichen (China former Foreign Minister) 156
Qing dynasty 108, 110, 112
Qin Huasan (China permanent representative to UN) 151–153
Qin Shihuangdi 108
Qing China 110, 112
  One third of world GDP 110

Racism 71, 124
Ramos, President Fidel (Philippines) 56
Ramos-Horta, East Timor President Jose 60
RAND/US Air Force 260
Reagan, President Ronald 64
Realpolitik 82
Reformation 44
Republican China 111
Resolution of the Sixth International Conference (1928) 14
Responsibility to Protect (R2P) 1, 4, 8, 41, 52–6, 58, 60, 62, 72, 78, 114, 118, 122, 150–61, 167, 168, 200
Review Conference of the Rome Statute (2010) 213
Righteous war 7, 87
Rome Statute 22, 25, 213, 214, 225, 227
Roosevelt, American President 18
Russia 8, 9, 22, 32, 61, 70, 113, 145, 146, 168, 170ff., 183, 203
Russo-Japanese War 9
Rwanda 8, 67, 68, 71, 118, 125, 134–6, 151, 180
  Government 134
  Hutus 135
  Rwandan Patriotic Front (RPF) 134
  Tutsi 134, 135
  UN Assistance Mission in Rwanda (UNAMIR) 68, 134, 136

Sadako Ogata (former UN High Commissioner for Refugees) 57, 204
Saiga Fumiko, Ms. 227
  First Asian female judge at ICC 227
Sameness (*Tong*) 101
San Francisco Peace Treaty (1951) 21, 195, 218, 228, 230
Sea of Japan 33
Sekampung 59
Self-defence, right to 10, 34, 37
Self-preservation, right to 10
Seoul 37, 68
September 11 attacks 8
Serfdom 71
Seven military classics 78
Shanghai Cooperation Organisation (SCO) 45, 113
Shanghai Spirit 45
Shintoism 44
Shinzo Abe, Chief Cabinet Secretary 36
Sichuan province 43
Sierra Leone 206
Singapore 18, 55
Sino-Indian border clashes 32
Sino-Japanese War 8, 9, 18
Six Party Talks 64, 257
Six-Way Talks 64
Slavery 66, 71
Solidarism 45, 46
Solomon Islands 60
Somalia 36, 67, 118, 125, 129–132, 135, 178, 180, 181, 197, 198, 208
  Mogadishu 67, 129
  Piracy 36, 197, 208
  United Nations Operation in Somalia (UNOSOM) 35, 66, 129, 130
  United Task Force 129–30
Somalia Syndrome 67
South China Sea 78, 113
South Korea (ROK) 4, 22, 28, 34–36, 38, 41, 55, 66, 70, 196, 242, 243
South Pacific 52, 59
South Vietnam 35
Southeast Asia 2, 47
Southern Kyrgyzstan 112
Southern Manchurian Railway 15
Soviet Union 17, 21, 29, 30, 32, 63, 196, 217, 222
Spanish Civil War (1936–1939) 17
Special Working group on the Crime of Aggression 225
Spratly Islands 32, 37
State of war, conditions for 10
Stettinius Jr., US Secretary of State Edward 57
Stimson doctrine 16
Stimson, US Secretary of State 16
Suárez 234
Sudan 62, 162, 165, 167, 188, 208
Sunshine Policy 38
Syria 32, 114, 118, 122, 150, 170–6, 180, 182, 183, 186, 187, 189, 208, 253, 259, 262
  Al-Assad, President Bashar 170, 171
  Annan Kofi (Arab league envoy) 174
  Arab League 172
  Chapter VII 173
  Houla 174
  Libya 171
  Massacres by Assad's forces 171

Regime 32
Resolution 2042 174
Resolution 2043 174
UN Supervision Mission in Syria (UNSMIS) 174

Taiwan Straits 37, 123, 186, 196
Taiwan 32, 33, 77, 82, 105, 112, 143, 147, 185, 186, 188
Tang Jiaxuan, Chinese Ambassador 184
Taoism 6
Taro Aso, Foreign Minister 36
Terauchi, General 21
Thailand 43, 55, 59, 60, 253
Than Shwe, Senior General 61
Tianxia 78, 90–92, 94, 99–101, 111, 112, 116
Tibet 43, 77, 78, 123, 143, 188
Tibetan monks, self-immolation of 112
Tibetans 185
Timor Leste 36, 206, 208
Tokyo Charter 20
Tokyo International Conference on African Development (TICAD) 207
Tokyo Trial 19–22, 214, 215, 217–21, 223, 228, 229, 231, 232
Bernard, Judge 219
Pal, Indian Justice Radhabinod 219, 220
Roling, Justice 219
Victor's justice 220
Tokyo Tribunal 19, 21
Tonkin War 8
Totalitarian dictatorships 70
Treaty of Nanjing (1842) 111
Treaty of Tanjin (1858) 111
Treaty of Utrecht 11
Treaty of Vienna 11
Treaty of Westphalia 7, 11, 120
Catholic versus Protestant states 7
Tributary system 91, 107
Truman 29
Turkey 127, 215, 222

Uighurs 185
UN Diplomatic Conference of the Establishment of an International Criminal Court (1998) 225
UN legislation 2, 72
UN Millennium Development Goals (MDGs) 207
UNESCO 45, 51
United Nations 3, 12, 18, 28–30, 40, 45, 48, 50, 54, 118, 121, 130, 131, 139, 142, 143, 146, 155, 156, 164–166, 176, 182, 189, 196, 207, 208, 219, 220, 222, 235, 241
General Assembly 23, 29, 48, 50, 54, 56, 114, 143, 151, 160, 184, 204, 206, 221–224
Regulation of use of force 25–7
United Nations Angola Verification Mission III (UNAVEM III) 35
United Nations Assistance Mission in Afghanistan (UNAMA) 35
United Nations Charter 3, 5, 18, 23ff., 30, 31, 33, 34, 37, 39–41, 48, 50, 55, 127, 128, 133, 145, 153, 158, 162, 175, 178, 195, 200, 222, 234, 241, 242, 244, 245, 249–251, 263
Art. 2(4) 3, 24, 25, 27, 33, 37, 48, 242
Art. 2(7) 127
Art. 24 18, 23
Art. 25 26
Art. 41 162
Art. 42 30, 249
Art. 51 27
United Nations Development Programme (UNDP) 56
1994 Human Development Report 58
Freedom from fear 58
Freedom from want 58
Human security, definition of 58
United Nations Integrated Mission to Timor-Leste (UNMIT) 35
United Nations Interim Force in Lebanon (UNIFIL) 35
United Nations Military Observer Group in India and Pakistan (UNMOGIP) 35
United Nations Mission for the Referendum in Western Sahara (MINURSO) 35
United Nations Mission in Liberia (UNMIL) 35
United Nations Mission in Nepal (UNMIN) 35
United Nations Observer Mission (UNOMIG) 35
United Nations Operations in Somalia (UNOSOM) 129
United Nations Operations in Somalia II (UNOSOM II) 35
United Nations Peacebuilding Commission (PBC) 206
United Nations Security Council 3, 18, 23–25, 27ff., 38, 39, 45, 48, 49, 53, 54, 56, 57, 61, 62, 68, 118ff., 167, 169ff., 186, 189, 199, 200, 206, 222, 224, 235, 241, 243, 249, 250, 263
Resolution 678 126
Resolution 688 127
Resolution 794 129
Resolution 814 130

Resolution 841 131
Resolution 940 132
Resolution 929 135
Resolution 743 136
Resolution 781 140
Resolution 1244 146
Resolution 1272 149
Resolution 1674 54, 62
Resolution 1769 166
Resolution 1874 38
Resolution 1973 168

UN Resolutions 30, 32, 56, 72, 126, 131, 138, 139, 141, 145, 160, 163, 171–173, 175, 189, 199, 200, 206, 221, 222, 249
General Assembly
Resolution 44/22 48
Resolution 2625 48, 49
Resolution 3314 48
Resolution A/63/L80 72
Security Council
Resolution 82 28
Resolution 83 28
Resolution 84 29
Resolution 660 126, 127
Resolution 678 32, 36, 126, 127, 133
Resolution 688 126, 127, 129, 133
Resolution 743 136
Resolution 781 140
Resolution 794 129, 130
Resolution 814 130
Resolution 816 140
Resolution 825 249
Resolution 841 131
Resolution 912 134
Resolution 918 134
Resolution 929 135
Resolution 940 132, 133
Resolution 964 133
Resolution 1160 143
Resolution 1244 146
Resolution 1264 149
Resolution 1272 149
Resolution 1556 162
Resolution 1674 54, 62, 159, 160
Resolution 1679 164
Resolution 1695 249
Resolution 1706 164, 165
Resolution 1718 38, 249, 250
Resolution 1769 166
Resolution 1874 38, 249, 250
Resolution 1970 167, 168, 170
Resolution 1973 168–170
Resolution 2042 174
Resolution 2043 174

United States 4, 16, 17, 19, 21, 22, 29, 30, 34, 35, 63, 64, 68, 77, 103–105, 112, 126, 128, 142, 196, 209, 215–217, 222, 227, 233–63
Universal Declaration of Human Rights (1948) 50, 51, 59
US National Security Strategy (2002) 239
2006 239
2010 239
Uruguay 14
Urumqi 112
US/China economic interdependence 103
Ussuri river 32
Uzbek 112

Versailles Peace Treaty 11–12
Vienna Convention on the Law of Treaties (1969) 48
Vietnam War 35
Vietnam 29, 54, 55, 60, 67, 87
Vietnam, Republic of 32
Virtue (*De Celüe*) 100, 101
Virtue, rule of, (*Dezhi*) 99
Virtues (*de*) 90
Vital interests, right to protect 10

Wang Guangya, Chinese Ambassador 156
War as art 81
War as tactics 81
War crimes 22, 52, 54, 89, 158, 159, 213, 217, 218, 228, 230
War of order 75–116
Warring States Period 6, 78, 89, 93, 108
Washington 193
Weapons of mass destruction (WMD) 34, 197, 241
Weber, Max 108
West Sea of Korea 39
Western neo-imperialism 46
Western values and perspectives 1
Western Zhou dynasty 98
Wilhelm II, German Kaiser 215
Trial of, envisaged 215–17
World Conference on Human Rights (1990) 44
World Summit (2005) 54, 62, 159
World Summit document 54, 56
World Summit Outcome Document (2005) 54, 158, 182, 204
World War I 7, 8, 11, 12, 86, 111, 213, 215
World War II 9, 11, 14, 17–19, 22, 62, 63, 146, 210, 214, 230
WTO 104
Wuwai 100

Wuzi 95
  Five types of war 95
  Reasons for war 95

Xinjiang 77, 78, 112, 143
  Uyghur minority 112
Xunzi 78

Yalu River 29
Yasekuni shrine 38
Yellow Sea 33
Yeonpyeong 39

Zaibatsu 21
Zongli Yamen 111

www.ingramcontent.com/pod-product-compliance
Lightning Source LLC
LaVergne TN
LVHW102103300926
849161LV00001B/12
* 9 7 8 9 0 0 4 2 4 9 0 4 2 *